Indirect Rule

Indirect Rule

The Making of US International Hierarchy

David A. Lake

Cornell University Press
Ithaca and London

First published 2024 by Cornell University Press

Library of Congress Cataloging-in-Publication Data

Names: Lake, David A., 1956- author.
Title: Indirect rule : the making of US international hierarchy /
    David A. Lake.
Description: Ithaca [New York] : Cornell University Press, 2023. | Includes
    bibliographical references and index.
Identifiers: LCCN 2023017916 (print) | LCCN 2023017917 (ebook) |
    ISBN 9781501773730 (hardcover) | ISBN 9781501773747 (paperback) |
    ISBN 9781501773761 (epub) | ISBN 9781501773754 (pdf)
Subjects: LCSH: World politics. | Power (Social sciences)—History. |
    Dependency--History. | United States—Foreign relations—Philosophy.
Classification: LCC JZ1480. L35 2023 (print) | LCC JZ1480 (ebook) |
    DDC 327.73—dc23/eng/20230427
LC record available at https://lccn.loc.gov/2023017916
LC ebook record available at https://lccn.loc.gov/2023017917

To Amily and Tammy,
who have brought so much joy into my life

Contents

Preface

My earliest political memory is as a small boy of perhaps eight standing in my backyard and thinking of how lucky I was to be an American born in the mid-twentieth century, a citizen of a country that was prosperous beyond historical measure, free and democratic, and esteemed by many around the world. What triggered this thought is now lost, and I will leave to the reader to consider just what an odd child I must have been to be contemplating such things at that age. Nonetheless, the moment has stayed with me.

My next political memory is the Vietnam War protests, seared into my mind by the 1968 Democratic convention in Chicago. One year too young to be drafted, but fully aware of the conflict abroad and at home, I wrestled for the next few years with the harm done by my country in a vain intervention in a faraway land.

My third political memory is coming home from my family's vacation in August 1971 and watching President Richard Nixon announce in a nationally televised address that the United States was officially ending the convertibility of the dollar into gold—closing the gold window, as it were—a move now interpreted as the beginning of the end of US international leadership.

I have lived almost my entire life, and certainly my entire professional life, with the contradiction between faith in America as a "city on a hill," a beacon to others and a source of good in the world, and the knowledge that it has too often been on the "wrong side of history," violating its ideals, supporting authoritarian rulers against their own people, and often acting in its narrow self-interest. I acknowledge this contradiction now out of an awareness I did not possess as an eight-year-old, including the privileges afforded me as a white male within American society. On the one hand, I admire the United States, reflected in my repeated scholarly efforts to understand its position and actions in the world through concepts like hegemony and, as here, international hierarchy. I fear the end of the Pax Americana or the liberal international order, as it is now sometimes called, constructed after World War II. On the other hand, I recognize that what we euphemistically call leadership can also manifest as domination and imperialism.

This book reflects my attempt to reconcile these two images of America that have long occupied my thoughts. The resolution I have reached is not particularly kind. It is that the United States and its people are neither inherently good nor bad, neither by nature promoters of democracy nor supporters of vicious dictators, neither by intent leaders nor imperialists. Rather, as a nation, we are opportunists who adapt to local conditions in pursuit of our self-interest through what I will call here indirect rule—our primary mechanism of international influence over the last 125 years. In some rare cases, indirect rule promotes democracy. In others, it sustains authoritarianism. Some might say this makes me a "realist," a label that carries little meaning beyond the simple assertion that nations act in their self-interest. Yet, I remain convinced that we can do better for ourselves and others if we understand more fully why and how we conduct ourselves in the world. This is the liberal idealist in me and why I study international politics. We have the potential to do great things, but we can also do great harm to others and ourselves by failing to recognize the sometimes pernicious consequences of international hierarchy and, importantly, indirect rule.

This book does not aim to set a new course for US foreign policy. Indirect rule will long remain a tool of international power for the United States as well as other countries. Rather, I aspire only to excavate a persistent practice that has largely escaped attention by both scholars and policymakers in the United States—and induce a degree of caution in its future pursuit.

Indirect Rule

Introduction

International influence is frequently exercised indirectly by manipulating the domestic politics of other states. When carried out on a sustained basis, this practice constitutes a form of international hierarchy best described as indirect rule. This mechanism of rule has existed for millennia, from the earliest multicity polities of Mesopotamia to Russia's near abroad today. It has also been a primary instrument of US international hierarchy for over a century, carried out in relations with countries in the Caribbean and Central America (CCA) in the early twentieth century, Western Europe in the mid-twentieth century, and the Arab Middle East (AME) in the late twentieth and early twenty-first centuries. Though the particulars differ across regions and countries and the political outcomes vary dramatically, the basic model of indirect rule remains similar. Through the lens of US history, this volume examines indirect rule as a method of international hierarchy, outlines its consequences for both domestic and international politics, and assesses how the costs and benefits of indirect rule condition the potential for international hierarchy in the first place.

In indirect rule, the dominant state forms an alliance with the group within the subordinate society whose interests are most closely aligned with its own: landed elites in the Caribbean, conservative parties in Western Europe, and monarchies and military regimes in the Middle East today. It then strengthens the political power of each group through regime guarantees, military and economic support, targeted policy concessions, or other forms of assistance. The now stronger group subsequently enacts foreign policies more favorable to itself and the dominant state—the United States in the cases here—in the face of greater resistance from other domestic groups. In short, the dominant state alters the balance of political power in the subordinate in favor of its like-minded ally at the expense of the domestic opposition.

The aid provided to the allied group is not a bribe or bargaining concession. Rather, it is necessary to sustain the ally in power against resistance from the rest of society. In this way, the dominant state and the allied group enter a mutually beneficial, self-interested, and seemingly voluntary relationship. The dominant state depends on the allied group to enact policies it prefers. The allied group depends on the dominant state to keep it in power despite domestic opposition. This mutual dependence ensures that both parties will live up to their policy commitments, obviating problems of credible commitment often found in other types of state-to-state interactions.

Indirect rule, however, also creates incentives for the allied group to act opportunistically against the interests of the dominant state, either exploiting it or entrapping it into conflicts it might otherwise avoid. Especially if its security is guaranteed, the allied group may be willing to take greater political risks than it otherwise would, doing less for its own defense at home or abroad or making greater demands on others. For the United States, this means allies free riding on US defense efforts, a critique leveled against Western European states throughout the Cold War and after, or being drawn into unwanted conflicts, whether these be domestic insurrections in the Caribbean or regional conflicts in the Middle East. To offset these incentives, the dominant state must retain discretion over the aid it provides and impose additional rules on the subordinate, thereby constraining its behaviors and actions. Critical rules imposed by the United States across regions include prohibiting cooperation with other great powers and independent military operations, at least without prior approval from Washington. In the CCA, the rules also extended into financial receiverships. It is here that mutual interests in policy coordination spill over into or, indeed, require international hierarchy. These additional rules are enforced largely by the alternatives of domestic or direct rule. If opportunism becomes too severe, the dominant state can either "walk away" from the subordinate and allow domestic politics to play out on its own, forfeiting the policy preferred by both it and the allied group, or impose its own policy preferences on the subordinate directly through war and occupation. The more attractive these alternatives are to the dominant state, the less room there is for the subordinate to act opportunistically. Indirect rule thus forms an international hierarchy enforced more or less by the next best alternative.

Indirect rule differs from standard bargaining theories in international relations (IR) in which formally equal and sovereign states coerce or induce others to alter their policies or use institutions to facilitate cooperation under anarchy. It also differs from constructivist accounts of norms structuring the social purposes of states, which in the contemporary world almost always cut against relations of international hierarchy and "intervention" in the internal affairs of others.[1] Rather, indirect rule is a "second face" of power mechanism,

---

1. Finnemore 2003.

an institutional or structural form of power that alters the incentives of actors and causes them to behave in ways they otherwise could not or would not choose.[2]

The Wrong Side of History

Although indirect rule is a common mechanism of international hierarchy used by many countries over many centuries, it has particular relevance for two perennial and related problems of US foreign policy. Indirect rule works, if you will, by inducing policy changes in the subordinate as desired by the dominant country, but it also produces two unintended by-products. These unintended consequences are inherent in all indirect rule. They are particularly problematic in the case of the United States.

First, while committed to democracy and pledged to its promotion abroad, through indirect rule the United States often ends up supporting authoritarian regimes and sometimes dreadful dictators. In all of the cases examined in this volume, the United States espoused support for democracy, but in the CCA (chapter 2) and AME (chapter 6) it has backed elite-based regimes that govern autocratically and repress the political and civil rights of their citizens. While democracy promotion is part of the American creed, practice often departs from principle.[3] The theory and evidence presented here explain why.

Under indirect rule, the allied group is rendered better off than otherwise, getting a policy it prefers to all alternatives with the costs borne by the dominant state. All other groups within the subordinate society—as a shorthand, the domestic opposition—always suffer from policies now less favorable to their interests. In equilibrium, assistance from the dominant state allows the allied group to suppress the opposition successfully. Repression is, as programmers would say, not a "bug" but a "feature" of indirect rule, though it varies in extent. When the allied group is large relative to society but unsure of its ability to govern against determined minorities, indirect rule is compatible with democracy and regarded as relatively legitimate, as I argue was the case in postwar Western Europe (chapter 4). Key in such cases is helping the allied group win elections, wherein the opposition is then "naturally" suppressed at the ballot box. But in many other cases, the allied group is a relatively small elite in an already precarious political position. To assist that group in retaining power while adopting policies even more favorable to its interests requires authoritarian rule. When its allies are small

---

2. On the faces of power, see Bachrach and Baratz 1962; Lukes 1977. On institutional and structural forms of power, see Barnett and Duvall 2005. For a related second face argument, see James and Lake 1989.

3. Smith 1994.

elites, however much the dominant state might endorse the principle of democracy, it will acquiesce and even support its elite allies in repressing the majority of society, as in the CCA and AME. Authoritarian powers like Russia or China have fewer qualms about indirect rule than democracies do. If they end up backing small repressive elites, it does not necessarily challenge their own principles nor their legitimacy at home. But for a democratic country like the United States, indirect rule can render it complicit in authoritarian rule and the suppression of human rights. Though the United States can benefit from indirect rule, its backing of authoritarian elites conflicts with its values, opens it to charges of hypocrisy, and renders indirect rule illegitimate in the eyes of many both at home and abroad.

Second, as a result of indirect rule, and especially in those cases where it backs small elites, the United States faces broad-based anti-Americanism and, in extreme cases, violent attacks from terrorist groups. Anti-Americanism befuddles many. Americans, myself included, like to think of their country as a benevolent hegemon—a "leader" of the free world—that provides an international order that improves the welfare of all, or at least aspires to. That US efforts are not always welcomed or recognized as virtuous often puzzles Americans, as exemplified by President George W. Bush's famous query after the attacks of 9/11: "Why do they hate us?" For President Bush, the answer lay in "our freedoms."[4] For others, the answer lies in cultural, religious, or ideological differences—a so-called clash of civilizations.[5] Without necessarily dismissing these factors, the analysis here suggests an alternative explanation.

As indirect rule reduces its welfare relative to feasible political alternatives, the domestic opposition can be expected to resist not only the now stronger allied group but also the patron—the dominant state—that allows that group to retain power. That is, the opposition will resist not only the local regime, the "near enemy," but also the dominant state, the "far enemy," a distinction popularized by al-Qaeda to justify its attacks on the United States.[6] Indeed, knowing that the regime stays in power and can adopt policies that render it worse off only with the support of the dominant state, the opposition will often turn its attention abroad. Even when the dominant state provides enough resources to suppress overt resistance, public attitudes will turn against the dominant state, creating in the case of the United States what is commonly known as anti-Americanism. Indirect rule may also provoke everyday acts of resistance—forms of opposition that are not sufficiently visible or acute to warrant repression but that eat away at the power of the elite and dominant state over time.[7] In some cases, indirect rule may also force an

---

4. From Bush's address before joint session of Congress, September 20, 2001.
5. Huntington 1996.
6. Gerges 2009.
7. Scott 1985.

opposition that sees little hope in addressing its grievances in the face of support from the dominant state to turn violent and direct its anger outward in transnational terrorism. Today, terrorist violence is a near constant threat to the United States because of its role in the AME. While indirect rule can work in the short run by shifting policy in the direction preferred by the United States, it also creates significant blowback in the form of anti-Americanism and, at an extreme, terrorism.[8]

Indirect rule is likely to remain a key mechanism of US international hierarchy now and into the future. A mechanism of rule that has endured for millennia is unlikely to be abandoned any time soon, even when it clashes with democratic values. A longer-term view that recognizes the inherent consequences of indirect rule, however, suggests that at least for some relationships, as Robert Jervis once wrote, the game may not be worth the candle.[9] I take up this question in the conclusion.

Hierarchy and International Relations

In recent decades, theories of international hierarchy have gained new prominence in the discipline of IR. Hierarchy is an ongoing authority relationship in which a ruler or, in our case, a dominant state, sets and enforces rules for a subordinate society.[10] To rule is to direct members of a subject community to alter their behavior on a continuing basis. Hierarchy is not just an occasional or one-off interaction but an enduring relationship of domination and subordination.

Since the founding of IR, the concept of international anarchy has played a central role in theories of world politics.[11] The construct was brought forward in Kenneth Waltz's third image of international politics and elaborated in his later systemic theory.[12] Waltz did not deny the possibility of hierarchy between states, but in pursuit of parsimony and since it did not apply to relations between great powers he dismissed it as unnecessary or unimportant for a systemic theory of international relations.[13] Following Waltz, the assumption of anarchy was given pride of place in IR by neoliberals and at least some constructivists, though with very different implications.[14]

---

8. Johnson 2000.
9. Jervis 1993.
10. Lake 1999; Lake 2009a.
11. Schmidt 1998. The concept was often left implicit. "Anarchy" is mentioned twice in Morgenthau's 1978 classic rendering of realism, but in both cases only as a synonym for chaos.
12. See Waltz 1959; Waltz 1979.
13. Waltz 1979, 114–116.
14. See Keohane 1984; Wendt 1992.

The assumption that interstate relations are characterized by anarchy eventually came under challenge.[15] To "see" international hierarchy, or the exercise of authority by one state over another, requires that we move outside theories of international politics as traditionally construed and broaden our understanding of the foundations of rule. The concept of anarchy in standard IR theory is typically rooted in a formal-legal conception of authority. As all states are assumed to possess equal status under international law, in Waltz's well-known phrase, it follows that "none is entitled to command; none is required to obey."[16] Though owing much to Max Weber's bureaucratic-rational conception of authority, law is only one possible foundation of rule. As Weber himself recognized, authority can be based on charisma (some exceptional quality of the leader), tradition (the way it always has been), or religion (divine right).[17] In IR, some scholars mirror these distinctions in focusing on "soft" power, great power status and the privileges that are assumed to follow, or manifest destiny and other rights countries claim as inspired by providence.[18] These are all ways of attempting to capture the essence of international hierarchy without violating the widely accepted assumption that relations between states are "anarchic."

While departing from the formal-legal conception of anarchy, the emergent literature on international hierarchy is far from unified.[19] Taking a broad conception of hierarchy as any ranked ordering, theorists have identified hierarchies of status (great, middle, and small powers), development (first, third, and fourth worlds), gender (masculinized and feminized states), race (often civilized and uncivilized or failed states), and more.[20] Other theorists take a longer view, probing historical systems of hierarchy and in some cases arguing that the post–Cold War international system is better conceptualized as one of US empire than as an anarchy.[21] This literature posits entire systems of centralized authority, or systems in which one state sets rules and others are expected to comply.

My own contributions to the hierarchy "turn" in IR have explored how dyadic relations between states vary in levels and types of authority.[22] This

---

15. Early critiques include Onuf and Klink 1989; Clark 1989; Milner 1991.
16. Waltz 1979, 88.
17. Weber 1978, chap. 3.
18. On soft power, see Nye 2004. On status, see Paul, Larson, and Wohlforth 2014; Renshon 2017; Simpson 2004. On divine sanction, see Mead 2001; Mead 2007.
19. See Kustermans and Horemans 2022. For a reasonably complete bibliography, though new works are appearing all the time, see Lake and Liu 2020.
20. On this broad conception of hierarchy, see Zarakol 2017 and the chapters therein. On racial hierarchy, see Barder 2021; Grovogui 1996; Sampson 2002; Vitalis 2015. For a more complete discussion and bibliography, see Freeman, Kim, and Lake 2022.
21. Donnelly 2006; Donnelly 2009; Reus-Smit 2005; Goh 2008; Bukovansky et al. 2012; Acharya 2014. See also Wight 1977; Buzan and Little 2000; Dunne 2003; Hobson 2014; Hobson and Sharman 2005; Kang 2003; Goh 2013; Kurz 2013.
22. Lake 1996; Lake 1999; Lake 2009a. For other dyadic conceptions, see, among others, Cooley 2005; Cooley and Spruyt 2009; Hancock 2009; Allen, Flynn, and VanDusky-Allen 2017; Butt 2013; Cha 2017; Chiozza 2013; Keene 2013; Hassan 2016; Musgrave and Nexon 2018.

view acknowledges the current international system is anarchic—there is no world government—but argues that it is a fallacy of division to assume that all relations between states are also anarchic. In this conception and, I would argue, reality, sovereignty is often restricted with dominant states ruling subordinate states in whole or in part. Rather than being anarchic, some—not all, but some—relations between states are characterized by varying degrees of authority.

Without minimizing these alternative conceptions, I ground my understanding of international hierarchy in a relational conception of authority drawn from social contract theory. As a social contract, rule is a bargain between the ruler and ruled, negotiated and renegotiated under the shadow of power. The ruler provides a social order of some benefit to the subordinate society and that society follows the rules of the order. In short, order is exchanged for compliance. Social contract theories, including my prior versions of the theory of international hierarchy, have been criticized for relying on consent by a society to its own subordination.[23] The criticism is not entirely wrong. Yet, hierarchy as I conceive it does not require consent or positive affirmation but is merely an equilibrium in a complex bargaining game. Given appropriate circumstances, the dominant state has incentives to rule and the subordinate society has incentives to comply, and a stable relationship exists when neither has cause to deviate from this set of actions. An equilibrium does not mean that, in some ideal world, the subordinate would desire a hierarchy or that it "wants" to comply with the rules imposed by the dominant state. Rather, it only implies that given the position in which the parties find themselves, neither the dominant state nor the subordinate society has an incentive to alter its behavior and thus their relationship. They accept hierarchy as a structure—a social fact, some might say—even if they would never choose that relationship entirely on their own. As analysts, our task is to explain when, how, and why this equilibrium is reached.

Many social contract theories, including my own, gloss over the fact that the bargain at the heart of any contract often has strong distributional implications for members of the subordinate society.[24] The critique of the voluntarism implicit in social contract theories is (or should be) directed at this oversight. Perhaps escaping from a Hobbesian state of nature—a war of all against all—might benefit everyone, but beyond this rudimentary level the bargains that sustain rule typically benefit some groups in society more than others and may, indeed, harm the welfare of some.[25] Rules are always written by someone for some purpose, most often by and for the ruler's supporters. Thus, rule creates winners and losers, with the former using their political

---

23. See Kustermans and Horemans 2022.
24. The bargain may also have distributive implications for members of the dominant society as well, though this is not the focus of the inquiry and theory here.
25. Hobbes 2017.

power to support the system from which they benefit and the latter using their (often limited) power to resist, ensuring that rule is always contested and evolving. Although I minimized these distributional implications in my past work on international hierarchy, they form the core of the theory of indirect rule elaborated in this book.

What is missing from all these conceptions of hierarchy—again, including my own—is a theory of process or an understanding of the mechanism by which one state exercises authority over other polities or states. How is it that one state rules others? How is international hierarchy created and maintained? The exercise of international authority is particularly problematic in the modern era when the norm of sovereign equality conflicts with hierarchy in practice. So, the question is, how does the exercise of authority between states actually work? Building from a conception of hierarchy as interstate authority, the answer offered here is indirect rule. That is, dominant states build authority and ensure compliance by promoting allies within subordinate societies that share their interests. But in promoting those allies, dominant states must also aim to control their subsequent actions.

The Theory in Brief

International hierarchy emerges when the interests of the dominant and subordinate states diverge and the dominant state possesses assets that are specific to its relationship with the subordinate. In a condition of closely aligned interests or "harmony," hierarchy is not necessary. Likewise, if there are no specific assets at risk, the dominant state has little incentive to pay the costs of governing the subordinate. When the interests of the dominant and subordinate states differ sufficiently, and the policies of the subordinate threaten to reduce the value of assets held by the dominant state, the dominant state has an incentive to rule the subordinate. To put this another way, the greater the divergence of interests and the greater the specific assets, the more the dominant state cares about the policies of the possible subordinate and the more it is willing to pay ensure a favorable outcome.

For simplicity, the theory in chapter 1 assumes there are two groups within the subordinate state, one whose policy interests are opposed to that of the dominant state—the opposition—and a second whose policy preferences are more closely aligned with those of the would-be dominant state—which I will call the allied group or client. When the opposition is powerful domestically, policy will reflect its interests rather than those of the allied group, creating an outcome that is relatively unfavorable to the dominant state. When the allied group is powerful and able to impose its preferences on society, policy will be closer to the preferences of the dominant state. In indirect rule, the dominant state offers the allied group political support in exchange for a more favorable policy. Key to the arrangement is the fact that the allied group cannot achieve its policy objectives on its own given domestic opposition, but with the aid of the dominant state it can successfully adopt a policy closer to its ideal. Aid from the dominant state, in essence, strengthens the political power of the allied group at home, allowing it to shift policy toward its ideal and, not coincidentally, toward that of the dominant state. Aid is most easily conceived as a bundle of resources transferred from the dominant to the subordinate state but can also include guarantees of political survival to the client in the face of resistance from the opposition or policy concessions on other issues. In whatever form, such aid constitutes a governance cost to the dominant state. The lower the governance costs, the more likely indirect rule is and the more favorable the policy adopted by the allied group will be.

The consequences of indirect rule, in turn, vary with the nature of the allied group. When the dominant state rules indirectly through a small elite, the allied group must govern autocratically and repress the rest of society. Both the elite and the dominant state, in this case, will be regarded by the majority of the public as illegitimate. In equilibrium, open revolt will be effectively suppressed, but relations will be plagued by everyday acts of resistance, manifested in the cases examined in this book as anti-Americanism. Conversely, when the majority of a society is more favorable to the policies desired by the dominant state but does not feel entirely confident in its ability to retain power—perhaps because of challenges from an extreme left or right—the dominant state not only can benefit from policies it prefers through indirect rule but can also support democracy at the same time. In so doing, it can earn a measure of legitimacy for its rule, mitigating any backlash and limiting anti-Americanism.

Indirect rule, however, also changes the incentives of the allied group in ways that may impose additional costs on the dominant state. Having strengthened the allied group, and especially if it has guaranteed the regime's survival, the dominant state may be exploited or entrapped by its ally. Oliver Williamson pithily described such actions as opportunism, which he defined as "self-interest seeking with guile."[26] The allied group may divert aid from the dominant state to purposes other than those for which it was intended. It may also accept greater risk in its relations with the domestic opposition or other states, confident that the dominant state will eventually have to come to its defense. Opportunism can be contained, in part, if the dominant state retains some discretion over the aid provided to the allied group, though this also weakens the efficacy of its aid in the first place. The dominant state can also impose additional rules on the allied group, such as limiting its ability to negotiate with other great powers, to conduct an independent foreign policy, or even to manage its own finances. These additional

---

26. Williamson 1985, 30.

rules designed to limit opportunism can often be quite restrictive and may even cause otherwise dependent elites to rail against the domination of their patron. Nonetheless, the discretion retained by the dominant state and the additional rules it imposes transforms policy cooperation between that state and the allied group into international hierarchy. Hierarchy necessarily comes into play to control opportunism.

International hierarchy through indirect rule is enforced by the relative appeal of the alternatives of domestic and direct rule. In domestic rule, which I treat here as a baseline, policy in the potentially subordinate state is set strictly by the groups within it. Groups vary in their interests and the power they can bring to bear on politics, either as a function of their position in the economy, the country's political institutions, or other factors. Importantly, in domestic rule the dominant state plays no role in setting policy. The subordinate adopts autonomously whatever policy its groups prefer and political structures allow, and the dominant state lives with the choice. At the same time, the dominant state also incurs no costs in attempting to govern the subordinate either directly or indirectly. As explained in chapter 1, domestic rule is likely preferred when the dominant state has few specific assets and does not care that much about policy, the allied group is both powerful *and* has policy preferences closely aligned with those of the dominant state, the costs of war and occupation in direct rule are high, or the governance costs of indirect rule are high.

Under direct rule, the dominant state imposes its own preferred policy on the subordinate. In governing directly, the imperial state enacts policy strictly according to its own interests rather than those of the subordinate population. Doing so, however, requires displacing any prior regime, often by force, and suppressing the entire society, which would otherwise resist the imposition of a policy that everyone prefers less than that adopted under domestic or indirect rule. In this way, direct rule is akin to war, which Carl von Clausewitz described more than a century and a half ago as "an act of force to compel our enemy to do our will."[27] The dominant state imposes the policy it most desires on the subordinate but at some significant cost of "fighting" and then "occupying" the country on a sustained basis. That these costs of direct rule can be quite large is suggested by the United States' occupation of Iraq (see chapter 7). Direct rule is most likely when domestic rule is extremely unattractive to the dominant state, for reasons just explained, or the costs of direct rule are unusually low. The power disparities that allowed European states to seize empires in ages past are now rare in international politics. Today, it is extremely difficult to impose "alien" rule and suppress the entirety of society for extended periods.[28] Given the costs of direct rule,

---

27. Clausewitz 1976, 75.
28. Hechter 2013.

this mode of hierarchy is most likely when the specific assets held by the dominant state are very large.

The alternatives of domestic and direct rule limit the scope of opportunism available to the subordinate state under indirect rule. While the allied group has incentives to adopt policies both it and the dominant state prefer, and thus has few incentives to "defect" from the arrangement, it still has incentives to act opportunistically. The additional rules imposed by the dominant state mitigate these incentives but are not self-enforcing. Rather, opportunism by the subordinate is limited by the dominant state's willingness to abandon indirect rule, allowing domestic actors to set policy through internal struggle alone, or to impose its own ideal policy and eliminate the subordinate's ability to act independently. The more attractive either domestic or direct rule is relative to indirect rule, the less range for opportunism the subordinate possesses. Indeed, if the expected returns for the dominant state from direct rule are nearly the same as those from indirect rule, for instance, the subordinate will be highly constrained and we should observe little opportunism. This was, I will argue, largely the case in the CCA in the early twentieth century (chapter 3). However, if domestic or direct rule is relatively unattractive, the subordinate has greater scope for opportunism and we should observe more behaviors that are "unwanted" but still tolerated by the dominant state, as appears to be the case in the AME (chapter 7). At an extreme, the subordinate may act in a sufficiently opportunistic fashion that the dominant state becomes nearly indifferent between indirect rule and the next best alternative.

When rule is indirect, international hierarchy is sometimes hard to distinguish from anarchy, and thus scholars and analysts may have underestimated its extent and importance in world politics. Under the "imperial" extreme, as in the European overseas empires, direct rule is obvious. A subject territory is claimed or seized, control established, governors and magistrates appointed, and edicts issued by the capital. Although there might be some powers delegated to local intermediaries, the power to determine those authorities as well as major questions of policy are reserved to the center. When Britain went to war in 1914 and 1939, for example, its empire and all its peoples and resources automatically went to war as well. When subordinates retain their sovereignty, however, and more or less comply with the wishes of the dominant state even in the absence of any explicit threat of coercion, we often assume we are observing voluntary cooperation in relations of anarchy, when in fact it may be hierarchy through indirect rule in action. When conditions align under indirect rule, allied groups appear to adopt policies preferred by the dominant state of their own volition. With the dominant state paying the governance costs of suppressing resistance by their domestic opponents, the allied group will actually encourage the external assistance that allows it to increase its political power and serve its interests. Finally, facing a now strengthened allied group, the opposition will choose not to revolt openly.

In equilibrium, all of this looks like "cooperation." Somewhat ironically, the more attractive this arrangement is to the dominant state, the more opportunism or "defection" by the subordinate we may observe, suggesting that international cooperation in general is problematic or fragile. In such cases, the lack of compliance is evidence not of a lack of hierarchy but of how attractive indirect rule is relative to the alternatives, and how much opportunism the dominant state is willing to accept to gain the policy of concern. Only by recognizing its subtle nature and how external support bolsters the political position of groups with sympathetic policy preferences can international hierarchy through indirect rule be seen and understood.

Summary of Cases

Indirect rule was first expressed as a coherent system of rule by Frederick Lugard based on his experience as a British colonial governor in Nigeria.[29] With typically small numbers of merchants limited to coastal entrepots protected by equally small numbers of troops, Britain could not hope to govern directly all of the colonial territories it claimed. Even before Lugard theorized the practice, Britain had long governed indirectly through local elites—sometimes manufacturing such leaders as "traditional" rulers.[30] Profiting from their positions as intermediaries between metropole and colony, these indigenous leaders maintained internal order while more or less complying with the dictates of the distant metropole. This was true even in India, the jewel of the British empire. Here the crown governed through the private British East India Company, which in turn ruled indirectly through local princes, zamindars, jagirs, and other aristocrats.[31] Although the subcontinent progressively succumbed to direct rule from London, in 1947, at the time of independence, 565 princely states still remained, governing 40 percent of the territory and 23 percent of the population of colonial India.[32] These political alliances allowed Britain to govern populations and territories often larger than itself for centuries. Indeed, one of the criticisms of indirect rule is that it worked too well, elevating local rulers—chiefs, clan leaders, nabobs—who today continue to block the consolidation of state authority.[33]

Indirect rule also characterized ancient empires in Mesopotamia, Egypt, China, Rome, and Byzantium, and was central even in the more recent Ottoman Empire.[34] The practice long predated Lugard. The Soviet Union

29. Lugard 1965.
30. See Mamdani 1996; Boone 2014.
31. Fisher 1991.
32. James 1997.
33. Boone 2003; Herbst 2000.
34. Burbank and Cooper 2010.

ruled Eastern Europe indirectly for forty-five years and today Russia contin-ues to exercise indirect rule over its near abroad, propping up dictators allied with Moscow and dependent on its support. Crucially, Russia ruled Ukraine indirectly in the immediate post-Soviet era. Only after the pro-Russian pup-pet Viktor Yanukovych was overthrown in the Maidan protests in 2014 and a pro-Western regime was installed did Russia attempt direct rule by seizing Crimea, promoting an insurgency in the Donbas region, and finally waging war on the entire country in 2022. As China expands its international inter-ests and hierarchies through its Belt-and-Road Initiative it is also beginning to implement indirect rule over at least some of its emerging subordinates, including Sri Lanka and the Solomon Islands.[35] Despite the empirical focus of this book, indirect rule and the theory developed here is by no means restricted to the United States.

The United States was selected for deep analysis in this volume not be-cause it is a particularly hard case through which to evaluate the theory but because neither scholars nor policymakers typically think of US policy toward other countries in terms of indirect rule. It is easy for Americans to dismiss the practice of indirect rule as something of the past or something done only by others. It is more difficult to deny its importance when, as I hope to show, it has been a primary form of US international hierarchy over the last century and still is today. Although most Americans do not like to think of themselves or their country as an imperial power, this only makes it all the more important to explore the "how" of international hierarchy in the US case. This norm against noticing, to borrow a phrase from Toni Morrison and a different context, rather than any other motivation justifies the focus here on the United States.[36]

Exploiting variation across countries and regions, I focus on cases of indi-rect rule to explore its operation and consequences. In many ways, countries in the CCA during the early twentieth century were exemplars for US indi-rect rule. The main foreign policy in contention was the commercialization of agriculture and integration into a globalizing economy. The United States wanted to expand exports overall but focused primarily on new markets to its south. Within CCA countries, the elites and the masses were divided over land tenure and ownership. Elites sought to drive tenants into a plantation economy directed toward exports of sugar, tobacco, and other primary crops, while peasants and small farmers resisted. The interests of the United States and the elites were relatively aligned though not perfectly congruent. While both favored increased trade, the United States wanted exclusive economic

---

35. See Cave 2022; Rowand 2022.
36. The phrase was originally used to refer to a norm against noticing race (Morrison 1992). It has been appropriated to highlight the overlooking of race in IR scholarship. See Vitalis 2000; Vitalis 2015; Freeman, Kim, and Lake 2022. I extend it here without, I hope, diluting its impact.

relationships and many elites wanted to retain traditional economic ties to Europe. The pace and extent of commercialization could be accelerated with US support even in the face of greater resistance from the broader population. By guaranteeing their regimes and adapting its own commercial policy to promote large-scale plantation agriculture, neither of which posed significant governance costs, the United States enabled regional elites to shift policy to their ideal. Indeed, though they never formally broke commercial ties to Europe, over time trade increasingly shifted to the United States, creating a solid regional economic block. In the end, the United States got pretty much everything it wanted. Once indirect rule took hold, the floodgates of US investment also opened, deepening dependence and ties to elites. A turning point was building the Panama Canal, a critical specific asset that was both a product of emerging indirect rule and a spur to greater US hierarchy. These elite regimes, in turn, necessarily governed autocratically and repressively.

Having guaranteed the elite regimes, however, the United States faced the potential for significant opportunism by its new clients. The United States had clear expectations about how its subordinates should conduct themselves, laid out in the Platt Amendment for Cuba and generalized to others through the Roosevelt Corollary to the Monroe Doctrine. These rules prohibited ties to European powers, asserted the right of US intervention, and imposed US-governed financial receiverships on unstable countries. The rules succeeded in constraining opportunism because of the real possibility for direct rule. The same ability to project force into the region that enabled the United States to guarantee regimes at low cost to itself also allowed Washington when necessary to seize control of a country, displace the existing regime, and rule directly for a time, a practice that became more common as its specific assets in the region expanded. When its rules were violated, the United States would sometimes intervene temporarily, simply replacing a wayward leader, but if opportunism was more severe it would occupy the country and govern directly for extended periods. Only in the case of Mexico did the United States accept both domestic rule and policies it deeply opposed because the country was too big to invade and the governance costs of supporting elites during a period of revolutionary change were too high. In other cases, with relatively aligned preferences, low governance costs, and a real constraint from the threat of direct rule, the United States got favorable policies at a cost it was willing to bear with very little opportunism by its clients. The mass publics, which suffered under autocratic and repressive rule, did not fare as well. The long-term result was high levels of anti-Americanism and resistance, manifested in new international law prohibiting intervention.

In US–Western European relations, the overriding issue was foreign policy orientations toward the emerging rivalry with the Soviet Union. By the late 1940s, the United States had come to see that its interests in economic expansion and international peace and stability required that it contain and deter its former wartime ally in Moscow, even at the risk of a prolonged Cold War. In Western Europe, with the exception of Great Britain, war-weary populations were somewhat evenly divided between conservative and pro-Western forces that advocated joining a new American-led order and a left bloc with socialists advocating neutrality in the Cold War and communists seeking to ally with the Soviet Union. The continent could easily have leaned in the direction preferred by the Social Democrats, forming a third force between the two superpowers. By bolstering the position of conservatives, who later constituted the political "center" in subordinates as indirect rule was consolidated, the United States tipped the political scales in its favor, producing a decisive shift toward the West. The US role in Western Europe deepened after the late 1940s and especially after 1951 not just because the Korean War unified the West around deterrence of the Soviet Union but also because the United States began investing in specific assets in its forward defense strategy, permanently stationing US troops on the continent through NATO. Much of what IR scholars normally associate with the Pax Americana was actually part of an intentional strategy by the United States to shift opinion and the balance of political forces within Western Europe. Given that there was no decisive majority supporting a Western orientation or neutrality, US indirect rule was both necessary and compatible with democracy.

While obtaining the policy it favored, the United States nonetheless faced significant opportunism by its new allies with few enforcement mechanisms. Facing free riding across the continent, it was also wary of being entrapped by Germany into supporting revanchist claims on its former territories in the east and lured by France and Britain into colonial wars. The allies had wide latitude on both counts, at least in the early postwar years, because neither direct nor domestic rule were nearly as attractive as indirect rule. The occupation of West Germany demonstrated just how impossible governing other developed states would be, and even there the United States rushed to shift from direct to indirect rule. Only in Great Britain were policy preferences sufficiently aligned both with the United States and between the Labour and Conservative parties that domestic rule was preferred. While Western Europe chafed under US-imposed rules, there was relatively little anti-Americanism in response, except for the extreme left and right, even though French resistance did increase over time. Because indirect rule in this instance was consistent with democracy, the United States' role in Europe was perceived as relatively legitimate.

In the AME, the United States rules indirectly but is deeply dissatisfied with the result. While US interests are more aligned with regional elites than broad publics, they are still relatively far apart. The United States wants stable access to oil and natural gas from the region and expanded trade and investment opportunities. Regional elites want regime stability to maximize economic rents from resource extraction or more closed economies where state or crony capitalism can channel wealth to the regime and its supporters. Local populations desire land and wealth redistribution, though since religion has been the one arena of less than complete government control these demands often follow sectarian lines. The United States pulls policy in its preferred direction by supporting elite regimes, but the policy outcome is far from what Washington desires. Despite its dissatisfaction, the United States still supports elite regimes that govern autocratically and repress the civil and political rights of their societies because indirect rule remains more attractive than the alternatives.

The United States is also dissatisfied with high levels of opportunism by its client regimes. Not only are policies unsatisfactory, but rulers take advantage of the near impossibility of direct rule and the fear of more extreme domestic oppositions to exploit and entrap the United States, further reducing its benefits from indirect rule. Often ignoring US rules imposed to control opportunism, local regimes engage in risky behavior and depend on the United States to protect them from regional rivals or domestic dissidents. The Afghanistan and Iraq wars demonstrate just how difficult it would be for the United States to govern countries directly (chapter 7). In both cases, the United States attempted direct rule and quickly sought to transition to indirect rule. When the high governance costs of supporting weak, unpopular leaders became too evident, the United States eventually walked away from its clients in both Kabul and Baghdad. Egypt under the Muslim Brotherhood equally shows that domestic rule will not be accepted when a favored and viable autocratic regime is available. Given that the alternatives are highly unattractive, the United States is plagued by rampant opportunism from its subordinates. In turn, regime opponents understand that the support of the United States helps their elite regimes remain in power and turn against the far enemy, embracing anti-Americanism and occasionally violence. In this case at least, I shall argue, it is unclear whether indirect rule is worth the effort.

Plan of the Book

Indirect rule will remain a key mechanism of international hierarchy both for the United States and other great powers like Russia in its near abroad and China as it expands its international commitments and influence. Yet, how this mode of international hierarchy works remains poorly understood. Chapter 1 explains the theory of indirect rule in detail. The three sets of chapters that follow focus on different regions and periods. For each region, a first chapter on indirect rule examines the interests of the actors, the mechanism of indirect rule, and the domestic political consequences. A second chapter on hierarchy then focuses on the international politics of indirect rule, especially the problem of opportunism and its solutions, the alternatives to indirect rule as constraints on opportunism by subordinate states, and the legitimacy of and resistance to indirect rule. The conclusion revisits the core argument and findings of the theory and then develops the implications of the analysis for IR theory and US policy. Though there are no easy choices in world politics, with the aid of this analysis we will hopefully understand the trade-offs and their consequences better than in the past.

Indirect Rule

Indirect rule is most simply characterized as the exercise of authority by proxy. For centuries, it has been a primary mechanism through which one state governs another on an ongoing basis.[1] Critical to this mode of hierarchy is the presence of an allied group within the subordinate society with a policy preference closer to that of the dominant state than the domestic opposition. Unable to enact its ideal policy against the resistance of the opposition unilaterally, the group collaborates with the dominant state to adopt a policy they both prefer but that the group cannot sustain on its own. In such an alliance, the dominant state transfers resources or otherwise strengthens the allied group in the domestic struggle with its political opponent. The now stronger group then enacts a policy more favorable to itself and the dominant state that nonetheless leaves others in the subordinate society worse off and aggrieved. This collaboration differs from simple bargaining between countries or even groups within countries as normally understood in the discipline of international relations (IR). There is no quid pro quo nor any risk of defection. Rather, the dominant state simply enables the allied group to act in ways both prefer, producing policy cooperation that is in their mutual self-interest.

In strengthening its ally, however, the dominant state also changes that group's incentives, opening the possibility that it may exploit the dominant state or entrap it into conflicts it might otherwise avoid. This potential for

---

1. The literature on indirect rule is quite extensive, especially single case studies. Many studies treat it as an internal characteristic of states. See Mamdani 1996; Naseemullah and Staniland 2016. For a general treatment, see Gerring et al. 2011. On client states in international relations, see Sylvan and Majeski 2009. On indirect control, see Padró i Miquel and Yared 2012; Berman and Lake 2019.

opportunism requires that the dominant state retain discretion in granting aid and impose a set of rules that limits the freedom of action available to the subordinate. These rules transform common interests over policy into international hierarchy. Indirect rule contrasts with domestic rule, where policy is made in a strictly autonomous process, and direct rule, in which the dominant state coerces the subordinate to adopt a policy it prefers. These alternatives serve to enforce the rules of hierarchy under indirect rule more or less stringently.

The consequences of indirect rule depend on the size of the allied group. When it is a small elite, the ally must govern autocratically and repress political opposition. Regardless of any normative preference, the dominant state supports that elite to obtain a policy it prefers despite broad-based resistance. When the allied group is relatively large, perhaps even a majority, indirect rule is compatible with democracy and may be recognized as legitimate by society.

This chapter outlines the theory of indirect rule, focusing on how support for an allied group induces policy cooperation and then requires at least a degree of international hierarchy. In order, the theory develops the key concepts of interests, governance costs, specific assets, opportunism and international hierarchy, and alternatives to indirect rule. Three text boxes throughout the chapter offer a brief formalization of each analytic contribution. Though readers may skip the boxes, they are necessary to show clearly the logic behind some of the propositions developed for empirical analysis.

Interests

We begin with the interests of states and groups within states, defined in terms of their respective preferences over the policy adopted by the subordinate polity. If policy preferences are closely aligned, states exist in a situation of harmony or, at worst, coordination. In such cases, policy cooperation under anarchy may be possible. If two people want to go to the same destination, neither needs to lead nor follow. The same for states. If they agree on objectives, cooperation is relatively easy and does not require rule.[2] When policy preferences are less aligned or, perhaps, diametrically opposed, the dominant state then has an incentive to influence the policy of the subordinate. Interests may diverge for many reasons. Countries may claim each other's territory, they may gain from freer trade but differ over the distribution of gains from specialization and exchange, or one state might impose a negative externality on the other by polluting the air and water or providing terrorists a safe haven on its territory.

---

2. See A. Stein 1990.

Interstate policy differences, in turn, are typically rooted in the interests of domestic groups and how they are aggregated and expressed through their national political institutions and practices. There may be some policy questions on which everyone agrees, such as avoiding nuclear annihilation, but on most issues of importance—or at least those that become politicized—there are groups with different interests and, in turn, different preferences over the policy adopted by their government. Differences may arise because of each group's position in the international economy, rendering members more or less open to trade and investment. Different policy preferences may also follow from attitudes toward security and risk, creating varying demands for defense and willingness to use force (including the taxes and expenditures that go along with such policies), or attitudes toward outgroups, resulting in greater or lesser willingness to cooperate with others. Differences may also arise from conflicting ideologies and norms, often arrayed along a left-right political spectrum but including attitudes toward the role of the state in the economy, redistribution of income and property, social hierarchies, and more. These differences can be mild or intense but are the essence of domestic and, in turn, international politics.

In all the cases that I will examine, groups and their policy preferences can be arrayed as in figure 1.1. For simplicity, I assume that policy differences can be reduced to a single dimension. The dominant state—the United States, in this study—has preferences at one extreme. That is, the dominant state would like the subordinate to adopt a policy at its own ideal point of $d=1$. An opposition that I will refer to generically as group B has preferences at the other extreme ($b=0$). Were the opposition successful in adopting a policy at its ideal point, the dominant state would be maximally unhappy or dissatisfied. Finally, an allied group—called group A—possesses policy preferences perceived to be more or less aligned with those of the dominant state ($b \leq a \leq d$). The distance between the ideal points of A and B reflects the divergence in domestic political preferences. The greater is a (the ideal point of the allied group), the more aligned are the preferences of the allied group and the dominant state. In the case of the Caribbean Basin countries discussed in chapter 2, for instance, the issue in dispute was the commercialization of agriculture, the opposition was landless peasants and wage laborers (group B), the allied group was the landed elite (group A), and the dominant state, of course, was the United States (D).

This is obviously a stark stylization of politics. In reality, there are multiple dimensions of policy over which states and groups disagree. Though I assume the dominant state has resolved its internal disagreements and formulated a "national" policy preference, there are likely multiple competing groups within the dominant state.[3] Within the subordinate state, individuals

---

3. Although clearly a simplification, this assumption is reasonable given that to reach a position of potential hierarchy the dominant state likely possesses a consolidated political system that aggregates group preferences in some coherent fashion.

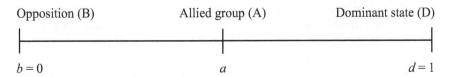

Figure 1.1 The actors and their interests (ideal points)

are distributed across the policy space and thus groups blend into one another, coalitions are fluid, and leaders may play individuals and groups off against one another to increase their room for maneuver.[4] Recognizing the complexity in any actual political system, this simple depiction nonetheless aims to capture the essence of indirect rule. Also important, however, is that the interests of the groups and the dominant state are not objectively defined but should be understood from the subjective viewpoints of each actor. In the cases in the remainder of this book, I attempt to describe the various interests at play in some detail. The possibility of error or bias in these subjectively defined interests is discussed in the conclusion. What matters for the theory and in these cases is the relative alignment of interests between the groups and the dominant state.

Given interests as arrayed in figure 1.1, and in the absence of any involvement by the dominant state, the potentially subordinate society determines its national policy (x_q) autonomously based on the interests and power of the two groups. Whatever their differences, in other words, the groups in the subordinate fight it out, so to speak, on their own. The determinants of this domestic bargain are collected here under the broad heading of the political power of the allied group relative to the opposition (π). Exactly what gives one group power is left open but can be considered a function of (a) the distribution of the population across the political spectrum; (b) who owns the means of production within society; (c) the fractionalization of the allied group, which reduces its ability to act coherently; (d) the opposition's mobilization potential; (e) political institutions and how they bias the aggregation of political preferences; (f) ideological polarization; (g) charismatic leadership, or other factors that influence bargaining between the groups. What creates power in any particular instance is also treated descriptively in subsequent chapters. Domestic politics is thus understood here very simply as a struggle between two groups with the outcome determined by the power of one group relative to the other. The more powerful the opposition is the closer the policy outcome will be to that group's ideal point (b), and the more powerful the allied group the closer the policy will be to a. No matter how powerful it may be, group A will never set policy to the right of its ideal

---

4. For a similar model with multiple groups in the subordinate, see Lake 2016.

point (that is $x_q \leq a$), which would reduce its welfare. In the absence of any international intervention, the outcome of this domestic bargaining game is the policy of the state. Importantly, that policy is the "best" that group A can achieve with its own efforts and resources.

Indirect rule shifts policy in the direction preferred by the dominant state by leveraging the differences in policy preferences between groups within the subordinate state. By supporting the group with policy preferences most closely aligned with its own, the dominant state enables its ally to enact a policy they both prefer against the opposition and resistance of the rest of the society. By transferring some quantity of resources to the allied group or expending effort to protect that group, thereby incurring governance costs (γ) as explained below, the dominant state effectively increases the political power of its ally. This enables the ally to enact a policy both prefer ($x_i > x_q$). This is the essence of indirect rule. By strengthening the hand of the allied group, the dominant state "pulls" policy in the direction that both it and the ally desire (see box 1). This policy cooperation is in the self-interest of both parties. Through its support, the dominant state enables the allied group to do what it otherwise cannot do on its own. Unlike in simple bargaining, there need be no quid pro quo between the dominant state and the allied group as it is in the self-interest of the dominant state to support the allied group (as we shall see below) and of the allied group to adopt a policy they both prefer. The dominant state need not worry about defection by the group as long as it supplies sufficient support to ensure the ally remains in power despite the new policy, nor need it worry about the allied group fulfilling any promise to enact the mutually preferred policy because it is in its self-interest to do so. Rather, both the dominant state and the allied group benefit from policy cooperation.

There are limits to how far the dominant state can shift policy, however, as its assistance provides no incentive for the allied group to offer a policy more attractive than what the group itself prefers. No matter how much the dominant state augments the power of the allied group, it will never voluntarily adopt a policy to the right of its ideal point (a) in figure 1.1. Indirect rule only enables the allied group to shift policy in its favor but does not itself transform the group's interests.[5]

This limit on policy under indirect rule implies that when the preferences of the dominant state and allied group are relatively similar, and the dominant state is willing to provide sufficient assistance to enable the ally to

---

5. Although it might seem intuitive that the dominant state could offer additional aid to "bribe" the allied group into enacting a policy even more favorable to itself, the ally would always have incentives to shirk or defect and return policy to its ideal point. This would bring us back to a standard bargaining model. What is distinctive about indirect rule, and what I want to emphasize here, is that support from the dominant state increases de facto the political power of the allied group and enables it to adopt mutually preferred policies rather than simply inducing a change in behavior by rewards.

BOX 1. INDIRECT RULE

Assume three actors: a dominant state (D), an opposition within the sub-ordinate state (B), and a group with preferences more or less aligned with those of the dominant state (A). Let the utilities of the actors with respect to any policy $x \in (0,1)$ be defined as

$$U_D(x) = \sigma x$$

$$U_B(x) = 1 - x$$

$$U_A(x) = -|a - x|$$

The specific assets held by D in the subordinate, which determine the "stakes" in the conflict or the intensity of the dominant state's policy preference, are represented by σ.

Under domestic rule, groups A and B must arrive at a policy settle-ment $x_q = \pi a$ strictly on their own, where $\pi \in (0,1)$ and represents the power of group A relative to group B. In indirect rule, D allies with A to enact a policy more attractive to both than otherwise possible. By paying governance costs γ, D enables the group to offer a policy $x_i \in (0,1)$ such that $x_i = \pi a + \gamma$. The sequence of moves is depicted in figure B.1. D offers A some level of support at cost γ, A then offers D a policy $x_i > x_q$. If D accepts the policy offer, A then decides the level of opportunism (η).

Since the difference $x_i - x_q$ is a function only of γ, the group will al-ways prefer policy at $x_i = a$ over any policy in which $x_i < a$. Thus, an increase in policy x_i over x_q is "free" to the members of group A. It is in the interests of both D and A to shift policy from x_q to a with no further restraints; neither D nor A has any incentive to defect on the arrange-ment. A will never offer D any $x_i > a$, however, as any such policy simply reduces the welfare of the group. This implies that policy is "capped" at group A's ideal point. Since A will never offer D any $x_i > a$, D will never offer A any $\gamma > a - x_q$. Indeed, in the absence of any budget constraint, D will offer A precisely $\gamma = a - x_q$, and policy will be $x_i = a$. There is always an opportunity cost to transferring resources to A, however, so D may choose not to provide a sufficiently large γ. This affects how much D is willing to pay to affect policy in the subordinate relative to other goals and is largely exogenous. The smaller the γ offered by D, the lower will be x_i. The governance costs to D will always be, therefore, $\gamma \leq a - x_q$.

As explained in the text, indirect rule creates the potential for oppor-tunism by A. Having accepted the resources, A then decides whether it

(continued)

BOX 1. (*continued*)

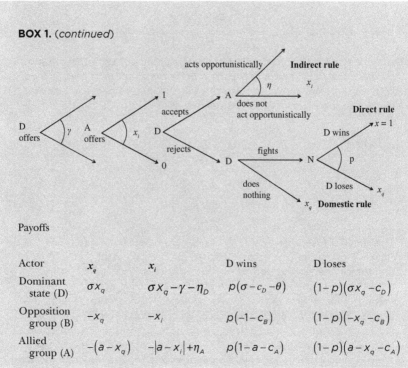

Payoffs

Actor	x_q	x_i	D wins	D loses
Dominant state (D)	σx_q	$\sigma x_q - \gamma - \eta_D$	$p(\sigma - c_D - \theta)$	$(1-p)(\sigma x_q - c_D)$
Opposition group (B)	$-x_q$	$-x_i$	$p(-1-c_B)$	$(1-p)(-x_q - c_B)$
Allied group (A)	$-(a - x_q)$	$-\lvert a - x_i \rvert + \eta_A$	$p(1 - a - c_A)$	$(1-p)(a - x_q - c_A)$

Figure B.1 The indirect rule game

will follow the rules or exploit or entrap D (η), creating a cost of opportunism imposed on D $(\eta_D = f\eta)$ and a benefit from opportunism for itself $(\eta_A = f\eta)$. The cost of opportunism to D and the benefit of opportunism to A need not be equal. Opportunism by its ally reduces the benefits of indirect rule by η_D for a payoff to D from indirect rule of $\sigma x_i - \gamma - \eta_D$. Direct rule and its payoffs are discussed in box 2.

shift policy to its ideal point, the dominant state will be relatively satisfied with the result of indirect rule. This state of affairs characterized relations between the United States and countries in the Caribbean Basin (chapter 2) and Western Europe (chapter 4) where the relatively aligned interests of the allied groups and the United States produced policy outcomes that were reasonably close to what Washington desired. When policy preferences are more distant from one another, the dominant state may still choose to rule indirectly and support its ally, but it will then be relatively disappointed with the resulting policy. We see this latter case in US relations with countries in the Arab Middle East in chapter 6. While Washington supports allied regimes in the region, they still enact policies that leave the United States relatively dissatisfied.

Shifting policy toward the ideal points of the allied group and the dominant state renders others in the subordinate society worse off than before. Although indirect rule increases the welfare of the dominant state and the allied group, it decreases the welfare of the opposition. In turn, the opposition can be expected to resist, up to and including challenging the allied group's hold on the government. In equilibrium, the support of the dominant state is sufficient to sustain its ally in power, but this does not necessarily imply that the opposition accepts this outcome. Opposition can take many forms, from everyday acts of resistance—subtle protests too small to provoke a response by the state but that eat away at its authority over time—to outright defiance, including violent protests or insurrections that must be suppressed by the ally with the support of the dominant state.[6] Equally, resistance will be directed not only at the allied group that enacts the harmful policy—the near enemy—but also at the dominant state that supports the ally and enables that policy—the far enemy.

Democracy and Legitimacy

The fact that the opposition is always worse off under indirect rule than domestic rule has implications—for both democracy and the legitimacy of indirect rule—that vary with the size of the opposition relative to the total population. The larger the opposition, the less likely it is that the subordinate state will be democratic under indirect rule. When the bulk of society is distant from the policy preferences of the dominant state and the subordinate is governed by a relatively small elite that retains power only with the support and assistance of the dominant state, it follows that the allied group must govern autocratically. Although with the aid of the dominant state the allied group may successfully repress dissent, when the opposition constitutes a large fraction of the society the allied group cannot hope to win free and fair elections. Thus, when the opposition is large, indirect rule requires some form of authoritarian rule and likely the suppression of fundamental political and civil rights. In turn, autocracy will persist with at least the acquiescence if not the active support of the dominant state. While the dominant state might otherwise espouse democracy and human rights—as did the United States in all the cases discussed here—the logic of indirect rule implies that it will support its ally in power even when the group is in the numerical minority. Thus, in the Caribbean Basin, indirect rule produced or reinforced authoritarian rule, as it has in the Middle East today. Conversely, when the group most sympathetic to the dominant state's preferred policies

---

6. On everyday acts of resistance, see Scott 1985.

constitutes a majority of the population, democracy is compatible with (but not required for) indirect rule. That is, when the allied group is relatively large, democracy is possible even under indirect rule. The opposition must still be suppressed, of course, but this will occur "naturally" at the ballot box or by manipulating the electoral system to ensure that the opposition cannot come to power through democratic means. We see this in postwar Western Europe, where new centrist majorities, orchestrated by the United States, favored allying with Washington over the neutralist policies advocated by left parties.

By the same logic, the larger the opposition, the less legitimate indirect rule will be. Although critics tend to treat international hierarchy in blunt terms, suggesting that all forms are morally wrong, the reality is quite nuanced. Indirect rule is always regarded as illegitimate by the opposition but can be legitimate in the eyes of the allied group. As in the case of democracy, the legitimacy of the relationship is determined by the balance between opponents and allies. We lack good theories of legitimacy, which is one of the more elusive concepts in political science.[7] Why some rulers are regarded as legitimate while others are not remains an open question, with any answer likely dependent on extant social norms.[8] It seems hard to conceive, however, that subordinates would regard indirect rule as legitimate if it systematically reduced their welfare relative to strictly domestic rule. This implies that those who benefit from indirect rule are more likely to regard that rule as legitimate, while those who are harmed are more likely to regard it as illegitimate. In this admittedly minimalist conception, legitimacy is the product of the equilibria identified by the theory. The policy bargain between the dominant state and allied group creates a measure of legitimacy or not, depending on who benefits.

What can vary, however, is the proportion of the population that is made worse off relative to feasible alternatives, which the theory helps us calibrate. Under indirect rule, the opposition is always worse off than otherwise. When this group is a larger proportion of the population, there will be fewer individuals within the subordinate society who regard indirect rule as legitimate and more who will regard it as inappropriate. Thus, when observing indirect rule in such a case, we would conclude that it is illegitimate, even if there are a few supportive voices from the allied group. As a result, not only will the subordinate be governed autocratically and repressively, but the opposition will recognize that this repression is made possible by the assistance of the

7. For various attempts to define and explain legitimacy, see Baynes 2001; Connolly 1984; Diggins 1991; Gerschewski 2018; Hurd 1999; Jost and Major 2001; Levi, Sacks, and Tyler 2009; Patty and Penn 2014; Rogowski 1974.

8. Theories of legitimacy tend to cluster in three camps: performance (output) legitimacy, procedural (input) legitimacy, and principled (normative) legitimacy (see Lake 2018b). Without dismissing the latter two, the minimalist definition used here focuses on performance legitimacy.

dominant state. Here, we would expect broad-based resistance to indirect rule, at least in principle if not manifested in practice, reflecting the public's assessment that hierarchy is illegitimate.

Conversely, the allied group benefits from indirect rule. When the allied group is relatively large as a share of the population, a majority might well regard indirect rule as legitimate. Of course, normative values might condition how these welfare effects are interpreted, but equally the welfare effects might influence the norms and ideologies held by society. This is particularly important in the current era when sovereignty is a normative standard to which many countries and even groups within countries aspire, though the meaning of that standard is itself contested.[9] The interplay of material conditions and norms is one of the most complex issues in the social sciences and not one to be resolved here. What we can say, however, is that indirect rule can be legitimate when the majority of society has preferences close to that of the dominant state but cannot implement those preferences on its own against the opposition of a determined minority. In such a case, the subordinate may or may not be democratic, but the majority will, in any event, support indirect rule because it strengthens its hand against a more extreme opposition. When this holds, indirect rule is likely to be regarded as at least somewhat legitimate by the subordinate society.

Thus, it is misleading to ask whether indirect rule itself is or is not legitimate. Rather, the question should be to what degree is it legitimate and for whom? Legitimacy is always difficult to observe in any systematic way. Especially when rulers are repressive, individuals may be reluctant to express their true sentiments, even in anonymous public opinion polls.[10] In international relations, illegitimate rule is reflected in various forms of anti-foreign sentiment, most concretely for this volume in anti-Americanism.[11] Defined as an attitude, anti-Americanism can be thought of as "a psychological tendency to hold negative views of the United States and of American society in general."[12] More precisely, it implies a particularized hostility toward the United States greater than that directed at other states and a generalized hatred of the United States that stands independent of the issue at hand.[13] Even if the opposition is not actively protesting against the regime and its patron, opponents will resent the role of the dominant state in supporting the allied group. This has long been a problem in US-Caribbean relations, suggesting that the US role in the region was broadly illegitimate. The same appears true today in the Arab Middle East. Anti-Americanism was much

9. Krasner 1999; Philpott 2001; Cooley and Spruyt 2009; Srivastava 2022.
10. For public opinion–based measures of legitimacy, see Gilley 2006; Gilley 2009. On the problem of preference falsification, see Kuran 1995.
11. On anti-Americanism, see McPherson 2003; McPherson 2006; Katzenstein and Keohane 2007b; Friedman 2012.
12. Katzenstein and Keohane 2007b, 12. Italics removed.
13. Friedman 2012, 5.

more confined and episodic in Western Europe after 1945, suggesting at least slightly broader legitimacy for US rule. These outcomes are examined in subsequent chapters.

Dynamics

A final implication of the interests of the actors as defined here is that the policy preferences of the groups supporting or opposing indirect rule may be dynamic and may change endogenously, or as a result of the policy adopted by the allied group.[14] Once in place, hierarchy changes the investment incentives of actors within the subordinate in ways that may, at an extreme, eventually transform indirect rule into domestic rule.

To the extent that indirect rule is credible and the policies it permits are expected to persist, actors within the subordinate will adjust their own investments in ways that expand domestic support for the allied group and its policies. This is most obvious (and easiest to see) when the dominant state demands the subordinate adopt a policy of free trade, though it might arise in other policy issues as well. Freer trade was a core demand of the United States in all of the cases examined in this volume. As freer trade is established and expected to endure, domestic actors will begin to reallocate their own investments according to the country's comparative advantage. Rather than producing inefficiently for the domestic market, entrepreneurs will begin to invest in new opportunities to export to foreign markets, especially in the dominant state. Once their assets are reallocated along the lines of comparative advantage, those actors may become dependent on access to the foreign market and, in turn, the relations with the dominant state that make that access possible. In recognition of this increased dependence, entrepreneurs and those employed in export sectors may shift their policy preference away from group B's ideal point closer to group A's, shrinking the heterogeneity of preferences within the population or equally expanding the size of group A. Reaping the gains from trade, members of the allied group will also increase their wealth and political power.[15] A similar process unfolds with foreign investments by the dominant state. As the dominant state invests in, say, production facilities within the subordinate, workers shift to that industry and become dependent on the jobs created. Likewise, military bases often become central to the local economy that provides food, services, and entertainment to the soldiers stationed on them.[16] Over time, to the extent that domestic actors within the subordinate become dependent on ties to the

---

14. Formally, the model explained in boxes 1 and 2 is a single period game. This dynamic extension is strictly informal.

15. Rogowski 1989.

16. Some of the services and entertainment may be reprehensible but still represent income for the local economy. See Enloe 1990; Cooley 2008.

dominant state and become more powerful, the subordinate society itself will also become vested in indirect rule and, eventually, may enact policies on its own that are compatible with those of the external patron.

An extreme case is the sugar industry in Puerto Rico. Prior to its incorporation as a US possession, Puerto Rico's primary export crop was coffee, grown on smallholder farms in the interior mountains. Once the United States seized the island in the Spanish-American War, the prospect of sugar entering the US market duty free caused investments to flood into that industry. By World War I, sugar was the dominant Puerto Rican export and the structure of the economy and society had radically changed. As sugar grew in importance, the resources and political influence of the landowning elites as well as workers in that industry expanded.[17] Ambivalence toward Washington soon gave way to support for a tight relationship with the United States—at least until the bottom fell out of the sugar market in the Great Depression.[18] Much the same kind of transformation occurred in West Germany after World War II as export industries became dependent on trade with the United States and its allies in Western Europe (see chapter 4).

This dynamic, however, can also operate in reverse. If the dominant state's support for the allied group is not credible, entrepreneurs within the subordinate may begin to hedge against indirect rule and invest in industries and assets likely to perform better under an alternative, more autonomously derived policy. In the cases below, and on the flipside of the freer trade typically demanded by the United States, this would imply new or continuing investments in comparatively disadvantaged industries that would thrive under more protectionist trade policies. We can see some elements of this hedging strategy playing out in the contemporary Arab Middle East (see chapter 6).

Governance Costs

Support for the allied group is always costly to the dominant state, referenced briefly above as the governance costs (γ) of indirect rule. Governance costs offset the benefits to the dominant state of more favorable policy in the subordinate. What matters here are the opportunity costs of committing material resources, time and effort, or political capital to supporting the allied group in a particular country. These are scarce resources that might be used by the dominant state for other international or domestic purposes. Presumably, the dominant state sets the governance costs it is willing to pay

---

17. See Ayala and Bernabé 2007; Gonzalez-Cruz 1998; Trías Monge 1997.

18. In this case of direct rule, the United States itself suppressed opposition, carried out a number of atrocities, and jailed political opponents. Puerto Rican nationalists attempted to assassinate President Harry Truman and carried out more than one hundred bombings in major US cities. For a brief history of Puerto Rican resistance to US rule, see Diaz 2022.

where the marginal cost equals the marginal benefit of an additional increment in policy, but these calculations require subjective valuations of policy that cannot be readily observed. The cases in the remainder of this volume attempt to justify assessments of these costs but can merely describe relative magnitudes and the direction of changes in policy. Indirect rule in the CCA became relatively more "expensive" during World War I and World War II, for instance, as resources were diverted to the war efforts.[19] The lower the opportunity costs of governing another state indirectly, the more likely we are to observe indirect rule. Likewise, if indirect rule is chosen, the more absolute resources the dominant state devotes to supporting the allied group, the more favorable will be the policy enacted for both the group and the dominant state. In short, the lower the governance costs of indirect rule, the more successful the dominant state will be in encouraging policy in its favor, up to and including setting policy at the allied group's ideal point.

Support for the allied group and, in turn, the governance costs incurred by the dominant state take four primary forms. First, the dominant state can guarantee the political survival of the allied group should it come under pressure or even attack from the opposition after implementing a policy it prefers. A guarantee of political survival allows the allied group to adopt a policy that it could not implement by itself without greater resistance from group B, including the risk of being overthrown. Here, the governance costs are simply the resources and effort necessary to defend the allied group against the opposition, which may require the dominant state to intervene militarily to protect or bolster the group and its leaders. This requires that the dominant state maintain a military infrastructure sufficient, at a minimum, to protect the allied regime and defeat the opposition and, at a maximum, to carry out military operations in defense of the allied group against popular protests or any insurgency. When the guarantee is credible, the opposition will be deterred and, despite its unhappiness over a policy far from its ideal, it will not choose to actually revolt. In this case, the dominant state may need only pay the fixed costs of maintaining the ability to intervene in support of its ally and not the marginal costs of an actual intervention. This suggests, moreover, that the infrastructure necessary to protect an allied group can apply to several subordinates simultaneously, further implying that hierarchy will tend to cluster within regions if societies share similar political interests and structures.[20]

Second, the dominant state may increase the ability of the allied group to suppress the opposition through various forms of what is today known as security force assistance. By training or even paying for local military and police forces, providing better equipment, or advising groups on intelligence operations, riot control, and counterinsurgency warfare, the dominant state

---

19. Butt 2013.
20. Lake 2009c.

can increase the capacity of its ally for domestic suppression. This allows the ally to repress the opposition more effectively as policy becomes more favorable to it, even when resistance would otherwise become more intense. In the contemporary era, security force assistance is often described in positive terms as building state capacity—a nice euphemism—but is better understood in the context of indirect rule as increasing the ally's ability to suppress opposition to its policies. Today, though much US security force assistance emphasizes professionalizing national militaries and encouraging norms of civilian control, this does not mean that the security forces cannot then be used by an allied regime to suppress domestic dissent.[21]

Third, the dominant state can augment the resources available to the allied group through foreign aid to buy off undecided citizens or even members of the opposition through more attractive domestic policies or "sidepayments."[22] It is through aid that leaders of the allied group may be best able to take advantage of the fluidity of coalitions to play individuals off against one another and increase the group's chances of retaining power. These transfers of typically more fungible resources may also take the form of loans with favorable conditions or concessions on other policy issues, including, as was frequent in the cases discussed here, trade concessions that benefit members of the allied group. Sidepayments will often appear—and be criticized by observers—as corruption, or the buying of political favors. This is accurate—and precisely the point. To sustain itself against resistance, the allied group must use sidepayments in ways that win political support from those inside the subordinate. This may take the form of public goods that benefit many, which is more likely in more democratic countries, or targeted assistance that benefits a particular constituency or individual, as might be expected in more autocratic states.[23] Though "bags of cash" delivered to leaders may be decried by advocates of good governance, such aid is sometimes the grease that allows the wheels of indirect rule to spin.

Fourth, the dominant state can assist in reconfiguring political institutions or reducing political fractionalization within the allied group itself. On the one hand, it can help redesign political institutions in ways that increase the allied group's ability to enact favored policies. All political institutions introduce more or less bias into the aggregation of individual interests into policy.[24] Who votes, the electoral rules (if elections are held), how votes are counted, and so on aggregate policy preferences in different ways. Short of direct democracy with universal suffrage and equal opportunities for voting, all institutions introduce some bias, especially as the selectorate is increasingly

---

21. See Berg 2022; Darden 2019; Martinez Machain 2021.
22. The literature on foreign aid is extensive. For several relevant contributions, see Bush 2015; Darden 2019; Zimmermann 2017.
23. On how internal or external resources are used to build support as the size of the selectorate varies, see Bueno de Mesquita et al. 2003; Bueno de Mesquita and Smith 2009.
24. Rogowski 1999.

narrowed.[25] Assisting the allied group to write institutional rules in its favor is not terribly costly, but to change the domestic political equilibrium and shift rules against the interests of the opposition will engender resistance and may require force, including the sorts of resource transfers to the allied group just discussed. On the other hand, factionalism within the allied group and the quality of the leadership will be of concern to the dominant state. In extreme cases where internal disputes threaten the unity of the allied group or an especially incompetent leader fails to maintain the necessary cohesion, the dominant state may also intervene directly to "fix" the regime by quelling infighting or even replacing a leader. In the cases discussed here, and for reasons explained in chapter 2, such interventions were largely confined to Central America and the Caribbean.

Despite these various forms of support that increase its political power, it is important to note that the allied group is no more secure in power under indirect rule than under domestic rule. When the dominant state provides aid that allows the allied group to shift policy toward its ideal point, the opposition is rendered worse off and will increase its resistance proportionately. In seeking to minimize the governance costs it must pay for a more favorable policy, in turn, the dominant state provides only enough assistance to enable the allied group to adopt a preferred policy. The allied group itself balances on a knife's edge, as it were, getting a policy it desires but always facing greater resistance from an opposition that might force it from power.

Specific Assets

The intensity of the dominant state's policy preferences vary as a function of the specific assets (σ) at risk due to the policy chosen by the subordinate state. Not all policy differences matter equally. In some cases, the policy chosen by the subordinate matters a lot to the dominant state, in other cases the policy of the subordinate does not matter much. The specific assets held by the dominant state determine the stakes of the relationship between the dominant and subordinate states.[26] The greater the specific assets held by the dominant state in the subordinate, or the greater the stakes, the greater the costs the dominant state is willing to bear to shift policy in its favored direction.

When there are no or few specific assets as risk, the policy of the subordinate has little consequence. Faced with an adverse change in policy, the dominant state simply changes partners and seeks to fulfill its interests through other relationships. As but one example, when during the US-China trade

---

25. On selectorates, see Roeder 1993; Shirk 1993; Bueno de Mesquita et al. 2003.

26. The core idea behind asset specificity originates in industrial organization. See Klein, Crawford, and Alchian 1978; Williamson 1975; Williamson 1985.

war Beijing placed tariffs on US soybeans in 2018, a homogenous good, it quickly replaced soybeans from the United States with those from Brazil, and the United States redirected its soybeans to markets previously filled by Brazilian producers. World soybean prices fell slightly for two years as supply chains were disrupted, but prices recovered and indeed soon exceeded their previous highs. Despite some short-term costs, markets adjusted rather quickly, China continued to consume soybeans, and even US farmers did not suffer significantly.[27] This is just one example of how homogenous goods on competitive international markets do not create dependence by one state on another, and thus create few incentives for either state to try to influence the policy of the other.[28] When assets are specific, however, the policy of the subordinate matters more because those assets are not easily replaced. The concept of an "asset" is important. Assets endure over some potentially infinite period, though they may also depreciate with time or use. As enduring items of value, they create long-lived interests that require some degree of ongoing rule and, in turn, offset the costs of establishing that rule. The greater the specific assets at risk, the more the dominant state is affected by the policy choices of the subordinate, and the more likely some form of international hierarchy will emerge.

Specific assets arise in many international interactions. Foreign investments in agricultural plantations, mines, and infrastructure like railroads, dams, bridges, and so on, are site-specific assets; once the investment is incurred, it cannot be moved and is, therefore, specific to the relationship between the home investor and host state. Such assets have long been characterized by an "obsolescing bargain" in which, prior to the investment, negotiating power lies with the investor, and after the investment is made negotiating power shifts to the host country, which may attempt to shift rents to itself by altering the terms of the original agreement.[29] More generally, this shift in bargaining power is known as the "hold-up" problem.[30] Portfolio investment has much the same quality; once the money is lent, bargaining leverage shifts to the borrower, who can threaten to default on the loan—thereby keeping the money that was originally lent without further repayment.[31] Assets such as strategic locations may also be specific to certain security relationships. Early in the nuclear era, for instance, US bombers and missiles with limited ranges needed to be deployed close to the Soviet Union. Turkey thus became an essential member of NATO with its valuable airfields and launch sites close

27. Trading Economics, n.d. On the rebound, see Lobosco 2022.

28. Keohane and Nye distinguish between sensitivity interdependence, as in the soybean example, and vulnerability interdependence, which follows here from specific assets (1977).

29. Vernon 1971; Moran 1974.

30. On the hold-up problem where subordinates want to make investments that may be at risk by policy changes in the dominant state, see Carnegie 2015.

31. Frieden shows how such site-specific investments were a leading factor in stimulating European overseas empires in the late nineteenth and early twentieth centuries (1994).

to targets in the Soviet Union. Once integrated into the US global defense posture, these specific assets created a potential hold-up problem, whereby Ankara might to seek to renegotiate the deal. As lift capacity increased and warheads were miniaturized, the value of sites in Turkey diminished and were de facto negotiated away in the aftermath of the Cuban missile crisis; what is "strategic" or specific at one moment may not be at another, depending on context. Many specific assets combine both economic and security elements and are important both for commerce and their military potential. These include canals (e.g., Panama and Suez) and various straits (e.g., Hormuz) that facilitate shipping and commerce but would also be valuable objects to control in war or industrial zones, such as the Ruhr. The concept of asset specificity nicely unifies strategic locations, as they are referred to in the literature on international security, and dependence, as it is known in the literature on international political economy.

While central to the calculations of the dominant state in determining whether to pay the governance costs of indirect rule, the relationship between rule and specific assets nonetheless poses a classic chicken-and-egg problem. To invest in specific assets—to build a military base or a banana plantation—often requires at least a degree of indirect rule or the prospect of it. If a state or its investors fear the asset will be seized or taxed more heavily upon completion, they will not invest. At the same time, a potentially dominant country will not pay the costs of rule unless there is a prospect of specific assets being acquired. In the real world, there is likely to be a feedback process at work over time. Expecting indirect rule and seizing some opportunity, an entrepreneur makes a small investment, and then lobbies the government of the dominant state to protect the assets so acquired; as that protection is extended, further investments are made; as investments expand even more, rule is eventually demanded despite its sometimes high costs, and so on. In this way, the old debate about whether trade follows the flag, or vice versa, is rendered moot.[32] This process can also evolve in reverse. Technological change can make once-specific assets less so, as in the case of Turkey just cited, or assets can depreciate and not be replaced, as with mines once depleted. In such instances, indirect rule can be expected to wane. Likewise, if the opportunity costs of governance increase, indirect rule will become less likely, policy will be more likely to shift in an unfavorable direction, and investors will halt further investments.

Over time, interests and rule coevolve such that the causal effect of one on the other is impossible to identify cleanly. What matters politically at any moment is the current stock of assets that are specific to the relationship with the subordinate. Whatever the exact causal process or sequence of events, the greater the specific assets the more likely we are to observe indirect rule.

---

32. Among many, see Pollins 1989; Keshk, Pollins, and Reuveny 2004.

But over the longer term it is important to acknowledge that the stock of investments is endogenous and will grow or decline as a function of indirect rule and the policy adopted by the subordinate. We find abundant evidence in chapter 2, for instance, for a positive relationship between specific assets and rule. Before 1898 and even as late as 1901 with the signing of the Hay-Pauncefote Treaty giving the United States the sole right to build a canal across the isthmus, the United States had few assets specific to countries in the Caribbean Basin and largely ignored the region. Once indirect rule began and investors poured into the area, the United States was drawn deeper and deeper into rule. As we shall also see in chapter 4, once the Cold War took hold and especially after the United States committed to a forward defense strategy on the continent, site-specific bases in Europe were crucial to the development of indirect rule. In the Middle East, protecting allied regimes and strategic assets in the region has led to a dramatic expansion of US bases around the Arabian Peninsula, which in turn have become additional specific assets that draw the United States further into indirect rule (chapter 6). In all the cases, specific assets beget hierarchy, and hierarchy begets greater investments in specific assets. Hierarchy and indirect rule may create vicious or virtuous circles—depending on one's point of view. Overall, however, the greater the specific assets at risk, the more intense the interests of the dominant state, and the greater costs it is willing to bear to create or maintain indirect rule, suggesting that hierarchy may create a "creeping" imperialism.

Opportunism and International Hierarchy

The dominant state, in strengthening the allied group and assisting it to enact a policy both prefer, also creates the possibility that the group may choose to act opportunistically or in ways that reduce the former's benefits from indirect rule. The potential for opportunism arises when a relationship like indirect rule changes the incentives of one or another of the parties, creating opportunities for one to act in ways that harm the other. Central to what economists term moral hazard is the implication that indirect rule allows the allied group in the subordinate state to accept more risk at the expense of the dominant state. The classic example of moral hazard is car insurance; once insured, a driver no longer bears the full costs of accidents and may drive in a more reckless manner. The same kind of problems arise in international relations. Given its increased political power, the allied group now has incentives to act in ways that may impose additional costs on the dominant state ($\eta_D = f\eta$). To control opportunism, at least in part, the dominant state imposes an international hierarchy on the subordinate state. Where policy cooperation is in the mutual interests of the ally and dominant state, opportunism requires an authority structure that limits the actions available to the subordinate state. It is here that otherwise cooperative relations between the ally and dominant state are transformed into international hierarchy.

Once a relationship of indirect rule is established, opportunism can take two primary forms. First, the subordinate may *exploit* the dominant state. If the dominant state lacks the necessary information, the allied group may be able to misrepresent the opposition as stronger than it really is, extracting greater aid than otherwise and then diverting some of that aid to other purposes. The allied group may also exploit time-inconsistency problems, in which promises made at one time are not carried out at another. After undertaking a loan, for instance, the subordinate may divert some or all of the money to other purposes, undermining its ability to repay in the future. Second, the subordinate may *entrap* the dominant state, prompting it to take actions it would have otherwise preferred not to take. Knowing the dominant state is more likely to come to its aid, the subordinate may act more aggressively (make larger demands) toward its domestic opposition or foreign competitors. Both exploitation and entrapment impose additional costs on the dominant state. Not all countries are equally likely to take risks that exacerbate conflicts with others or that threaten their reputation for financial probity. Nonetheless, under indirect rule the potential for exploitation or entrapment is always present.

In turn, opportunism is anticipated by the dominant state and can be mitigated at least in part through international hierarchy. One means to control opportunism is for the dominant state to retain discretion over the terms on which support is provided, leaving the implicit contract underlying indirect rule incomplete with the ultimate authority or residual rights of decision-making under its control.[33] Security guarantees, for instance, may be left ambiguous so that the dominant country retains the right to determine whether or not circumstances require it to come to the aid of the subordinate. Even in the case of multilateral security institutions such as NATO, for instance, although the United States has committed in principle to the defense of member states, it retains discretion over what circumstances and to what extent it will come to their aid. With some uncertainty over what exactly the dominant state will do, the subordinate is less likely to seek to exploit or entrap it. Likewise, credit rationing can limit risks of default, or credit may be issued only in increments contingent on fulfilling certain conditions as defined by the dominant state. Arms sales can be structured so that the subordinate remains dependent on spare parts and maintenance, which can be turned on and off like a spigot. In all of these forms of support for the allied group, the dominant state retains the residual rights of control.

---

33. On residual rights, see Williamson 1975; Williamson 1985. For Williamson, this is the defining characteristic of hierarchy.

A second means to limit opportunism is to impose rules on the subordinate restricting its choices and actions. As we shall see, a common rule imposed by the United States on its subordinates prohibits relations with other potentially dominant states, which would increase their bargaining power vis-à-vis Washington. A second rule prohibits independent military actions by subordinates, which limits the potential for entrapment. In the Caribbean Basin, the United States also imposed customs receiverships on highly indebted countries, giving it first claim on the most important source of government revenue. As these rules do, in fact, constrain the subordinate's freedom of action and ability to take advantage of the dominant state, they often elicit complaints of domination not only by the opposition but the allied group as well.

The greater the discretion of the dominant state and the more extensive the rules imposed on the subordinate, the greater the degree of hierarchy the dominant state possesses. Enforcing contracts within a relationship of indirect rule remains problematic, however. Rewarding the ally for forgoing opportunism or engaging in "good" behavior raises the governance costs of indirect rule, which likely means a less favorable policy at the margin. Equally, cutting aid to punish opportunism weakens the allied group, which in turn means that it can enact only a policy less favorable to itself and the dominant state. To combat opportunism by punishing the ally means sacrificing the policy gains that motivate indirect rule in the first place. With the dominant state having committed to the allied group and increased its political power, the group can now "bite the hand that feeds it" with a degree of impunity. The main instruments of rule enforcement under indirect rule, thus, are the threat to "walk away" and allow domestic rule to prevail or to impose direct rule on the subordinate. In walking away from indirect rule, the dominant state forfeits the preferred policy but so does the allied group. In all cases, therefore, the allied group must balance its gains from policy under indirect rule against the benefits obtained by opportunism, ideally limiting the level of opportunism to one that allows indirect rule to continue. In direct rule, the dominant state imposes its preferred policy with some probability but at greater cost, and the allied group loses both on policy and opportunities to exploit or entrap its patron as decisions are made in the metropole. This implies that the more attractive either domestic or direct rule is relative to indirect rule, the less able the allied group is to act opportunistically. Conversely, the more beneficial indirect rule is relative to the alternatives, the greater the scope for the allied group to engage in opportunism. It is the alternatives to indirect rule that prevent opportunism by the allied group from getting out of hand. Indeed, we can expect the allied group to maximize the benefits it can extract from the dominant state, even up to the point where the latter is indifferent to the choice between indirect rule and the next best alternative.

Alternatives to Indirect Rule

Indirect rule is bounded by domestic rule, explained above as the domestic game, and direct rule. Under certain parameter values these may be viable alternatives to indirect rule and selected by the dominant state. Indirect and direct rule, to be clear, are different mechanisms of international hierarchy and all three, including domestic rule, are imperfect substitutes for one another. Nonetheless, domestic and direct rule condition where and when we can expect to observe indirect rule and, in turn, determine the scope of opportunism. These alternatives also serve to enforce the rules of hierarchy imposed by the dominant state.

In domestic rule, as above, policy is set by the policy preferences and power of the domestic groups without cost to the dominant state $\left(x_q = \pi a\right)$.[34] Should the governance costs of indirect rule be too large, or opportunism by the subordinate become too costly, the dominant state can simply abandon the relationship. Though it sacrifices a more preferred policy, it saves on governance costs and any opportunism. The allied group is also made worse off if the dominant state withdraws aid provided under indirect rule, as policy reverts to that under domestic rule $\left(x_q < x_i\right)$. It is the dominant state's threat of withdrawing support that in part keeps opportunism within acceptable limits.

Alternatively, the dominant state can rule directly and impose its own preferred policy (d=1) on the subordinate. By ruling directly and setting policy for the subordinate, the dominant state also eliminates its ability to act opportunistically. In short, under direct rule, the sovereignty of the subordinate polity is transferred to the dominant state. Even if the dominant state delegates some authority to the subordinate, it retains the ultimate or supreme authority to determine what powers if any the subordinate possesses. Direct rule is analytically distinct from indirect rule as sovereignty is sited in the imperial state.[35]

To establish direct rule and impose its own preferred policy on the subordinate, the dominant state must typically remove an existing regime from power and in all cases suppress opposition from groups within the polity,

---

34. Domestic and indirect rule are analytically separable: the dominant state either intervenes in support of the allied group or not. Indirect rule varies in extent by how far the dominant state "pulls" policy in its favored direction, given the allied group's ideal point, and this is a function of the governance costs it is willing to pay for this policy. But any effort by the dominant state to increase the political power of the allied group transforms domestic into indirect rule.

35. The two mechanisms of hierarchy may blur together in practice if the dominant state abdicates by transferring some decision-making authorities to local actors. If decision-making powers cannot be retracted, then sovereignty is shared between the dominant state and the subordinate state, creating a hybrid form of hierarchy. Restricted to a single dimension of policy preferences, the theory here does not consider these hybrid forms.

including resistance from what would otherwise be the allied group.[36] The costs to the dominant state of direct rule thus include the costs of "war" (c_D) necessary to impose its ideal point on the subordinate society and "occupying" the country to ensure compliance with that policy (θ).[37] Recognizing these costs, the dominant state can credibly threaten war and demand policy concessions from the subordinate whenever the expected gains from direct rule (x_W) are greater than the policy enacted under domestic rule or the net gains from indirect rule. Given that direct rule implies a policy less preferred by all groups in the subordinate society than that of indirect rule, the costs of war and occupation will always be larger than governance costs. That is, even the allied group will resist direct rule as policy is now more extreme than what it would prefer $(d > a)$. While the dominant state gets a policy it prefers over that possible in indirect rule, it must now suppress all of the subordinate society rather than just the opposition.

The greater the probability that the dominant state will succeed in imposing its preferred policy, or the lower the costs of using force to do so, the more likely is direct rule (see box 2). Conversely, when the probability of success is low or the costs of imposition are high, the more likely the dominant state will choose domestic or indirect rule. Likewise, the greater the specific assets at risk and the more intense its policy preferences, the greater the costs the dominant state is willing to bear to achieve its ideal policy. If specific assets are important enough, direct rule may be preferred to indirect rule even when conditions are otherwise unfavorable. That is, when the stakes of the relationship are very large and the dominant state has very intense policy preferences, it may be willing to bear the higher costs of war and occupation in order to impose its ideal policy on the subordinate. This suggests that direct rule will only be credible when specific assets are very large.

Indirect rule is, thus, bounded on either side by possible domestic or direct rule. If the governance costs of indirect rule are too high, or opportunism by the subordinate is too costly, the dominant state always has the option of allowing domestic politics within the subordinate to unfold autonomously. The dominant state does not prefer this outcome, but it may be willing to accept it if indirect rule is too costly to sustain. We see this in the case of Mexico discussed in chapter 3. Alternatively, the dominant state has the option of ruling the subordinate directly and imposing its ideal policy on the entire society while at the same time eliminating the potential for opportunism. This was the case in Nicaragua, Haiti, and the Dominican Republic after the opening of the Panama Canal (also in chapter 3). Overall, when the governance costs of indirect rule are not too high and war is not credible, indirect rule

---

36. In the cases considered in later chapters, the United States sometimes left a nominal government in place but otherwise ruled directly under martial law.

37. On the bargaining model of war from which this discussion is drawn, see Fearon 1995; Powell 1999; Powell 2006.

BOX 2. ALTERNATIVES TO INDIRECT RULE

Turning to the full game illustrated in box 1 and figure B.1, we can now compare the choice of indirect rule and domestic and direct rule. The indirect rule subgame is as explained in box 1 (the upper branch of the game tree). If the dominant state rejects x_i, it can then (1) do nothing, allowing groups A and B to set a strictly domestically derived policy at $x_q = \pi a$ (domestic rule) or (2) attempt to impose its ideal point on the subordinate state forcibly through "war" at some exogenous cost to each party to the fighting (c) (direct rule).

If the dominant state chooses to fight, nature draws randomly from some exogenous probability distribution whether the dominant state wins (p) and imposes its ideal point d on the subordinate state or loses ($1-p$) and policy reverts once again to the domestic alternative x_q. If the dominant state wins the war, it rules directly. The logic of direct rule follows the now standard rationalist model of war, with one exception. If it wins, D also pays a cost for setting policy at $d=1$ and repressing ongoing resistance by the society equal to θ, which I refer to as occupation costs. Direct rule is more extensive than just "war." That is, in imposing its ideal point D must now suppress the subordinate population, all of which—including group A—will resist the policy set at the extreme of D's ideal point. By construction, governance costs will always be less than occupation costs; that is, $\gamma < \theta$. In direct rule, the subordinate loses any ability to act opportunistically but D must pay more to govern it directly. The larger is θ, the less attractive direct rule will be.

In this full information model, we should never observe war. Since fighting is costly, there must exist some bargaining range, here between $p(\sigma - c_D)$ and $p + c_A + c_B$ that all sides would prefer to actually fighting (see figure B.2). To avoid the costs of fighting, D will prefer any policy in the subordinate greater than what it could expect to get from war, or

$$x_w = p(\sigma - c_D - \theta) + (1-p)(\sigma x_q - c_D)$$

The higher the probability of victory for D (p), the smaller the costs of fighting (c_D), the lower the occupation costs (θ), or the greater the specific assets at risk (σ), the greater is x_w. Since indirect rule will not provide an $x_i > a$, this suggests the following:

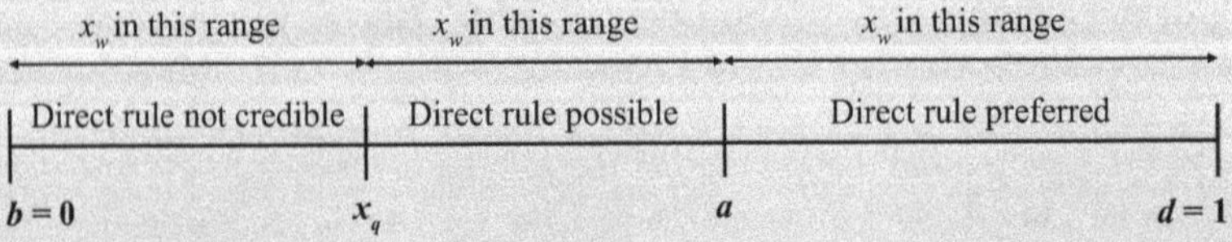

x_w in this range	x_w in this range	x_w in this range
Direct rule not credible	Direct rule possible	Direct rule preferred
$b = 0$	x_q	a	$d = 1$

Figure B.2 Direct rule

If $x_w \le x_q$, war is never a credible option and direct rule is strictly less preferred than domestic rule. Alternatively, when $x_w \ge a$, war and direct rule will be preferred in expectation. In the middling range, both indirect and direct rule may be possible depending on the costs and policies enacted under each. Since $\gamma < \theta$ and there are positive costs to fighting (c_D), direct rule is possible in this range only when specific assets (σ) are large.

Solving this relatively simple game of complete information by backward induction implies that the dominant state will prefer indirect rule over the alternatives of domestic or direct rule if and only if

$$\sigma x_i - \gamma - \eta_D \ge \sigma x_q$$

and

$$\sigma x_i - \gamma - \eta_D \ge x_w.$$

will prevail but the subordinate will have greater room to act opportunistically against the interests of the dominant state.

Theoretical Reprise

The theory is summarized in figure 1.2 with reference to the domestic attributes of the subordinate state, the ideal policy (a) and power (π) of the allied group.[38] A partial set of propositions that follow from the theory is listed in box 3. When the allied group's policy preferences are relatively aligned with those of the dominant state and that group is powerful (a is high, π is high, and x_q is high), domestic rule is likely to be preferred to indirect or direct rule. Indeed, as interests converge with the dominant state ($a \cong 1$) and the allied group is sufficiently powerful to impose its ideal on society ($\pi \cong 1$), domestic rule will always be preferred to any form of international hierarchy. Short of this situation of "harmony," even relatively aligned and powerful allied groups may gain from assistance that allows them to move policy closer to the group's ideal point and that of the dominant state. In all cases, the lower the governance costs, the more likely indirect rule is to prevail (the threshold defined by γ contracts toward the northeast corner of the diagram); as governance costs increase, the range over which domestic

---

38. For notation, see boxes 1 and 2, this chapter.

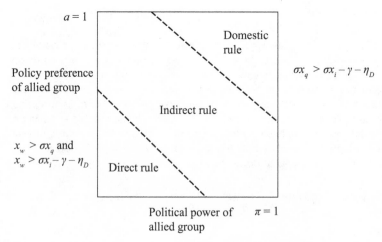

Figure 1.2 Form of rule conditional on preference alignment and allied group power

rule will be preferred to indirect rule expands (threshold moves outward to-ward the southwest corner) (proposition 5 of box 3). When the allied group's preferences are aligned but the group is weak (a is high, π is low, and x_q is low), the dominant state can gain by providing resources to that group and pulling policy toward its ideal point. Whenever interests (a) are closely aligned—that is, in these first two scenarios—or the governance costs of indirect rule are low, the dominant state is likely to be relatively satisfied with the policy adopted by the allied group with its support (propositions 1 and 6). When the allied group is powerful but its preferences are not well aligned with that of the dominant state (a is low, π is high, and x_q is low), indirect rule may also be pursued but for different reasons; the dominant state may still gain by paying a governance cost to shift policy toward the allied group's ideal point (a), but it will be relatively dissatisfied with the result. Indirect rule is also conditioned in an important way by the extent of specific assets of the dominant state at risk in the subordinate state (σ) (proposition 7). The greater the specific assets, the greater the governance costs the dominant state is willing to bear to shift policy in its favor through indirect rule. In all cases, moreover, the opposition will be less satisfied under indirect rule than domestic rule and can be expected to resist not only the allied group but the dominant state as well (proposition 2).

In supporting the allied group, the dominant state also creates incentives for that group to act opportunistically. Under indirect rule, the dominant state always faces a tradeoff between inducing a policy it prefers (x_i) and the risk the allied group will act in self-interested ways that undermine the gains from that policy (η_D). The dominant state, in response, imposes a hierarchy on the subordinate to limit opportunism, the rules of which are enforced by

BOX 3. SUMMARY OF PROPOSITIONS

Proposition 1: The more aligned are the policy preferences of the dominant state and allied group (the greater is a), the more satisfied the dominant state will be with the policy enacted under indirect rule. Conversely, the less aligned their policy preferences are, the less satisfied the dominant state will be.

Proposition 2: Resistance by the opposition to indirect rule will be directed not just at the allied group but also at the dominant state that supports the ally.

Proposition 3: The larger the opposition group under indirect rule, the more authoritarian the regime will be. Conversely, the larger the allied group under indirect rule, the more likely the regime will be democratic.

Proposition 4: The larger the opposition group, the less legitimate will be indirect rule. The larger the allied group, the more legitimate will be indirect rule.

Proposition 5: The lower the opportunity costs of governing through indirect rule (γ), the more likely is indirect rule. The higher the governance costs, the more likely is domestic or direct rule.

Proposition 6: The lower the opportunity costs of governing through indirect rule (γ), the more favorable the policy enacted for both the allied group (up to its ideal point) and the dominant state.

Proposition 7: The fewer the specific assets of the dominant state in the subordinate or the less intense its policy preferences (the lower is σ), the more likely is domestic rule. As the specific assets held by the dominant state increase (the greater is σ), indirect rule will be preferred to domestic rule and, beyond some level of σ, direct rule will be preferred to indirect rule.

Proposition 8: The greater the policy benefit of indirect rule ($\sigma x_i - \gamma$) relative to the payoffs from domestic (σx_q) or direct $\left(x_w\right)$ rule, the greater the scope for opportunism $\left(\eta\right)$ by the allied group.

Proposition 9: The greater the policy benefit of indirect rule ($\sigma x_i - \gamma$) relative to the payoffs from domestic (σx_q) or direct $\left(x_w\right)$ rule, the greater the hierarchy extended by the dominant state over the subordinate.

the alternatives of domestic rule or direct rule (propositions 8 and 9). As the probability of victory or the costs of war and occupation decrease, the likelihood of direct rule increases (the threshold dividing indirect and direct rule expands toward the northeast). As with indirect rule, the greater the specific assets at risk, the greater the costs the dominant state is willing to bear to achieve its preferred policy, and the more credible will be threats of direct rule (proposition 7).

Finally, and perhaps most importantly, though the opposition has been treated largely as a passive actor in the theory with the allied group and the dominant state investing enough to suppress resistance as policy moves in their favor, the opposition always opposes indirect rule and even more so direct rule. It may not welcome domestic rule, either. Even in these cases if it lacks political power policy will favor the allied group. But any support from the dominant state under indirect rule pulls policy even further away from the opposition's ideal point and reduces the welfare of members of the group. As a consequence, the opposition will always oppose the allied group's relationship with the dominant state. This does not mean that the opposition will necessarily rebel against the allied group or the dominant state that supports it. Indeed, under indirect rule, the dominant state provides just enough assistance to the allied group to suppress challenges from the opposition given any policy. Even if members of the opposition resist, overt rebellions will be out of equilibrium and rare. Nonetheless, it follows that when the allied group is relatively small, it must rule autocratically. If conditions support indirect rule, the dominant state will still assist the allied group, despite whatever misgivings it might have about the lack of democracy and the violations of civil and political rights that must follow (proposition 3). The relationship of indirect rule will then be regarded as broadly illegitimate (proposition 4). Conversely, if the allied group is sufficiently large, democracy is compatible with indirect rule. In this case, a majority may embrace the assistance of the dominant state that allows it to govern despite the resistance of the relatively small opposition, and the relationship may be seen as legitimate or even desirable. Each combination of variables represents an equilibrium in which the actors—the dominant state, the allied group, and the opposition—do not have an incentive to change their behavior. An actor might not like the equilibrium, wishing that the allied group was stronger or that war could be fought at less cost, but given the parameters they are stuck where they are. This does not detract from the fact that in the cases I explore here, the opposition is often a simmering volcano of anti-Americanism.

Empirical Strategy

The method used throughout the following chapters is that of an analytic narrative.[39] Such narratives seek to explain specific events by combining the analytical tools of economists and political scientists with the discursive method of historians. In this book, the theory was informed by the history of US foreign policy. Historians and other observers already know quite a bit

---

39. On analytic narratives as a method, see Bates et al. 1998; Elster 2000; Bates et al. 2000; Kiser and Welser 2007; Arias 2011; Monglin 2016. Analytical narratives, of course, were employed long before they were recognized as a specific method.

about US hierarchy, even if they do not employ the terms or model as here, and past works based on close readings of primary sources have had to come to grips with questions of rule by the United States over its subordinates. My claim is not to a new history of US foreign policy. Rather, what we lack—and what I aim to provide—is a theory for understanding how US international hierarchy has worked over the last century to induce subordinates to enact policies favored by the United States and to comply with rules largely laid down in Washington across different political settings, and how the practice of indirect rule generated more or less resistance. At the same time, this book generalizes the notion of indirect rule and calls attention to problems of indirect rule that are often overlooked.

In any analytic narrative, the primary criterion for evaluation is verisimilitude, or the fit between theory and facts, although it can be extended further to include uncovering "new facts" predicted by theory.[40] In addition to revealing the commonalities across these cases, the theory highlights the degree and nature of US rule, the specific assets at risk that require some degree of international hierarchy, and the domestic collaborators who benefit from indirect rule. Perhaps most important, it challenges notions of cooperation in IR, especially in the case of postwar US-European relations that are often seen as the core of a voluntary Pax Americana successfully created and managed despite the challenges of anarchy. While the empirical chapters are hopefully effective in persuading readers how indirect rule works and that the theory is capturing some significant variation in form and extent, they do not constitute a test of that theory by any standard criteria. Rather, the cases should be considered plausibility probes to assess whether additional effort in refining the theory and, especially, developing more rigorous tests will be worthwhile.[41] There are three main reasons for treating the empirical material here with some caution.

First, the focus of the empirical chapters is on indirect rule and its consequences. The main purpose of the volume is to identify theoretically and explore empirically how indirect rule operates to produce international hierarchy and its consequences. In pursuing this ambition, I concentrate on cases where indirect rule is observed. In many regions of the world even now, the United States does not seek to exercise authority over other states, accepting anarchy in relations with great power competitors it cannot dominate or even small states in regions where it has few specific assets and, therefore, only marginal interests. In the Caribbean and Central America in the early twentieth century, Western Europe after 1945, and the Arab Middle East since at least 1979, the United States has exercised indirect rule to varying extents and in different ways that, we shall see, are consistent with the theory. Focusing on indirect rule and how it varies across countries and

---

40. On new facts as a measure of a progressive research program, see Lakatos 1978.
41. Eckstein 1991, 147–153.

regions allows a full assessment of propositions on how satisfied the United States is with the policy adopted by the subordinate, the level of autocracy and repression, or degrees of resistance and anti-Americanism. Within and across the cases, there is sufficient variation in the interests of the actors, their political power, the governance costs of indirect rule, and other factors that we can draw some initial conclusions. Focusing on cases of indirect rule, however, becomes problematic when attempting to account for the alternative forms of rule. Domestic and direct rule are primarily important for this study as constraints on opportunism by the subordinate; the more attractive the alternatives to indirect rule, the less room the subordinate has to exploit or entrap the dominant state. Nonetheless, to understand how constraining these alternatives are, I must also theorize and assess the conditions that make domestic or direct rule more or less attractive and likely to be observed in the historical record. The variation within the region discussed in each section is suggestive, but due to the initial selection criteria any conclusions about the determinants of different forms of international hierarchy must remain tentative.

Second, specific assets, one of the key variables in the theory, are partially endogenous and, therefore, cannot be treated in a causal manner.[42] Specific assets are sometimes "natural," deriving from geography or other physical attributes. The Strait of Hormuz described in chapter 6 is perhaps the best example. But most other specific assets are products of actors deciding to invest resources, their returns being contingent on the policy of the subordinate over the life of those assets. As explained above, this forms a "chicken-and-egg" problem that makes it difficult to identify which came first, the specific asset that needed to be governed, or the hierarchy that permitted investments in specific assets. The United States could begin construction on the Panama Canal, for instance, only once Washington was reasonably certain it could induce favorable policies in regional states and therefore safeguard its interests over the lifespan of what was then one of the largest infrastructure projects in human history (chapter 2). Once hierarchy was extended over the region, however, there was a tremendous influx of additional investment in other specific assets. In such cases, specific assets do not cause hierarchy any more than hierarchy causes specific assets. In all three regions examined here, once the "chicken-and-egg" problem was resolved, there followed an expansion in the specific assets and the breadth and depth of international hierarchy in ways consistent with the theory but lacking any exogenous or singular cause.

Finally, other variables in the theory are difficult to operationalize in any systematic fashion. Coding variables here requires context-specific knowledge

---

42. Over the very long term, we might also consider that governance costs and the costs of war and occupation are also endogenous, reflecting prior decisions to build the military capability to project power over distance in order to create international hierarchies.

and sometimes can only be assessed through theoretically disciplined coun-terfactuals. Governance costs, for instance, come in varied forms, may be observable only in "out-of-equilibrium" events when the opposition actually revolts and the dominant state must respond, and in all cases lack a com-mon metric. Thus, we can observe what the United States actually does in any given case, including the kinds and levels of support given to the allied group, but we cannot measure precisely the total cost of governance under indirect rule. The same for the costs of direct rule. Similarly, in ongoing cases of indirect rule the policy that would have been adopted autonomously under domestic rule is not actually observed, and thus cannot be estimated empirically either ex ante for the actors in the game or ex post for external observers such as ourselves. To establish the counterfactual, we must rely on reasoned speculation about what would have happened in the absence of indirect rule.

Perhaps most important, policy preferences and especially the divergence in the interests of groups within and between countries are critical for the theory of indirect rule. Yet, interests are always difficult to specify. What we can see in the historical record are the choices made by groups and states, but all interesting questions of politics involve at least a degree of strategic interaction between two or more parties. Choices in turn are based on an actor's understanding of the actions available to it and the other relevant par-ties, its conception of its own interests, its beliefs about the interests of other parties, and the available information.[43] In a given strategic setting, what an actor chooses is often different from what it "wants." As a result, one can-not easily reason backward from choices to preferences. As a methodological problem, we can assume interests, posit them deductively on the basis of other theories, or attempt to infer preferences from choices.[44] Throughout this volume, I use a combination of the last two methods to identify prefer-ences. I begin from theories of open economy politics to deduce the distri-butional implications of increased economic openness, a goal desired by the United States in all of the cases examined here, and then use counterfactual reasoning informed by the theory to generate insights into what the broader interests of the parties might have been.[45] I also draw heavily on the work of historians to ascertain what the United States and potential subordinates—and the groups in both—desired to achieve in each period. The first chap-ter in each regional case begins with a survey of the interests of the United States and groups within the subordinate states. There is no objective way to determine whether the interests as characterized are correct—whatever that might mean. In each case, we can only judge whether the interests described

43. Lake and Powell 1999.
44. Frieden 1999.
45. On open economy politics, see Bates 1997; Frieden and Rogowski 1996; Hiscox 2002; Lake 2009b.

are reasonable, conform with what historians have concluded, accord with subsequent behavior, and help us understand the politics of international hierarchy.

This strategy runs the risk of bias in the subjective perceptions of interests by the actors being reproduced in the histories used to help identify those interests. Interests are defined here from the viewpoints of the actors themselves. As we shall see in the cases, and discuss in the conclusion, there is likely a non-theorized tendency in the dominant state to "other" the opposition in subordinates or exaggerate the differences in their interests. In deciding to ally with one group, decision-makers and publics in the dominant state may come to see the opposition as "alien," inherently hostile, or more distant from themselves than they are in some objective sense. Since most of the histories of US foreign policy—and especially those relied on for this study—are written by US historians, any bias in the perceived interests may be reproduced in those histories. This does not matter significantly for the analysis here, though it will make indirect or direct rule more likely than otherwise, but any exaggeration in the difference between the dominant state and the opposition will matter for policy recommendations going forward. If differences between the United States and opposition groups in subordinate states are systematically exaggerated, domestic rule might be more attractive and indirect rule less attractive than is perceived through our subjective and biased assessments. I take up this challenge in the conclusion.

All of this is complicated by the fact that when rule is indirect international hierarchy is sometimes hard to see. This is the true value of the theory here. It grinds a new set of lenses through which we can see what was previously obscured. By focusing on the larger pattern of compliance and how external support bolsters the political position of groups with sympathetic policy preferences that could not otherwise survive in office, international hierarchy through indirect rule can be revealed.

Indirect rule is a distinct form of international power and influence. It differs from how interstate relations are often understood in IR. It is not a bargain between two states in which some compromise is reached, each has incentives to defect, and monitoring and enforcement are central problems. Rather, indirect rule is an ongoing relationship in which the dominant state enables the allied group in the subordinate to achieve and retain political power and, in so doing, enact policies both prefer to at least the strictly domestic alternative. It is not coercive, an exchange of favors or a threatened "do this or else," but a deal in which the dominant state provides support and the allied group acts in its self-interest to provide a policy that both actors desire. There is no incentive to defect from the deal itself, but there are problems of opportunism in which the allied group may exploit or entrap the dominant state. To safeguard itself, the dominant state retains discretion over the terms of the relationship and imposes additional rules on the subordinate that transform policy cooperation into international hierarchy. With all of this as prolegomenon, we can now turn the theory to the question of how indirect rule works in actual cases and with what consequences.

2

Indirect Rule in the Caribbean and Central America

Historians have long characterized US policy in the Caribbean and Central America (CCA) in the late nineteenth and early twentieth centuries as imperialist, and the region as a US empire or, more accurately, an informal empire. We also know that this policy led to a century or more of brutal authoritarian repression and anti-Americanism. The fact of US domination is not new or in dispute, nor are its consequences.

The usual explanation for this international hierarchy focuses on US power—the colossus to the north. But this is almost a truism and falls short as an explanation. The United States could have ruled directly in a formal empire, much as European countries did during this period. Instead, the United States mostly ruled indirectly, allying with local elites who then enacted policies that both preferred to the strictly domestic policy alternative.

Historians point to two factors for this relative "restraint," yet neither explanation is sufficient. One focuses on the United States' national identity as an anti-imperialist nation. While there were anti-imperialists in the United States in the late nineteenth and early twentieth centuries, there were many important imperialists as well, including presidents and other influential policymakers.[1] Americans also overcame their reluctance for empire in acquiring the Philippines, Guam, and Puerto Rico as "possessions," and ruled directly in Nicaragua, Haiti, and the Dominican Republic for extended periods. If the United States was an anti-imperialist nation, it was remarkably selective in applying this principle.

---

1. On imperialism and US national identity, see Ninkovich 2001. On the anti-imperialists, see Beisner 1968.

A second explanation attributes the reluctance of the United States to acquire territory in the CCA to racism. But this factor is even more complicated than the first, as it was used to justify both imperialism and its opposite, and therefore cannot explain either. There is no doubt that many if not most Americans of the era were deeply racist, seeing people of color in the Caribbean Basin as inherently inferior and incapable of self-government and thus requiring some form of oversight by a "civilized" country, as President Theodore Roosevelt would declare in 1904. For imperialists, in a variant of the "white man's burden" used to justify European colonialism, the need for supervision implied that subordinate countries needed to be governed directly by the United States. For anti-imperialists, this same racism required a hands-off approach for fear that any association would ultimately bring people of color into the union on equal terms, thus they favored some form of indirect rule in alliance with elites of Spanish descent. Racism mattered, rendering the opposition more "alien" than the elites in the eyes of decision-makers in Washington, but by itself cannot explain the choice between direct and indirect rule.

Even if we accept these explanations for the lack of direct rule, they do not explain the choice of indirect rule and how it operated in the region. This chapter surveys the interests that allowed indirect rule to flourish in the CCA, the forms of support provided by the United States to the regional elites, and the domestic political consequences of indirect rule. The next chapter examines the international hierarchy created by the United States to govern the region and the politics of resistance.

Interests

The primary interest of the United States in the CCA during the early twentieth century was economic expansion, both in trade and finance. This interest in expanded economic exchange was reciprocated by landowning elites throughout the region. In this regard, at least, the policy preferences of the United States and the group that would become its ally in the region were relatively well aligned. Yet, as its specific assets in the region expanded, the United States became more sensitive to the policy choices of its subordinates, doubled down on its strategy of indirect rule, and as we shall see in the next chapter became more willing to use direct rule when opportunism by its allies became too severe.

While recognizing that local variations existed, political interests in the CCA can be described in general terms (see figure 2.1). The main issue in contention was the means and pace of integration into an increasingly globalized economy. The United States sought expanded trade and investment opportunities in the Caribbean Basin ($d=1$). Landed elites strove to commercialize agriculture, pushing tenants off small farms and expanding crops for

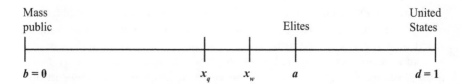

Figure 2.1 Configuration of US and CCA interests

export ($b \leq a \leq d$). Mass publics, mostly peasants and wage laborers, focused more on local conditions but opposed the economic dislocations forced upon them ($b{=}0$). Though relatively powerful and able to impose something close to their ideal policy on the majority of society (x_q), landed elites were restrained by a fear of popular uprisings. By allying with the United States, elites could shift policy further in their favor and that of Washington.

Interests in the United States

The United States turned to the CCA during the first great depression of 1873–1896.[2] During this period, the United States suffered through three severe recessions brought on by increasing production, especially from innovations in manufacturing, the mechanization of agriculture, and falling transportation costs. The closure of European markets to US grain exports exacerbated the problem.[3] Insufficient demand in the United States led to deflation and demands for currency reform, including calls for going off the gold standard or adopting bimetallism.[4] The political manifestation of this economic crisis was the Populist movement championed by three-time presidential candidate William Jennings Bryan. Many embraced the expansion of US exports and the investment of "surplus" capital abroad as solutions to the crisis. With Europe facing its own difficulties and becoming increasingly protectionist, the United States turned toward new markets in its backyard, namely the CCA. This was not necessarily the best or most vibrant market, but it was the one most readily available to US exporters and investors.[5]

There were important sectional differences within the United States.[6] The South, still concentrated in tobacco and cotton, often saw itself in competition with Caribbean producers. The nascent cane sugar industry in Louisiana,

---

2. Hoffman 1970.
3. Ashley 1920. The relationship between European protectionism and US exports is discussed at length in Lake 1988, chap. 3.
4. Frieden 1997.
5. The definitive account is still LaFeber 1963. On more ideological explanations for US expansion, see Rosenberg 1982; Schoultz 2018.
6. On sectionalism in the United States, see Bensel 1984. On sectionalism and US foreign policy, see Trubowitz 1998; Narizny 2007.

along with sugar beet farmers in Colorado, opposed any economic strategy that relied on greater trade with the CCA. The Midwest produced grains and meat largely for domestic consumption and export to Europe. Yet, as the infamous Coalition of Iron and Rye formed in Germany and similar protectionist movements sprouted across the continent, midwestern farmers began to seek new markets elsewhere.[7] Finally, the Northeast was the manufacturing center of the country. Though it still had trouble competing with established European industries, it saw Latin America in general and the Caribbean in particular as ripe markets for US goods. Given that the Northeast was the most populous region in the United States, no one could win a national election without the support of its voters, making the region decisive in setting policy. Along with midwestern farmers, the Northeast defined the nation's interest as one of overseas economic expansion.

US Specific Assets

As it expanded into the Caribbean, the United States acquired specific assets that were vulnerable to changes in policy. As its specific assets increased, it became ever more important to ensure that "friendly" governments that would support and not threaten US interests in the region remained in power. Foremost among these assets was the Panama Canal. In fact, the tortured history of the canal foundered on precisely the problem of site specificity.[8] In practice, progress stalled on the question of who would control the canal: Britain and the United States (under the Clayton-Bulwer Treaty of 1850), France (under the first attempt led by Ferdinand de Lesseps in the 1880s), or just the United States. Construction began only once Washington had negotiated exclusive control in the Hay-Pauncefote Treaty of 1901, in which Britain gave up its claim to joint governance. Given the required investment, the United States needed a compliant regime in whichever country it chose to build the canal. Both Nicaragua, which had been the long-preferred route, and Colombia, of which Panama was a province, proved to be difficult negotiating partners. Seeing an opportunity, President Roosevelt spurred a revolt in Panama in 1903 and immediately recognized the new state. Understanding its dependence on Washington, the new Panamanian government gave Roosevelt favorable terms in the Hay-Bunau-Varilla Treaty, signed just two weeks after the declaration of independence, which charged far less for transit rights than previously demanded by Colombia and granted the United States de facto sovereignty over the canal zone. Only once the question of control was finally sorted out did construction begin in 1904.

The United States also understood early on that a peer competitor could seize control of any canal—and could likely do so more easily from forward

7. Lake 1989.
8. Gibson 2014, 231.

bases in the region. Once the canal moved from vision to reality, protecting it became a central pillar of US policy in the region, including foreclosing the other possible route across the isthmus through Nicaragua (see chapter 3). By extension, protecting the canal also meant controlling the two primary transit routes from the Atlantic to the Caribbean, namely the Windward Passage separating Cuba and the island of Hispaniola (Haiti and the Dominican Republic) and the Mona Passage separating Hispaniola and Puerto Rico, making these three islands critical choke points that, along with Panama (and Nicaragua), needed to be incorporated in the informal empire.[9] Military planners foresaw the need to control Haiti and the Dominican Republic as early as 1904.[10] As Secretary of State Elihu Root wrote privately in 1905, "The inevitable effect of our building the Canal must be to require us to police the surrounding premises. In the nature of things, trade and control, and the obligation to keep order which go with them, must come our way."[11] As we shall see in the next chapter, the United States resorted to direct rule only when internal instability combined with European meddling in these crucial states threatened access to the canal.

Other US investments in the Caribbean went almost entirely into resource extraction, infrastructure (mainly railroads), and plantation agriculture, all sectors also characterized by high asset specificity and vulnerable to changes in national policy (see table 2.1). With the promise of US hierarchy following the building of the Panama Canal, US entrepreneurs poured into the region. US investments grew rapidly during this period, more than doubling between 1897, before the Spanish-American War, and 1908, when the canal was well underway, and quadrupling by 1914 when the canal opened. The same pattern emerged in portfolio investment, which grew from $274 million in 1908 to $310 million in 1914, mostly in government loans. Having invested in these site-specific assets, the United States was vulnerable to political changes in Caribbean states where new regimes might seek to renegotiate the terms of any past investment by demanding a greater share of the profits or even expropriating the asset in its entirety.[12] Likewise, once money is lent, borrowing countries will always have a temptation to appropriate at least some of the value by defaulting on the loan or demanding what is now called a "haircut" of revised terms. As these investments moved forward, and the risks increased, the intensity of US policy preferences also increased.

Following the Spanish-American War and the start of construction on the Panama Canal, US interests in the Caribbean did not change dramatically in substance but did become progressively more intense as its site-specific

---

9. McPherson 2014, 4; Trías Monge 1997, 23; Ninkovich 2001, 123.
10. McPherson 2014, 5.
11. Quoted in LaFeber 1983, 37.
12. Stallings 1987.

TABLE 2.1
US investments in the Caribbean Basin, 1897–1934
(Current dollars; percentages of US worldwide total in each category)

	1897		1908		1914		1919		1924		1929		1935	
	Amount	Percent	Amount	Percent	Amount	Percent	Amount	Percent	Amount	Percent	Amount	Percent	Amount	Percent
Portfolio investment														
Caribbean Basin			273.7	27.8	310	32.8	306.5	10.7	389.6	8.0	429.8	5.3	433.6	6.2
Foreign direct investment by country														
Cuba and West Indies	49.0	7.7	195.5	11.9	281.3	10.6	567.3	14.6	993.2	18.4	1025.5	13.6	731.3	10.1
Mexico	200.2	31.6	416.4	25.4	587.1	22.1	643.6	16.6	735.4	13.6	709.2	9.4	651.7	9.0
Central America	21.2	3.3	37.9	2.3	89.6	3.4	112.5	2.9	143.5	2.7	250.9	3.3	160	2.2
CCA total	270.4	42.6	649.8	39.7	958	36.1	1323.4	34.1	1872.1	34.7	1985.6	26.3	1543	21.4
Non-site specific														
Selling organizations	5.5	2.2	7.5	1.2	13.5	1.5	16	1.3	20	1.1	24.9	1.4	0.0	0.0
Manufacturing	3.0	1.2	28	4.7	30	3.3	34	2.7	37	2.1	60.6	3.4	58	4.0
Oil distribution	1.0	0.4	3	0.5	3	0.3	10	0.8	10	0.6	9.5	0.5	9	0.6
Resource extraction														
Oil production	2.5	1.0	52	8.7	88	9.6	208	16.6	285	15.9	261.5	14.6	261.5	18.2
Precious metals and stones	52.0	20.5	127.6	21.2	150.2	16.4	113.5	9.0	119	6.6	123	6.9	112	7.8
Industrial minerals	21.0	8.3	122	20.3	178.2	19.4	144.3	11.5	146.5	8.2	151.4	8.5	154.9	10.8
Infrastructure														
Railroads	128.3	50.6	109	18.1	172.1	18.7	207.6	16.5	257.7	14.4	230.1	12.9	186.3	13.0
Public utilities	5.6	2.2	46.2	7.7	94.7	10.3	96.5	7.7	157.4	8.8	227.9	12.7	227.4	15.8
Plantation agriculture														
Sugar	22	8.7	54	9.0	112	12.2	350	27.9	663	37.0	637.5	35.6	363.5	25.3
Fruit	10.5	4.1	31.5	5.2	61.8	6.7	72.5	5.8	94	5.2	61.3	3.4	63.1	4.4
Rubber	2	0.8	20	3.3	15	1.6	3	0.2	2	0.1	1.5	0.1	1	0.1

Source: Lewis 1938, appendix D, 606; and appendix E, table 605.4, 654–655. All recalculations by author. Miscellaneous sectors dropped so totals by sector will not equal totals by region.

assets expanded. Once this process began, the policies of states in the CCA mattered more to Washington than before, and the United States became increasingly willing to bear higher costs to protect those assets. Informal empire spurred investment and investment spurred informal empire.

Interests in the Caribbean

The overriding interest of all CCA countries was integration into the global economy. Caribbean states are among the world's smallest and most open economies; only Mexico is an exception to this condition. During the colonial era, countries in the region developed as highly specialized producers of primary products. Because they exported minerals or unprocessed agricultural goods to Europe and imported whatever manufactures they could afford under mercantilist trade restrictions, none of the regional economies enjoyed a diversified, self-sustaining engine for growth—again, with the possible exception of Mexico.[13] Even agriculture for domestic consumption was less than what was required for subsistence and there was virtually no local industry. To acquire the rudiments of life in the Caribbean required exports to pay for essential imports.[14] This was especially true for elites who could afford manufactured goods. As the first period of globalization took off in the late nineteenth century, the attraction of deepening integration could not be resisted.[15]

Almost everywhere on the Caribbean littoral, there were two main lines of cleavage, one between elites and masses and a second within the elites. In the first, landowning elites sought to expand commercial agriculture, which in turn displaced peasants and small farmers. Caribbean societies were likely among the most unequal in the world.[16] Whether exploiting land titles granted under colonialism or exerting superior political power, elites consolidated their control and pushed peasants off the land and into wage labor, a trend that accelerated across the region during what is known as the liberal reform period (1870–1940), and especially during the years leading up to World War I. There were, of course, exceptions to this rule. After achieving independence, Haiti redistributed land and moved toward smallholder (mostly subsistence) farming, but it too was constrained by the need to make labor available for the sugar plantations to earn the export revenues required for the survival of all, but especially the unusually avaricious elites. Costa Rica specialized in smallholder coffee farming and therefore escaped the need to repress labor that later plagued so many other countries in the region.[17] But

---

13. Bulmer-Thomas 2012, 107–108.
14. Hopkins 2018, 389 and 428.
15. O'Rourke and Williamson 2000.
16. Bulmer-Thomas 2012, 13–14. See also Prados de la Escosura 2007; de Ferranti et al. 2004; Moatsos et al. 2014. On inequality today, see Hoffman and Centeno 2003.
17. Mahoney 2001. The elites nonetheless retained economic power and political control through their dominance of coffee processing, commerce, and all-important credit (Yashar 1997, 56–58).

for most islands and Central American republics, elites controlled the means of production (land) and sought to expand exports of primary products.

Peasants and wage laborers in agriculture formed the opposition. Largely illiterate, rural, and dispersed in small communities across the countryside, and typically employed in backbreaking physical labor for low pay, workers for the most part focused on the conditions of their daily lives. Although wages were higher for cane workers, work in the sugar mills was especially dangerous.[18] Employment was also sporadic, peaking at harvest season and often nonexistent at other times of the year. Protests accordingly centered on working conditions and, sometimes, on living conditions on the plantations, though the two were often fused. These were mostly local events, spurred by a particularly oppressive overseer or owner. The only general demand of peasants and agricultural workers was for land redistribution, especially for limiting or even breaking up the largest holdings. It was the underlying economic inequality that split the masses from the elites throughout the region and, in turn, made indirect rule possible.

How distant US interests were from landless peasants and wage laborers remains a matter of some dispute. On the one hand, publics appear not to have mobilized around ties to the United States or international politics generally. Indeed, if there was any attitude toward the United States it was generally one of optimism that a liberal democracy might favor their struggle and improve their working conditions. On the other hand, the United States saw itself as quite distant from the concerns of these disenfranchised groups. With US citizens and firms investing in the same plantations as local elites, economic interests appear to be a sufficient explanation for this perception. At the same time, it is impossible to discount the role of racism in determining perceived interests. In this era, racism permeated US society, especially in the Jim Crow South but elsewhere as well. Even President Woodrow Wilson, otherwise a leading Progressive, was deeply racist; he resegregated the federal workforce and dismissed Japan's appeal for racial equality at the Versailles Peace Conference that created the League of Nations, attitudes and actions that carried over into relations with the CCA and likely contributed to the increased frequency of military interventions during his presidency. That landed elites in the CCA were largely drawn from Spanish colonialists and their descendants while the great mass of society was Black or indigenous surely played some role in leading the United States to see its interests as more closely aligned with elites than laborers. Almost by default, the United States assumed landed elites were its most reliable allies in the region.

The second line of cleavage was between members of the elite, though any line drawn through a class will necessarily be blurry. Historically, elites across the region were split between conservative and liberal parties, often overlapping with the cleavage between peninsulares, on the one hand, and

---

18. Trías Monge 1997, 16.

criollos, on the other. For the most part, conservatives were drawn from the colonial elite, tied politically and economically to the metropole, dependent on mercantilist trade practices, and allied with corporatist institutions, primarily the Catholic Church. Importantly, both conservatives and the church tended to benefit from communal landholdings and supported traditional patronage relations with the peasantry. First generation liberals, emerging around the time of independence from Spain, drew upon Enlightenment thought, championed human equality, and promoted market-based reforms. Also drawn from the landed elite and wealthy merchant class, though with fewer ties to Spain and blinded by racism, these early liberals never sought cross-class coalitions with peasants or indigenous communities and thus never achieved significant political power. By 1870 or so, however, liberals and conservatives had largely converged, at least in the ways that mattered to the United States. By mid-century, second generation liberals in the region—heavily influenced by Auguste Comte's philosophical positivism and, later, social Darwinism—developed an "elitist vision of society that was deeply imbued with classism and racism."[19] Though maintaining the rhetoric of egalitarianism and advocating for more "modern" political institutions, liberals came to be skeptical of fundamental social and economic reforms. Pushing to transform communal land into private property wherever possible, liberals supported the development of plantation agriculture for export. Conservatives also embraced commercial agriculture and economic integration, if somewhat more reluctantly due to the social changes they introduced. Though they opposed rapid privatization of land and sided with the church in the treatment of ecclesiastical property, they too supported the move toward export crops. By the turn of the twentieth century, partisan differences were small, individuals changed parties as local advantages waxed and waned, and politics became more personalist than ideological.[20] Nonetheless, elites remained highly fractionalized throughout this period, almost uniquely so compared to the other regions considered in this volume. Fractionalization exacerbated rent-seeking by individuals within the elite and, as I explain in chapter 3, sometimes pulled the United States into internal conflicts it might have wished to avoid.

Indirect Rule

Political systems within the CCA were highly skewed in favor of elites. Peasants, landless laborers, and workers more generally comprised about 90 percent of the population in most of these societies, with landed elites, merchants, and a small professional class comprising the other 10 percent.

---

19. Mahoney 2001, 68.
20. Mahoney 2001, 69.

After centuries of slavery and geographic isolation, and absent any organization to represent their interests, the masses lacked significant political power and possessed only a limited ability to act collectively. With plantations dispersed around the island and workers locked into semifeudal conditions, for instance, Cuban laborers might never meet anyone from another plantation or village—never mind plan or carry out successful nationwide political movements.[21] Nonetheless, elites lived in constant fear of mass unrest, a not unreasonable worry given the history of slave revolts across the region. While they exploited workers to the fullest extent, the lives of elites were precarious despite or perhaps because of the fact that they dominated their political systems.

The United States did not find a tabula rasa when it entered the CCA beginning in the 1890s. In almost no case had national elites been reliant on their own resources. European imperial powers had always favored landed elites, allowing them to survive politically despite their minority status. As it engaged the region, the United States did not create but inherited the role of regime guarantor. Thus, the counterfactual of what elites might have done and what policies they might have enacted without assistance from some foreign power is hard to estimate. Nonetheless, it seems reasonable to assume that any autonomous Caribbean political system would have been skewed against the interests of the majority of the population and toward those of the elite, although without external support elites would have been forced to limit their exploitation of peasants and landless laborers in light of the potential for further revolts. That is, while elites did have the upper hand in the struggle over land and employment, without external support they would likely have had to slow the process of commercialization and reduce the pace by which tenant farmers on small plots were displaced into wage labor on plantations.

With several prominent exceptions, discussed in the next chapter, the United States ruled countries in the CCA indirectly through alliances with local elites. Indirect rule was made possible by the similar (though not identical) interests of the United States and the regional elites outlined above and the willingness of Washington to, first, guarantee the political survival of elite regimes during a period of rapid economic and social change, and second, offer policy concessions that increased the economic benefits and political power of the elites. As Secretary of State Robert Olds declared in 1926, "We do control the destinies of Central America and we do so for the reason that the national interest absolutely dictates such a course. . . . Central America has always understood that governments which we recognize and support stay in power while those we do not recognize and support fail."[22]

---

21. Thomas 2010.
22. Quoted in Loveman 2010, 234.

Governance Costs

To support its elite allies, Washington extended de facto guarantees of regime survival. While elites were politically powerful, dominating politics in the face of the broad but unorganized opposition, they were still constrained in the pace and extent of commercialization by the threat of rebellion. With a regime guarantee from Washington, which shared interests in commercializing agriculture, the elite could more easily shift policy in its favor and that of the United States.

During the informal empire in the CCA, Washington intervened relatively frequently to suppress threats to its allies or protect its own investments. While in the Arab Middle East and other more recent cases (see chapter 6) the United States typically gives allied regimes security force assistance and relies on the regime itself to police the opposition, in the CCA this form of aid was employed only toward the end of the period considered here when the United States began training various national guard units. Through the 1920s, the United States more often relied on its own military forces to protect its clients. This was possible because the United States could quickly and easily deploy troops from its own territory or the Panama Canal Zone, and because international norms had not yet turned against external military interventions—indeed, as we shall see in chapter 3, this norm developed in response to frequent US interventions in the region.[23] Given the small size of countries in the CCA relative to the United States, sending a frigate to the main port or landing a few hundred marines was usually enough to quell any violence, signal Washington's support for a regime, or spur a coup by a preferred candidate.

Evidence for this regime guarantee can be found in the interventions carried out by the United States, but these must be carefully parsed. Interventions occurred for several, sometimes overlapping reasons. Some interventions aimed only to defend American lives and interests—meaning investments by US entrepreneurs or banks; this was in all cases the publicly stated justification. Other interventions were undoubtedly to defend the regime against domestic opponents whether US investments were targeted or not. Still other interventions, however, were cases of entrapment in which the United States was drawn into intra-elite disputes (see chapter 3). In these instances, the United States was particularly likely to intervene when troublesome leaders either failed to comply with the rules of the informal empire or were so disruptive that they threatened to undermine the solidarity and power of the elite as an ally.

Every history of US-CCA relations highlights the number of interventions carried out by the United States before 1932, after which the Good Neighbor policy supposedly broke the pattern. Interpreting the meaning of

---

23. On norms of intervention, see Finnemore 2003.

these interventions is more fraught, however. First off, what counts as an intervention varies. Some historians count twenty such events, mostly those in which US troops were deployed on foreign soil and stayed for some extended period. Others count forty-plus interventions. One historian cites an implausible 6,000 possible "interventions."[24] Interpreting interventions is complicated by the fact that peasant rebellions—that is, revolts by the "opposition"—were often stimulated by elite conflicts during which publics saw opportunities to press demands on the elites or were intra-elite struggles that simply mobilized large numbers of workers through traditional patronage ties. The most comprehensive listing of US "displays of force" in the region was compiled by the Congressional Research Service and is abstracted in table 2.2 (table 2.2.A in this chapter's appendix provides more information on each case). Based on the available histories—often sketchy in their details—I identify those that appear aimed directly at suppressing unrest by opposition actors and those seeking to replace particular leaders within the elite, recognizing that some may include both goals. The null category includes those interventions in which the United States appears to have acted only to protect its citizens or their property. Deciding whether an intervention was designed to replace a leader is difficult. Negotiations between the United States and various factions often unfolded over time, and a coup or pressure on leaders to step aside may not coincide perfectly with the often limited periods of overt US intervention. In coding the cases, I focus on "irregular" exits and entries of leaders as defined by the Archigos dataset that occurred within two months of the intervention, with many but not all occurring within the period of the intervention.[25] I also note whether the intervention occurs in the same year as a foreign imposed regime change (FIRC), as coded from three different sources.[26] Between 1880 and 1940, there were many irregular exits and entries and a few FIRCs that did not coincide with US uses of force, in some of which the United States undoubtedly played a role. When a case falls within a relatively narrow window around the display of force, it is more likely that the United States had some hand in the transition. Conversely, there may be "regular" transitions in which the United States also exercised some influence, convincing an incumbent not to extend his term or seek reelection, promoting a favored candidate over others, and so on. Focusing only on irregular transitions immediately before or after a display of force is likely capturing the minimum number of cases of US involvement rather than the maximum.

---

24. McPherson 2014, 1.
25. See Goemans, Gleditsch, and Chiozza 2009.
26. Owen 2010, 18; Willard-Foster 2019, 249–250; Monten and Downes 2013, online appendix A. All FIRCs coincided with these interventions except for one identified by Willard-Foster in the Dominican Republic in 1912. Unfortunately, FIRCs are only coded by year, not specific dates.

TABLE 2.2
US military interventions in the CCA, 1880–1940

		Replace leader		
		No	Yes	
Suppress opposition	No	12	10	22
	Yes	7	12	19
		19	22	41

Source: Derived from table 2.2.A.

As table 2.2 shows, roughly one-quarter of the forty-one interventions were directed neither at suppressing political unrest by non-government actors nor at replacing leaders; cases in the upper left cell usually involved territorial disputes or protecting US citizens and assets. In ten cases in the upper right cell the United States intervened to replace a leader absent any effort to suppress unrest, constituting cases of "pure" elite replacement. These appear to be cases in which the United States was entrapped into intra-elite contests, discussed more in the following chapter. In the seven cases in the lower left cell the United States intervened to assist in putting down opposition unrest but did not replace the incumbent leader, all of which appear to have honored the regime guarantee. In the final twelve cases, the leader was replaced while the United States was also attempting to suppress some form of domestic instability. In nineteen cases, then, the United States intervened in a relatively neutral fashion to protect its own interests or on behalf of the current government to suppress political unrest. In twenty-two cases, Washington used force during a period of leadership transition and, though details are often not available, likely played some role in these events. The pattern is consistent with the United States mostly intervening to assist leaders in maintaining power in the face of resistance or replacing leaders who either refused to follow the rules set by the United States or provoked factional conflicts that undermined elite power. Nonetheless, how many of these interventions by the United States were "necessary" under indirect rule to sustain its elite allies and how many were cases of entrapment that might otherwise have been avoided is difficult to discern. A fair conclusion is that both types of cases occurred, with entrapment imposing additional costs on the United States beyond what was required for indirect rule itself.

Importantly, as the specific assets accumulated by the United States in the region increased, so did the number of interventions, which peaked during World War I and persisted into the early 1930s. The pattern of interventions by year is illustrated in figure 2.2. This is consistent with the increase in specific assets accumulated over the period and the corresponding increase in the intensity of US interests. As the Panama Canal neared completion in 1914, the United States became more concerned with the policies adopted

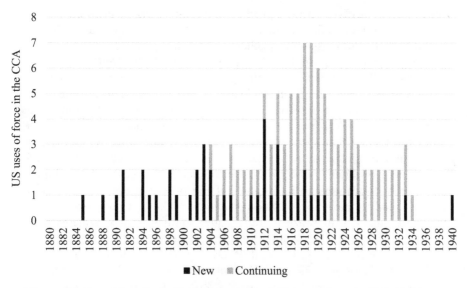

Figure 2.2 Uses of force by the United States in the CCA, by year between 1880–1940

by states in the region. It is noteworthy that the duration of interventions also increased over time, with episodic displays of force being replaced by multi-year interventions, often including periods of direct rule (see chapter 3). One plausible interpretation of the gradual decline in the number of new interventions after 1919 is that Caribbean elites and societies "learned" the extent of the US commitment to stability in the region and acted according-ly.[27] Several of these prolonged interventions constitute cases of direct rule, discussed in the following chapter.

The governance costs to the United States of these military interventions appear to have been relatively low. As historian Frank Ninkovich writes, "be-cause the United States possessed overwhelming power and there were few serious costs associated with throwing its weight around, intervention in its heyday seemed to operate as if by some involuntary conditioned reflex."[28] Given its military superiority, the United States could intervene easily, albeit at some cost to itself (see chapter 3). While this would have allowed it to rule directly if it so chose, it also allowed Washington to secure indirect rule at little cost to itself.

Elites also benefited from US tariff concessions in addition to the US defense of their regimes. Given increasing specialization in export crops produced on large elite-owned plantations and the repression of labor that allowed the gains from trade to be captured by those same landowners,

---

27. Tulchin 1971.
28. Ninkovich 2001, 93.

reductions in tariffs on tropical products not only redirected economic transactions to the United States, consistent with US objectives, but also concentrated benefits within that group allied with Washington.

Certain tropical products had long entered the United States duty free,
especially coffee and cacao, even though, like sugar, they were potential revenue sources. Given the fiscal implications, not taxing these products was
very much a political decision. Under the McKinley Act of 1890 and the
Dingley Act of 1897, sugar, molasses, coffee, tea, and hides were allowed to
enter the United States duty free in return for concessions on US exports
of live animals, grains, meat products, bridge-building materials, cottonseed
and related products, railway cars, and timber and iron for shipbuilding.
Retaliatory duties were to be imposed if the president determined that a
nation failed to make appropriate reductions.[29] The first reciprocity agreement was signed with Brazil in 1891. Agreements were also reached with
Spain for Cuba and Puerto Rico; with the United Kingdom for Barbados,
Jamaica, Leeward Islands, Trinidad, Windward Islands, and British Guiana;
and with El Salvador, Nicaragua, Honduras, and Guatemala.[30] With the exception of tea, all these products were primarily imported from countries
on the Caribbean littoral. The duty on sugar was reinstituted in 1894 and
the duty on hides was restored in 1897. Nonetheless, other products of the
region remained duty free.

Sugar was the most controversial item in the tariff both at home and
abroad. The tariff on sugar was, by far, the single largest source of US government revenue. Eliminated in the McKinley tariff, the duty was restored under
the Democrats four years later both for revenue—fixing the federal deficit
that opened when the duty was repealed—and as a concession to senators
from Louisiana, where it remained in subsequent Republican tariffs under
pressure from the nascent sugar beet industry in Colorado. Yet, the tariff on
sugar created opportunities for bilateral concessions for political purposes.
Sugar was the largest export commodity from the region, and indeed the
health of Caribbean economies depended almost entirely on the quantity of
sugar produced and its price in any given year. Under a commercial treaty
enacted in 1903, Cuban sugar and tobacco (leaf form only) enjoyed a 20 percent reduction in the tariff paid by other producers.[31] The overall effect of

---

29. Of all the countries determined to discriminate unjustly against US goods, only
Colombia, Haiti, and Venezuela refused to grant the United States tariff concessions and,
thus, were subjected to the retaliatory duties specified in the act.

30. US sugar producers were granted a "bounty" to offset the reduction in tariffs. Democrats
differed on the level of protection but concurred on the need to expand exports. In the
Wilson-Gorman Tariff of 1894, the Democrats adopted a strategy of diffuse reciprocity, lowering duties unilaterally on raw materials typically imported from Latin America, expecting
this would lead to greater US exports (LaFeber 1963, 160). For more extensive discussions of
reciprocity, see Lake 1988, 100–102 and 126–131.

31. Bulmer-Thomas 2012, 93 and 207.

US policy was that from the early 1900s nearly all goods from CCA countries entered the United States either duty free or on concessionary terms.

Trade concessions on tropical products were targeted benefits for land-owning elites in the region, making them almost ideal for compensating US allies while not increasing the political power of other groups in society. The dependence of sugar producers on the US market increased dramatically.[32] Yet, the benefits were highly concentrated. Workers gained little. Real wages for agricultural workers were essentially stagnant after 1870 even as invest-ment, production, and exports expanded. Indeed, in Barbados, where re-cords are most complete, the real wage in 1900 was identical to that in 1838.[33] In conditions of excess labor and subsistence wages, fluctuations in the de-mand and prices for commodities resulted not in higher or lower wages for workers but only in increases and decreases in employment. With most of the gains going to wealthy elites, average workers most likely suffered declines in real income during the years of US indirect rule.[34] Thus, tariff concessions were a boon mostly for the landed elites who profited from increased pro-duction and prices for agricultural commodities and secured their allegiance to Washington.[35]

There were some costs to the United States from these trade concessions, but they were mostly political rather than economic. Except for sugar, as noted, the United States produced few tropical products. Nonetheless, pro-tection was the primary partisan issue of the era.[36] Republicans favored high and nearly prohibitive tariffs on imports, while the Democrats advocated freer trade. As tariffs still accounted for more than 50 percent of all govern-ment revenue in the 1890s, however, no one envisioned anything like the free trade of the post–World War II era. Reducing the tariff on any prod-uct was always politically fraught either because it removed protection from the domestic industry or, in the case of tropical products, reduced revenue. Nonetheless, the governance cost of the concessions in exchange for locking Caribbean elites further into the informal empire appears to have been mod-est. Together, the low cost of interventions to protect elite regimes and the trade concessions to benefit these same elites meant that the governance costs of indirect rule were relatively low. Given the alignment of interests between elite allies and the United States and low governance costs, Washington was able to pull policy quite close to the ideal of elites and its own preferences, leaving it quite satisfied with the results of its support.

---

32. Bulmer-Thomas 2012, 211, figure 8.2 and tables C.15 and C.22.
33. Bulmer-Thomas 2012, 74–75, figure 3.5 and table A.8.
34. Bulmer-Thomas 2012, 259, figure 10.1.
35. Some of the gains, of course, were shared with US investors who poured into the re-gion, especially Cuba and Puerto Rico. US investment in sugar production alone rose from approximately $22 million in 1897 to $112 million in 1914 and $663 million in 1924 (Lewis 1938, appendix D, 578–604).
36. Terrill 1973.

Indirect Rule in Cuba

Cuba exemplifies indirect rule in the CCA. The jewel of the Spanish empire, by the 1820s the island was the richest colony and the largest sugar producer in the world.[37] It was also highly unequal in land and wealth. In 1899, the largest 2 percent of farms held over 40 percent of all land on the island, with 90 percent of all sugar and tobacco produced by white farmers.[38] To put this another way, nearly all of the country's two most valuable export crops were produced by large landowners of Spanish descent. In part because of this inequality, Cuba had long been unstable with multiple elite factions competing for power.[39] Social and economic cleavages divided criollos from peninsulares; merchants from planters; smaller planters in the east from larger planters in the west; and ranchers, coffee farmers, and sugar plantation owners from each other. These divisions were manifest in the "first" war for independence in 1868, and only festered afterward in the division between liberals, who demanded independence, and the conservative Constitutionalist Union Party, which desired to maintain ties with Spain.[40] In the face of this continuing instability, the United States imposed itself into an already blazing conflict with Spain, sending the USS Maine into the maelstrom and then using its sinking as a justification to seize Spanish possessions.

The debate over how to rule Cuba began even before the Spanish-American War. Though imperialists wanted full control under US direct rule, in the end the United States settled on a system of indirect rule that was enormously favorable to US interests. Accordingly, once the United States was victorious a military government was declared, which lasted until May 1902, when Cuba obtained its independence under the tight restrictions of the Platt Amendment as incorporated into the Cuban constitution (see chapter 3).

Famously, the Teller Amendment to the declaration of war against Spain prohibited the United States from the permanent annexation of Cuba and promised "to leave the government and control of the island to its people."[41] Historians often attribute the Teller Amendment to domestic political considerations in the United States, but this explanation is inadequate. Worried that annexation would allow duty-free entry of Cuban sugar, Senator Henry Teller (R-CO), representing the nascent beet sugar industry of his state, wanted to limit competition from the world's lowest-cost producer, and thus sought to take annexation off the table. Yet, some other means of limiting imports of sugar from Cuba could have been found, or alternatively a bounty could have been paid to domestic sugar producers as under the McKinley

---

37. Thomas 2010, 41.
38. Thomas 2010, 247 and 251.
39. Thomas 2010, 158. See also Hopkins 2018, 349–351 and 584.
40. Thomas 2010, 147.
41. Trías Monge 1997, 25.

Tariff of 1890. Under the US occupation that began on January 1, 1899, military officials under orders from President William McKinley rapidly expanded US economic investments on the island, especially into the sugar industry, creating a politically influential counterweight within a few years to the beet sugar producers. Indeed, according to historian A. G. Hopkins, the strategy of Leonard Wood, the US occupation authority in Cuba following the Spanish-American War, "was to pack as many US companies and as much foreign investment into Cuba as he could in the short time before he was obliged to hand power to an independent Cuban administration," encouraging investments in sugar plantations and associated enterprises, including railways and utilities. By the early twentieth century, following the end of the US occupation, 60 percent of all rural land in Cuba was owned by US investors and corporations.[42] This made for a not insignificant pressure group in favor of retaining control over the island. Even if the Teller Amendment was decisive in 1898, it cannot explain why some rationale was not found by 1902 to justify continued US occupation. Finally, the 1903 commercial treaty granted Cuban sugar entry into the US market with an advantage over beet sugar.[43] Rather, the Teller Amendment represented a compromise between the imperialists and those in Congress who supported a free Cuba. Critically, McKinley did not recognize the Cuban rebels as a legitimate government in order to maintain his freedom of action and promised that the US military would remain on the island until Cuba had "complete tranquility," a sufficiently ambiguous phrase to countenance a variety of outcomes. Indeed, by the end of the war, even Senator Teller favored some form of long-term oversight of the island's politics.[44]

Looming over all these negotiations, however, was the recognition that the island was ungovernable under direct rule, or at least incapable of being suppressed at a cost the United States was willing to bear. Where indirect rule promised an alliance with the elite, direct rule would have required repressing not only the landless laborers and workers but also the elite that had been mobilized to fight for independence.[45] As discussed in chapter 3, the Spanish-American War was a substantial undertaking for the US military.

---

42. The General Sugar Company, owned by City Bank (New York), alone held over one million acres of land, hundreds of miles of railroad, a dozen sugar mills, and was responsible for one quarter of the country's annual production (Hudson 2017, 202).

43. Thomas 2010, 266.

44. Ninkovich 2001, 94–95.

45. Racism played a key role in limiting US direct rule. Although Cuba had a far smaller slave population relative to the total population than any other island in the Caribbean and a larger white population than elsewhere, its substantial black and mulatto population thwarted annexationists. Senator Orville Platt, the architect of US-Cuban relations after independence, argued that "the people of Cuba, by reason of race and characteristic, cannot be easily assimilated by us. . . . Their presence in the American union, as a state, would be most disturbing." John W. Foster, a former secretary of state, echoed Platt, asking, "with the negro problem in our Southern States pressing upon us for solution . . . do we desire to aggravate the situation by adding a million more of the despised race to our voting population?" (P. Smith 1996, 51).

More important, perhaps, Cubans had successfully mobilized to fight for their own independence from Spain and were better prepared to resist direct rule than other societies in the region. Though the United States would likely have won any contest, it would have incurred some substantial costs in subduing the population on a permanent basis. Even under the occupation, the United States kept over 24,000 troops in Cuba to maintain order, though stationed in disease-free urban zones. Given the substantially mobilized society, annexation would have only resulted in continuing resistance, which the United States was ill-prepared to suppress.

Instead, the United States moved quickly to indirect rule. Tomás Estrada Palma, who once favored outright annexation by the United States, became president on the termination of the military government on May 20, 1902. Yet, his pro-American rule was fragile. As elsewhere in the region, the United States supported the regime by offering favorable terms on exports and by guaranteeing its security, though not the position of any particular leader. The security guarantee is notable in the frequent interventions into Cuban politics that protected the allied regime and supposedly stabilized the country. The United States intervened three times to restore order, protect its assets, and shape the outcomes of domestic political struggles. The first intervention arose from a contested election in December 1905, soon after the US withdrawal. Although he might have won fairly, Estrada stole the election. General José Miguel Gómez, the governor of Santa Clara province, protested to the United States and, receiving no response, led an armed revolt. The opposition force of 24,000 vastly outnumbered the Cuban Rural Guard of 3,000. Estrada then petitioned the United States to send forces to preserve life and property, although he was really interested in the preservation of his presidency.[46] In September 1906, Roosevelt sent two warships and secretary of war William Howard Taft to mediate. With the United States having lost faith in his leadership, Estrada and his vice president subsequently resigned. In the absence of an administration, Taft named himself provisional governor, succeeded by Charles Magoon in October.[47] Under the oversight of 5,600 US troops, the United States held new elections, which were won by Gómez. After his inauguration in January 1909, the US provisional government and troops withdrew.

Though a genuinely popular figure, Gómez turned out to be an incompetent leader.[48] He was confronted first by an insurrection of veterans who demanded the removal of government officials who had supported Spain in 1898, and then a second insurrection by Black Cubans under the leadership of Evaristo Estenoz of the Independent Party of Color, who were protesting their unequal treatment despite having fought for independence. Alarmed

46. Gibson 2014, 229.
47. Schoultz 2018, 38; Earwicker 2013a.
48. Thomas 2010, 365.

by these events, one of the few times when the opposition actually threat-ened the regime, the United States dispatched three gunboats and landed troops at Guantanamo, with additional troops at Daiquirí to protect US sugar plantations. Estenoz was killed in June 1912 and US forces withdrew in July. Though the United States played no overt role in the election, conservative and highly pro-American Mario García Menocal was elected later that year.

In 1916, Menocal engaged in obvious voting fraud in his reelection bid, with ballot boxes intercepted by the government and results withheld from the public; 800,000 votes were cast from a pool of 500,000 eligible voters.[49] Protests by liberals, including former president Gómez, were brushed off by President Woodrow Wilson, who backed Menocal. Gómez then led a sec-ond insurrection starting February 1917, and the United States responded by again sending three battleships and landing marines at Guantanamo and elsewhere to protect the sugar plantations. At Menocal's request, 2,500 US troops remained in Cuba. US-supervised elections were held in 1920, but Gómez boycotted in protest, leaving the presidency to another liberal, Alfredo Zayas. Even before the election, Sumner Wells, then head of the Division of Latin American Affairs at the Department of State, drew up a list of desirable characteristics for any Cuban president, the most important of which was "his thorough acquaintance with the desires of this [US] govern-ment . . . [and] his amenability to suggestion of advice which might be made to him by the American legation."[50] As a victory "present," the United States gave Zayas fifteen memoranda detailing reforms and reiterating the US right to monitor their implementation, including the right to approve of Zayas's cabinet choices.[51] With Zayas's consent to these terms, US forces withdrew in January 1922.

The United States also supported the regime with targeted trade conces-sions. As noted, under the 1903 commercial treaty Cuban sugar and tobacco received a 20 percent reduction in the tariff paid by other producers, greatly benefiting Cuban growers and securing their dominant position in the US market.[52] Indeed, after World War I, the discounted tariff on Cuban sugar was essentially the effective rate as virtually all US dutiable imports came from the island.[53] As noted by historian A. G. Hopkins, the development of the sugar industry "turned the export economy decisively toward the United States," giving it unparalleled influence even after the island regained its nominal

---

49. Thomas 2010, 317.

50. Quoted in Thomas 2010, 330. Brackets in the original.

51. Earwicker 2013b, 127.

52. Bulmer-Thomas 2012, 93 and 207.

53. Taussig 1931, 457–458. This advantageous system was replaced by quotas in 1934 under the Agricultural Assistance Administration formed by President Franklin D. Roosevelt in the New Deal, which not unexpectedly favored domestic and insular producers to the detriment of Cuban growers—a trend reversed during World War II when world supply dramatically declined (see Irwin 2014).

independence. Under the property system in Cuba, however, these concessions also furthered specialization in sugar and tobacco for export, concentrated the benefits of trade on plantation owners, and limited economic
opportunities for now landless peasants and workers. In the Economic
Defense Act of 1914, and at the instigation of US bankers, Cuba demonetized
all foreign currencies previously circulating in the country and tied the national currency to the US dollar, meaning that all international transactions
were now paid in dollars rather than Spanish gold.[54] During a visit to the
United States in April 1925, president-elect Gerardo Machado declared that
the role of government in Cuba was to defend foreign capital, pledged "an
absolute guarantee" for businesses operating in the country, and on assuming
office one month later carried out a widespread crackdown on communists
and union organizers.[55] Backed by the security guarantee from Washington
and bought off by the sugar concessions in the US tariff schedule, Cuba was
an example of indirect rule in stark form.

Consequences of Indirect Rule

The United States was enormously successful in pulling policy in the CCA
in its preferred direction. This is, of course, a subjective judgement. How
quickly and extensively regional elites might have been able to commercialize
agriculture without the support of the United States is difficult to estimate.
The most direct measure of elite influence might be land consolidation, for
which we lack data. One excellent proxy measure, though, is sugar production, which is carried out more efficiently on plantations and requires a measure of capital for processing that is typically unavailable to smallholders.
During this period of expanding indirect rule, sugar exports from Caribbean
countries alone rose from 1.6 billion pounds in 1900 to 7 billion pounds in
1914, expanding during the war to 14 billion pounds in the mid-1920s. Sugar
exports as a percentage of all exports rose from 35 percent in 1900 to more
than 80 percent in 1920, though this was driven in part by extraordinary
price increases due to shortages in Europe during the war.[56] Other commodities, especially tobacco, followed a similar trajectory.

Overall, trade in the Caribbean grew by 89.3 percent between 1900 and
1913, which was then the fastest rate of growth in the world with the exception
of Canada, and by 62.3 percent between 1921 and 1929, just before the Great

---

54. Hudson 2017, 138–139, 204.
55. Hudson 2017, 213–217. One year later, however, Machado turned on the US banks he
had previously pledged to support.
56. Bulmer-Thomas 2012, 230–231. The real price of sugar increased fourfold during the
war (Bulmer-Thomas 2012, 242–243, figure 9.4).

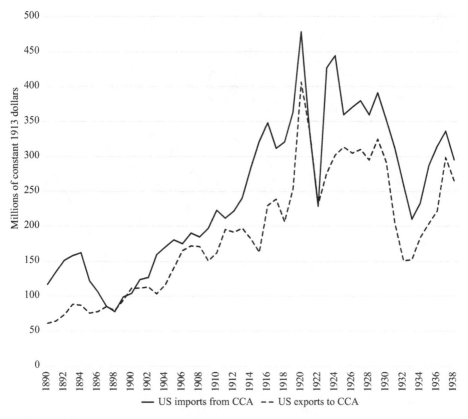

Figure 2.3 US trade with the CCA, 1890–1938

Source: Trade data in current dollars from Bureau of the Census 1975 (Series M 87–102, pp. 250–251). Converted to constant dollars using indices derived from Federico and Tena Junguito 2018.

Depression.[57] Although the United States was nearly always in a balance of trade deficit with the region, importing more than it was exporting to the CCA, trade with the United States grew especially fast (see figure 2.3). Between 1898 and 1913, US imports from the CCA grew 208 percent in real terms and exports to the region grew by 147 percent, far greater than the overall increase in trade.

The United States also gradually shifted trade away from Europe. As indicated in figure 2.4, beginning before 1900, the United States took more than 50 percent of all exports from Caribbean Basin countries, reaching a high of almost 74 percent in 1920. US exports to the region displaced those from Europe more slowly, passing the 50 percent mark only in 1908. Altogether, the United States reoriented economic activity away from the former colonial

---

57. Bulmer-Thomas 2012, 201, table 8.1. This remarkable rate of growth is all the more impressive considering that global trade in manufactures typically grows more rapidly than trade in primary products (Bulmer-Thomas 2012, 323).

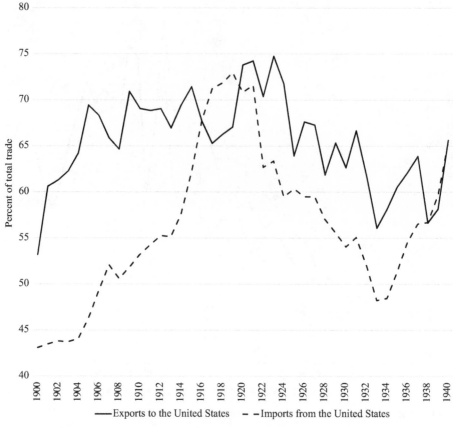

Figure 2.4 Domination of Caribbean trade by the United States, 1900–1940

Source: Bulmer-Thomas 2012, tables C15 and C22.

powers toward itself. To the extent that the United States wanted to expand trade with its neighbors and preferred exclusive economic regions, it got most of what it wanted in alliance with regional elites who wanted the same.

We see similar patterns in US investments in the CCA during this period. As already noted, investments in specific assets are a driver of indirect rule, and led the United States to place increasing importance on the policy adopted by its subordinates. At the same time, the expansion of investments reflects Washington's confidence in the position of its allies. Without an expectation that elites in this case would continue to rule indirectly, the United States would have been hesitant to invest in the region. Table 2.1 above shows that portfolio investment (government bonds and loans) increased substantially over time, peaking before the Great Depression (an increase of 57 percent between 1908 and 1929) and accounting for roughly one-third of total US portfolio investment before World War I. Foreign direct investment (FDI) in the CCA as a whole increased even faster at 634 percent between 1897 and

1929, mostly going to Mexico early in the period but shifting to Cuba and the West Indies over time. The vast majority of FDI went into resource extraction and infrastructure early in the 1900s, then switched to plantation agriculture and sugar production during and after the war. Motivated by profit opportunities, these investments by private actors would likely not have occurred if they were not protected by allied regimes that were, in turn, protected by the United States.

While the United States succeeded in obtaining policies it desired, indirect rule had severe consequences for mass publics within the CCA. Countries in the region were less democratic than elsewhere in Latin America at that time and more likely to repress human rights. These consequences reflect the bargain made between the United States and local elites to implement policies that both preferred and to suppress the opposition to those policies, including actions by the United States to put down insurrections.

In principle, the United States supported liberal democracy in Latin America, including in the CCA. Its belief that it is a shining example on a hill that others should emulate has always been part of the American creed. An important consequence of elite-led indirect rule, however, is that regimes will be autocratic and repressive. This follows logically from the selection process. Distant from the policy preferences of their own populations, and more aligned with US than with local interests, these elites were necessarily unpopular. If free and fair elections under a broad franchise had actually been held, none of the elite factions would have likely won the popular vote. US allies, therefore, were forced to govern autocratically. Despite its expressed preference for democracy, the United States came to support and, indeed, protect some of history's most vicious dictators. Preferring "military dictatorships to indigenous radicalism," writes historian Walter LaFeber, US "support for relatively open elections gave way to accepting repression."[58] The United States was not opposed to democracy, it was just a lesser priority than the policies it wished states in the CCA to adopt, and it was willing to sublimate this goal as necessary to keep its allies in power.[59]

As figure 2.5 indicates, states throughout the CCA scored about the same as the rest of the world (largely Europe and North America at this time) on a common measure of democracy but much lower than in South America. Likewise, countries in the Caribbean Basin were also more repressive on average than elsewhere. Regimes in the CCA were more likely to abuse human rights than other countries in general or in South America in particular. The stark difference with South America suggests that the lack of democracy or human rights was not simply the residual influence of institutions constructed

---

58. LaFeber 1983, 74.
59. See Drake 1991.

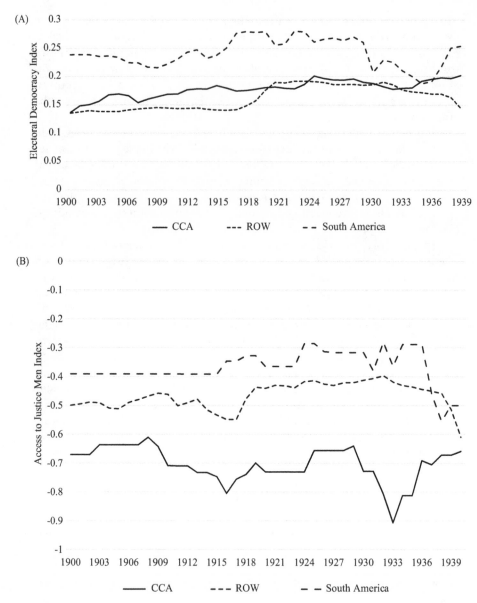

Figure 2.5 Democracy and human rights in the CCA compared to rest of world (ROW) and South American averages, 1900–1940. Caribbean Basin countries are Correlates of War (COW) code 40 (Cuba) to 101 (Venezuela) and South American countries are COW code 110 (Guyana) to 165 (Uruguay). Global is all countries except the CCA and South America, in this period meaning mostly North America and Europe. Panel A: VDem Electoral Democracy Index (v2x_polyarchy). Higher scores achieved when suffrage is extensive, political and civil society organizations can operate freely, elections are clean and not marred by fraud or

Figure 2.5 (*continued*) systematic irregularities, and elections affect the composition of the chief executive of the country. In between elections, there is freedom of expression and an independent media capable of presenting alternative views on political matters. Very similar patterns are found in virtually all other measures of democracy. Panel B: VDem Access to Justice Men Index (v2clacjstm). Higher scores achieved to the extent men can bring cases before the courts without risk to their personal safety, trials are fair, and men have effective ability to seek redress if public authorities violate their rights, including the rights to counsel, defense, and appeal. Very similar patterns are found for nearly all other measures of human rights practices.

---

under Spanish rule.[60] The evidence on democracy and repression, in short, is consistent with the model of indirect rule and unpopular elite regimes backed by the United States. Although the United States might in principle extol the virtues of democracy, in fact it did little to promote liberal political institutions and practices. This was not just an oversight or even malign neglect, but a predictable consequence of indirect rule through small elites.

With relatively aligned preferences, the United States and its elite allies in the CCA got much of what they wanted in the early twentieth century. Commercial agriculture grew rapidly and US trade expanded. Elite regimes remained secure despite enacting policies increasingly unfavorable to the masses, indeed, pushing smallholders off the land and into wage labor while plantation owners kept real wages fixed even as exports and profits rose. In turn, the United States could support elite regimes at relatively little cost to itself, principally having to defend regimes on an occasional basis and granting tariff concessions that posed little harm to US domestic producers. All this was in the mutual self-interest of the United States and its allies. By supporting elites, the United States could pull policy in the direction they both favored at a cost it was willing to bear.

In supporting elite regimes, however, the United States not only failed to promote democracy and human rights but ended up backing autocrats who often severely repressed their societies. Indeed, by the 1930s, when the United States pledged not to intervene in their affairs any longer, many regimes in the CCA were led by some of the most odious but pro-American dictators on record, including General Rafael Leónidas Trujillo y Molina in the Dominican Republic and Anastasio Somoza in Nicaragua. By guaranteeing the survival of their regimes against domestic opposition, the United States also opened itself to greater opportunism, which required greater hierarchy, a topic taken up in the next chapter.

---

60. On the distinct nature and long-term consequences of Spanish rule, see Sokoloff and Engerman 2000.

Appendix to Chapter 2

TABLE 2.2.A
Displays of military force in the CCA by the United States, 1880–1940

	Country/ year of intervention	Suppress opposition	Irregular leader-ship transition and Foreign Imposed Regime Change (FIRC)	Brief description
1	Panama 1/18–1/19/1885	Yes	None	During period of French construction of the canal, Panamanian liberals launched a secessionist rebellion against Colombia. Under guise of protecting US-financed railroad, troops land to put down revolt and reestablish US military dominance given French presence.
2	Haiti 12/20/1888	No	Irregular entry 10/16/1888	Display of force to persuade Haiti to return US steamer charged with breach of blockade during period of political instability.
3	Haiti 1891	Yes	None	Troops protect interests in guano on Navassa Island following rebellion by Haitian workers and trial of rebels for murder in United States; sovereignty of island long disputed between United States and Haiti.
4	Nicaragua 7/6–8/7/1894	No	None	Granted autonomy under treaty between Britain and Nicaragua, the latter invades and seizes control over Bluefields in early 1894; joint US-British intervention forces the withdrawal of Nicaraguan forces; on departure of US-British troops, Nicaragua invades a second time and retains control after paying indemnity to Britain.
5	Colombia 3/8–3/9/1895	Yes	None	Troops deploy at Bocas del Toro in current Panama to crush labor strike against US banana planters.
6	Nicaragua 5/2–5/4/1896	No	None	Troops protect US holdings in Corinto during political unrest.

7	Nicaragua 2/7–2/8/1898	No	None	Troops protect interests at San Juan del Sur; on standby in case of attack, given President Zelaya's extension of his term of office, US troops enter the city at request of consulate and withdraw the next day.
8	Spanish-American War 1898/Cuba 1898–1902	No	FIRC[1]	United States seizes Cuba and Puerto Rico from Spain. US troops remain in Cuba until 1902.
9	Nicaragua 2/22–3/5/1899	No	None	During insurrection, troops protect interests at San Juan del Norte and Bluefields; aim to prevent rebels and government from destroying US property.
10	Colombia 11/20–12/4/1901	No	None	Troops protect US property on isthmus and keep transit lines open during Panama secession.
11	Colombia 4/16–4/23/1902	No	None	US forces protect US lives and property at Bocas del Toro during Panama secession.
12	Colombia 9/19–11/18/1902	No	None	United States places armed guards on all trains crossing the isthmus to keep the railroad line open and stations ships on both sides of Panama to prevent the landing of Colombian troops during Panama secession.
13	Honduras 3/23–3/31/1903	Yes	Irregular exit 1/30 and irregular entry on 2/1	Troops protect US consulate and steamship wharf at Puerto Cortez during revolutionary activity.
14	Dominican Republic 3/30–4/21/1903	Yes	Irregular exit and entry on 4/18	In support of the government, troops protect US interests in Santo Domingo during revolutionary outbreak.
15	Panama 11/4/1903–1/21/1914	Yes	Irregular entry on 11/3	Troops intervene to support independence from Colombia; and again to protect US interests and forestall a coup.
16	Dominican Republic 1/2–2/11/1904	Yes	None	During revolutionary activity, US and British forces establish ceasefire zone in support of government; US troops protect US interests in several cities.

(continued)

TABLE 2.2.A (*continued*)
Displays of military force in the CCA by the United States, 1880–1940

	Country/ year of intervention	Suppress opposition	Irregular leadership transition and Foreign Imposed Regime Change (FIRC)	Brief description
17	Cuba 9/1906–1/23/1909	Yes	Irregular exit 9/28 and FIRC[1,2]	Following fraudulent reelection of Moderate Party leader Estrada Palma, liberals led by Miguel Gómez revolt; Estrada Palma requests US intervention but subsequently resigns. After US-designed reforms, Gómez elected.
18	Honduras 3/18–6/8/1907	Yes	Irregular exit on 4/11 and irregular entry on 4/18	To protect US interests during a war between Honduras and Nicaragua, troops were stationed in Trujillo, Ceiba, Puerto Cortez, San Pedro, Laguna, and Choloma.
19	Nicaragua 5/19–9/4/1910	No	Irregular exit and entry 8/20, irregular exit and entry 8/29, and FIRC[2,3]	United States backs insurgents seeking to overthrow Zelaya's handpicked successor, José Madriz, forcing him out of office; replaced by Juan José Estrada.
20	Honduras 1/26/1911	No	Irregular exit and entry on 3/28 and FIRC[2,3]	Insurrection supported by US investors overthrows Miguel Dávila with implicit support of US government; troops seize key ports and supervise transitional government that elects Manuel Bonilla.
21	Panama 1912	No	None	On request by both political parties, troops supervise elections.
22	Honduras 1912	No	FIRC[3]	Forces land temporarily to prevent seizure by the government of a US-owned railroad.
23	Cuba 6/5–8/5/1912	Yes	None	Troops deployed to press Gómez to address Independent Party of Color uprising and protect sugar plantations.
24	Nicaragua 11/1912–8/5/1925	Yes	FIRC[3]	In midst of domestic insurgency and unrest, troops deployed to protect US-backed president Adolfo Díaz.
25	Mexico 9/5–9/7/1913	No	None	Troops land at Ciaris Estero to evacuate US citizens during civil strife.

#	Country and dates			Description
26	Haiti 1/29–2/9; 2/20–2/21;10/19/1914	No	Irregular exit 1/27, irregular entry 2/8, irregular exit and entry 10/19	Naval forces protect US nationals threatened by civil unrest.
27	Dominican Republic 6–7/1914	Yes	Foreign imposed exit 8/27 and FIRC[2,3]	During ongoing insurrection, US troops deploy to contain rebels sponsored by and operating out of Haiti. United States forces resignation of president.
28	Mexico 1914–1917	No	Irregular exit 7/15/1914, irregular entry 10/19/1915, and FIRC[3]	Ongoing hostilities during the Mexican Revolution, including two US military interventions.
29	Haiti 7/28/1915–8/15/1934	No	Irregular exit 7/26 and FIRC[1,2,3]	Following assassination of president, marines occupy country and declare martial law.
30	Dominican Republic 5/1916–9/1924	No	Foreign imposed exit 5/8/1916, irregular entry 7/12/1924, and FIRC[1,2,3]	With successive presidents de facto vetoed by the United States, troops occupy country, shut Congress, and declare martial law.
31	Cuba 1917–9/1922	Yes	FIRC[1,2]	Following fraudulent election of Mario Menocal, liberals attempt coup blocked by US marines; former liberal Alfredo Zayas elected in 1920 with support of Menocal's conservative party.
32	Mexico 1918–1919	No	None	After withdrawal of John J. Pershing, United States pursues bandits into Mexican territory at least nine times.
33	Panama 1918–1920	Yes	None	Troops police Veraguas Province according to treaty stipulations to protect US interests, especially United Fruit plantations, during election disturbances and subsequent unrest.
34	Honduras 9/8–9/12/1919	Yes	Irregular exit 9/9 and FIRC[3]	Troops deployed during attempted revolution to maintain order in neutral zone.

(continued)

TABLE 2.2.A (*continued*)
Displays of military force in the CCA by the United States, 1880–1940

	Country/ year of intervention	Suppress opposition	Irregular leadership transition and Foreign Imposed Regime Change (FIRC)	Brief description
35	Guatemala 4/9–4/27/1920	No	Irregular exit and entry 4/15	Troops protect US interests during fighting between unionists and government.
36	Panama-Costa Rica 1921	No	None	Naval squadrons deployed on both sides of the isthmus to prevent war over a boundary dispute.
37	Honduras 2/28–3/31/1924	No	Irregular exit and entry 2/1 and FIRC[2]	Troops protect US interests during election hostilities.
38	Honduras 4/19–4/21/1925	No	None	Troops protect foreigners at La Ceiba during political upheaval.
39	Panama 10/12–10/23/1925	Yes	None	Troops landed to keep order and protect US interests during strikes and rent riots and secessionist revolt in Darién.
40	Nicaragua 5/7/1926–1/3/1933	Yes	FIRC[2,3]	Prompted by civil war between liberals and conservatives, United States returns and restores Díaz to office as president; insurgency begins under Augusto César Sandino.
41	Cuba 1933	Yes	Irregular exit and entry 8/12, irregular exit 9/5, irregular entry 9/10	Naval demonstration to support President Gerardo Machado during attempted revolution.

Source: Compiled from Torreon 2017; McPherson 2013. Instances identified by Torreon, unless otherwise noted, and coded from Torreon and McPherson. Leader transitions from Goemans, Gleditsch, and Chiozza Archigos 4.1. FIRCs coded from 1 = Owen 2010, 18; 2 = Willard-Foster 2019, 249–250; 3 = Monten and Downes 2013 online appendix.

3

Hierarchy in the Caribbean and Central America

Interests alone might have allowed for effective cooperation between the United States and elites in the Caribbean and Central America as both sides saw potential gains from expanding markets. Had regional elites been able to commercialize agriculture at the rate they desired without the regime guarantees and favorable tariff policies of the United States, indirect rule might not have been necessary. If so, some kind of free trade zone or a customs union might have sufficed. Indeed, just such a union was envisioned by Secretary of State William Blaine in the 1880s.[1] Though regional elites were powerful, they were not powerful enough to impose their policy preferences on the mass of society. Constrained as they were by the fear of peasant insurrections, fueled by the memory of the slave revolts of the early nineteenth century, regional elites would have had to moderate their policies without external support. Through indirect rule, the United States changed the politics and possibilities within its client states.

In guaranteeing the political survival of local elites, however, the United States also created the potential for them to act opportunistically in ways that would undercut Washington's benefits from indirect rule. To limit this potential, the United States imposed a set of rules on its subordinate states, enforced by the very real possibility of direct rule should its injunctions be violated. Only in the case of Mexico, where indirect rule was impossibly costly during the revolutionary period, did the United States accept domestic rule. In turn, the United States faced resistance from mass publics, mostly in the form of anti-Americanism, and by the end of the period even opposition from elites to the interventions that enforced the rules of the informal

---

1. LaFeber 1963, 104–114.

empire. This chapter outlines the potential for opportunism and the rules imposed by the United States, considers the alternatives to indirect rule, and explores the various forms of resistance in the region.

Opportunism and the Rules of the Informal Empire

In supporting the landed elites, the United States exposed itself to possible opportunism by those same allies. Knowing that it preferred indirect rule to the alternatives, and increasingly so as its specific assets in the region increased, elites aimed to exploit the United States by diverting its assistance toward other ends and entrapping it into their internal struggles. As a consequence, the United States needed to set rules that would limit the ability of these elites to act in ways it opposed.

Opportunism

Exploitation was a potential problem at the level both of individual leaders and of the elites as a whole. Elite fractionalization created incentives for individual leaders to exploit the United States by extracting "rents" for themselves or their support coalitions. Some leaders were particularly avaricious. Others were politically weak and needed additional resources to consolidate their personal support coalitions. Given the tendency toward personalist rule and typically short tenures in office in the CCA, leaders frequently ransacked the public treasury, diverting tariff revenues and US loans into their private pockets.[2] With previous leaders often depleting the public fisc, even honest presidents often lacked the funds necessary to repay past loans. Elites as a class failed to reform their political systems to reduce fractionalization, which perpetuated the lack of state capacity. This was more common in finance than other types of investment.[3]

The United States also feared entrapment into internal conflicts between elites. Given that regional states lacked the ability to project power, Washington did not much fear being pulled into territorial conflicts, although the regional ambitions of President José Santos Zelaya of Nicaragua did pose a problem that led to his eventual ouster. Not without reason, however, it did worry about being dragged into conflicts between elite factions. Not only did private rent-seeking render elite regimes less effective at repressing their oppositions, but it fueled intra-elite infighting. These struggles often turned violent, with various factions mobilizing peasants through traditional patronage arrangements—thereby threatening elite dominance necessary for indirect rule—or appealing to Washington for support. The risk of entrapment

---

2. On loan diversions in Cuba, see Hudson 2017, 246.
3. On US financial control, see Hudson 2017.

was real and constant, and the United States found itself drawn into domestic struggles with some regularity. As discussed in the previous chapter, some number of interventions occurred not to suppress the opposition to indirect rule but as a result of entrapment, although it remains unclear exactly how one might differentiate these interventions from others.

Finally, the threats of exploitation and entrapment were exacerbated by the potential for European meddling in US-Caribbean relations. By offering CCA countries an alternative source of support and especially loans, Europeans powers might have allowed elites to play one potentially dominant state off against another. This would have had the effect of weakening the rules of informal empire subsequently imposed on US subordinates. Indeed, relations between European and regional states were actively sought by both sides. Europeans wanted to sustain their empires and lucrative CCA colonies or, at least, nurture postcolonial ties. In attempting to counterbalance the domination of the United States, countries in the CCA sought to retain or develop ties to other major powers in Europe. By having an "outside option," countries hoped to bargain more effectively with the United States. With alternative markets for their goods in Europe and alternative lenders in London, Paris, or Berlin, countries in the CCA could diversify their economies and limit the control over their finances exerted by the United States.

Given these conditions, the United States harbored well-founded fears of foreign meddling in its emerging sphere of influence. Europeans continued to play an important role in the region far longer than is commonly appreciated.[4] In the mid-1890s, as Peter Smith writes, the Caribbean was still "essentially a European lake."[5] The great turning point in hemispheric relations was the Venezuelan border crisis of 1895, in which the United States forced Britain to arbitrate its border with Caracas. Left undefined at independence, the boundary between Venezuela and the British colony of Guiana was the subject of periodic disputes. As tensions rose once again, Secretary of State Richard Olney demanded that London enter arbitration, famously declaring that "today, the United States is practically sovereign on this continent, and its fiat is law upon the subjects to which it confines its interposition." This was a rather startling claim of suzerainty, and the British, at least, were incredulous at this unilateral assertion of US international authority over the hemisphere. The response was fast and critical. "Her Majesty's Government," wrote foreign secretary Lord Salisbury, "[is] not prepared to admit that the interests of the United States are necessarily concerned in every frontier dispute which may arise between any two States who possess dominion in the Western Hemisphere."[6] But faced with threats of war from the administration

---

4. Loveman 2010, 5. By contrast, Ninkovich suggests that "the fear of foreign intervention was more hypothetical than real" (2001, 119).

5. P. Smith 1996, 28.

6. Quoted in Loveman 2010, 160.

of Grover Cleveland, and looking to retrench from the Americas to deal with emerging threats in Europe, Britain eventually agreed.[7] Nonetheless, as late as 1903, even after the United States had claimed Puerto Rico in its war with Spain, Germany was developing plans to take the island as a staging area to invade the eastern seaboard of the United States.[8] Fears that the German community in Haiti would draw the island into Berlin's sphere were constant through World War I. The most famous case of European aggrandizement, of course, is the Zimmermann Telegram supposedly sent from the German Foreign Office in 1917, offering an alliance and assistance to Mexico in re-claiming its "lost territory" in Texas, New Mexico, and Arizona if, in return, it would open a second front against the United States were Washington to join the war in Europe.[9] Actions like the Zimmermann Telegram showed just how disruptive European involvement could be to the informal empire being built by the United States. Overall, the United States faced real risks that its gains from indirect rule would be undermined by its elite allies acting alone or in concert with European competitors.

The Rules of the Informal Empire

To limit opportunism, the United States set forth rules to limit the behav-ior of its subordinates. The first formal articulation of these rules was the Platt Amendment to the Army Appropriations Bill of 1901, defining the con-ditions under which Cuba could gain its independence after the Spanish-American War (see chapter 2). Originally drafted by Secretary of War Elihu Root, the amendment was written into the Cuban constitution by the United States.[10] Root was contemplating something like the amendment as early as January of that year, when he outlined similar terms to Secretary of State John Hay and extended them in a note to General Leonard Wood, who was then in command of the occupation authority in Cuba. With their approval, Senator Orville Platt introduced the amendment, which was passed in the

7. LaFeber 1963, 278 and 315. Indeed, once Britain ceded its authority over the region, relations with the United States grew so warm that by 1898 and the outbreak of the war with Spain many speculated that London and Washington had entered a secret alliance, and the previously Anglophobic and now-former secretary of state Olney began referring to England as the United States' "best friend." See Rock 1989, 28. On the reconciliation between the United States and Britain, see Lobell 2003. In a challenging alternative interpretation, see Vucetic 2011. He argues that war between the United States and Britain over Venezuela was unthinkable because of a common Anglo-Saxon identity, partly forged during this crisis.
8. Loveman 2010, 168–169n60.
9. Loveman 2010, 168 and 209. There is continuing debate about the authenticity of the telegram, largely because the timing seems fortuitous. Intercepted by British intelligence in January 1917 just before Germany began to expand its submarine attacks on ships from the United States and other neutral countries and released on March 1 in the midst of the naval campaign, the Zimmermann Telegram may not have been decisive but certainly bolstered public support for entering the war.
10. Thomas 2010, 263.

Senate on February 27 and the House on March 1. The Cuban constitutional convention initially rejected the terms of the amendment, only to be told, on the one hand, that US troops would not be withdrawn until it was enacted into the constitution and, on the other hand, that if approved the United States would proceed with the negotiation of a favorable commercial treaty. The treaty was finally enacted in 1903 and privileged Cuban sugar. The terms of the Platt Amendment were clear. The Cuban government would (1) never enter into any treaty with foreign powers that impaired the independence of Cuba or allowed any bases or other ports on the island, (2) not undertake any debt beyond what could be repaid from ordinary revenues, (3) "consent that the United States may exercise the right to intervene for the preservation of Cuban independence [or] the maintenance of a government adequate for the protection of life, property and individual liberty," (4) validate all acts of the US military government, (5) enact sanitation and measures for disease eradication, making future interventions safer for US troops, and (6) grant the United States naval bases. The provisions of the Platt Amendment were not repealed until the Cuban-American Treaty of Relations of 1934 and its provisions were not removed from the constitution until 1940. The United States leased Guantanamo Bay indefinitely under the last clause, and the lease remains in effect.[11] The Platt Amendment led one historian to conclude that although "a sovereign nation in name, Cuba was in fact a protectorate of the United States," and another to note that "in essence, the Platt Amendment gave Cubans permission to rule themselves as long as they allowed the United States to veto any decision they made."[12] Nonetheless, President Theodore Roosevelt declared the Platt Amendment a success in 1904. "If every country washed by the Caribbean Sea would show the progress in stable and just civilization which with the aid of the Platt amendment Cuba has shown since our troops left the island," he claimed in his annual message to Congress, "all question of interference by this Nation with their affairs would be at an end."[13] In other words, as long as Cuba abided by the rules of the informal empire, the United States would not use force against it.

Though later cases were less codified, the Platt Amendment served as a template for indirect rule in the region. Indeed, the rules were informally generalized by President Roosevelt in his famous corollary to the Monroe Doctrine. In the context of a debt default by the Dominican Republic in 1904, Roosevelt declared in sweeping terms:

> Any country whose people conduct themselves well, can count upon our hearty friendship. If a nation shows that it knows how to act with reasonable efficiency and decency in social and political matters, if it

---

11. Thomas 2010, 262–267.
12. P. Smith 1996, 36; Kinzer 2006, 43.
13. Quoted in Schoultz 1998, 197; also Gibson 2014, 228.

keeps order and pays its obligations, it need fear no interference from the United States. Chronic wrong-doing, or an impotence which results in a general loosening of the ties of society, may in America, as elsewhere, ultimately require intervention by some civilized nation, and in the western hemisphere the adherence of the United States to the Monroe Doctrine may force the United States, however reluctantly, in flagrant cases of such wrong-doing or impotence, to the exercise of an international police power.[14]

Such a stark claim of international authority was and still is nearly unprecedented in international politics. Importantly, the United States reserved to itself to decide whether subordinates were actually following the rules of "civilized" society.

Not only were subordinates subject to US oversight and potential intervention, but the United States also typically demanded and received control over their finances. First implemented in the Dominican Republic in 1905, the United States eventually imposed customs receiverships on nearly all the major countries in the CCA. As Alan McPherson notes, the goal of what came to be called dollar diplomacy was "not to enrich US corporations—though that did occur—but to transfer debt from Europe to Wall Street and thus bolster regime stability."[15] In the modal response, default or near default would prompt the United States to (1) underwrite new loans in New York to pay off European creditors; (2) establish control over the customs revenues on which the new loans were secured, often by seizing the customs houses and staffing them with US citizens and sometimes even US government officials; (3) privilege repayment of the new loans over all other obligations, using the first 40 to 45 percent of all tariff revenues for this purpose; (4) appoint a US citizen to serve as a "financial adviser" to the government, often with veto power over expenditures; and (5) restrict further borrowing from other countries without US approval.[16] With relatively honest Americans in charge of collecting import duties, this practice was reputed to generate revenues sufficient not only to pay the banks on a timely basis but to provide the governments with even higher incomes than before.[17] At the very least, it limited how much any regime could divert to its own ends. US banks also typically acted as central repositories for local government funds, were charged with holding revenues as deposits and distributing salaries to employees on payday, and managed nearly all issues of government bonds.[18] The net effect was

---

14. Quoted in P. Smith 1996, 38.
15. McPherson 2014, 6.
16. Loveman 2010, 179. See also E. Kaplan 1998, 60 and 70. Customs revenues were normally about 90 percent of national revenues in countries of the region (P. Smith 1996, 66).
17. Maurer disputes this claim, arguing that only in the case of the Dominican Republic did receiverships generate more revenue than previously collected (2013, 90–91 and 183).
18. Hudson 2017.

to grant Washington unprecedented control over the finances of otherwise sovereign states.[19] Although individual leaders and elites as a whole chafed against these financial restrictions, they were accepted as the price of US support for their regimes.

Alternatives to Indirect Rule

Countries in the CCA largely complied with the rules instituted by the United States. They did not form relations with European countries, nor did they grant basing rights to any. Mexico did not even respond to the Zimmermann Telegram. They accepted the customs receiverships, though not always without protest. And they acquiesced to the US military interventions, at least until they became cases of direct rule later in the period. It was not that elites necessarily agreed with these restrictions. It was the distinct possibility of US occupation that appears to have limited the ability of subordinates to act opportunistically. The threat of direct rule was apparently sufficient to induce relatively high rates of compliance or, to say the same thing, low rates of opportunism, at least compared to the other regions examined in this study.

Direct Rule

Rather than engaging in indirect rule, the United States might have used its military power to impose its ideal policy on countries in the CCA under direct rule. This was, after all, the era in which the Europeans were dividing up Africa and transforming informal empires in the Middle East into formal colonies. The practice of imperialism elsewhere suggests that direct rule by the United States was possible. Nor was the United States entirely opposed to the possibility. Imperialism seized the popular imagination in 1898, including that of future president Roosevelt. Many apparently thought that to be a great power in this era required an empire and that war, especially against "backwards" peoples, would be cheap, quick, and easily won. In practice, though, the United States avoided direct rule except when specific assets were high and under threat, as in Nicaragua, Haiti, and the Dominican Republic.

The Costs of War and Occupation
To assess direct rule requires comparing the costs of war and occupation to the issues in dispute as well as the alternatives of indirect and domestic rule. The fact that the policy preferences of regional elites and the United States were relatively aligned placed real limits on the policy difference that might be obtained under indirect and direct rule. Despite the enthusiasm

---

19. On the indirect effects of US economists as an epistemic community that instilled ideas of financial rectitude in the countries of Latin America, see Drake 1989.

of Roosevelt and others, perhaps propelled by the not unreasonable belief that the United States would likely win any war in which it fully engaged, the costs of war and occupation nonetheless appear to have been substantial, at least compared to the conflict of interest between the United States and Caribbean elites. This conflicts with intuition and many histories of the period in which the United States is understood to be the nascent superpower, easily dominating its "backyard." Thus, determining the costs of war requires careful consideration, even more so because actual wars were both exceptional and rare. These costs were substantial, but not so high that they precluded direct rule under some conditions. While less preferred than indirect rule for the United States, direct rule remained a possibility.

The largest conflict fought in the region was the Spanish-American War of 1898. Though instructive, this war is an imperfect analogy for the costs of direct rule. It was, after all, fought not against a local military but against a European power, though one suffering a great geographical disadvantage and unable to offer any serious military resistance.[20] Equally important, as explained in chapter 2, the United States entered rather late into an ongoing war for independence in which Cuban revolutionaries were already on the verge of success; even if the US intervention was decisive in the end, it is important to note that the United States fought with rather than against substantial indigenous forces. Thus the counterfactual of a US war to impose its preferred policy against an independent country in the region remains difficult to estimate.

For Spain, the war was quite costly. At the height of the fighting, it fielded 196,000 troops in Cuba (for a total of 206,000 in the Caribbean as a whole) and suffered 700 to 800 casualties killed in action and another 15,000 dead from disease. The United States, in turn, deployed 72,339 troops to Cuba and suffered 385 fatalities from combat and another 2,000 or so from disease. This was a significant deployment. On the eve of war, the entire US Army totaled only 28,183 men, and was then immediately expanded to a total of 65,700. This meant that most US soldiers in Cuba were recruited as volunteers from the various state militias, including of course Roosevelt and his infamous Rough Riders. Nonetheless, the soldiers sent to Cuba alone were approximately triple the size of the prewar standing army. The epidemic of yellow fever that set in among US troops was especially difficult for military operations, forcing the army out of the interior of the country to the somewhat healthier coastal areas. Without a modern understanding of disease vectors, large portions of the country were essentially off-limits to US forces.[21] The financial cost of the war was also significant, totaling $283 million, or approximately 1.1 percent of GDP in the peak year. This is roughly equivalent to annual spending in the twenty-first century wars in Iraq and Afghanistan

20. Ninkovich 2001, 26.
21. Trask 1996, 324–335.

combined (1.2 percent of GDP in the peak year).[22] Later, long-term occupations by the United States in Nicaragua, Haiti, and the Dominican Republic were considerably less expensive, requiring a maximum of 5,500 US troops in the case of Nicaragua during the revolt led by Augusto Sandino.

There is no clear way to calibrate the costs of directly ruling subordinate countries. In absolute terms, the costs of the Spanish-American War were clearly lower than in World Wars I or II, which were great power wars for dominance of the international system that the United States was ultimately willing to join. The real question, however, are the costs of fighting and occupying a country relative to the issue in dispute, and focusing on the absolute magnitude of the costs, even relative to other wars, is misleading. What matters for the imposition of direct rule is the costs of war and occupation relative to the policy Washington might have imposed. The United States certainly wanted the Europeans to withdraw from hemispheric affairs and was willing to incur some significant costs in order to expel Spain from Cuba, which was the most valuable island in the Caribbean and the one that was closest to the United States. But the policy preferences of Cuban elites were relatively similar to those of the United States. What the United States might obtain by direct rule was not that different from what it might get if elites were to impose their own ideal policies on the rest of society. This pushed the United States to indirect rule wherever possible. Direct rule in the CCA, however, remained a possibility—unlike in many regions of the world, both then and now. Even if seldom employed, this potential served to constrain opportunism by elites. Indeed, the United States imposed direct rule mostly when its specific assets, especially the Panama Canal and its approaches, were threatened by local regimes.

Protecting Specific Assets: Nicaragua

Specific assets exert their effect on rule through policy. The greater the specific assets, the greater the stakes in the relationship between the dominant and subordinate states, and the greater the costs the dominant state is willing to bear to obtain the policies it desires. This implies that beyond some point the dominant state may be willing to pay the costs for direct rule to obtain its most preferred policy. In all of the cases of direct rule—Nicaragua between 1912 and 1924 and again in 1926 to 1932, Haiti between 1915 and 1934, and the Dominican Republic between 1916 and 1924—specific assets were high enough to render direct rule a possibility despite its higher costs.[23]

---

22. By contrast, World War I cost 13.6 percent of GDP and World War II cost 35.8 percent of GDP (Daggett 2010).

23. Puerto Rico, the only other case of direct rule in this period, is an interesting exception that, unfortunately, must be skipped for reasons of space. Acquired as a by-product of the Spanish-American War, Puerto Rico lacked significant resistance to US direct rule and, thus, incurred very low costs of occupation. These costs fell further as the Puerto Rican economy was reoriented from smallholder farmers dependent on trade with Spain to large elite-owned plantations benefiting from duty-free sugar exports to the United States. On Puerto Rico, see Ayala and Bernabé 2007; Gonzalez-Cruz 1998; Trías Monge 1997.

All three countries occupied strategic approaches or posed an alternative to the Panama Canal. At the same time, as opportunism increases, or becomes too severe, the net gains from indirect rule decline and direct rule will be preferred even if it is more costly than indirect rule. It was this conjuncture of high specific assets and increasing opportunism that drove direct rule in these cases. This is not a natural experiment, of course, as neither the canal nor other investments were exogenous, but the opening of the Panama Canal in 1914 along with increasing site-specific investments (see chapter 2) raised the stakes and suddenly made the United States less tolerant of opportunism. The timing of this dramatic shift to direct rule in these cases appears not to be coincidental.

Nicaragua exemplifies this switch to direct rule. As an alternate route across the isthmus, by train or a second canal, Nicaragua was of long-standing concern to Washington, leading to successive occupations by the United States.[24] Nicaragua was ruled indirectly by the United States from 1894, when Washington displaced Britain from its position of influence and a revolution brought President José Santos Zelaya to power. Historians differ in their descriptions of Zelaya. For some, he was a nationalist and liberal hero who stood up to the United States, for others he was a "depraved and brutal dictator, a contemptible little tyrant . . . best known for his persecution of foreigners."[25] Supported by the United States, however, he was a loyal ally for over a decade. In 1898, the American ambassador in Managua wrote that Zelaya "has given the people of Nicaragua as good a government as they will permit him," and more important, noted that "foreigners who attend to their own business, and do not meddle with politics which does not concern them, are fully protected."[26]

Yet, after the United States chose the Panama route for its canal, relations quickly soured. As one historian observed, "To the State Department, Nicaragua was no longer a country that needed to be coddled or cared for in preparation for future usefulness. Rather, it was now a country that needed to be watched carefully and kept in line."[27] Or as another remarked in wry understatement, "support for Zelaya waned after he appeared to take Nicaraguan sovereignty too seriously."[28] Starting in 1903, Zelaya began targeting US investors, canceling a contract with the George Emery Company for logging rights when the firm failed to fulfill its commitments, threatening to confiscate the assets of the La Luz y Los Angeles Mining Company, and waffling on his support for United Fruit when local growers went on strike.[29] He also entertained ambitions against Guatemala and El Salvador, disrupting

---

24. For historical background, see Bemis 1943, 161–166. See also Tulchin and Walter 1991.
25. E. Kaplan 1998, 38. For a more favorable treatment, see Kinzer 2006, chap. 3.
26. Quoted in Kinzer 2006, 60.
27. John Ellis Findling, quoted in Kinzer 2006. See Schoultz 1998, 210–211.
28. McCune 2019, 3.
29. Maurer 2013, 105. On the Emery concession, see Hudson 2017, 155.

regional politics.[30] When Zelaya borrowed heavily from European banks to build a railroad across the isthmus, an effort the United States sought to block, President Taft announced that the United States could no longer "tolerate and deal with such a medieval despot."[31] When Zelaya reached out to Germany and Japan to sell Nicaragua's transit rights for a second canal, his fate was sealed.[32] For his temerity in courting extra-regional powers and breaking one of the cardinal rules of the informal empire, Zelaya lost favor with the United States.

As was common in the region, Nicaraguan politics had long been split between liberals and conservatives. The traditional landed oligarchy and the Catholic Church formed the conservative party; urban elites formed the liberal party.[33] Yet, both parties remained highly personalist and clientelist and drew some peasant support.[34] Zelaya was a liberal, as were the most visible opponents of US rule in Nicaragua. When the United States intervened in the country beginning in 1912, it did so in support of conservatives who, representing no more than one-third of the population, were "the least electable party."[35]

With the backing of the United States and funded by US companies in Nicaragua, General Juan José Estrada, a provincial governor, hired American mercenaries to help overthrow Zelaya, setting off a civil war and revolution that lasted from 1910 to the US invasion two years later.[36] Adolfo Díaz, then chief accountant for the Philadelphia-based La Luz y Los Angeles Mining Company, served as treasurer for the rebellion, lending the rebels $600,000 for weapons and supplies, supposedly out of his $1,000 per year salary.[37] After two Americans were captured laying a mine in the San Juan River and executed, the Taft administration demanded Zelaya's ouster.[38] When a new president, José Madriz, also attempted to suppress the rebellion, the United States intervened, prohibiting government forces from firing upon the insurgents within what it declared to be a "neutral zone" because stray bullets "might accidentally hit American citizens" (who were, of course, mercenaries fighting with the rebels). Estrada's insurgents quickly won and marched to Managua, sending a telegram along the way to Secretary of State Philander C. Knox—who, as a lawyer in Pittsburgh, had previously represented the La Luz y Los Angeles Mining Company—assuring Americans of "the warm regard

---

30. Schoultz 1998, 210–211.
31. Quoted in Kinzer 2006, 66. Maurer 2013, 109.
32. E. Kaplan 1998, 38.
33. McCune 2019, 2.
34. McPherson 2014, 13–14.
35. McPherson 2014, 53, 74 and 214.
36. Castro 2013, 431.
37. Maurer 2013, 108–110. US interests contributed over $1 million to the revolt.
38. The United States insisted that the Americans had the stature of belligerents and therefore were entitled to prisoner of war status, and thus the executions made Zelaya into a war criminal—at least in their eyes (Kinzer 2006, 67). See also Schoultz 1998, 212.

entertained for them by the victorious party of the revolution."[39] Estrada was sworn in as president eight months after Zelaya's resignation, with Díaz as his vice president, completing what Stephen Kinzer describes as "the first real American coup."[40] Estrada turned out to be a paranoid alcoholic who, according to the US minister in Managua, resigned "in a fit of drunken insanity" and fled the country after only five months in office.[41] Díaz replaced Estrada and served as a loyal agent of the United States from 1911 to 1917 and again from 1926 to 1929. Díaz even offered his country to the United States as a protectorate in 1912 in exchange for new loans. The formerly anti-imperialist secretary of state William Jennings Bryan urged President Wilson to accept, arguing that "it will give us the right to do that which we might be called upon to do anyhow."[42] When a revolt broke out, led by former minister of war Luis Mena Vado and liberal general Benjamin Zeledon, the United States landed 2,600 troops to protect Díaz and remained until 1925.[43]

With US protection, the Díaz regime was secured. US forces imposed martial law during most of period, transforming this case from one of indirect rule into a form of direct rule, although Nicaragua retained its formal sovereignty throughout. In turn, Díaz adopted the policies desired by the United States. As one US mining investor wrote in 1912, the Díaz "government will be run from Washington more than from Managua."[44] Once engaged in Nicaraguan affairs, the United States imposed the usual customs receivership.[45] On the positive side, this stabilized the currency and, as Zelaya had been provoking his neighbors, the US presence permitted a dramatic reduction in military spending.[46] In exchange for new bank loans, the Bryan-Chamorro Treaty approved in 1914 granted the United States the right of first refusal on any future canal built through Nicaragua, removing the threat of external influence in the region and preserving the monopoly held by the Panama Canal.[47] As elsewhere in the region, Brown Brothers and Seligman assumed de facto control over the central bank, the Banco Nacional de Nicaragua, with James Brown's signature, in fact, gracing the national currency.[48] The loans and customs receivership proved to be, as Secretary of State

---

39. Quoted in Kinzer 2006, 69–70.

40. Kinzer 2006, 70.

41. Quoted in Schoultz 1998, 216. See also Maurer 2013, 111.

42. Quoted in LaFeber 1983, 53.

43. McCune 2019, 4; LaFeber 1994, 262; Hudson 2017, 157. Castro (2013, 433) lists over 3,000 troops.

44. Quoted in McPherson 2014, 16.

45. Maurer 2013, 111; Castro 2013, 432. The United States did not obtain control over the state rum and tobacco monopolies or property taxes (Schoultz 1998, 221).

46. McPherson 2014, 55.

47. Castro 2013, 433. The first draft of the treaty contained language quite similar to the Platt Amendment imposed on Cuba, which was accepted by Díaz. Ironically, the language was unacceptable to the Democratic majority in the US Senate and was removed from the final treaty (Schoultz 2018, 60–61).

48. Hudson 2017, 158.

Knox wrote to the chair of the Senate Committee on Foreign relations, "of vast commercial advantage." Where the United States took only 31 percent of Nicaraguan exports in 1911, it took over 85 percent by 1917, 91 percent of which entered the United States duty free.[49]

Díaz's liberal opponents, as well as the majority of the population, rejected the US role in Nicaragua, creating a festering sore of anti-Americanism that persists to the present day. In 1911, the US minister found "an overwhelming majority of Nicaraguans . . . antagonistic to the United States because of the loans" undertaken by Díaz and the customs receivership. Even some conservatives, no longer able to plunder the government fisc, turned against Díaz and the United States. According to McPherson, "the deals united Nicaraguans in hostility, a stunning feat considering their extreme partisanship." A goodwill trip by Secretary of State Knox in March 1912 triggered significant anti-American protests, with violent demonstrations sponsored by liberals who accused Díaz of an "Americanizing mania."[50] When rumors began flying about an impending assassination, Knox fled the country.[51] Between 1913 and the first withdrawal of US troops starting in 1924, Nicaragua experienced at least ten significant rebellions, all put down by the United States with armed force.[52] Such repression led to widespread resentment, especially as the US Marines and the newly created National Guard—trained and equipped by the United States, one of the first instances of what is now called security force assistance—became increasingly brutal.[53] Resistance only subsided after the United States reduced its occupation force from approximately 3,000 troops to a legation guard of 100. Indeed, as late as 1924, a US naval officer stationed in Nicaragua observed "a noticeable increase in anti-American feeling, shown both by individuals and newspaper articles" and bemoaned the fact that the local police showed no "initiative in bringing the offenders to justice."[54] As expected, direct rule, which imposed a policy more favorable to the United States and less favorable to the locals than might have been achieved under indirect rule, united all Nicaraguans including elites against the occupation.

Relatively free elections were held under US supervision in 1924, with the moderate conservative Carlos Solórzano winning the presidency and liberal Juan Bautista Sacasa the vice presidency. Happy with the result, the United States withdrew its troops soon thereafter. Within months of the US withdrawal, however, the defeated candidate Emiliano Chamorro led a coup,

49. Quoted in Schoultz 1998, 217–218. Percent entering the United States duty free calculated from Department of Commerce 1918, 364.
50. McPherson 2014, 15.
51. Maurer 2013, 112.
52. Castro 2013, 434.
53. McPherson 2014, 19.
54. Quoted in McPherson 2014, 58.

forcing Solórzano to resign and Sacasa to flee the country.[55] Despite some mild pressure from US authorities to step down, no real action was taken given Chamorro's ties to US financial interests.[56] Liberals under Sacasa and General José María Moncada revolted, causing the United States to send troops to protect Standard Fruit Company plantations near the coast. After a US-imposed ceasefire and peace conference on the *USS Denver*, Chamorro resigned and Díaz was reinstalled as president. On November 15, 1926, after liberals including Sacasa, Moncada, and Sandino refused to disarm, Díaz requested that the United States once again send troops for his protection, beginning another seven-year occupation.[57]

All this sparked the only true popular rebellion in the region, led by Sandino, a liberal member of the elite who cultivated support from peasants and backed their interests in exchange for the ability to operate anonymously in the countryside.[58] Breaking with the liberals in 1928, Sandino increasingly described his movement in class terms and attacked foreign-owned mines—destroying the La Luz y Los Angeles mine in April 1928 with twenty-five cases of dynamite.[59] Even 5,500 US marines were unable to capture the so-called bandits, largely because of the support of rural peasants for Sandino.[60] Indeed, in the province of Segovia, Sandino's base, between 50 and 95 percent of the population was reportedly Sandinista. The United States lost more soldiers in fighting Sandino than in all of the occupations of Haiti, the Dominican Republic, and Nicaragua between 1912 and 1925, combined.[61]

After the 1928 elections, the most free and fair in Nicaraguan history, resistance to US rule and support for Sandino began to wane. The marines drew their forces down to 2,500 from over 5,000, with the remainder finally leaving in 1932.[62] In November 1932, Sacasa won the presidential election, after which Sandino agreed to peace talks. Sandino laid down his arms and, under a grant of amnesty, began working with the Nicaraguan government. Sandino was executed in 1934 after being seized by the head of the National Guard, Anastasio Somoza. After Somoza grabbed power in 1936, elected officials appealed to Washington for assistance, only to be told by the State Department—without, apparently, a hint of irony—that it was contrary to US policy to intervene in Nicaraguan affairs. The Somoza family ruled Nicaragua for the next forty-three years under a brutal dictatorship.

---

55. McPherson 2014, 215.
56. Gomez and Hilgert 2013, 436.
57. McPherson 2014, 74.
58. Sandino also appears to have gotten support from urban conservatives who may have hoped that a defeat of the US Marines would allow the return of caudillo rule (McPherson 2014, 137).
59. McPherson 2014, 83–85.
60. LaFeber 1994, 361.
61. McPherson 2014, 80.
62. McPherson 2014, 226 and 232.

Nicaragua and other similar cases demonstrate that the United States was willing to undertake direct rule, impose its preferred policy, and bear the costs of occupation when necessary to protect its interests and assets and when leaders blatantly challenged the rules of the informal empire. Such prolonged occupations, however, occurred only in those countries (Haiti and the Dominican Republic, as well as Nicaragua) where specific assets were especially high, mostly driven by concerns over the canal, and domestic political instability threatened the elite's ability to retain control. The possibility of direct rule, however, helps explain why allied regimes throughout the region were tightly constrained and limited in how far they could exploit or entrap the United States, lest they themselves become objects of US intervention.

Domestic Rule

Mexico is the great anomaly in the CCA. After attempting to create at least a measure of indirect rule during the Mexican Revolution—a period of acute political instability—the United States abandoned the effort and learned to live with a Mexico that could and did set policy according to its domestic interests and institutions and that largely ignored the rules of the informal empire applied elsewhere in the region.[63] In terms of the model in chapter 1, Mexico hovered ambiguously around x_q, the domestic alternative. What it might have done had it not been "so far from God, so close to the United States," as President Porfirio Díaz supposedly said, is hard to determine.[64] Certainly, many Mexicans felt like they were subordinate to Washington. But in the end, Mexico adopted policies that the United States would not have tolerated in other countries within the region, and Washington did not react strongly. Yes, the United States huffed and puffed and threatened, and intervened twice at the height of the Mexican Revolution, but when land reform was adopted in 1917 and the oil industry was nationalized in 1937 the US reaction was comparatively mild.[65]

It is useful to inquire as to why this anomaly arose and persisted. One answer is relatively simple. As Noel Maurer writes, "Mexico was a partial exception to the logic of empire for a very simple reason: it was too big to invade."[66] While this prevented direct rule, indirect rule proved to be equally difficult. Especially in the midst of the revolution, guaranteeing any regime at a cost the United States was willing to pay would have been nearly impossible. As a large and diversified economy, moreover, Mexico was less dependent on export-led growth and its exports competed more directly with US products than other CCA states. Unlike elsewhere in the

---

63. For an overview, see Meyer 1991.
64. Jay 1996.
65. For an overview, see Bemis 1943, chap. 10.
66. Maurer 2013, 137.

region, small concessions on tariffs on tropical products were nowhere near enough to tip elites into allying with the United States. This was not a case where opportunism drove the United States to "walk away" from indirect rule, though the effect would have been similar. Rather, the governance costs of indirect rule were simply too high to justify the effort to stabilize the country with a pro-American elite faction. Perhaps more than any other, this case shows the limits of indirect rule.

In the early twentieth century, Mexico was similar to other CCA countries in its essential economic and political structure, a legacy of the Spanish encomienda system put in place under colonial rule. Although its product structure differed in important ways, Mexico was characterized by the same inequalities in the distribution of land and wealth, with the country divided between a small elite of large landowners and a mass of campesinos or landless peasants. The state was controlled by landed elites and vulnerable to personalist rule. After overturning the constitution of 1857, Díaz ruled the country from 1887 to 1911, a remarkable period of political stability and economic growth.[67] Importantly, he did not challenge US interests in the region while in power. He was forced to flee the country early in the revolutionary period.

The United States also invested heavily in Mexico in site-specific assets. Mexico was by far the leading destination in the CCA for US investors, accounting for more than one-quarter of all FDI in this period (see table 2.1). Most of these investments were in oil production, copper mining, railways, and land for agricultural exports, all site-specific industries vulnerable to changes in government policy. As a result of these investments, Americans owned 43 percent of all land by value in Mexico.[68] Major investments by Americans meant that the United States had relatively intense preferences regarding policies adopted by the Mexican government, which all else considered should have spurred some form of hierarchy.

Mexico differed from its neighbors, however, in being substantially larger in terms of its population and territory. It was no match for the United States, of course, having lost almost half of its population and territory to its northern neighbor by 1848. Though considerably poorer per capita than Cuba, it was much larger than other states invaded by the United States around the same time. This greater size and population raised the costs to the United States of any attempt to dominate the country. While a few hundred marines might insure a pro-American regime in a small island state, Mexico required a very different approach. A final war plan for invading Mexico published by the US military in July 1914—well into the revolutionary period—envisioned a force of 352,985 soldiers at a cost of $238 million, at a time when the active-duty military in the United States was only 98,544 strong and the entire US

---

67. Schoultz 1998, 192.
68. LaFeber 1994, 278.

defense budget was $347 million. The annual cost of any occupation, it was estimated, would come to about 2.6 percent of US GDP.[69] As these figures suggest, the costs of defeating the Mexican military and then suppressing resistance from peasants and workers as well as elites across such a large territory were likely to be very high. Direct rule was largely out of the question. These same costs, however, meant that interventions to protect a regime or replace an incompetent leader also rendered the governance costs of indirect rule relatively high compared to elsewhere in the CCA.

The limits on indirect rule are best seen in the context of the Mexican Revolution and its extended aftermath.[70] This was an intense period of social and economic change similar to that occurring across the region during the liberal reform period. Rising opposition to the despotic and increasingly senile Díaz crystalized under Francisco I. Madero, a relative moderate. In calling for a national uprising on November 20, 1910, Madero aimed mainly to restore the constitution of 1857 and abolish unlimited presidential terms. A second movement led by Emiliano Zapata in southern Mexico went further in calling for the breakup of the encomienda system and land redistribution to peasants, leading to a split in the anti-Díaz movement that would plague the revolution going forward. The more radical program championed by Zapata also drew support from northern rebel leaders, including Pascual Orozco and Francisco "Pancho" Villa, with the latter playing a starring role later in the revolution (and then, in caricature, as the quintessential villain in many Hollywood movies). Zapata's proposed Plan de Ayala is a particularly clear example of what landless peasants elsewhere in the region might have demanded if they had been able to organize sufficiently to do so. After Díaz fled the country, Madero easily won the election in 1911, but was assassinated by General Victoriano Huerta in a counterrevolutionary coup approved by the outgoing administration of President William Howard Taft.[71] This spurred Zapata and Villa into new action, and Huerta was eventually driven from office and succeeded by Venustiano Carranza, a moderate follower of Madero and rival of Villa. Carranza led a constitutional convention in 1917, assassinated Zapata in 1919, and was himself assassinated in 1920. He was followed in office by former colonel Alvaro Obregón and eventually Plutarco Elías Calles in 1924, after which the period of acute violence and unrest ended.

As elsewhere, domestic instability in Mexico was a concern of the United States, especially given its site-specific investments. The limited efforts by the United States to support favored candidates, however, also illustrate the larger costs of attempting indirect rule. US president Woodrow Wilson

---

69. Maurer 2013, 141–142.
70. Buchenau 2015.
71. Maurer 2013, 137; Knock 1992, 25. After firing the US ambassador appointed by Taft, Wilson imposed an arms embargo and hoped to mediate between Huerta and Madero's Constitutionalist Party successors. The arms embargo was lifted in February 1914.

strongly opposed Huerta, objecting to his use of force to seize power. As the revolution took hold, Wilson looked for an opportunity to shape the course of events, which presented itself in April 1914 when seven US sailors were arrested.[72] Wilson had sent US warships to take up positions off Tampico, Mexico's most important port for the export of petroleum. The naval presence was intended to provide some security for US oil firms and their employees and implicitly to challenge Huerta.[73] While on shore to purchase supplies, the US sailors wandered into a restricted area and were detained. Although Huerta quickly released the sailors, Wilson demanded an apology to satisfy American "honor."[74] When this demand was rejected, as anticipated, Wilson asked Congress for authorization to use force against Mexico. While Congress investigated the incident, Wilson learned that a German ship was en route to Veracruz to deliver weapons for Huerta. He then ordered the US Navy to occupy Veracruz, seize the customshouse, and commandeer the cargo of the German ship, landing 787 marines and armed sailors for this purpose.[75] The United States assumed incorrectly that the Mexicans would not resist, but fighting immediately broke out.[76] Wilson then sent reinforcements, including five more battleships and another 3,000 marines. When the Mexicans blocked US moves by deploying 15,000 soldiers west of the city, Wilson sent an additional 4,000 marines. This now very significant US deployment, far larger than any other intervention in the region except for the Spanish-American War, occupied Veracruz for seven months at the cost of 17 American and 126 Mexican lives, all lost in small clashes. The mission became a stalemate.[77] Ironically, the German ship unloaded its cargo at Puerto Mexico, further south. During the Veracruz crisis, Zapata expanded his guerrilla war in the south, a radical labor movement took up arms in Mexico City, and the northern rebels under Villa marched on central Mexico, eventually reaching the capital and forcing Huerta to resign. In the end, Wilson's objective of removing Huerta was achieved, but the US role in this affair is greatly debated. At best, by locking Huerta's forces up in Veracruz, the United States simply diverted them away from the other fronts and blocked the delivery of additional supplies. Overall, the US intervention served mostly to stoke anti-Americanism not only among the supporters of Huerta but also other Mexicans.[78]

The United States then lost whatever control over events it might have exercised. When Carranza took office and began to implement a more radical

---

72. On Wilson's motivations, see Knock 1992, 27.
73. Britton 2013, 391.
74. LaFeber 1983, 280; Knock claims that Wilson demanded a twenty-one-gun salute (1992, 27).
75. Maurer 2013, 139.
76. Britton 2013, 392.
77. Britton 2013, 392.
78. Maurer 2013, 139.

program than anticipated, Wilson shifted his support to Villa, another radical. As Carranza steadily defeated his forces, Villa attempted to disrupt the military balance "by terrorizing Arizona and New Mexico in the hope that Wilson's military retaliation would undermine Carranza."[79] This plan backfired. After Villa attacked the town of Columbus, New Mexico in March 1916, killing 197 Americans, Wilson had to shift strategy once again, and sent 7,000 soldiers under the command of General John Pershing into Mexico to capture his former ally. After chasing Villa and his fighters around the deserts of northern Mexico for eleven months, and after several clashes with Carranza's military forces, Wilson finally withdrew US troops in early 1917 in anticipation of joining World War I. Villa was never apprehended.

Both the stalemated occupation of Veracruz and the unsuccessful pursuit of Villa demonstrate clearly the difficulty in using force to try to impose any semblance of rule on Mexico.[80] As these fruitless efforts suggest, putting an ally in power and defending that ally against opponents was well-nigh impossible, or at least impossible at a governance cost the United States was willing to pay, especially as the opportunity costs of the resources necessary to rule Mexico indirectly rose as the United States prepared to enter the war in Europe. Washington was also unwilling to make the kinds of trade concessions that were successful elsewhere. Even as the United States invested in Mexico's oil industry, its mineral, cotton, and nascent manufactures competed directly with US products, and thus were excluded from preferential tariff treatment. The model used elsewhere in the region appeared out of reach in Mexico.

Without any real alternative, the United States had to accept the results of Mexico's internal politics, creating a rare case of domestic rule in the CCA. As noted, Carranza steered to the "left" immediately after taking office, authoring a new constitution that contained elements deeply disturbing to US investors. Among other provisions, Article 27 proclaimed all land and the subsoil the patrimony of the nation, which could be used by foreigners only with the consent of the federal government. Article 123 recognized the right of workers to form labor unions and bargain collectively for wages and improved working conditions. When adopted in February 1917, the Mexican constitution was one of the most progressive in the world. Crucially, these progressive elements were opposed by some elites in Mexico, suggesting that domestic rule in this case produced a policy result far from their interests and those of the United States. By forfeiting indirect rule, elites got less than they might have wanted. US investors in Mexico, in turn, lobbied for a forceful

---

79. LaFeber 1994, 280. Knock suggests that Villa was convinced that Carranza and Wilson had reached an agreement that would have made Mexico a protectorate of the United States, though there has never been any evidence that such an agreement was contemplated (1992, 82).
80. LaFeber 1994, 280.

response. In 1919, Senator Albert Fall (R-NM) held widely publicized hearings that cited continued instability, land redistribution, and labor rights as justifications for new military operations against Mexico. With the revelation of the military's Plan Green, a previously secret contingency plan setting strategic guidelines for an invasion of Mexico, rumors circulated widely in 1926 and 1927 about preparations for another invasion.[81] Tensions remained high until the Calles-Morrow Agreement of 1928, which reaffirmed the rights of oil companies in the territories they had worked prior to 1917.[82] Yet, through all of these changes in Mexican policy and demands by US business that their interests be defended, the United States largely failed to react.

The conflict over foreign property rights flared again in 1937, precipitated by a strike by Mexican oil workers for pay equal to their American counterparts doing the same jobs. President Lázaro Cárdenas attempted to settle the issue by drawing up a new labor agreement, but it was rejected by the oil companies. In response, Cárdenas nationalized the oil firms, promising to pay fair compensation. The US government response was mixed, but certainly limited. On the one hand, it stated publicly that it had no objection to nationalization if Mexico agreed to compensate the oil companies. On the other hand, this was the first major nationalization of US investments anywhere in the world, setting a precedent for future actions. Accordingly, Secretary of State Cordell Hull advocated a stronger response, including a boycott of Mexican silver. Given that Mexico was then fully on a silver standard, this would have devastated the value of its currency. Hull eventually backed down under pressure from the US Treasury Department, which feared disrupting the emerging international economic recovery. The United States supported the oil companies, despite their extravagant claims about the value of the expropriated assets, until the outbreak of World War II, at which time it forced a settlement on the firms for a fraction of what British investors would later receive.[83]

Even if it was reluctant to defend its economic interests in Mexico, the United States might have been expected to react more strongly to challenges from its southern neighbor to its national security. Germany's outreach to Mexico in the Zimmermann Telegram did pose a clear threat to the United States. Issued while Pershing was chasing Villa around northern Mexico, and while Wilson was contemplating when and how to join the war in Europe, the offer by a budding enemy to a contiguous country then under attack by the United States was interpreted by Washington and the American public as especially menacing. The Zimmermann Telegram did contribute to US support for declaring war on Germany. Surprisingly, however, it provoked no reaction by the United States against Mexico. Mexico had just approved a

---

81. Britton 2013, 393.
82. LaFeber 1994, 359–360.
83. Office of the Historian, n.d. See also Maurer 2011.

new constitution striking at the interests of US investors and now it was being courted by a country against which the United States was about to declare war. Yet, there were no warnings, counterthreats, or retaliation against Mexico. This reaction, of course, might have been different had Mexico attempted to take Germany up on its offer. Actually allying with an extra-regional power might have provoked the United States into responding more dramatically. In contrast to the cases of Nicaragua, Haiti, and the Dominican Republic, when far less dramatic foreign overtures were made, the United States appeared content—or forced by the high costs of indirect and direct rule—to allow Mexican politics to unfold in their own way. As President Wilson stated when removing US troops from Veracruz, "if the Mexicans want to raise hell, let them raise hell. We have nothing to do with it. It is their government, it is their hell."[84]

Resistance

Both the cases of direct rule in Nicaragua, the Dominican Republic, and Haiti, and the case of domestic rule in Mexico make clear that alternatives to indirect rule were possible and even preferred when specific assets were too large or governance costs were high. These alternatives, especially direct rule, suggest that most countries in the CCA were tightly constrained in the extent to which they could exploit or entrap the United States. Washington did get entangled in some domestic disputes it might have otherwise avoided, though how often and to what extent is difficult to ascertain. But this analysis suggests that by and large, countries in the region did comply with the rules of the informal empire, in part because of the real possibility of direct or domestic rule that would have left elites disadvantaged either way. Indirect rule reinforced the economic and political power of elites, although it alienated publics and fomented anti-Americanism. Elites also chafed against the rules of the informal empire. As interventions expanded into direct rule, even they looked for ways to resist US domination.

Anti-Americanism

The legacy of repressive rule in the CCA generated much of the anti-Americanism that continues to burden US relations with Latin America today. Landless laborers and workers opposed to US backing of their repressive elite regimes likely never regarded US indirect rule in the Caribbean as legitimate, especially as hopes for democracy faded. Though we lack any systemic

---

84. Quoted in McPherson 2014, 266.

polling evidence before the 1950s or even 1960s, it seems safe to describe the United States as extremely unpopular in the CCA.[85]

The decades after 1898 are generally described as increasingly hostile to the United States. In but one telling piece of evidence from the time of the Mexican Revolution, a country where the United States never succeeded in establishing indirect rule, US consul Samuel E. Magill at Guadalajara reported to Secretary of State Knox in 1911 that the "anti-American sentiment is almost universal among rich and poor alike." Consul Charles M. Freeman at Durango concurred, writing that "this district is 95% anti-American, and that is a most conservative estimate for I have yet to meet a Mexican who has any love for the people of the United States as a whole."[86] These reports suggest that even in relations with Mexico, the United States managed to alienate large parts of the population, including members of the elite.

We also see resistance to the United States in cases of direct rule. These are, admittedly, extreme cases but, given the large deployments of US troops, also the best documented. Throughout, even though newspapers were heavily censored and therefore are an unreliable measure, there is evidence of hostility and everyday acts of resistance to US occupation. One US captain deployed in Nicaragua described a mob blocking his train during an attempt to rescue a detachment of conservative soldiers. "All along the streets they showed their hostility," he wrote in his diary, "even women spat at us, many women were armed with rifles and machetes." Another mob forced a different group of US soldiers from their train and then forced them to walk the fifty-five miles back to Managua. Fear of working with US troops pervaded society; one telegraph worker took his own life rather than send a message for the United States.[87] As already noted, Secretary of State Knox was forced to flee the country due to angry mobs and assassination threats. Resistance appears to have increased over time. In 1924, a Navy major stationed in Nicaragua described "a noticeable increase in the anti-American feeling, shown both by individuals and newspaper articles."[88] That same year, as US troops prepared to leave for the first time, a Marine intelligence officer described the results of the occupation. While the conservatives supported the United States, he wrote, "the Liberal Party denounces American influence, proclaims American bankers as robbers, speaks of American officials as grafters and men of little honor and is preaching a gospel of national independence."[89]

---

85. On anti-Americanism in later periods, see McPherson 2003; McPherson 2006. On the causes and variation in anti-Americanism, see Baker and Cupery 2013; Azpuru and Boniface 2015. At least some of this later anti-Americanism is likely a residual of earlier anti-Americanism.
86. Quoted in P. Smith 1996, 106.
87. Quoted in McPherson 2014, 19.
88. Quoted in McPherson 2014, 58.
89. Quoted in McPherson 2014, 214.

As Peter Smith explains, the "creeds of resistance" that arose "contained a series of interlocking assumptions. To uphold the sovereignty of young and fragile republics in Latin America was to be a nationalist. To be a nationalist was to be anti-imperialist. To be anti-imperialist, as US power grew, was to become anti-American, anti-*gringo*, and anti-*yanqui* . . . the logic was ineluctable." He continues, "Virtually by definition, a nationalist movement in quest of social justice would have to be anti-American."[90] Even in the depths of the Great Depression, with revolutionary activities threatening to topple governments in the region, the United States remained unpopular. With the Good Neighbor policy well in hand, Secretary of State Henry Stimson could still agonize over the US role, writing, "I am getting quite blue over the bad way in which all Latin America is showing up." As he saw it, the countries themselves could not keep order "and yet if we try to take the lead for them, at once there is a cry against American domination and imperialism."[91]

A Turn to International Law

As dissatisfaction with US indirect and especially direct rule built, opponents of US rule turned to international law to constrain US interventions and resist US domination. With political change blocked by the US allied elites, societies had few political avenues available to them. The increase in extended US military occupations also turned elites against the United States from the 1920s. As its specific assets increased and the United States increasingly chose direct rule under extended military occupations, even elites came to oppose US military interventions.[92] In Haiti, for instance, the US-installed president complained bitterly about Washington's control over customs revenues.[93]

The primary vehicle for challenging the United States and its self-proclaimed right of intervention were the Pan-American Conferences.[94] First held under US auspices in 1889 to develop hemispheric solidarity and expand US influence in the region, they eventually became a springboard for regional resistance to US hierarchy.[95] For the longest time, the United States refused to consider constraints on its freedom of action. Assertions of power and privilege such as the US seizure of territory from Mexico, the US seizure of Cuba from Spain, and the "liberation" of Panama from Colombia greatly worried and offended other states in the region.[96] Though acquiescing to an exclusive US sphere of influence, and in fact not directly protesting US occupations when they occurred, these states were nonetheless reluctant to

---

90. P. Smith 1996, 105–106.
91. Quoted in LaFeber 1983, 64.
92. McPherson 2014, 199.
93. McPherson 2014, 133.
94. See Bemis 1943, chaps. 13–15.
95. On the early conference, see LaFeber 1994, 175.
96. Blakeslee 1917; Castle 1939.

acknowledge special rights for the United States.[97] As historian Samuel Flagg Bemis observed, "it was the supreme diplomatic objective of the twenty Latin American republics to write [the doctrine of non-intervention] into a code of 'American international law' and to get the United States to ratify it."[98] While the principle of non-intervention was a topic of constant agitation in hemispheric relations throughout this period, the United States consistently rejected the idea.

The issue came to a head at the Sixth International Conference of American States in Havana in 1928. The timing here is important. Though long desired, the movement to outlaw intervention gathered steam only after sporadic US interventions evolved into prolonged occupations in Nicaragua, Haiti, and the Dominican Republic. At the sixth conference, the Latin American states submitted a resolution that "no state has a right to intervene in the internal affairs of another." The United States strenuously objected to this on the grounds that it did, in fact, have a right to intervene to protect the lives of its nationals should internal order break down. Although the United States was able to force the withdrawal of the proposal, only four of the twenty other delegations supported the US position.

Under increasing international pressure, the United States eventually had a change of heart. Following the Havana conference, the State Department commissioned a memo by Undersecretary J. Reuben Clark to review US rights of intervention. The Clark memorandum, released the following year, reasserted the Monroe Doctrine but accepted that the Roosevelt Corollary had been misapplied and could not justify intervention. At the same time, however, Clark's new interpretation claimed a right of intervention for purposes of self-defense and self-preservation of people and property derived from international law itself.[99] Shifting the foundation of the practice, however, did not quell the dissent. Only under the new Good Neighbor policy did United States finally relent. At the Seventh International American Conference held in Montevideo in 1933, the United States finally joined the other states of the hemisphere in the Convention on the Rights and Duties of States, in which Article 8 states that "no state has the right to intervene in the internal or external affairs of others." Although the United States finally bent on this principle, it continued to reserve all rights by "the law of nations as generally recognized"—just as stated in the Clark memorandum. Finally, in 1936, the United States conceded completely. At the Eighth International American Conference in Buenos Aires, the United States accepted the additional protocol, which declared "inadmissible the intervention of any [high

---

97. On the absence of protests elsewhere in the region against occupation, see McPherson 2014, 213.

98. Bemis 1943, 237–238.

99. Loveman 2010, 236–238; LaFeber 1994, 358–359.

contracting party], directly or indirectly, and for whatever reason, in the internal or external affairs of any other of the Parties."[100]

This turn in US policy coincided with and, indeed, was the core of the Good Neighbor policy. The shift began under President Herbert Hoover, who realized that US interventions and support for odious dictators was spurring anti-Americanism throughout the CCA and Latin America more generally.[101] Indeed, Hoover "refrained from intervening in Panama, Peru, Honduras, and El Salvador in response to events that in the past would have drawn the marines."[102] In ending the occupation of Haiti, however, Hoover was also puzzled by the lack of gratitude for the services rendered by the United States and defended the rights of US investors.[103] President Franklin Roosevelt continued this policy shift and gave it the Good Neighbor label, getting perhaps undue credit for initiating this new approach to hemispheric relations. US leaders eventually recognized that US interventions were doing more harm than good. Not only did interventions breed resentment from all sides in the subordinate states, but Washington kept getting pulled unnecessarily into domestic disputes. It had to escape the politics of entrapment and eventually did so by committing not to intervene in the internal affairs of subordinate states any longer.

Enthusiasm for the Good Neighbor policy should be tempered, however. While significant, it can also be seen as representing the success of indirect rule.[104] By the 1930s, pro-American regimes prevailed throughout the CCA and were increasingly institutionalized. Some regimes were also led by extremely repressive dictators still allied with the United States, including General Rafael Leónidas Trujillo y Molina in the Dominican Republic and Anastasio Somoza in Nicaragua. These repressive regimes lasted into the 1960s and 1970s. Moreover, although it did so less frequently, the United States did not stop intervening entirely, backing a coup in Guatemala in 1954, underwriting various attempts to overthrow Fidel Castro after the Cuban Revolution, spurring the assassination of Trujillo in 1960 for seeking new support from the Soviet Union, invading the Dominican Republic in 1965, and of course supporting the government in the civil war in El Salvador (1979–1992) and the Contras in Nicaragua after the revolution (1981–1990). Under the Good Neighbor policy, the United States widened the scope for countries in the CCA to rule themselves, although their freedom of action remained constrained by the potential for indirect and even direct rule. In the

---

100. Cabranes 1967, 1153–1154.
101. Loveman dates the beginning of the turn from the mid-1920s (2010, 241); see also Tulchin 1971.
102. McPherson 2014, 247.
103. Hudson 2017, 266–267.
104. See Tulchin 1971.

end, relations between Washington and states in the CCA gradually evolved toward a form of indirect rule "lite," in which the United States promised to meddle less often in their domestic affairs as long as the countries followed the rules of the informal empire.

With only a few exceptions, the United States ruled the Caribbean Basin indirectly in the early twentieth century. Through its support for elites, the United States obtained policies it favored but also needed to confront possible opportunism by its allies. It imposed a set of rules on subordinates to limit exploitation and entrapment and enforced those rules mostly through the threat of direct rule, as manifested in the occupations of Nicaragua, Haiti, and the Dominican Republic. As its specific assets in the region increased, the United States became more concerned with the policies adopted by its subordinates and more willing to bear higher costs for controlling them. When regimes and individual leaders deviated from the rules of the informal empire, the United States intervened and, in extreme cases, governed the country directly under martial law for extended periods. If the costs of direct or indirect rule were too high, the United States was also willing to countenance domestic rule, as in Mexico, leaving the country to sort out its own internal conflicts and elites to accept progressive reforms not found elsewhere in the region.

The consequences of indirect rule were autocratic and repressive regimes, anti-Americanism, and ultimately resistance to US interventions through the creation of new international laws and norms. In practice, these consequences were bundled together, each reinforcing the others, and are hard to differentiate. Elite-based regimes had to govern autocratically, and US support for these regimes necessarily implicated the United States in the repression they exerted over their societies. Mass opposition was largely and successfully suppressed during the period reviewed here, but it did not prevent anti-Americanism from simmering under the surface and occasionally boiling over. As direct rule expanded, even elites came to oppose US intervention. Nonetheless, given their relatively aligned interests, Washington largely got the policies it wanted from its elite allies, with the United States and countries in the CCA becoming much more economically integrated. Constrained by the prospect of direct rule, Caribbean countries also accepted US fiscal oversight and control and eschewed foreign ties. In the end, indirect rule "worked" in producing policies favored by the United States while limiting opportunism, but we are still today dealing with the lingering effects of anti-Americanism.

4

Indirect Rule in Western Europe

The Pax Americana, as relations between Western states after World War II are commonly known by scholars of international relations, is normally understood as an exceptional regional order in which benevolent hegemony or US leadership produced extensive international cooperation despite the condition of international anarchy.[1] For some, the common threat from the Soviet Union, itself rooted in the structure of bipolarity, drove the West together under a US security umbrella.[2] For others, shared liberalism, cultural heritage, or economic interests created the basis for unprecedented international cooperation.[3] For still others, common interests mattered but it was the provision of key public goods or the creation of international institutions by the United States that allowed problems of collective action to be overcome.[4] These long-standing explanations capture important parts of the postwar order. This was an era of broadly shared interests. There was unprecedented cooperation between states. The role of the United States was important in formulating common policies. However, the reality was more complicated and, I will argue, more open-ended than these explanations suggest. This chapter and the next alter the focus and emphasis of these standard narratives in two ways.

First, while conservative parties in Western Europe had policy preferences closely aligned with those of the United States, left parties had more distant preferences, favoring at least neutral foreign policies that promised a third

---

1. Ikenberry 2001; Ikenberry 2011. This system has also been characterized as a Pacific Security Community. See Deutsch 1957; Adler and Barnett 1998.
2. Waltz 1979; Gaddis 1982; Gaddis 1987.
3. Ikenberry 2011; P. Jackson 2006.
4. Kindleberger 1973; Krasner 1976; Gilpin 1977; Keohane 1984.

way between the two superpowers or, at an extreme, collaboration with the Soviet Union. With possible coalitions almost evenly balanced on the continent, cooperation with the United States was not a foregone conclusion. History should not be read backwards. Rather, the United States put a heavy thumb on the political scale, so to speak, and tipped the balance toward those groups whose preferences on foreign policy were closest to its own. By linking aid to market-oriented economic reforms and heavily subsidizing security, which reduced the costs of siding with Washington in the Cold War, the United States facilitated the rise of coalitions across Western Europe by the early 1950s that, as they eventually constituted majorities within each society, became what we regard today as "centrist." When electoral outcomes were in doubt, the United States also intervened covertly to ensure that at least centrist and preferably center-right parties won. These centrist coalitions then enacted policies favored by the United States, creating a Western economic and security bloc ruled indirectly by Washington. Once consolidated around a pro-Western orientation, indirect rule was compatible with democracy, even in West Germany, which was ruled directly after the war under the occupation but transitioned to indirect rule by the mid-1950s.

Second, relations between the United States and its so-called allies were not relations between equals. Though the fact is often obscured by euphemisms, it is difficult to characterize interactions between the United States and its allies as entirely voluntary cooperation by partners under anarchy. As discussed at greater length in the next chapter, the United States imposed an international hierarchy on Western Europe with Washington at the helm. Fearing exploitation, especially in the form of free riding, and entrapment into European and colonial conflicts, the United States needed to safeguard itself against opportunism by its allies. This required a set of additional rules limiting the scope for independent action by the Western Europeans that prohibited bilateral relations with the Soviet Union and autonomous military operations unless approved by Washington in advance. Although true anti-Americanism really only arose within the far left and right within Western Europe, these rules nevertheless grated on subordinates. The impossibility of direct rule, proven in the occupation of Germany, and the possibility that domestic rule would see West European states drifting away from the US orbit meant that its allies had broad scope to act opportunistically despite the rules issued by the United States. This was especially the case in France under President Charles de Gaulle, which resisted US hierarchy with few penalties. Nonetheless, the United States persisted with indirect rule until pro-Western majorities took hold across the continent.

The Pax Americana was not just a happy coincidence or the product of an entirely apolitical process. The United States intentionally manipulated the domestic politics of its Western European subordinates until they came to want what Washington wanted them to want, and they then agreed to live within additional rules intended to limit opportunism. Rather than anarchic cooperation led by a benevolent hegemon and reinforced by international institutions, the Pax Americana was a set of hierarchical relationships managed in the crucial postwar years through indirect rule. It was, as Geir Lundestad famously described it, an "invited empire."[5] This chapter examines the foundations of indirect rule and its domestic political consequences. The next chapter focuses on the formation and workings of international hierarchy and resistance to the United States.

Interests

Political interests in the United States and most Western European countries after the war can be described in general terms as in figure 4.1. The United States preferred policies of economic liberalism and market-enhancing reforms as well as collective security designed to contain and deter the Soviet Union ($d=1$). These policy preferences were opposed by the far left, which were largely communist parties aligned with the Soviet Union ($b=0$). Center-right parties were more closely aligned with the United States ($b \leq a \leq d$). Given the strength of the left after the war, strictly domestic rule would likely have produced social democratic governments and policies that favored a neutral course between the United States and Soviet Union in the emerging Cold War (x_q). That the interests of center-right parties in Western Europe were relatively aligned with those of the United States was crucial to the success of the Pax Americana. Also important was that many European societies were somewhat evenly divided between left and center-right, suggesting that policy was very much "in play" and open to influence by the United States in ways that were eventually consistent with democracy. The center parties themselves and the center and center-right coalitions that prevailed across the continent by the early 1950s were both the foundation and product of indirect rule.

Interests in the United States

The United States itself was relatively united on its postwar foreign policy goals.[6] This was the vaunted era of bipartisanship, itself something of a myth, no doubt, but not without foundation. The so-called Eastern establishment ruled in Washington. Prewar isolationists, like Senator Arthur Vandenberg (R-MI), became postwar internationalists. Voters knew little and cared less about foreign policy, although this was partly endogenous since, if

---

5. Lundestad 1986; Lundestad 1990.
6. Leffler 1992, 140 and 341. This bipartisanship can be easily exaggerated, however. See Block 1977; Pollard 1985. On the "selling" of internationalism during and after World War II, see Wertheim 2020.

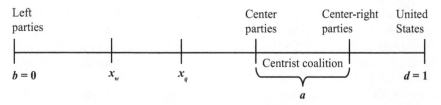

Figure 4.1 Configuration of US and Western European interests

elites do not disagree, the public does not feel the need to engage.[7] Sectional differences, at least over foreign policy, were small.[8] This was, quite literally, a period in which foreign policy did (almost) stop at the water's edge.

The United States had three basic interests in the postwar period. The first was US prosperity, which was understood to require exports to its traditional markets in Western Europe. Producing approximately half the goods in the world in 1945, a function both of the collapse of the European economies and the expansion of US production to fill demand during the war, the United States knew it could not sustain its factories and farms without foreign markets. This required economic recovery abroad to build markets for US exports, imports from others so that trade partners could pay for US goods, and monetary stability with sufficient liquidity to sustain growth.

The second interest was maintaining peace in Europe. The consequences of war on the continent were all too clear to Americans. To prevent another conflagration, some means was necessary to restrain great power competition and resolve the disputes that would inevitably arise in the future. It was also clear to Americans that their first interest in prosperity could not be realized without peace. In this way, these first two interests were deeply connected. Disputes were to be addressed, at least in part, by the United Nations, which through its charter established principles for the peaceful conduct of interstate relations. The United Nations was supplemented early on by European initiatives, which the United States actively supported. The first of these was the Brussels Pact of 1948, negotiated by British Labour leader Ernest Bevin with an eye toward sustaining US engagement in Europe. An agreement between Britain, France, and the low countries as a Western proto-collective security organization, it laid the foundation for NATO. The United States also encouraged efforts by Jean Monet, Robert Schuman, and others to build an integrated Europe, starting with the European Coal and Steel Community (ECSC) in 1951. Political and economic integration were seen as essential in building a "new" Europe.

---

7. Zaller 1992.
8. Trubowitz 1998.

The third interest—and the last to manifest itself—was to contain and deter the Soviet Union. There is a long-standing debate about who caused the Cold War.[9] Certainly, Americans at the time were insufficiently attentive to how US actions might be interpreted by Moscow. Just as certainly, as the Soviet Union consolidated its control over its self-proclaimed sphere of influence in Eastern Europe, sought to expand in Iran in 1946, obstructed quadripartite rule in Germany, destroyed any lingering hopes for cooperation during the Berlin Crisis of 1948–1949, and finally gave a green light to North Korea's invasion of South Korea in 1950, the United States not unreasonably came to perceive its former wartime ally as a major threat to its own sphere of influence in Western Europe.[10] As early as 1946, with General Lucius Clay's warning that war with the Soviet Union could erupt at any time and George Kennan's Long Telegram interpreting the Soviet Union's purported imperialism as part of an innate Russian character, the United States began to embrace a policy of containing the Soviet Union. Containment morphed into deterrence with the military build-up envisioned in Truman's NSC-68 (1950) and the beginning of the Korean War, until it became the overriding objective of US foreign policy.

This third interest in deterring the Soviet Union transformed the first two interests and their respective institutional forms. Though never designed to welcome the Soviet Union and its command economy, the Bretton Woods institutions and the General Agreements on Tariffs and Trade (GATT) were consolidated as Western organizations limited to members of the US sphere and, later, used as instruments of outreach to the new states of the developing world. Europe now needed to be kept peaceful and made prosperous not just to avoid a future war but to create a common front against communism. Importantly, even West Germany needed to be rehabilitated as a US ally to bear some of the burden of deterring Soviet expansionism—its capabilities were essential to successful international economic and security cooperation. In turn, rearming West Germany required deepening economic and political integration in Europe and binding the former enemy into institutions both within Europe, like the ECSC and the Customs Union (formed in 1958), and with the United States, such as NATO. Deterrence did not so much alter other US interests as limit their scope to Western Europe and deepen those interests to include a permanent military presence on the continent. Evolving between 1945 and 1951, US interests eventually solidified into an integrated whole that saw prosperity and peace within its sphere linked to collective security abroad.

---

9. For a realist account, see Kennan 1951. For revisionist accounts, see W. Williams 1972; LaFeber 1985. For a post-revisionist account, see Leffler 1992. Post–Cold War accounts tend to support the realist version (see Gaddis 1997; Gaddis 2005).

10. Leffler 1992, 103–104.

US Specific Assets

As the United States began investing in specific assets in Western Europe after 1945, and especially with the permanent stationing of US troops on the continent in 1951, the intensity of US interests in Western Europe grew rapidly and it became increasingly concerned with the political orientation of its allies in the emerging Cold War. Unlike in the Caribbean Basin examined in chapter 2, the specific assets of concern in postwar Europe were largely military. Although US foreign direct investment flowed into Europe during the postwar years, it was mostly in manufacturing, which was protected by brand name when producing for the host market or integrated into global supply chains, and therefore at least partly self-insured against expropriation.[11] European firms also invested in the United States, creating a rare mutual-hostage situation that could be managed reciprocally. But to deter the Soviet Union from invading the US sphere required significant deployments of US military forces along with all the equipment and infrastructure required to fight a major war. To avoid another Pearl Harbor, US military planners wanted an active defense based on forward-deployed forces that would fight far from the homeland.[12] To signal its resolve to Moscow—and its subordinates—the United States also needed to deploy those troops on the frontlines of any conflict, with the majority going to West Germany.

With the permanent stationing of US troops in Western Europe, the United States was hostage to the whims of European politics. In the immediate postwar period, the United States did not envision permanent bases in Europe. Adopting a peripheral defense strategy, Washington's planners insisted on a global network of naval and air bases, including in Europe. Naval bases in Italy were essential to the control of the Mediterranean and, with it, the Suez Canal and sites beyond.[13] Given the limited range of US bombers (and their fighter escorts), the nuclear deterrent required air bases close to the Soviet Union. The same was true for missile launch sites, which were eventually built in Turkey, making it an essential member of NATO.[14] As the Cold War began to heat up and NATO developed a military command structure, however, the United States switched to a forward defense-in-depth doctrine that relied upon permanent deployments of soldiers and bases on the continent. Permanent deployments of US forces required large bases to house, feed, and train the troops and stockpile equipment and ordinance. Although there was some flexibility in their exact placement, once the bases were constructed at great expense they became quintessential specific assets. This

---

11. On how brand and vertical integration protect multinational corporations from opportunism, see Caves 2007, esp. 1–27.

12. Leffler 1992, 41 and 56.

13. Pisani 1991, 107 and 110–111.

14. This included bases in the Middle East (Leffler 1992, 112–113 and 226). On technological changes that obviated, in part, the need for forward bases, see Harkavy 1993.

decision followed the "Great Debate" that unfolded in fall 1950 and spring 1951 between the Truman administration, which wanted to station troops in Western Europe on a permanent basis, and conservative Republicans lead by Senator Robert Taft (R-OH) who advocated for an offshore balancing role that relied primarily on air and sea power. With the outbreak of the Korean War in June 1950 and the passage of the Senate resolution in April 1951 sending four additional divisions of US troops to Europe under NATO auspices, the United States greatly expanded its role on the continent. From a high of roughly 3 million US troops on V-E Day, US forces gradually declined to a low of just over 120,000 in 1950. At this point the tide reversed and US forces rose to a peak of almost 439,000 in 1957. Between 1950 and 1953, US troops in West Germany alone increased from just under 98,000 to over 250,000. By the time of the Korean War, managing and, indeed, controlling the foreign policies of their allies in Western Europe had become a priority for US decision-makers. Once the United States had decided on defense-in-depth in Europe, any change in policy by its West European allies threatened to undermine US strategy in its entirety. Ensuring that its allies remained committed to economic and political integration with the West, in general, and the United States, in particular, became a key priority for Washington. Above all, this meant preventing left parties either allied with the Soviet Union or advocating neutrality in the emerging Cold War from coming to power. The timing here is important. Although the United States was concerned with the political orientation of Western Europe after the war, if only to deny the resources and factors of the continent to the Soviet Union, it engaged more deeply in shaping the domestic politics of its ostensible allies through indirect rule only after the Great Debate was resolved.

Interests in Western Europe

While US interests after the war were expansive, envisioning a new international order, Western Europeans had more limited goals. The first and by far the most important interest in Europe was economic and social recovery. The war was devastating. Even at the height of the war effort in 1943, for instance, the average adult in Germany consumed 2,078 calories per day. In June 1945, the official ration in the American occupation zone was 860 calories per day. For all of 1945, the population of Vienna subsisted on an average of 800 calories per day.[15] Disease ripped through the weakened, homeless, and displaced populations. During an outbreak of dysentery in Berlin in July 1945, for instance, the rate of infant mortality rose to 66 percent—that is, two out of every three infants died in their first year. As Jeffry Frieden writes, "The war on the Continent had thrown back the winners' economies

---

15. Judt 2005, 21.

twenty-five years (in terms of output per capita), while those of the losers had lost forty, fifty, even seventy-five years. German living standards before the war were comparable to those of Great Britain and about four-fifths of the United States; by 1946 they had sunk to barely one-third of British and one-quarter of American levels, roughly comparable to Spain or Peru."[16] Though Germany might have been the most affected, similar conditions existed everywhere in Europe. The interests of Europeans were clear. Above all, they just wanted to survive and reconstruct their lives.

Europeans also shared with the United States an interest in building a new, more peaceful international order that would prevent new conflicts. There was, however, little agreement on how to do this, and the differences created an opening through which the United States could rule indirectly. While a consensus emerged relatively quickly within the United States about the threat posed by the Soviet Union, Western Europe was more divided. There were four main political streams in postwar politics across Western Europe. The exact party composition and strength varied by country, but identifiable clusters existed almost everywhere. Communists, who had gained strength as the vanguard of the various wartime resistance movements, occupied the far left, and generally followed Moscow's lead on foreign policy. Maintaining that social revolutions would bring about a more harmonious international order, the communists were surprisingly strong—at least in American eyes—capturing 28.6 percent of the vote in France in 1946 and joining the coalition government and receiving 19 percent of the vote in Italy.[17] Socialist or Social Democratic parties represented the non-communist working classes, along with some professional groups and intellectuals. Social Democrats mostly abandoned Marxism after the war, if they had not done so before, but favored strong state intervention in the economy. More important here, they advocated non-alignment in world politics, particularly in regard to the emerging East-West split.[18] In their view, by steering a middle course between the superpowers, Europe could serve as a bridge between Washington and Moscow and avoid entanglement in their rivalry while preserving peace on the continent. The British Labour Party was the principal outlier on this score, with crucial implications for the form of rule (see chapter 5). Conservatives in the form of Christian Democratic or liberal parties captured the center-right, favoring free market policies and economic integration as well as close relations with the United States. After the war, conservative parties generally avoided class-based appeals and instead emphasized traditional social values and a return to political stability and "normalcy," but shared with the United States a strident anti-communism that

---

16. Frieden 2006, 261.
17. Judt 2005, 80.
18. On Marxism, see Mazower 1998, 290.

bled into resistance to the Soviet Union.[19] Finally, there was lingering if often covert support for the far right. This was especially true in France, where the wartime split between conservatives who joined the Vichy regime and the Gaullists who opposed the Nazis allowed the latter to remain a more vibrant presence than elsewhere. With most far-right parties formally or informally disbanded, even very conservative voters tended to support the center-right parties, but these supporters might still have been mobilized as a political force if given the chance.

Torn between ideologies and parties, Europe could have gone in almost any direction after the war: to the far left in a pro-Soviet direction, to the center-left and neutrality in the Cold War, or toward the center-right and an alliance with the United States. During the early postwar years, continental politics appeared to be tipping toward the first of these alternatives. The strongest parties were those with clear anti-fascist credentials, and these were, in practice, the communists who would ally with Moscow. Also quite strong were socialists who promised economic nationalization and planning at home and neutrality abroad.[20] On their own, many European countries would likely have clustered around neutrality. Although there were clear differences between the United States and left opponents in Western Europe, it is likely that some of these policy differences were exaggerated from a fear of communism in the United States. This was, after all, the era of strident anti-communism and McCarthyism. The fear of communism at home and abroad, sublimated during the war when the Soviet Union was an ally against Nazi Germany, returned with a vengeance by the late 1940s and early 1950s. Whether the opposition in West European states was as distant from its interests as the United States believed at the time is difficult to calibrate, but many Americans at least perceived the left in Europe as irrevocably hostile to the United States and left governments as likely to act against US interests. This fear, exaggerated or not, drove the United States closer to its eventual center-right allies, resulting in indirect rule and international hierarchy. In elevating newly constituted centrist coalitions to power across Western Europe, the United States brought anti-communist allies to the fore who then enacted the security cooperation and economic and political integration desired by Washington.

Indirect Rule

With significant popular support for left parties and latent support for far-right parties, it was by no means clear that pro-American center or center-right majorities would prevail in Western Europe, especially given the hardships of

19. Judt 2005, 80.
20. Judt 2005, 66.

the war and its aftermath.[21] Counterfactuals are always difficult to estimate. Nonetheless, consider what might have happened had the United States withdrawn its troops permanently from Europe as originally planned. An offshore balancing role by Washington would have left the United Nations as the primary forum for the rehabilitation of Europe and the restoration of peace, with possible vetoes from the Soviet Union and France who, for different reasons, would have disagreed with the US vision for the future of Germany. Under this scenario, there is little doubt that Europe would have been dominated by left parties or drifted increasingly to the left. As the most legitimate anti-fascist parties and with a plausible claim to represent the median voter in most countries, socialist and communist parties had emerged strengthened from the war almost everywhere. In Belgium, membership in the Communist Party rose from 9,000 before the war to 100,000 in November 1945, and within a similar time period from 10,000 to 53,000 in Holland, from 17,000 to 70,000 in Greece, and from 5,000 to 1.7 million in Italy. In 1945, French and Italian communists were already more that 20 percent of the electorate, and in Belgium, Denmark, Norway, Holland, and Sweden, communists comprised approximately 10 percent of all voters.[22] On the continent, the most likely political outcome would have been a united front of communists and socialists. If this had not happened immediately, then it very likely would have as the devastation of the war was exacerbated by the harsh winter of 1946–1947. Even in West Germany, where the Social Democratic Party (SPD) eventually broke with the communists, the desire for an inclusive left party remained strong, and in Britain, where the Churchill led the country to victory under a wartime coalition, Labour decisively won the first postwar election.[23]

Assuming a leftward tilt, there are three plausible counterfactuals. First, and most distant from US interests, united front governments might have allowed communists to seize power and align their countries with the Soviet Union. This was the pattern throughout Eastern Europe where, through alliances with local communist collaborators, the Soviet Union established a particularly deep international hierarchy through indirect rule. This occurred only in those areas controlled by Soviet troops at the end of war, but it was not entirely out of the question in Western Europe given appropriate conditions. Second, and still distant from US preferences, socialist or social democratic parties might have won elections and adopted a neutral stance in the emerging Cold War. This too was to be avoided at all costs. As Secretary of State Dean Acheson declared before the Senate Foreign Relations Committee,

21. Levin 2020.
22. Leffler 1992, 7.
23. Bessel 2009, 304.

"neutralism is a shortcut to suicide."[24] These first two scenarios were greatly feared by US officials in 1946, especially after Secretary of State George Marshall's tour of Europe on his return from the Moscow foreign minister's conference. Even if the first counterfactual of communist rule strains credulity, the second embodied the position of virtually every socialist party after the war and was likely the most natural result of strictly domestic rule. Third, and most favorable to the United States, was an independent European response to contain the Soviet Union and isolate Germany. Although British foreign minister Ernest Bevin clearly understood the need to involve the United States and advocated on this basis for the Brussels Pact, whether other centrist parties would have won elections and gravitated to this position is unclear. This most optimistic of scenarios might have resembled the Western Union of the United Kingdom, the Benelux countries, and France. Left entirely on their own, this is likely the best the United States could have hoped for from an autonomous Europe.

In either the second or third scenarios, however, Germany would have remained an element of contention. Without US reassurances, France would have remained opposed—or become even more stridently so—to German reindustrialization, reintegration, and certainly remilitarization. The Western Union would never have become the European Defense Community, vetoed even as it was by Paris, and without Germany Europe's ability to deter the Soviet Union would have been dramatically reduced. Alienated from Western Europe, Germany would likely have tilted further left and accepted Soviet offers of unification in return for neutrality. This last possibility was nearly a certainty—or believed to be a certainty by US officials. None of these scenarios would have been attractive to the United States. Under any feasible alternative, Western Europe would have spun out of the US orbit. Under even the outcome most attractive to Washington, Germany would have been excluded and, at best, neutralized.

Governance Costs

To ensure that Western Europe, at least, was pulled in its favored direction, the United States unfurled a strategy that was designed to increase support for the economic and foreign policies preferred by conservative parties who, over time, along with related groups, would come to constitute the political "center." Indirect rule in Western Europe required a less heavy-handed approach than it had in the other regions where it backed small elites against popular desires, but the United States nonetheless acted consciously to move European societies in its preferred direction. As historian Melvyn Leffler writes, "the Truman administration did not force changes in the political

---

24. Quoted in Leffler 1992, 17.

regimes of West European countries. Instead, US officials structured incentives and invited symbiotic relationships with European parties that saw their own self-interest served by informal alliances with the United States."[25] To rule indirectly, the United States had to ensure that pro-American parties governed in Western Europe, ideally with majority support in free and open elections but, in the end, by any means necessary. Once centrist coalitions came to the fore and solidified their power, Western European democracy and indirect rule were rendered compatible.

To build support for governments that would favor and adopt the policies preferred by the United States, Washington undertook several efforts—three indirect and one direct—which together constituted the governance costs (γ) of indirect rule. Most generally, it adopted policies that, by sparking economic growth, strengthened the political power of conservatives, allowing allied parties to defeat their opponents. Economic aid, an open economy that facilitated export-led growth, and security assurances and subsidies all bolstered the position of pro-American groups within Europe. For instance, "Instead of bludgeoning the French," historian Frank Costigliola explains, "the United States lured them with aid" to the tune of almost $1 billion per year between 1945 and 1954. According to US officials, the preferred method for shaping French policy was "finding, or creating through persuasion, influential groups in [the] French Government who want to see instituted . . . [what] we have in mind and working with them towards its accomplishment."[26] When required, however, the United States also intervened directly in national elections to ensure that its preferred parties won.

Many of these indirect policies have been discussed at length in the existing literature as core elements of the Pax Americana. What is important here is how these actions shaped the domestic political balance within subordinate states, locking in groups and eventually majorities that shared a vision for the postwar order with the United States. Washington knew that a measure of stability and prosperity was essential to win support for pro-American parties. A starving Europe would go to the left or far right, not to the center. Historian Deborah Kisatsky concludes that "between 1945 and 1991, when the Cold War ended, the United States poured billions of dollars into Italy [alone] in the form of recovery assistance, export-import credits, military aid, and technical support, in order to prop up anti-communists against radical forces."[27] Moreover, the aid provided needed to be clearly and obviously associated with the United States. Western Europeans needed to know where their bread was being buttered, and that future aid depended on their political choices. When Paris wanted to avoid embarrassing publicity in signing the Marshall Plan agreement, widely perceived as being an American dictate, the

25. Leffler 1992, 158. See also Herring 2008, 318–320.
26. Costigliola 1992, 44–45.
27. Kisatsky 2005, 113.

United States embassy insisted on a public ceremony with widespread press and radio coverage to ensure that the French appreciated their benefactors.[28]

Indirect US policies that favored conservative parties took three general forms. First, the United States provided reconstruction aid to all Western European countries, but it came with clear strings attached that mandated market-oriented policies. The single largest program was the Marshall Plan. Over the course of the program between 1948/1949 and 1951, Marshall Plan aid totaled about $12.6 billion in late 1940s dollars (approximately $100 billion in today's dollars), or roughly 0.5 percent of US GDP on an annual basis.[29] This sum helped finance imports of fuel ($1.567 billion); food, feed, and fertilizer ($3.192 billion); raw materials and semi-manufactured products ($3.430 billion); and machines, vehicles, and equipment ($1.853 billion).[30] These imports provided the inputs necessary to restart industry and agriculture. The sum was large but not necessarily decisive; most investment during the period was generated from internal sources, not from US aid.[31] What made the Marshall Plan so important, however, was linking aid to economic liberalization. Critical to this effort was the European Payments Union, begun with $350 million of Marshall Plan money, which allowed for multilateral clearing of trade balances and eliminated discriminatory trade measures between members.[32] Also important was the Committee of European Economic Co-operation, formed to create the integrated request for aid demanded by the United States.[33] Aid recipients had to agree to liberalize trade and commit to the goal of European economic integration, which was then implemented through the European Payments Union and Committee of European Economic Co-operation. As Michael Hogan argues, "Marshall Planners were . . . interested . . . in cutting the web of exchange controls, quotas, and import licenses and the tangled network of over two hundred bilateral trade and payments agreements that stifled intra-European commerce and prevented the most efficient use of local resources."[34]

Countries accepting Marshall Plan aid were also required to sign bilateral agreements with the United States in which they agreed to decontrol prices, stabilize exchange rates, and balance budgets, all actions aimed at creating the macroeconomic conditions believed necessary for effective market economies.[35] Linking aid to policy in this way undercut programs of economic planning and nationalization championed by socialists on the

---

28. Costigliola 1992, 64.
29. Gardner 2001, 120.
30. Hogan 1987, 415.
31. Hogan 1987, 431.
32. Eichengreen 2001, 135; Hogan 1987, 323.
33. Mazower 1998, 295. The Committee of European Economic Co-operation was later renamed the Organization for European Economic Co-operation and, later still, the Organization for Economic Co-operation and Development.
34. Hogan 1987, 19.
35. Eichengreen 2001, 133.

continent. Critical here were the use of counterpart funds. To receive Marshall Plan aid, recipients were required to deposit an equal amount of local currency in a counterpart fund. These funds were to be used by local governments for their own purposes but were subject to a veto by the US Economic Cooperation Administration.[36] During the plan's first year, the Economic Cooperation Administration blocked efforts to use counterpart funds for social welfare programs, which were viewed as inflationary. Rather, it directed local governments to use their funds to pay down foreign debt, balance their budgets, and restrain wages, thereby making their exports more competitive and reducing their trade deficits.[37] Counterpart funds were also used to sponsor trips by European business and labor leaders to the United States in hopes of "modernizing" their industries and industrial practices.[38]

Most generally, the United States made clear to Marshall Plan recipients that aid was contingent on the nature of their regimes. Although historians have searched in vain for a "smoking gun" order from Washington to any European capital demanding that communist parties be excluded from government, there were implicit threats to cut off aid if the communists won.[39] Domestic rule, which would have set policy far from US preferences, would not be supported by Washington. In 1946, even before the Marshall Plan was developed, Acheson announced that nations fighting to preserve their independence and democratic institutions would receive priority in the distribution of aid, a thinly veiled encouragement or threat, depending on one's view, to the Italians and French to exclude communist parties from their coalitions.[40] During Ambassador-Extraordinary Leon Blum's visit to Washington to negotiate a 1946 loan to France, Treasury Secretary Fred Vinson advised the socialist leader that US aid would flow more freely if his party were to join an anti-communist coalition and the communists were to be ousted from important economic posts in the cabinet.[41] Even though there were no direct orders from Washington to expel the communists, there were enough hints and suggestions that it is perhaps not a coincidence that communists were dropped from coalition governments in France, Italy, and Belgium in the days and weeks before the Marshall Plan was passed. Later, European conservatives frequently cited the possible loss of Marshall Plan aid if they or their market-oriented reforms were opposed at the election booth.[42] Overall, the widespread impression that aid was contingent on market-oriented

---

36. The threat to cut off these funds was not credible because it might bring about the economic collapse that they were designed to forestall (Wall 2001, 169).

37. McCormick 1989, 78–79; Esposito 1994. For a more skeptical view of the utility of counterpart funds, see Pollard 1985, 158.

38. Eichengreen 2001, 134.

39. Wall 2001, 170; LaFeber 1994, 480. The threats by Washington were not made public for fear of popular backlash (Costigliola 1992, 65).

40. Leffler 1992, 157.

41. Pollard 1985, 76; Patrick 2001, 233.

42. Eichengreen 2001, 133.

economic reforms bolstered the electoral fortunes of those groups most closely aligned with US interests in Europe. Economic recovery after the war, although it proceeded more slowly than desired, also reinforced support for market-oriented policies and those parties that supported them.

While the United States was ultimately successful in reshaping politics in Western Europe, providing aid was a major postwar governance cost, and US public support was initially soft. While the Marshall Plan is broadly praised in retrospect, it took over a year to put together the coalition of international business, major investment banks, trade unions, and leading farm associations within the United States to pass the bill.[43] Even then, Congress was hardly unanimous in its support, with the House voting 329 to 74 and the Senate 69 to 17 in favor. US conservatives argued and voted against reauthorization every year.

Second, the United States created conditions for export-led growth that tied Western Europeans to the US market and to each other. With the only prosperous economy after the war, the United States accepted that it had to be the engine for European recovery. It could have exploited its fortuitous position and imposed a positive optimal tariff, one of the few circumstances in which any country had sufficient market power to drive prices to its advantage.[44] Instead, as historian Melvyn Leffler writes, "from the perspective of postwar Washington, a viable international economy was the surest way to defend the health of core industrial nations and to protect friendly governments from internal disorders and nationalist impulses that might impel them to gravitate eastward."[45]

Not only did the United States demand that Europeans dismantle the bilateral agreements inhibiting trade, but it also led the effort to open international markets through the GATT. Although tariff reductions were negotiated reciprocally, and US duties were still on average high at the beginning, the United States gave Western Europe generous terms, reducing its duties by larger amounts in the early negotiations and recognizing that European concessions would not be meaningful until their currencies returned to full convertibility—something that did not actually take place until 1958.[46] The founding Geneva Round of the GATT in 1947 included twenty-three countries and 45,000 tariff concessions on over $10 billion of traded goods. At the start of this round, 60 percent of imports to the United States entered duty free. The United States also reduced tariffs on 53 percent of the remaining goods by ranges of 36 to 50 percent and froze another 20 percent at then-current levels.[47] Of equal importance, the United States strongly encouraged

43. Gardner 2001, 122; Hogan 1987, 191.
44. Gowa 1994.
45. Leffler 1992, 10.
46. Bown and Irwin 2015.
47. Barton et al. 2006, 41.

Western European countries to set their exchange rates to the dollar on favorable terms after 1949, giving their goods a competitive advantage on international markets.[48] Recognizing an acute dollar shortage, the United States also purposely ran a balance of payments deficit to provide liquidity to the international monetary system. Finally, rather than blocking European integration as a violation of the unconditional most-favored-nation principle, the United States championed efforts to create first the ECSC and later the Common Market. Indeed, it granted the ECSC a $100 million loan when it opened in 1952 and wrote into the GATT specific provisions that exempted customs unions from the unconditional most-favored-nation rule if internal duties were reduced to zero, prodding Europe toward the Common Market and complete free trade.[49] This combination of policies led to an unprecedented period of prosperity in which trade grew rapidly, outpacing industrial production.

The United States benefited from freer trade, of course, so the governance costs of this policy dimension were not huge. Rather, the costs were more political than economic. In a narrow economic sense, US leadership was hardly altruistic in opening the international economy. It maintained a positive trade balance with the strongest and most competitive industries through 1971, which was offset by military expenditures in Europe and long-term capital investment. The same favorable exchange rates that allowed Europeans to export also made investing in Europe attractive to US firms, who set up foreign factories on the cheap to jump the remaining tariff barriers into the Common Market. The role of the dollar as a reserve asset also allowed the United States to finance its payments deficit by simply printing more dollars, obviating the need for domestic adjustment and giving Washington what French minister of finance Valéry Giscard d'Estaing later called an "exorbitant privilege."[50] Nonetheless, there were real political costs to the United States that limited its generosity. Protectionist forces at home killed the International Trade Organization, for instance, and exempted a range of uncompetitive industries from tariff reductions entirely.[51] To open European markets, Washington had to be willing to pay the political costs of disappointing special interests that had, in the past, been protected by trade barriers and might otherwise have expected continued insulation from international market forces. While the United States as a whole benefited from open markets, not all sectors and industries gained equally, and some suffered directly. That Democratic and Republican administrations alike were willing to bear the political costs of disappointing protectionist constituents suggests the importance they placed on rebuilding the international

---

48. Hogan 1987, 210 and 264.
49. Frieden 2006, 286.
50. Eichengreen 2011.
51. Barton et al. 2006, 41.

economy and, by backing centrist coalitions, locking their allies into cooperation with the United States.

Finally, the United States alleviated European security concerns, both in deterring the Soviet Union and in pacifying relations between the allies. Through NATO, the United States aimed at the first, and through facilitating economic cooperation within Western Europe it attempted the second.[52] To meet both goals, it provided military aid that dwarfed the Marshall Plan and substituted its own forces for local security efforts. The Mutual Defense Assistance Act, enacted in October 1949, was intended as a military complement to the Marshall Plan and the grease that would make NATO work.[53] Both the Mutual Defense Assistance Act and Marshall Plan were integrated into and succeeded by the Mutual Security Act of 1951. Together, these military assistance programs provided billions in aid to NATO members. This combination of deterrence, pacification of Europe, and massive military aid reduced the burden of defense on European taxpayers and allowed an expansion of the social welfare state and deeper economic integration.[54] This subsidized security, in turn, undercut the case for neutralism in European foreign policies by reducing the cost of siding with Washington in the Cold War. In return for giving up a degree of autonomy in foreign policy, Western Europe got security "on the cheap," freeing up resources for other priorities. Some of what is often understood as European "free riding" on the United States, in other words, was built into indirect rule as a means of seducing voters into supporting parties aligned with Washington.

Assessing the security benefits that the United States provided to Western Europe is difficult, of course. How these benefits are perceived depends on the policy preferences of different factions within each European country and on counterfactuals that cut to the core of debates over the origins of the Cold War. Providing collective security within the West was clearly of benefit to all countries and factions. Absent a US presence on the continent, fear of German revanchism would have limited all other forms of cooperation, including economic integration, and required the members of the Western Union to arm, if only defensively, in order to ward off any possible threat from Bonn or, if the country had unified, Berlin. The pluralistic security community that would render the use of force unimaginable between member states depended in its early stages on the engagement and possibly the presence of the United States.[55] The security benefits from deterring the Soviet Union, however, are more varied, and in fact depend on one's perspective. To communists who might otherwise have taken their countries into the Soviet orbit, integration under the US defense umbrella was a net negative.

---

52. Hogan 1987, 22 and 27.
53. Ismay 1954, chap. 3.
54. Judt 2005, 304.
55. Deutsch 1957.

For communist parties, the Soviet Union was not a threat and, indeed, any role it might have played in Western politics would likely have strengthened their hand against their domestic opponents. That left parties eventually embraced the western alliance—the Italian Communist Party accepted NATO in 1983[56]—does not mean that they wanted the kind of protection against the Soviet Union that the United States was offering in the late 1940s and early 1950s. For socialists advocating neutrality, the Soviet Union was, again, not a significant threat and, in fact, US policies of containment and then deterrence were equally problematic, understood as needlessly escalating tensions with Moscow. The US defense umbrella was an unmitigated benefit only for conservatives who opposed communism at home and abroad. If one shared the view of US cold warriors that the Soviet Union was inherently imperialist—and after the Prague coup and the Berlin Crisis this meant most Americans and many Western Europeans—the deterrence provided by the United States was indeed a positive contribution. But these distributional effects of the US military role in Western Europe were, in some ways, precisely the point. By reducing the costs of security for Western Europeans, the United States tipped voters at the margin into the conservative camp.

Providing security to Europe was costly to the United States in two ways. One was the direct cost in higher defense expenditures. Estimating these costs once again requires an examination of the counterfactual. Assuming the Cold War would have broken out in any event, one comparison might be the costs of offshore balancing versus those for permanently stationing US troops in Europe. Since the unilateralists relied mostly on the threat of nuclear annihilation to deter the Soviet Union, and nuclear weapons were relatively inexpensive, as President Dwight D. Eisenhower later recognized, US forward deployments were likely more costly than the alternative, though the effectiveness of the two strategies might still be debated. A second comparison might be defense expenditures in the United States and Europe. This is not a perfect measure, however, as it ignores the counterfactuals noted above and does not capture what European defense expenditures might have been had the United States not deployed troops on the continent. Nonetheless, between 1950 and 1960, the United States expended 9.63 percent of its GDP on defense while Britain spent 7.73, France spent 7.21, and West Germany (1955–1960, post-occupation) spent 3.88 percent of GDP. Overall, in substituting its troops and equipment for local efforts, the United States spent about 2.5 percent more of its GDP on defense than did the other major European powers.[57] As noted, burden-sharing has always been a contentious

56. *New York Times* 1983.

57. Calculated from COW National Material Capabilities dataset (NMC v6). See Singer, Bremer, and Stuckey 1972. During the Korean War, the United States spent about 0.5 percent more of its GDP on defense than immediately before and after. The war cannot account for the substantially higher US defense expenditures compared to Europe.

issue within NATO. We know the United States formed a privileged group within the alliance and almost inevitably would have provided a greater share of the public good of defense.[58] Yet, the relevant question is how the community was defined, with the free-riding problem kicking in only once the United States was committed to collective security.

The second and indirect cost to the United States of its security umbrella was an increased risk of war with the Soviet Union. This is, of course, impossible to measure in dollar terms and depends again on the relevant counterfactual. A useful way to think about this cost is as the problem of extended deterrence. Throughout the Cold War, the United States aimed to defend Western Europe by threatening nuclear war should the Soviet Union launch even a conventional attack against its allies. To the extent that the US policy of extended deterrence was credible, any Soviet strike against Western Europe would also have to include automatic strikes on the United States. The same logic holds for conventional war in Europe. In essence, the United States put itself at risk to defend Bonn and Paris. Any policy of deterrence against the Soviet Union carried some risk, and extended deterrence might have occurred even if the unilateralists had won in Washington and the United States had pursued only an offshore balancing role. Nonetheless, a forward defense on the continent surely increased the risk of US involvement should war break out. Indeed, as Thomas Schelling famously argued, stationing troops in an exposed tripwire position in Berlin was actually intended to maximize this risk.[59]

Reconstruction aid, export-led growth, and military assistance all contributed to the political success of centrist and center-right parties in Europe and pulled European policies toward US interests, but at some real cost to the United States. When these indirect means failed to ensure victory by groups in Europe aligned with the United States, however, Washington undertook to manipulate electoral outcomes directly. Starting in 1948, as the Cold War took off, the United States committed to shaping electoral contests in ways that undermined votes for communist parties, especially in France and Italy where the left was strongest, and bolstered popular support for center-right regimes. Some of this effort was also undertaken in association with US labor unions, largely because they too feared the expansion of communist influence in Europe and because their participation would mask direct US involvement.[60] None of these direct actions were especially costly, and were often paid from counterpart funds under the Marshall Plan or underwritten by private foundations in the United States.[61] They were also of dubious effectiveness, and at best mattered at the electoral margins rather than in any

---

58. Olson and Zeckhauser 1966; Hartley and Sandler 1999.
59. Schelling 1966, 47.
60. Barnes 1981, 404; Kisatsky 2005, 21; Pisani 1991, 119.
61. Pisani 1991, 73.

decisive fashion. Nonetheless, they illustrate the lengths to which the United States was willing to go to support parties aligned with its interests and to help push politics and thus policies in the direction preferred by Washington.

Direct efforts at electoral manipulation remain a bit of a mystery, even today. They are often noted but rarely described in detail.[62] These operations were among the very first undertaken by the covert action division of the CIA.[63] The US government knew that if such activities were discovered they would undermine support for democracy in Europe and weaken the very parties that Washington was trying to support. With communist parties garnering the largest single bloc of voters in the early postwar elections in France and Italy, the CIA concluded that "economic aid alone and even improvement in the standard of living was by no means an adequate answer to the internal threat." In an ex-post justification, the CIA explained that "it was felt . . . that consideration should be given to new techniques to deprive the French and Italian communists of their power, recognizing that these parties constituted a continuing threat to democratic government and the NATO forces in Western Europe." The United States needed to act, in turn, because "both the Italian and French governments have evidenced over reluctance to proceed forthrightly against their local communist parties."[64]

Accordingly, the United States undertook a variety of direct actions to undermine support for left parties in Western Europe, some heavy-handed, others naïve and unsophisticated. In the case of Italy, emigration to the United States and remittances from those migrants were critical to the health of the economy.[65] In an attempt to suppress communist influence, US officials denied immigration visas to known communists and, in turn, US Communist Party members of Italian descent were publicly threatened with deportation. To support the conservatives, the United States also gave the Christian Democratic government twenty-nine merchant ships and additional arms just before the 1948 elections.[66] The Voice of America broadcast propaganda in Italy and the US government promoted anti-Soviet films. Recognizing that it would be best to speak to Italians through people and organizations that were identifiably Italian, the United States also recruited prominent Italian Americans to publicly support the Christian Democrats.[67] In France, the United States funded a similar propaganda effort, employing 289 US and French specialists, as the Psychological Strategy Board declared, to "influence men's minds and wills." In addition to the usual distribution of news and magazines that portrayed the United States in the best possible light,

62. Mazower 1998, 289.

63. Pisani 1991, 6, 59, 67 and 70.

64. Quoted in O'Rourke 2018, 110.

65. On the efforts of the CIA to encourage emigration from Italy to South America in order to reduce the "excess" population, see Pisani 1991, 111 and 114.

66. Leffler 1992, 196–197; Pisani 1991, 117.

67. Herring 2008, 321. On speaking through indigenous groups, see Pisani 1991, 92.

the propaganda effort subsidized the production of French magazines and funded the powerful Congress for Cultural Freedom and the government-affiliated Democratic Union for Peace and Liberty.[68] Although these were public actions in the sense that propaganda must be read by the public to be effective, the source of funding for these activities was not publicly disclosed.

In addition, the United States undertook a variety of more covert activities to shape electoral outcomes. In NSC-4A (1947), Truman authorized the CIA to undertake preventive action to ensure that the communists would not win at the ballot box in Italy or France.[69] In Italy, $10 million was diverted from the counterpart fund before the 1948 elections to pay for bribes and local campaigns by conservative candidates.[70] A November 1949 CIA policy statement reveals deep US involvement in the Italian trade union movement. Leaders of moderate unions were instructed to "carry out our (American) objectives in the light of local circumstances as they see them," with the CIA noting clearly that "assistance" would be provided. The creation of an anti-communist labor front in 1950 was also supported by the CIA and, in this case, the State Department.[71] With the communists polling 37 percent of the vote in advance of the June 1953 elections in Italy, the CIA went into overdrive, allocating $25 million per year to William Colby, the future CIA director then deployed in Italy, to ensure the communists did not win. Working closely with the Catholic Church, Colby funneled money to conservative parties and related organizations.[72] As historian Trevor Barnes concludes, "the strident anti-communism of the Christian Democrats [was] stimulated and sustained by infusions of CIA money."[73] By one estimate, the United States spent more than $65 million over the first postwar decades on psychological warfare in support of Christian Democratic candidates in Italy's national and local elections.[74]

In 1947 the United States also began covert operations to split the French trade union movement, then dominated by communists.[75] Supported by funding from the US garment workers union, the Worker's Force (Force Ouvrière), a moderate faction, defected from the communist-dominated General Confederation of Labor. When union funding began to run out, the CIA took over, providing Force Ouvrière with approximately a million dollars per year.[76] The CIA gave additional support to the French Confederation of Christian Workers. Through the splitting of the trade union movement,

---

68. Costigliola 1992, 85–90.
69. Barnes 1981, 412.
70. Barnes 1981; Kisatsky 2005, 117.
71. Barnes 1982, 662.
72. Barnes 1981, 663.
73. Barnes 1981, 664.
74. Kisatsky 2005, 113.
75. Costigliola 1992, 66–67.
76. Barnes 1981, 413. See also Pisani 1991, 100.

French politics were transformed and the communists lost momentum as a political force.[77] The CIA also reportedly bribed at least one member of several French cabinets on a continuing basis and considered a larger attempt to sway opinion over the European Defense Community in the Chamber of Deputies with bribes to lawmakers.[78]

Finally, Truman authorized the US military to act in the event of a communist coup.[79] If necessary, US officials decided, military force would be used to prevent France and Italy from falling under Soviet rule, though in the end more subtle forms of intervention proved sufficient.[80] Although the CIA and US government more generally "were euphoric" about the operations, what effect they had on any given election is not obvious. Although their advance in Italy does appear to have halted by the 1950s, the communists might well have lost even if the CIA had not intervened.[81] Nonetheless, the US program of election manipulation lasted throughout the initial postwar period until new centrist governments were consolidated across the continent.

The Federal Republic of Germany

The politics of indirect rule are particularly stark in the case of the Federal Republic of Germany (FRG). This is the only case of US direct rule in Europe during the twentieth century, and it evolved rapidly into indirect rule over the 1950s and eventually into domestic rule by the late 1960s or 1970s. Why direct rule was adopted and then abandoned is discussed in chapter 5. Here, the case of West Germany serves as an especially clear example of how indirect rule worked in practice.

The problem of ensuring West German allegiance became acute by 1951 when the United States fully embraced its forward defense strategy and agreed to the permanent placement of US troops in Europe, mostly in West Germany. Thus, by the early 1950s, the Federal Republic had become critical to US defense policy. Any move toward neutrality would have caused the whole defense strategy to unravel, and so some means of controlling the future of West German politics had to be implemented. After a period of direct rule under occupation authorities, the solution to the "German problem," as it was called, was ensuring that pro-American, Western-oriented factions rose to power and secured a hold on the population, permitting a shift to indirect rule as elsewhere on the continent.

Within the US and British postwar occupation zones, politics quickly solidified into two coalitions. Left groups clustered around and strengthened

---

77. P. Williams 1966, 37.
78. Barnes 1982, 660.
79. Pollard 1985, 76.
80. Leffler 1992, 196.
81. Barnes 1981, 413; LaFeber 1994, 483.

the historic SPD.[82] The communists were not as important a force in western Germany as they were elsewhere in Europe at the time. Despite industry concentrated in the Ruhr, the western regions of Germany were not sites of historic communist strength. Moreover, unlike in France and especially Eastern Europe, the communists did not lead the resistance to the Nazi regime and thus could not claim a vanguard position in the new era. The raping and pillaging carried out by Russian troops as they fought across Eastern Europe, which drove so many refugees into the western zones of Germany, also did not endear communists to the general population. The combined communist/socialist party in eastern Germany, the Socialist Unity Party, got less than half the vote in the Soviet zone elections of October 1946, and less than 20 percent of the votes in Berlin, which suggests just how unpopular the communists were. The larger concern was what might emerge on the political right. Under the Weimar Republic, the right had been highly factionalized, with no equivalent to the SPD. Given that Catholics predominated in the western sectors after the war, some politicians advocated for a Catholic party, but others, including Konrad Adenauer, the first chancellor of the Federal Republic, successfully argued for a unifying appeal based on common Christian principles.[83] Lacking a significant presence able to sustain a separate party, Protestants went along with this catch-all conception of the Christian Democratic Union (CDU). Although keeping a separate identity, and somewhat more conservative on social issues, the Bavarian Christian Social Union fused with the CDU, ultimately creating the CDU/CSU.[84] The Free Democratic Party (FDP) took a classically liberal (i.e., conservative) but secular position, occupying a strategic place between the SPD and CDU/CSU and allowing it to govern in coalition with either. With far-right parties prohibited by law and delegitimated in practice, right-wing voters gravitated to the CDU/CSU.[85] Within the possibilities set by the postwar structure of West Germany, facilitated by the force and vision of party leaders, two major groupings took shape occupying the center left and center right.

Two lines of cleavage separated the SPD from the CDU/CSU. Domestically, the SPD held fast to a traditional conception of socialism, including the nationalization of critical industries and promotion of worker's rights. This implied, in turn, support for a strong central government and a large role for the state in the economy.[86] Under the leadership of future economics

---

82. Botting 2005, 358.

83. Judt 2005, 267; Heidenheimer 1966, 61; Granieri 2003, 13–15.

84. As a catch-all party, the CDU/CSU solidified only slowly. It was not until October 1950, a year after Adenauer was elected chancellor, that the CDU actually became a unified party (Bessel 2009, 311).

85. The National Democratic Party (1945–1949) and Socialist Reich Party (1950–1953) were far-right parties advocating an autocratic state along the Nazi model but were eventually outlawed (see Kisatsky 2005, 17).

86. Weymar 1957, 238–239.

minister Ludwig Erhard, the CDU/CSU championed a program for a social market economy that embraced a role for government planning and guidance but emphasized private enterprise and free market principles.[87]

Internationally, the SPD strongly advocated the reunification of Germany and neutrality in the emerging Cold War. The commitment to neutrality was a combination of ideology and strategic calculus. The SPD would be stronger politically in a unified rather than a divided Germany. To ally with the United States would also make the pursuit of socialism problematic. Perhaps most important, though, to gain Soviet consent to a unified Germany the SPD accepted that Germany would have to adhere to strict neutrality in world affairs.[88] Reunification was a top priority, SPD leader Kurt Schumacher believed, and neutralism was a price that he was willing and even eager to pay for it.[89] Upon breaking with the SPD fragment in East Germany over the question of merging with the communists, Schumacher was permitted by the Western occupation authorities to reform the SPD as a national party, with himself as leader.[90] As the only SPD leader who remained in Germany during the Nazi era and did not collaborate with the regime, Schumacher had enormous prestige and influence. In strenuously advocating for socialism and German unity at all costs, Schumacher was probably close to the center of German opinion in the first years after the war.[91] Although it is difficult to know for certain, it is likely that this would have been the position of the median voter in the absence of US engagement in German politics. In the late 1940s, the SPD was clearly more popular than the CDU/CSU and pulling ahead at the ballot box.[92]

By contrast, the CDU/CSU platform committed Germany to binding itself as much as possible to the West—the policy of *westbindung*. Only in this way, the CDU/CSU argued, could Germany become a fully sovereign state and be accepted as an equal member of the international community. Accordingly, the CDU/CSU embraced every opening for deeper integration with the West: the ECSC, the European Defense Community, NATO, and more. No German politician could fail to support the ultimate goal of national unification. Yet, if *westbindung* required an interim division of Germany into East and West, this was for the CDU/CSU an acceptable compromise. As a member of the British occupation authority astutely observed about Adenauer, "In every speech, [he] proclaimed his dedication to the ideal of a united Germany.

---

87. Figures prominent in the early CDU emphasized the "social" aspect of the social market economy, calling for a "socialism based on Christian responsibility." Under Adenauer, the emphasis shifted to the "market" side of the equation (Bessel 2009, 317–318).

88. Judt 2005, 126.

89. Kisatsky 2005, 17.

90. The US occupation permitted parties, including the communists, only on a local basis until rather late (Mazower 1998, 243–244). Only the SPD and CDU were allowed to organize as national parties.

91. Leffler 1992, 453.

92. Levin 2020, 57–59.

By every action he did his best to make it politically impossible."[93] For the CDU/CSU, sovereignty was the highest goal and if this required dividing the country and binding the western portions to Europe, so be it. Reunification, if it was to be obtained, would follow rather than precede integration.[94]

The CDU/CSU platform was clearly closer to the interests of the United States than that of the SPD. In the immediate aftermath of the war, the United States focused almost entirely on reconstruction and humanitarian welfare to stabilize the economy and society in order to forestall more radical alternatives of the left or right. The Military Occupation Authority of the United States avoided favoring either the SPD or the CDU/CSU, as its leadership was convinced that any interference—even against the communists—would undermine public support for democracy.[95] Nonetheless, as the parties were legalized and began to take their modern form, the United States began to back the CDU/CSU in subtle ways.[96] Lacking local knowledge, the United States relied on high-ranking bishops and business leaders in Germany to suggest reliable administrators after the war, nearly all of whom were conservative (and frequently former Nazis) and now aligned with the Christian Democrats. US officials then pressed local leaders in Stuttgart, Frankfurt, and other cities to support Christian Democratic candidates and to include CDU and FDP members on their city councils. They also urged the Bizonal Economic Council to accept proportional representation, which, in practice, favored CDU and FDP candidates at the expense of the SPD.[97]

Especially as new bases and specific assets were developed in Germany after the Great Debate at home, US support shifted more clearly toward the CDU and Adenauer. On the one hand, Schumacher came to be perceived as an arrogant nationalist who refused to accept US rules. Indeed, his strident demands for neutrality and critique of allied policy convinced Acheson that Schumacher was a "fanatic of a dangerous and pure type."[98] On the other hand, Adenauer, according to historian Deborah Kisatsky, "appeared to epitomize the United States' best hopes for postwar Germany" and was, in turn, particularly solicitous toward the United States.[99] As the British observed, "Adenauer considers that his bread is spread entirely with American butter."[100] Even before the first federal election in 1949, Adenauer was brought in to negotiate the Petersberg Agreement with the Allied High Commission, which ended the dismantling of German factories and gave him

---

93. Quoted in C. Williams 2000, 341.
94. Leffler 1992, 454.
95. J. Smith 1990, 241, 294, 370. Clay's emphasis on democracy was not necessarily shared by military and diplomatic leaders in the United States.
96. Kisatsky 2005, 17.
97. Kisatsky 2005, 28–29.
98. Granieri 2003, 34.
99. Kisatsky 2005, 17.
100. Quoted in C. Williams 2000, 350.

a popular victory. He was also appointed chair of the Parliamentary Council, charged with writing the Basic Law.[101] The seeds of Adenauer's dominance were sown, even if they would take some years to sprout.

Despite favoring Adenauer, the United States took a relatively "hands off" approach to the first national elections in 1949. Perhaps this was because with the Korean War not yet on the horizon, the Cold War was not yet hot enough; because Germany was still under direct rule, and the Allied High Commission could veto any policy it chose; or because the difference between the SPD and CDU-CSU was not as clear as it soon became.[102] Whatever the reason, and admittedly the picture here is unclear, there is little evidence that the United States intervened directly in the first federal election, though the State Department around this time undertook a program of support for conservatives and an active propaganda campaign against Soviet calls for a neutral Germany.[103] Adenauer led a frenetic campaign, however, amazingly so as he was already seventy-three. When the ballots were counted, the CDU/CSU had won the largest number of seats at 139, as opposed to 131 for the SPD—a small difference, illustrating the fairly even balance between center-left and center-right politics. With 202 seats required for a majority, some within the CDU/CSU argued for a grand coalition with the SPD to ensure stability in the new regime. This was the result preferred at the time by the United States.[104] But with the SPD demanding the economics ministry in any coalition government, Adenauer held out for the social market economy on which the CDU/CSU had run in the election and cobbled together a coalition with the other conservative parties, including the FDP (52 seats), the German Party (17 seats), and the Bavarian Party (17 seats).[105] The communists received only 15 seats and later became a fringe party, receiving only 2.2 percent of the vote in 1953 and being banned by the Constitutional Court in 1956.[106] Soon after the election, and clearly summarizing the principle that would guide him over the next sixteen years as chancellor, Adenauer wrote that his "primary goal" was "to develop a close relationship with our neighbors in the Western world, especially with the United States," while also moving "with all our energy to see that Germany be admitted as a member of the European federation with equal rights and responsibilities."[107]

In the second federal election in September 1953 the United States clearly sided with the CDU/CSU, placing its thumb firmly on the center-right side

---

101. Granieri 2003, 34; Weymar 1957, 235.
102. The Allied Control Commission continued to exist formally, though it became inactive, and was replaced in West Germany by the Allied High Commission (the United States, Britain, and France) in 1949.
103. Kisatsky 2005, 46.
104. Levin 2020, 61.
105. Weymar 1957, 280.
106. Weymar 1957, 283–284; Judt 2005, 269.
107. Quoted in Granieri 2003, 30.

of the political scale.[108] While the United States initially had leaned toward the CDU/CSU but without actively favoring Adenauer, by 1951 the SPD had come out firmly against the ECSC and the European Defense Community, with Schumacher declaring that whoever approved the European Defense Community "ceases to be a true German." By 1953 the Korean War and the resolution of the Great Debate within the United States had led to a dramatic expansion of the US military presence, most of which was concentrated in West Germany.[109] Coming to office with President Eisenhower, Secretary of State John Foster Dulles leaned decisively toward Adenauer despite the fact that the president had some misgivings.[110] Washington now clearly backed the Christian Democrats and especially Adenauer as its favored ally. In late January 1953, Deputy US High Commissioner Samuel Reber wrote Dulles that "Adenauer is the symbol of what we are trying to achieve in Germany." The chancellor's position would be strengthened, Reber continued, were he "invited to visit the United States at an early date." Dulles and Eisenhower agreed. Americans should make clear, Dulles said, that US officials "were putting their money . . . so to speak, betting, on Konrad Adenauer." Eisenhower called Adenauer "our ace-in-the-hole," and agreed that the United States should "do almost anything to help" the chancellor with his reelection.[111] In mid-March 1953, through back channels, Adenauer requested help from the Eisenhower administration in the upcoming election and provided the White House with a list of actions it could undertake to raise his chances, most of which the administration agreed to fulfill.

Seeking to elevate Adenauer in the eyes of his fellow citizens, the United States as proposed invited the chancellor to visit Washington in April. The visit was replete with displays of German-American friendship. Laying a wreath at the Tomb of the Unknown Soldier at Arlington National Cemetery, Adenauer said it "symbolized the end of the years of enmity" between the two nations and "showed the world that . . . an era of friendship had begun in which the Federal Republic was accepted once more in the circle and company of the free peoples"—exactly the message he wanted to send his constituents back home. Mostly, Adenauer reflected, the visit demonstrated "that he could deal effectively with the Americans" and had "succeeded in raising Germany to the level of an equal."[112] Equally important, before the election the administration and Adenauer agreed to revive the 1923 US-German Treaty of Friendship, Commerce, and Consular Relations, suspended during the war; transformed Allied parole boards for war criminals into joint German-Allied boards, which eventually expedited the release of

---

108. Kisatsky 2005, 18.
109. Levin 2020, 61.
110. Levin 2020, 65.
111. Quoted in Kisatsky 2005, 53.
112. Quotes from Kisatsky 2005, 52–54. See also Granieri 2003, 62.

many Germans from detention; provided food aid to East Germany during the 1953 uprising in ways that Adenauer could take credit for; and scheduled a four-power conference with the Soviet Union to suggest progress on unification.[113] On its own, the United States also expanded assistance to publishers, business groups, and veteran's organizations that opposed neutrality. In addition, Eisenhower sent the chancellor an open letter expressing his conviction that Germany's integration into Europe provided the only path to "peaceful reunification."[114] Just days before the election, Dulles placed the entire weight of the United States on Adenauer's side. At a press conference, he stated outright that a defeat for Adenauer "would have catastrophic consequences for the prospects for German unification and the restoration of sovereignty." Such a defeat could "trigger off such confusion in Germany that further delays in German efforts for reunification and freedom would be unavoidable."[115]

While some US officials feared that such heavy-handed intervention would create a domestic backlash against the chancellor, Adenauer was adamant "that the West German public were either so grateful for past US actions or so certain of their dependence on it for their future security that the reverse would be true." In the months preceding the election, Adenauer took "every possible opportunity to demonstrate to the German public the friendliness of the US government toward him."[116] After this "love affair" played out in the public domain, the CDU/CSU vote share increased to 45.2 percent as compared in 31 percent in 1949, a gain of 105 seats in the Bundestag.[117] Although the counterfactual is unknowable, Dov Levin concludes that "the overall effect of the American intervention is quite sizeable."[118]

With power securely in the hands of the CDU/CSU, the United States and its allies could now safely return full sovereignty to the Federal Republic and rely as elsewhere in Europe on indirect rule. As the Federal Republic succeeded, the CDU/CSU along with Adenauer increased their support, indicating that Germans, at least, saw the country as being on the right track. As Arnold Heidenheimer observed, "after the early 1950s there was no longer any doubt that the political structures were coming to be regarded as legitimate by a rapidly increasing majority of the population."[119]

Indirect rule was furthered by the evolution of the SPD. With Germany now integrated into Europe and the Pax Americana, the SPD began a slow transition to the center, adopting the Bad Godesberg program in 1959, which

---

113. Levin 2020, 67–76. Few expected the four-power conference to produce any results; this was almost entirely for show to support Adenauer.
114. Kisatsky 2005, 55.
115. Quotes from C. Williams 2000, 407. See also Kisatsky 2005, 25.
116. Levin 2020, 78.
117. Judt 2005, 267.
118. Levin 2020, 209.
119. Heidenheimer 1966, 81.

rejected the goal of replacing capitalism, gave up on nationalization, accepted private ownership, and eschewed any residual Marxism in its ideology while declaring for ethical socialism based on humanistic principles. More important here, the SPD also accepted rearmament and reconciled itself to Germany's membership in NATO, which it had opposed as late as 1955.[120] With *westbindung* having succeeded in integrating the FRG into the West, and with society now dependent on continued access to Western markets and the United States for security, the SPD compromised on what had been core principles. Indeed, in the 1965 election, Adenauer, now retired and increasingly at odds with his former US supporters, complained that "the Social Democrats had become more American than the Americans."[121] Steadily improving its electoral performance under the moderate Willy Brandt, the SPD entered a "grand coalition" with the CDU/CSU in 1966.[122] By effectively consolidating a majority around economic and security integration with the West, thus creating a new center for German politics that had not previously existed, the United States could depend on the Federal Republic to follow policies that Washington preferred—no matter which party was in power.

Consequences of Indirect Rule

Indirect rule was remarkably successful. Given the alignment between US interests and those of center-right parties in Western Europe, policies adopted by its allies on the continent clearly embraced Washington's aspirations. Western Europe was now integrated into an American-led order. Perhaps more than any other single indicator, the eventual dominance of centrist coalitions demonstrates the success of US indirect rule. By the early 1950s, centrist and center-right coalitions broadly aligned with US policy prevailed across nearly all of Western Europe. Table 4.1 lists governments by "party families," country, and year for the original European members of NATO. Although they were often part of coalition governments immediately after the war, left parties were soon excluded from power. In using a relatively light touch, the United States was able to tip the balance of power within its allies in the direction it preferred in a way that was eventually compatible with democracy. Indeed, perhaps as a result of successful indirect rule, Western European countries have not only become consolidated democracies but have also been in the forefront of protecting human rights globally.

The overall result of reconstruction aid, economic integration and freer trade, and subsidized security was to ignite a period of growth in Europe that was nearly without precedent in human history, exceeded only by the

---

120. Granieri 2003, 85 and 132.
121. Quoted in Granieri 2003, 205.
122. Judt 2005, 269.

TABLE 4.1
Western European national governments by party families, 1946–1956

(Original members of NATO with the exception of Portugal, which was a dictatorship during this period)

	1946	1947	1948	1949	1950	1951	1952	1953	1954	1955	1956
Belgium	**Mixed** LIB/SOC **Mixed** SD/SOC/LIB	**Mixed** SD/SOC/LIB **Center** CD/SD	**Center** CD/SD	**Center** CD/SD **Center-Right** CD/LIB	**Center-Right** CD/LIB **Center-Right** CD	**Center-Right** CD	**Center-Right** CD	**Center-Right** CD	**Center-Right** CD **Centrist** SD/LIB	**Center** SD/LIB	**Center** SD/LIB
Denmark	**Mixed** SD/CON/ LIB/RW	**Mixed** SD/CON/ LIB/RW **Center-Left** SD	**Center-Left** SD	**Center-Left** SD	**Center-Left** SD	**Center** SD/LIB/ CON	**Center** SD/LIB/ CON	**Center** SD/LIB/ CON	**Center** SD/LIB/ CON	**Center** SD/LIB/ CON **Center-Left** SD	**Center-Left** SD
France	**Mixed** CD/SOC/ SD/CON	**Mixed** CD/SOC/ SD/CON **Mixed** SOC/CD/ SD/CON	**Mixed** SOC/CD/ SD/ CON **Center** CD/SD/ CON	**Center** CD/SD/ CON	**Center** CD/SD/CON **Center** CD/CON/SD	**Center** CD/CON/ SD	**Center** CD/CON/ SD	**Center** CD/CON/ SD	**Center** CD/CON/ SD	**Center** CD/CON/ SD	**Center** SD/CON
Germany (Federal Republic)				**Center-Right** CD/LIB/ CON	**Center-Right** CD/LIB/CON	**Center-Right** CD/LIB/ CON	**Center-Right** CD/LIB/ CON	**Center-Right** CD/LIB/ CON **Center-Right** CD/LIB/ CON/ RW	**Center-Right** CD/LIB/ CON/ RW	**Center-Right** CD/LIB/ CON/ RW **Center-Right** CD/LIB/ CON	**Center-Right** CD/LIB/ CON **Center-Right** CD/CON/ LIB
Iceland	**Mixed** CON/ SOC/ SD	**Mixed** CON/SOC/ SD **Mixed** CON/AGR/ SOC	**Mixed** CON/ AGR/ SOC	**Mixed** CON/AGR/ SOC **Center-Right** CON	**Center-Right** CON **Center-Right** CON/AGR	**Center-Right** CON/AGR	**Center-Right** CON/AGR	**Center-Right** CON/AGR	**Center-Right** CON/AGR	**Center-Right** CON/AGR	**Center-Right** CON/AGR **Mixed** AGR/SOC/ SD

	1	2	3	4	5	6	7	8	9	10	11
Italy	**Mixed** CON/SD/SOC/LIB	**Mixed** CON/SD/LIB **Mixed** CON/SOC/SD/LIB	**Mixed** CON/SOC/SD/LIB **Center** CD/SD/LIB	**Center** CD/SD/LIB	**Center** CD/SD/LIB	**Center** CD/SD/LIB **Center-Right** CD/LIB	**Center-Right** CD/LIB	**Center-Right** CD/LIB **Center-Right** CD	**Center-Right** CD **Center** CD/SD/LIB	**Center** CD/SD/LIB	**Center** CD/SD/LIB
Luxembourg	**Mixed** CD/SD/LIB/SOC	**Mixed** CD/SD/LIB/SOC **Center-Right** CD/LIB	**Center-Right** CD/LIB	**Center-Right** CD/LIB	**Center-Right** CD/LIB	**Center-Right** CD/LIB	**Center** CD/SD	**Center** CD/SD	**Center** CD/SD	**Center** CD/SD	**Center** CD/SD
Netherlands	**Center** SD/CD/LIB **Center** CD/SD/LIB	**Center** CD/SD/LIB	**Center** CD/SD/LIB **Center** SD/CD/LIB	**Center** SD/CD/LIB	**Center** SD/CD/LIB	**Center** SD/CD/LIB	**Center** SD/CD/LIB **Center** SD/CD	**Center** SD/CD	**Center** SD/CD	**Center** SD/CD	**Center** SD/CD
Norway	**Center** SD/CON/LIB/AGR	**Center** SD/CON/LIB/AGR	**Center** SD/CON/LIB/AGR **Center-Left** SD	**Center** SD/CON/LIB/AGR **Center-Left** SD	**Center-Left** SD	**Center-Left** SD	**Center-Left** SD	**Center-Left** SD	**Center-Left** SD	**Center-Left** SD	**Center-Left** SD
United Kingdom	**Center-Left** SD	**Center-Left** SD	**Center-Left** SD	**Center-Left** SD	**Center-Left** SD **Center-Right** CON	**Center-Right** CON	**Center-Right** CON	**Center-Right** CON	**Center-Right** CON	**Center-Right** CON	**Center-Right** CON

CD=Christian Democrat; LIB=Liberal; CON=Conservative; RW=Right Wing; SD=Social Democrat; SOC=Socialist/Communist; AGR=Agrarian

Source: ParlGov Project, n.d.

rapid growth of the East Asian "tigers" during their periods of export-led industrialization. It is, of course, impossible to distill the effects of any one program or cause during this period of unusually high growth as much was changing simultaneously in these years. But the combined effect of these various efforts and innovations produced an economic boom that dramatically increased standards of living in Western Europe in only a couple of decades. Between 1913 and 1950, a period covering both world wars, per capita economic growth in Western Europe averaged only 1.1 percent per annum, with Germany achieving only a 0.3 percent annual growth rate over this period. By contrast and reflecting the recovery, Western European income per capita increased by 4.5 percent per year between 1950 and 1973, with West Germany averaging 5 percent over these so-called miracle years. Another way to gauge success is to compare per capita income levels in Western Europe to those in the United States. On the eve of the Great Depression, the future members of the EU-15 averaged 66 percent of US income per capita, falling to 47 percent by 1950—less than half the US standard of living. By 1973, Western Europe had returned to its historic level of 65 percent even as the United States continued to grow.[123]

By encouraging trade and specialization, the United States induced publics across Western Europe to support the US-led international order. Dependent on export markets in the United States and other European countries, and in turn dependent on imports from those same countries, Western Europeans came to understand that their political interests were tied to the support and goodwill of the United States and required continued cooperation with their neighbors. If the war and its aftermath had destroyed the old economic and political interests vested in comparatively disadvantaged industries that demanded autarky and empire, a new set of vested interests emerged around freer international trade, open markets, and international cooperation.[124] Over time, export-led growth expanded the relative size of the comparatively advantaged industries, shrank (in relative terms) comparatively disadvantaged sectors, and shifted the domestic balance of political power increasingly in the interests of the former, reinforcing the constituency in favor of freer trade and stronger relations with the United States and its other subordinates.[125] This dynamic lock-in effect of international hierarchy was anticipated in chapter 1.

The general pattern can be illustrated again in the case of the FRG in the decade or so following the war. Germany is likely an extreme case, of course,

123. Eichengreen 2008, 16–18. By further comparison, earlier growth rates for Western Europe were 1.7 percent between 1820 and 1870 and 2.1 percent between 1870 and 1913. Per capita income levels in Europe would have been even higher by 1973 but Europeans chose to work fewer hours. See Baily and Kirkegaard 2004, 36.

124. On war destroying vested interests, see Olson 1982.

125. On how economic integration transforms domestic political balances of power, see Rogowski 1989.

having both lost its eastern territories and suffered devastating losses during the war. Nonetheless, the composition of the German economy changed dramatically as specialization and export-led growth took hold.[126] Two comparisons are important. By 1949, the Federal Republic had lost half the agricultural land of prewar Germany, most dramatically in regions of the east known for growing rye, barley, and oats. Nearly all manufacturing industries also declined by roughly similar amounts. Between 1949 and 1960, agriculture recovered in absolute terms, with the largest increases in wine and meat production—not grains. Manufactures boomed, however, with automobiles leading the way followed by pig iron and steel production. Exports of manufactures returned to their historic share of all exports, with motor vehicles the fastest growing sector. As Germany both shrank in size and increasingly specialized in manufactures and especially automobiles, its economy and politics were transformed. The "German miracle" was not just a recovery across the board, but a massive transformation of the country into an industrial powerhouse. Economic integration made this possible. Similar transformations occurred elsewhere, especially in some of the smaller and more open economies. The period of growth and rising prosperity across the West caused European politics—so plastic immediately after the war—to harden around those parties that adopted policies largely favorable to the United States. The fact that Western Europe emerged as a bastion of democracy and human rights after the war requires little documentation here.

The legitimacy of US indirect rule, like the dog that does not bark, is hard to interpret. Some underlying tensions are revealed in the need to speak of the US role in Western Europe through euphemisms. The United States never called itself an empire and rarely a hegemon, preferring instead "leader of the free world," partner, ally, or at most primus inter pares—first among equals. To declare its domination outright would have conflicted with principles of sovereignty and cooperation. Although differences with the United States emerged over time, most dramatically in the 1980s when Washington's attempt to station intermediate range ballistic missiles in Europe set off massive demonstrations across the continent, during the period discussed here most Western Europeans appear to have accepted US indirect rule and even quietly acknowledged it, although they did not (and still do not) want to call it by its name.

It is often argued that institutions within and between countries created the postwar international order and, institutions being sticky, allowed it to persist.

---

126. In an ideal world, we might have more disaggregated economic statistics. These are, however, the only data that both carry over from prewar Germany to the postwar Federal Republic and are adjusted for changes in territory. Calculated in real output and as shares of exports, these data are not distorted further by price and exchange rate changes. See Rahlf 2016. Data are available from Rahlf et al. 2015.

This may be true. But the analysis here calls attention to the underlying social formations on which those institutions were but a superstructure. By the early 1950s, centrist coalitions were firmly ensconced throughout Western Europe and the invited empire of the United States was broadly supported and therefore compatible with democracy. The United States did not get everything it might have desired, but it got most of what it wanted. It all looked voluntary, like cooperation under anarchy. But if we look deeper, we can see the hand shaping circumstances in ways that brought governments to power through democratic means that largely wanted to adopt policies favored by the United States. This is the power of indirect rule.

5

Hierarchy in Western Europe

The Pax Americana was structured around a set of international regimes, especially in trade, finance, human rights, and collective security. As posited in neoliberal international theory, these regimes reduced transaction costs, provided information, and facilitated cooperation between largely like-minded states.[1] The previous chapter showed how the mutual interests that allowed these regimes to succeed were constructed. They did not arise naturally or entirely of their own accord, but they were actively shaped by the United States through indirect rule.

But this is only half the story. Precisely because indirect rule was beneficial to the United States, Washington had to be concerned with opportunism by its allies. Common interests only take a country so far, and indeed create opportunities for "partners" to exploit or entrap even a superpower that is dependent on the cooperation founded on those interests. To safeguard itself, the United States had to impose additional rules to limit opportunism, transforming policy cooperation into international hierarchy and the "invited empire."[2] Beside generally recognized regimes that have garnered so much attention in the current literature, the United States created a parallel set of rules, generally informal and left implicit, that limited the foreign policy options available to Western Europeans. While compliance was generally good, US allies had considerable leeway in following the rules given the impossibly high costs of direct rule and worries about domestic rule on the continent. This fact is most dramatically exposed by France, which explicitly resisted US domination. This chapter examines the international politics of opportunism, hierarchy, and resistance in this order.

---

1. Keohane 1984; Haftendorn, Keohane, and Wallander 1999.
2. Lundestad 1986; Lundestad 1990.

Opportunism and the Rules of the Invited Empire

After securing reliable allies in Western Europe through indirect rule, the United States faced two forms of opportunism that required limits on the foreign policies of its subordinates. Even with the preferences of center and center-right coalitions well aligned with those of the United States, some degree of rule was still necessary. In attempting to control opportunism, mutual interests were transformed into international hierarchy. Beyond the regimes normally construed as the basis of the Pax Americana—the Bretton Woods institutions, the General Agreement on Tariffs and Trade, even NATO—the United States mandated that its new subordinates contribute to the common defense, an expectation not formally included in the North Atlantic Treaty, and prohibited the pursuit of independent foreign policy initiatives, especially with regard to their former empires and the Soviet Union.

In deterring any expansion by the Soviet Union, the United States simultaneously protected its subordinates, including those countries that were some distance from the front lines and did not have US bases and troops on their soil. For the Soviet Union to invade France in a conventional war, even more so Portugal, would require attacking through Germany. The US defense umbrella created general protection for Western Europe, not just for individual countries. Collective security was, thus, a club good provided largely by one member or a positive externality produced by US efforts to deter the Soviet Union. This external security guarantee, in turn, created incentives for subordinates to free ride on the United States.[3] Knowing that the United States was committed to their defense, subordinates could simply spend less on their militaries—which they did.[4] Indeed, this was a benefit that compensated states, in part, for giving up their autonomy and deferring to policies made in Washington. It also lowered the "price" of allying with the United States in the Cold War, undercutting one of the arguments of left parties that militarization would divert efforts and resources from building more extensive social welfare programs. But the United States still wanted and needed its allies to contribute to collective security, which they had less incentive to do once the US security umbrella unfolded. This led to the first rule of US international hierarchy that allies must share the burden of defense.

In the early postwar years, questions of burden-sharing largely revolved around rearming West Germany and, more generally, its status in the new regional order. Initially, the victors shared many goals with regards to Germany. The Morgenthau Plan, proposed by the US secretary of the treasury and approved by President Franklin Delano Roosevelt and Prime Minister Winston Churchill at their Quebec summit in 1944, aimed to transform Germany into a pastoral economy and strictly limit its industrial capacity. Soon after the war,

---

3. On free riding in alliances, see Olson and Zeckhauser 1966; Hartley and Sandler 1999.
4. Lake 2009a, 140–148.

however, the United States came to recognize the need to restart the German economy in order to stop the spread of communism and lessen the financial burden on US taxpayers, an idea strongly promoted by General Lucius Clay, then military governor in the US occupation zone.[5] By April 1947, the United States had fully embraced rehabilitation with new guidelines (JCS 1769/1) stating that "the complete resurgence of German industry, particularly coal mining, is essential for economic recovery of France—whose security is inseparable from the combined security of the United States, Canada, and Great Britain. The economic revival of Germany is therefore of primary importance from the viewpoint of United States security."[6] While an intended beneficiary of this turn in policy, France did not agree with this new American line. The prospect of an economically and militarily revived Germany "terrified" the French.[7] Along with the Soviet Union, France obstructed quadripartite governance, figuring that the longer Germany remained fragmented into zones the weaker it would be. Most importantly, France fought tooth-and-nail against German rearmament, delaying the question even in the face of US pressure; proposing the integration of West Germany into the European Defense Community—which it rejected some years later; and finally agreeing under duress to rearm Germany but only under NATO auspices. In the end, German rearmament was a compromise between the United States and France. Free riding and the demand that Western Europeans contribute more to collective security through NATO was an issue throughout the Cold War—and remains one today.

The external security guarantee also created incentives for subordinates to engage in risky behavior. This is the problem of entrapment in alliances.[8] Since a subordinate would not bear the full cost of any war it provoked, it might make increased demands on others that could lead to confrontations the United States would prefer to avoid. Early in the postwar period, the United States was especially concerned about Germany confronting the Soviet Union over its lost territories in Poland or even its new allies about control over the Saar and Ruhr regions.[9] Fearing entrapment, the United States imposed a second rule on its subordinates that prohibited independent military action. This rule was promoted, first, through the deployment of large US forces interspersed between possible rivals, especially the West and the Soviet Union, and then through the integrated command structure of NATO. Washington also manipulated military supplies to ensure continued dependence on the United States. Second, the United States interposed

---

5. On Clay's struggles with Washington, see J. Smith 1990, esp. 238. See also LaFeber 1994, 461.

6. Quoted in Leffler 1992, 148.

7. Leffler 1992, 322.

8. Snyder 1984. Economists refer to this incentive as moral hazard.

9. By the same logic, Poland became subordinate to the Soviet Union to protect itself from German revanchism. Mazower 1998, 217.

itself diplomatically between the Soviet Union and its allies, insisting that all negotiations with Moscow go through Washington. Somewhat surprisingly, the allies largely accepted this restriction. Although France wanted more autonomy from Washington, according to historian Frank Costigliola, "the French government did not seriously challenge Washington's leadership in negotiating with the Soviets."[10]

The United States was also worried that ties and commitments between European states and their colonies might entrap it into peripheral conflicts, such as those arising for France in Indochina and Algeria or for Britain in its empire.[11] Here, too, the United States sought to prohibit Western European countries from engaging in independent military actions. The single largest violation of this prohibition—the example that proves the rule—was the Suez Crisis of 1956. Following President Gamal Abdel Nassar's nationalization of the canal, Israel, Great Britain, and France hatched an elaborate plot to reverse the move and, ultimately, overthrow his regime. Fearing that any intervention would increase Nassar's stature and propel Egypt further into the Soviet orbit, President Dwight D. Eisenhower repeatedly warned the Europeans against such a move and, once the invasion began, threatened to bankrupt Britain, then in the throes of another financial crisis.[12] When Prime Minister Anthony Eden pleaded with Eisenhower to permit British troops to clear the canal and remain in Egypt as peacekeepers, the president responded with a blunt threat. "If you don't get out of Port Said tomorrow," the president wrote, "I'll cause a run on the pound and drive it down to zero."[13] It was not so much that the United States disagreed with the objectives of its European allies in this case—it too opposed Nassar and wished to see him removed. Rather, Eisenhower was clearly opposed to the means undertaken and, most importantly, was furious with London and Paris for not getting permission for the incursion. As Eisenhower concluded at the time, "nothing justifies double-crossing us."[14] Following Britain's promise to withdraw, which infuriated both France and Israel, the United States approved a $561 million loan from the IMF and an additional line of credit for $738 million and waived a payment of $143 million on a wartime loan due on December 31.[15] Britain, at least, was clearly brought to heel.

It was precisely to control the potential for both forms of opportunism by alliance members that the United Stated had to impose some form of hierarchy. While boosting centrist coalitions to produce allies in the Cold War, it needed to exert more or less control on the foreign policies of its

---

10. Costigliola 1992, 96.
11. Judt 2005, 289.
12. Ambrose 1990, 422. See also McDermott 1998, chap. 6.
13. Quoted in Buruma 2020, 77.
14. Quoted in Nichols 2011, 203–204.
15. Judt 2005, 297; Nichols 2011, 274.

subordinates to limit the problems of exploitation and entrapment. The Western Europeans, in other words, could not be permitted to conduct entirely autonomous or independent foreign policies. Had US forces not been permanently stationed on the frontiers, cooperation based on mutual interests might have been sufficient. But the more deeply the United States committed to the defense of its allies, the greater the risk of opportunism and the greater the need for some form of international hierarchy. Europeans were not free to set policy according to their own lights but had to contribute to the common defense and follow a channel on relations with Moscow and with their former colonies marked out by the United States. The deal that emerged was that the United States would provide a regional order of collective security and economic integration in return for a leading role in relations with the Soviet Union and within the alliance. Special responsibilities in return for special privileges.

Alternatives to Indirect Rule

The fact that indirect rule was so beneficial to the United States compared to the alternatives of domestic or direct rule posed problems for Washington in enforcing the rules of its hierarchy. Free riding within the alliance was a perennial problem. While Washington admonished or perhaps more accurately hectored NATO members to contribute more to the collective defense, and did succeed in rearming West Germany, the United States always bore a disproportionate burden.[16] Washington could threaten to reduce its own spending or withdraw from the continent, but such threats were not credible. Likewise, limiting independent foreign policy initiatives by allies was difficult. While the United States bludgeoned Britain into compliance over Suez, for instance, it did not similarly threaten to bankrupt France. More telling, once France withdrew from Vietnam after Dien Bien Phu in 1954, the United States ended up replacing the French presence in a postcolonial conflict it would later regret. Had the United States been better placed to walk away from indirect rule and default to domestic rule, it might have reduced the scope for opportunism by its allies. As it was, the United States was forced to tolerate free riding on a long-term basis and occasional entrapment because the alternatives to indirect rule were typically worse. This is especially true when the costs of war and occupation are measured against the policies adopted by Western Europeans under indirect rule and those that might have been imposed by the United States under direct rule.

---

16. Olson and Zeckhauser 1966; Hartley and Sandler 1999.

Direct Rule

The United States could have attempted to force Europeans into abiding by its preferred policies, using its military and economic might to impose direct rule on former allies and enemies. The idea that, having fought a war to defeat the Axis countries, the United States would then turn on its allies—even just its Western allies—and attempt to impose direct rule, however, strains credulity. The costs of World War II were steep and would likely be even more so against its victorious if weakened allies. Overall, threats of war would simply not have been credible.

As noted in chapter 4, the United States did govern West Germany directly under the postwar occupation, transitioning to indirect rule by the early 1950s. Direct rule was possible in this instance only because the costs of war had been absorbed in the process of defeating the Nazis and were therefore sunk with regard to the postwar era. Direct rule was preferred in the early postwar period, in turn, because of a divergence of interests that was expected to continue after the war. In light of Germany's history, no one believed US and German policy preferences would be well aligned, at least at first. To bring Germany into the fold, so to speak, required direct rule. But even so, the costs of occupation rendered permanent rule out of the question, prompting a quick transition to indirect rule once a center-right regime was consolidated (chapter 4).

Germany was originally to be divided into four zones administered by the United States, Britain, France, and the Soviet Union but governed as a single unit under the Allied Control Council, in which the sovereignty of the country initially resided.[17] The Allied Control Council broke down in 1946–1947, with Britain and the United States merging their zones in January 1947 and later adding the French zone. Following the Berlin Blockade of June 1948 to May 1949, the three Western zones merged to form the Federal Republic of Germany (FRG) in May 1949 and the Soviet zone became the German Democratic Republic (GDR) in October 1949. In the FRG, the occupation continued until May 5, 1955, when the General Treaty entered into force. At this time, the allied military governors were replaced by civilian high commissioners with reduced powers. Full and unrestricted sovereignty was returned to Germany only with reunification and the Treaty on Final Settlement with Respect to Germany, which became law in March 1991. Long after 1955, the FRG remained a "semisovereign" state.[18]

Following the defeat of the German military, the allied powers issued the so-called Berlin Declaration in June 1945 in which they assumed "supreme authority with respect to Germany, including all powers possessed by the German Government." Military governors reigned in each of the occupation

---

17. J. Smith 1990, 254–258, 266.
18. Katzenstein 1987.

zones, with the Allied Control Council acting as a parallel governance body. With the breakdown of the Allied Control Council, the Western allies created the Allied High Commission in September 1949, which remained in operation until 1955. The Occupation Statute and subsequent Petersberg Agreement specified the prerogatives of the Western allies, including the right to veto military, economic, and foreign policies of importance. Under the Allied Control Council and Allied High Commission the allies mandated the denazification of German society, demilitarization of the Wehrmacht and arms industries, democratization (in the Western zones), decentralization in a federal system, and disassembly of industrial plants and equipment (mostly by France and the Soviet Union, a policy that ended in the FRG in 1951). Banning all political activity immediately after the war, with military "civil affairs" officers taking direct control over the administration of towns and districts, the allies eventually began to rebuild German administrative capacity from the ground up, creating representative councils for towns and cities (though with members selected by the military authorities). Elections for local councils began in October 1946. The first parliamentary elections in the FRG were held in 1949. Through 1955, additional powers were increasingly delegated to the government of the FRG but ultimate authority and sovereignty continued to be held by the Allied High Commission. The occupation was just about the clearest case of direct rule that can be found.

Direct rule in Germany, however, was always a waning form of hierarchy. Even though the costs of war were discounted, the costs of occupation were still understood to be unacceptable over the long run. The main costs of the occupation were not for military troops but for the rehabilitation of Germany. Clay, at least, understood what Secretary of State Colin Powell later called the "Pottery Barn Rule" in the case of the Iraq War—you break it, you own it. As long as it was responsible for Germany, Clay maintained, the United States had to provide for the well-being of the people lest they revolt, what the theory in chapter 1 refers to as occupation costs. Despite imposing some taxes on Germany, the United States was contributing four times more to the occupation than it was able to raise in revenue from the impoverished Germans themselves. Between 1945 and 1955, when the occupation formally ended, the United States contributed more than $4 billion in economic aid to the Federal Republic, or roughly $400 million (approximately $5.2 billion in 2020 dollars) per year.[19] Reinforcing these estimates, in 1946 Britain paid some £80 million (roughly $4.4 billion in 2020 dollars) toward the "upkeep" of its zone in Germany.[20] These costs were simply unsustainable over the

---

19. In Japan, where the United States carried out a similar occupation, estimates suggest that the United States spent more than $365 million per year (approximately $4.8 billion in 2020 dollars), which rose each year rather than falling as the country rebuilt. Lake 1999, 190.

20. Botting 2005, 181 and 350. Combined, the United States and Britain were spending approximately $600 million per year in their occupation zones.

long run. If this was true in Germany, where the costs of imposing its policy preferences on a population were absorbed in defeating the Nazi regime, the costs of war and occupation elsewhere were simply too high to even consider direct rule as a viable solution to the problem of opportunism by subordinates. The more likely alternative to indirect rule was domestic rule.

Domestic Rule

Great Britain, permitted to govern itself largely free from US control, is the exception to indirect rule in Western Europe, an anomaly that once again proves the rule. Britain benefited from the various forms of economic and security aid provided to all of Western Europe after the war. Nonetheless, throughout the period Britain was more of a partner than a subordinate. The United States did not attempt to manipulate Britain's internal politics and allowed autonomous political processes to unfold for two critical reasons. First, United States and British policy preferences were more closely aligned than elsewhere. Indeed, Britain was instrumental in drawing the United States into its role as leader of the so-called western alliance. Second, the similarity in the foreign policy preferences of the two major political parties in Britain—Labour and Conservative—limited the ability of the United States to impose indirect rule, even had it wanted to. Tipping the balance of political power in one direction or the other would have produced little difference in Britain's foreign policy. These unique circumstances were not found on the continent, where left parties took a very different political stance than Labour. In France and elsewhere, domestic politics were much less favorable to Washington, requiring indirect rule while at the same time allowing the continental states range for greater opportunism.

Unlike in other European countries where center-right and left parties differed in their preferred policies toward the Cold War, the Conservative and Labour parties agreed on Britain's interests in the postwar system. For five years, the parties had governed together in a wartime coalition with Churchill as prime minister and Clement Attlee as deputy prime minister. At war's end, the coalition was dissolved, but not over issues of foreign policy. As a symbolic but important example, Britain's first postwar election results were announced in the middle of the Potsdam Conference, attended by the United States, the Soviet Union, and Great Britain. Churchill and Attlee were both present during the first half of the conference, Attlee as a mostly silent observer. Both flew back to Britain for the counting of the ballots, which, to nearly everyone's surprise, elevated Attlee to prime minister by a large majority. Only Attlee returned to Potsdam. But there was no change in the British negotiating position, only a change from Churchill's bombastic ramblings to Attlee's more focused interventions. Attlee did not even have time to formulate a cabinet before returning to Germany, never mind put together a new policy, but the new prime minister had participated in the formulation of Britain's foreign policy during the coalition and, in that supposed British tradition, just carried on. Labour favored far more socially progressive economic policies—nationalization of key industries, a national health service, and more, though the party was probably closer to President Roosevelt's New Deal than to socialism per se—but on foreign policy the two British parties were remarkably similar.[21] Indeed, when the new foreign secretary Ernest Bevin spoke for the first time at the second half of the Potsdam summit, "it was as though Churchill had never left."[22]

Not only were the two countries' interests generally aligned, but Britain also intentionally sublimated any differences that might have existed to US interests, at least as British officials understood them. As Churchill confided to Anthony Eden, his foreign secretary during the war, his "whole system is founded on partnership with Roosevelt."[23] More graphically, in upbraiding Charles de Gaulle for his independence as the leader of Free France, Churchill lectured the general, "Look here! I am the leader of a strong and unbeaten nation. Yet every morning when I wake my first thought is how I can please President Roosevelt."[24] This sense that Britain had to follow Washington's lead continued after the war.

Although some in the Labour Party aspired to greater independence in foreign policy, Attlee recognized Britain's dependence on the United States.[25] Indeed, his foreign secretary, Ernest Bevin, receives substantial credit as the orchestrator of the United States commitment to Europe.[26] As Don Cook writes, "The British knew full well, better than the Americans, that they could no longer hold a European balance of power. The primary aim of British postwar policy, therefore, had to be to ensure that American power was not withdrawn from Europe."[27] Bevin slowly and purposively sowed the seeds of what eventually became NATO. The Labour leader demonstrated early leadership in responding to Secretary of State Marshall's plan, though it was more a vaguely formulated invitation. Grasping the significance of Marshall's offer of aid if Europe could organize itself, Bevin immediately contacted other European leaders and organized the Committee on European Economic Co-operation to coordinate their request.[28] In planning for postwar security policy, Attlee and Bevin saw the Soviet Union as a threat to

---

21. Bew 2017, 389; Clarke 2008, 333. A minority in the Labour Party advocated neutrality as well, but Attlee and Bevin forcefully denounced this position (Judt 2005, 111).
22. Clarke 2008, 356. See also Bew 2017, 301 and 354.
23. Quoted in Clarke 2008, 8.
24. Quoted in J. Jackson 2018, 302. Churchill's rant supposedly concluded with the admonition, "Your situation is very different. Why then should your first waking thought be how can you snap your fingers at the British and the Americans."
25. Judt 2005, 111–112.
26. Bew 2017, 425.
27. Cook 1989, 11.
28. Adonis 2020, loc. 252–253.

Europe before many Americans did.[29] Following the London foreign ministers conference in November 1947, Bevin approached Secretary of State
Marshall with the idea of a security arrangement between the two countries.
The secretary of state was intrigued, but faced substantial resistance at home,
including from within his own department. Bevin continued to nurture the
seeds of a possible alliance. After Marshall indicated a desire to see Europe
demonstrate some initiative on its own, Bevin responded with the Treaty of
Brussels in March 1948 between Britain, France (the two were already allied through the Treaty of Dunkirk in 1947), Belgium, Luxembourg, and the
Netherlands.[30] As relations with the Soviet Union turned increasingly tense,
and after Truman's election in November 1948, negotiations on the North
Atlantic Treaty were quickly completed. Nonetheless, without Bevin's leadership, the treaty would likely not have happened. While many historians focus
on Soviet moves that antagonized or worried the United States, Britain's efforts to draw the United States into the alliance were equally important and
a reflection of their common interests.

Ironically, where the policy preferences of London and Washington did
differ, the United States had to resort to financial coercion to force compliance with its preferences. One issue on which London and Washington disagreed vehemently was the future of Britain's empire. Throughout the war,
Britain had fought with one eye on its empire, both as a source of resources
and manpower and as a political unit integral to its great power status. As
then prime minister Winston Churchill famously declared, "I have not become the King's first minister in order to preside over the liquidation of the
British Empire."[31] The United States was far less attached to the idea of empire than many Europeans and, fearing communist expansion into colonies
demanding independence after the war, supported decolonization except
where it was likely to result in pro-Soviet regimes.[32] Dismantling the empires
would also render the Europeans more dependent on the United States and
reduce the risk that they or even Washington would be pulled into peripheral conflicts. Throughout the war, US leaders were at pains to make clear
to the British and the American public that the country was not fighting to
preserve Europe's empires.

During this time, the United States and Britain clashed dramatically over
the issue of Britain's imperial preferences. The United States had begun working toward lower tariffs on trade within the British empire from the 1930s,
and continued to dismantle the system of preferential duties during the war.
The Atlantic Charter signed by FDR and Churchill in 1941 stated that one

29. On the Soviet threat, see Bew 2017, 315 and 417. On the need to involve the United
States, see Bew 2017, 366.
30. Costigliola 1992, 70; Bew 2017, 462.
31. Quoted in Clarke 2008. On imperial preferences, see 13–14.
32. Hager and Lake 2000.

of the war's aims was to ensure "access, on equal terms, to the trade and raw materials of the world." Though Churchill managed to insert the proviso that any such rules would have to be consistent with "existing obligations," by which of course he meant the empire, the careful wording was understood by both sides to mean the end of discriminatory tariffs such as those maintained by Britain with its colonies.[33] The United States continued to exert pressure on Britain over imperial preferences through the Lend-Lease Act, critical to the war effort, which explicitly committed both countries (meaning Britain) to "the elimination of all forms of discriminatory treatment in international commerce."[34]

Although pledged to eliminate imperial preferences, Britain was slow to implement any change in policy. The United States delivered the knock-out blow in 1946. Britain was in desperate financial straits as a result of the war. As historian Peter Clarke writes, "It was not just that the British bet the farm [during the war]: they also mortgaged it to the Americans."[35] Britain emerged from the war greatly weakened. Not only had it sold most of its foreign assets, reducing its postwar income stream, and borrowed heavily from the United States, it had also imported goods from its empire with a promise to pay in the future, accumulating the so-called Sterling balances of approximately £3 billion ($12 billion at the prevailing exchange rate), with the majority owed to India. Between the sale of assets and accumulation of overseas debts, 28 percent of the country's total wealth disappeared in the war. Such was the price of victory.[36] In producing for the war and to sustain its population, Britain had also forfeited its export markets, which had mostly been picked up by the Americans.[37] Any recovery of its economy and global stature depended on assistance from or at least the forbearance of the United States as its main creditor. The United States took advantage of Britain's financial weakness to extract important concessions that would bring London into compliance with its rules for the postwar order.

With victory in Europe in May 1945, Britain anticipated a prolonged phase two of the Lend-Lease program lasting up to eighteen months, until Japan was defeated as well. The atomic bombs dropped on Hiroshima and Nagasaki in August 1945, however, brought the Pacific war to a quick conclusion. Congress promptly terminated the Lend-Lease program in September 1945. Goods already in the pipeline to Britain, worth approximately $1.1 billion,

---

33. Within days of signing the charter, Churchill made plain that he had no intention of implementing its platitudes, at least as they applied to the empire (Clarke 2008, 91). On the rewriting of the text, see Buruma 2020, 25; McKinstry 2019, 267–271.

34. Frieden 2006, 256. See also LaFeber 1994, 415. The United States tied Lend-Lease aid to postwar civil aviation as well, as it wanted access to airfields equal to the British worldwide, including within the empire (Clarke 2008, 104).

35. Clarke 2008, 3.

36. Clarke 2008, 402–403.

37. In 1944, for instance, British exports paid for about 1 percent of British imports (Clarke 2008, 28).

were sold at 10 percent of their nominal value, but no further assistance was to be forthcoming. Caught by surprise, London was unprepared to cover its now looming balance of payments deficit. Lord John Maynard Keynes, negotiating on behalf of the treasury, immediately proposed a phase three of the Lend-Lease program that envisioned expanded exports, domestic austerity, and continued aid based on "justice" in recognition of the unilateral British war effort before 1941.[38] This plan was quickly shut down by the Truman administration. With no phase three of the Lend-Lease program, Britain was in desperate straits.[39]

With Keynes again the lead negotiator, the United States finally agreed to a new loan of $3.75 billion at 2 percent interest, on the condition that London abide by its earlier agreement to phase out imperial preferences and reduce tariffs on US goods, although this was likely to worsen Britain's balance of trade.[40] This pledge was finally implemented through the GATT, which extended most-favored-nation status to all members, including the United States, essentially ending preferences within the empire.[41] Rather than aiding Britain, the United States extracted full value from the loan to force London to comply with its rules on trade. Critics within Britain complained that "we have sold the empire for a trifling sum. Henceforth the United States of America reaps where we have sown." But as Attlee explained, "you can criticize the loan and the arrangement surrounding it—and we fought inch by inch throughout the negotiations—but the fact remains we couldn't do without it. The critics could shout. We had to run things."[42] With imperial preferences resolved, at least for the moment, unconditional US aid through the Marshall Plan began to flow and, in turn, took some of the financial pressure off Britain—serving in Bevin's words as "a life-line to sinking men."[43]

Although there is no formal accounting of "quid pro quos" in US relations with various European states during this period, the historical record is replete with instances of coercion in US-British relations that appear to be absent elsewhere, the Suez Crisis being perhaps the most dramatic

---

38. Clarke 2008, 314–315 and 403; Bew 2017, 373.

39. Clarke 2008, 511.

40. Bew 2017, 380; Frieden 2006, 266; LaFeber 1994, 458; Clarke 2008, 376. Canada extended another $1.19 billion at the same rate. Britain also had to allow the pound to be freely convertible into dollars within eighteen months, as originally envisioned in the Bretton Woods Agreement (Clarke 2008, 376, 400). Although there were no formal requirements, in the runup to the loan Britain made a number of other concessions desired by the United States, including referring the question of Palestine to the United Nations, withdrawing British troops from Greece, and quitting India (Clarke 2008, 376, 476–477).

41. In practice, some imperial preferences remained intact until Britain joined the Common Market in 1973, but the commitment to eliminating preferences was essential to getting the 1946 loan through Congress (Clarke 2008, 395 and 511).

42. Quotes from Bew 2017, 385.

43. Quoted in Clarke 2008, 491–492.

example.[44] Britain's overarching lesson from the Suez affair, as Tony Judt writes, was that it "must never again find itself on the wrong side of an argument with Washington . . . however ambivalent they might feel about particular US actions, British governments would henceforth cleave loyally to US positions."[45] Nonetheless, in this rare instance cutting off aid to enforce concessions by Britain was possible because the Conservative and Labour parties were both acceptable allies for the United States. Where elsewhere threats to cut support would weaken the groups most favorable to Washington, possibly bringing left governments to power, in the case of Britain the United States was free to use its financial strength to enforce its rules on colonial ties and independent foreign policy actions. Shared interests between London and Washington, as well as between Conservatives and Labour in Britain, permitted the "special relationship" to prosper even under domestic rule. But Britain also learned well the rules of the invited empire. Surprisingly, other states for whom domestic rule was less attractive for the United States—especially France—had much greater leeway in their foreign policies.

Resistance

Any system of rule will create opposition and resistance, even if it may be suppressed and, therefore, largely invisible. Yet, democracy and broad public support for the Pax Americana suggest that US-led indirect rule is likely be regarded as relatively legitimate, as appears to have been the case. In the case of postwar Western Europe, the opposition to US indirect rule came from both the far left and far right of the political spectrum. With the majority of the population in what came to be seen as the center, indirect rule was compatible with democracy, but those on the extremes resented and resisted US domination.

Multilateralism

The United States attempted to preempt resistance in Western Europe by building new multilateral institutions. Multilateralism is often described as a distinguishing feature of the Pax Americana. Defined as "an institutional form that coordinates relations among three or more states on the basis of generalized principles of conduct . . . without regard to the particularistic interests of the parties," it implies "indivisibility among members of a

---

44. We do not have a complete inventory of coercive events with regards to Europe. Historians may have focused on those targeted at Britain because they seem anomalous given the "special relationship," in which case the secondary literature is providing a biased sample. Here, though, these coercive attempts follow precisely from the aligned interests that rendered indirect rule ineffective.

45. Judt 2005, 299.

collectivity" and diffuse reciprocity.[46] In the context of indirect rule, multilateralism is a far-sighted form of what G. John Ikenberry calls "self-binding," which limits US actions that might be perceived by subordinates as harming their interests.[47] Understood in this way, multilateralism gives subordinate states an institutional basis for "voice"—an opportunity and sometimes a forum for those subject to rules from Washington to raise concerns and objections about the conduct of US foreign policy.[48] If subordinates are prohibited from conducting an independent foreign policy with the Soviet Union, for instance, multilateralism allows for input by others into how the United States manages relations with Moscow on behalf of the collective.

Nonetheless, it is important to recognize that in no case from the Bretton Woods institutions to NATO did the United States allow its allies to possess a veto over US policy or the ability to demand a particular course of action. Even the North Atlantic Treaty, which lays out the terms of one of the most important multilateral institutions, states that an attack on one is an attack on all—a clear example of indivisibility and diffuse reciprocity—but commits each member, including the United States, to take only "such action as it deems necessary."[49] Moreover, with the supreme allied commander always an American general reporting to the president, any action recommended or taken by NATO has always been subject to a US veto. While the treaty and institution carry a presumption of collective defense, and the United States would suffer a cost to its reputation and credibility should it fail to respond to any external aggression, no state has an obligation to respond in a particular way or to allow others to determine its response. By granting members voice, multilateralism masked the inequality in the US international hierarchy, but it did not transform relations between members into those between equals.

Anti-Americanism

Despite multilateralism's purpose of diffusing resistance, there was always some anti-Americanism and pushback against US hierarchy in Western Europe, which deepened as time went on. With anti-Americanism less pervasive than sometimes averred, and far less salient than in other regions covered in this volume, it was never a serious limitation on US-West European relations.

The extent of opposition to US indirect rule is hard to assess exactly. Within the United States, any criticism of US policy by foreigners was often attributed to anti-Americanism. Relatedly, any failure to recognize or appreciate what was in the eyes of Americans, at least, the fundamentally benevolent

---

46. Ruggie 1993, 11.
47. Ikenberry 2001.
48. On voice, see Hirschman 1970.
49. North Atlantic Treaty, Article 5.

nature of US actions toward Europe was also attributed to an underlying hostility. However, neither criticism nor failing to extol the virtues of US rule should be mistaken for the general psychological tendency that is anti-Americanism. While there was certainly criticism of US policy, which reached a height during the period after the Suez Crisis, there appears to have been relatively little hostility toward the United States or Americans in general.[50]

In surveys in West Germany between 1950 and 1956, for instance, 78 to 83 percent of respondents supported cooperation with the United States, with only 3 percent opposed, and 57 to 69 percent expressed overall positive opinions toward the United States, with only 2 to 4 percent indicating negative opinions. The latter contrasts with 18 to 46 percent and 62 to 80 percent expressing negative opinions toward France and Russia, respectively.[51] In 1956, only 36 percent of French, 18 percent of West Germans, 16 percent of Italians, and 13 percent of British respondents considered the interests of their countries to be in conflict with those of the United States.[52] And while there was an elitist anti-Americanism in Europe, which was common in France and among intellectuals, more educated Europeans were on average less critical of the United States than others.[53] Perceptions of the United States were fraught, no doubt, and some US policies were undoubtedly deserving of criticism, but there appears to have been at worst a thin layer of true anti-Americanism. Anti-Americanism during this period appears to have been less a reality and more a product of the sensitivity of Americans to any questioning of their motives. This contrasts with attitudes in the Caribbean Basin and Middle East examined in other chapters.

Opportunistic Resistance

Once centrist coalitions were consolidated and US hierarchy had achieved a measure of broad-based legitimacy, indirect rule was compatible with democracy. Nonetheless, some Europeans went beyond superficial anti-Americanism to actively resist US hierarchy, most visibly in France. Importantly, resistance centered not around the so-called Atlantic Alliance of shared interests but on the rules of the invited empire that aimed to limit exploitation and especially entrapment. For all Western European nations, but especially for France, constraints on autonomy in foreign policy rankled deeply. France's actions could simply be interpreted as opportunism but are considered here as resistance because of how Paris, and President Charles de Gaulle in particular, presented them. These were not subtle actions designed to gain

---

50. Isernia 2007, 82–83; Friedman 2012, 97.
51. Friedman 2012, 99.
52. Costigliola 1992, 84.
53. On cultural anti-Americanism, see Judt 2005, 353. On education and anti-Americanism, see Isernia 2007, 87.

some advantage from the United States though everyday acts of resistance, hoping to escape notice, but acts carried out publicly and declaratively in defiance of Washington. Nevertheless, given the difference between indirect rule and domestic and direct rule, there was very little the United States could do to constrain French policy. Indeed, France's defiance became so severe that, in the end, when France withdrew from the NATO command structure, the United States barely reacted.

As the most conservative and nationalist government in the invited empire, it is not surprising that France would lead the active resistance to US indirect rule. Resistance did not come exclusively from France or de Gaulle as president, of course, but together they assumed a vanguard position in attempting to limit US power. As Costigliola writes, "more than any other ally, France attempted to maintain a foreign policy at least partially independent of the United States," and this is where the rules of the invited empire mattered most.[54] Concerned most prominently with restoring France's international status and glory as a great power and demanding that the United States treat it as an equal, de Gaulle sought to thwart US international hierarchy during his presidency and steer a more independent course in foreign affairs. Such overt resistance was possible because the domestic political instability of the Fourth Republic essentially forced the United States to accept de Gaulle as the lesser evil. The general had long been a thorn in the side of US decision-makers, and they were delighted that he was kept in the shadows during the Fourth Republic. But as the country teetered on the edge of collapse during the Algerian War, with the military on the verge of staging a coup, chaos threatened. The fear that France might "go" communist loomed in Washington's thoughts, making domestic rule once again unattractive. Once de Gaulle came to power in 1958, he was tolerated by Washington only because of the lack of any viable non-communist alternative.[55]

The United States supported centrists within the Fourth Republic with some success. From 1948 on, when the communists were expelled from the government, France was governed by various coalitions of Christian Democrat, Social Democrat, and conservative parties. Nonetheless, the political institutions of the Fourth Republic were never sufficiently strong to stop the constant cycling of personnel within the centrist governments of France, with one cabinet constantly replacing the other but without any real change in the parties in government. Understanding himself to be the embodiment of the French nation, de Gaulle refused to participate in party politics. Nonetheless, he continued to wield influence over the far right. Few political moves were made without his sanction. When the war in Algeria finally broke the Fourth Republic, de Gaulle reemerged as perhaps the only

---

54. Costigliola 1992, 1.
55. J. Jackson 2018, 477. See also Wall 1977.

possible leader capable of holding the country together.[56] De Gaulle immediately strengthened the role of the presidency in the new Fifth Republic, inaugurated in 1958, and led France for the next decade.

De Gaulle demanded above all that France be recognized as a great power, equal at least to Great Britain. With US support for centrists under the Fourth Republic, the left and far right were excluded from power and united in opposition to the role of the United States. De Gaulle successfully capitalized on this anti-Americanism to promote independence and greater autonomy for France in world affairs. Drawing on his wartime experience and France's subsequent defeat in Algeria, de Gaulle was convinced he could not trust Britain or the United States to defend French interests.[57] In this, he was likely correct. The United States and de Gaulle had different goals: the former wanted to limit the independent actions of its European subordinates, while the latter wanted to restore France's glory, though "grandeur was as much a state of mind and a sense of ambition as a concrete objective."[58] Though not wanting to go it alone, de Gaulle believed that only by having an equal voice and vote could he defend France's interests within the alliance. Immediately after the war, he publicly warned about Soviet expansionism; within a decade he came to believe the Cold War was unacceptable, especially as it divided Europe into two blocks and undermined the old European balance of power system.[59] As Cold War tensions slowly declined over the 1950s and early 1960s, de Gaulle struck out at US dominance in five acts of resistance; the cumulative impact of this level of opportunism was to leave Washington indifferent as to whether France remained part of the alliance or not.

First, France developed an independent nuclear deterrent aimed at the Soviet Union named the Force de frappe (strike force) and later the Force de dissuasion (force for deterrence). The decision to develop France's own nuclear weapons was taken in 1954 by the administration of Pierre Mendes-France, suggesting that a strategy of resistance began early. The program and especially the triad of delivery systems (air, land, and sea), however, was accelerated under de Gaulle.[60] The first test of an atomic bomb occurred in Algeria in 1960, with the first operational weapons deployed in 1964. France tested its first hydrogen bomb in 1968. It eventually developed the world's third largest nuclear arsenal, though still far smaller than that of the United States or the Soviet Union. This was always primarily a countervalue force, meaning that its intended targets were Soviet cities.

---

56. J. Jackson 2018, 467–473.
57. Buruma 2020, 78; J. Jackson 2018, 481.
58. J. Jackson 2018, 566.
59. J. Jackson 2018, 412.
60. J. Jackson 2018, 599.

The French nuclear program was motivated at least in part by the pursuit of grandeur.[61] If France wanted to be the equal of the great powers, it believed it needed to have its own nuclear deterrent.[62] Beyond grandeur, however, France and de Gaulle also believed strongly that the United States and NATO more generally could not be trusted to defend France in the event of a major war in Europe.[63] With a small second-strike capability, France believed it could deter possible Soviet attacks.[64] The United States, in turn, opposed the independent French capability for fear of entrapment. If there was any possibility that the United States would actually honor its commitment to defend France, then any Soviet first- or even second-strike attack on France would require that Moscow simultaneously attack US nuclear forces as well. Thus, at least as perceived in Washington, by building an independent nuclear capability France gained a finger on America's nuclear trigger.[65] De Gaulle usually justified France's nuclear program as emancipating Europe from its dependence on American protection, but it was precisely for this reason that it was opposed by the United States.[66] In the end, Washington could not stop France's nuclear program—an important example of the limits of US control over its allies.

Second, de Gaulle withdrew France from the NATO command structure. The far right had always been skeptical of the Atlantic Alliance.[67] As the 1950s progressed, according to Costigliola, "the French bitterly complained that they had committed their nation to NATO, only to receive little in return. Both the war in Algeria and the Suez crisis, which grew out of that conflict, strengthened this nationalist, neutralist sentiment in France."[68] In February 1958, before his return to power, de Gaulle declared: "If I governed France, I would quit NATO. NATO is against our independence and our interest."[69] Soon thereafter, the new president sent a secret memo to British prime minister Harold Macmillan and President Eisenhower, declaring that France cannot "consider that NATO in its present form meets the conditions of security of the free world and notably its own."[70] De Gaulle questioned the principle of NATO integration and especially the implied subordination of French forces to a US supreme commander, and demanded tripartite leadership of the alliance, which would have created a two-tiered NATO with the

---

61. Peet 1964, 27.
62. Martin 2011, 235.
63. The Suez Crisis was important in convincing France that its interests were not aligned with those of the United States (Costigliola 1992, 115).
64. Peet 1964, 29.
65. Peet 1964, 28.
66. J. Jackson 2018, 601.
67. On early tensions with France on the creation of NATO, going beyond de Gaulle, see Raflik 2011; Costigliola 1992, 70–71.
68. Costigliola 1992, 112.
69. Quoted in Nuenlist 2011, 221.
70. Quoted in J. Jackson 2018, 497.

United States, Britain, and France at the top and the other members relegated to a secondary position.[71] Tripartism was rejected both by the smaller members of the alliance, including West Germany, and by the United States, with Secretary of State John Foster Dulles making Washington's position clear in a December 1958 meeting with the general.[72]

When his vision of a reformed NATO was rejected, de Gaulle began to disengage. He withdrew France's Mediterranean fleet from NATO (March 1959), rejected France's participation in NATO's integrated air defense and the storing of US nuclear weapons on French territory (June 1959), announced that troops returning from Algeria would not be integrated into NATO (1962), withdrew the Atlantic fleet from NATO (1963), and decided that all French ships would be excluded from NATO's integrated naval command (1964). In March 1966, de Gaulle declared that France would withdraw completely from NATO's integrated military structure. France would no longer host NATO headquarters, French troops in West Germany would no longer report to NATO, and all foreign troops in France would have to leave by April 1967.[73] Notably, he did not quit the alliance itself, but the withdrawal helped cement France as a great power, at least in de Gaulle's mind, as it earned his country a distinctive status, establishing a de facto decision-making structure within the alliance of 14+1.[74]

Third, in seeking to position Europe as a third force in world politics, de Gaulle attempted to form an independent political and security structure. Movement toward a European community was already occurring. By the time de Gaulle returned to power, the ECSC was a success and had been joined by the European Economic Community, formed by the Treaty of Rome in 1957. In the same month that he sent his NATO memo to the United States and Britain, de Gaulle raised the possibility of closer political cooperation with the other five European Economic Community members. These discussions eventually became the Fouchet Plan, first proposed in late 1961 and revised thereafter. The plan, which proposed common foreign and defense policies and a series of intergovernmental institutions, was clearly intended as an alternative to NATO and US domination. Given that German chancellor Konrad Adenauer was increasingly disillusioned with his Anglo-American partners, the plan was received with some interest in Bonn but was rejected outright by the Benelux countries for fear it would diminish both NATO and the European Economic Community, which was, of course, de Gaulle's intention. De Gaulle's veto in January 1963 of Britain's application to join the European Economic Community simply reinforced fears of domination by

---

71. Martin 2011, 234–235.
72. An "official" response to tripartism by the United States was delivered only in September 1960, after de Gaulle had already begun withdrawing from aspects of the alliance (Martin 2011, 224).
73. J. Jackson 2018, 671–673.
74. Martin 2011, 235.

Paris.[75] With the failure of the Fouchet Plan, de Gaulle turned to a Franco-German Treaty, signed in January 1963, which aimed to improve security and defense cooperation between the two largest states in the European Economic Community. West Germany, however, was reluctant to break with the United States and NATO and saw the treaty not as an alternative to the Atlantic Alliance but as a way of restraining Gaullist tendencies within the organization. De Gaulle quickly became disillusioned with his German counterpart. In a July 1964 meeting with the new chancellor Ludwig Erhard, he forced a clear choice. "Either you [West Germany] follow a policy subordinated to the US or you adopt a policy that is European and independent of the US, but not hostile to them."[76] Not surprisingly, Erhard choose Washington over Paris, signaling there could be no common European policy separate from that of the United States and no immediate prospects of reforming NATO along the lines demanded by de Gaulle. This failure helped spur de Gaulle to his final decision to withdraw from the integrated NATO command.

Fourth, de Gaulle reached out to the Soviet Union in an attempt to establish an independent channel to Moscow that would position France and Europe more generally between the two superpowers. This was, in many ways, the most direct challenge to US hierarchy. Expecting communism to wane and the Soviet bloc (including ties to China) to fragment, de Gaulle believed conditions were ripe for a rapprochement with the Soviet Union. Having withdrawn from NATO, which he understood as a credible signal of his independence from the United States, de Gaulle expected Russia to welcome an overture. As historian Garret Martin writes, "France's withdrawal from NATO, and its policy towards the Eastern Bloc, were therefore not separate policies but two sides of the same coin, both aiming to end the division of Europe and restore full sovereignty and independence to all its states."[77] De Gaulle envisioned US troops exiting the continent and the Soviet Union leaving East Germany, permitting reunification, and restoring independence to the satellite states. France and Russia would then become the main pillars of a new European balance of power system.[78]

De Gaulle's overture, however, was not reciprocated. During a state visit to Moscow in June 1966, initially constructive talks ended on a sour note when the Russians demanded that France recognize the GDR in exchange for improved relations, a price de Gaulle was not willing to pay. When, during a visit to Gdansk in 1967, de Gaulle called for the Polish people to become more independent of the Soviet Union, he was sharply rebuked by the Polish leader, Władysław Gomułka. Less than a year later, Warsaw Pact troops invaded Czechoslovakia, making clear that the Soviet Union was far from

---

75. Martin 2011, 237.
76. Quoted in Martin 2011, 237.
77. Martin 2011, 239.
78. Martin 2011, 240.

ready to abandon its informal empire in Eastern Europe. De Gaulle's plan collapsed. What the United States might have done had de Gaulle's attempt at independence succeeded is an open question.

Finally, in what was not so much an attack on the United States as a refusal to cooperate with Washington, de Gaulle sought to alter the unique role of the dollar. In this, he was indirectly successful. Here, de Gaulle did not seek renewed glory for France or the franc, but simply "to curb Washington's influence by any means possible."[79] Under the Bretton Woods monetary regime as it functioned in practice, the dollar was the primary reserve asset. At a news conference in February 1965, de Gaulle attacked the Bretton Woods system as "abusive and dangerous" because of the exorbitant privilege it granted the United States.[80] Instead, de Gaulle argued, the international monetary system should return to a gold standard. In attacking the dollar in various ways and rejecting efforts by other European states to support its value, de Gaulle did help undermine the prestige and position of the United States and weakened one of the central pillars of the US-dominated international economy.

Although his opportunism was costly to the United States, de Gaulle's grand vision for France failed, and along with it any organized opposition to US hierarchy. As recent biographer Julian Jackson concludes, "In the end, de Gaulle had achieved neither a reorganization of the Atlantic Alliance nor a political organization of Europe around a common defense policy," and had failed to overcome the structure of bipolarity in which both France and Europe were embedded. Central to this failure was de Gaulle's very ambition, which threatened his European partners. His neighbors were ready to join a European economic bloc, but they were unwilling to abandon the open global economy and the United States, especially the security umbrella it provided. As Jackson continues, "If France resented the domination of America, Holland, Belgium or Italy might reasonably feel the same about France. De Gaulle tried to play on two stages—the great power one and the European one—but France was not big enough for the first, too big for the second."[81] Leading the resistance, France nonetheless stayed within the order created and led by the United States. As one analyst put it, "Franco-American relations were strained but never close to the breaking point."[82] Tellingly, his efforts to forge a new, more autonomous Europe free from US rule failed because other allies refused to follow de Gaulle's lead. Despite his efforts, other Europeans were unwilling to break with the United States. In the end, Western Europe was too well integrated into the invited empire.

---

79. Cohen 2019, 152.
80. Eichengreen 2011, 52.
81. J. Jackson 2018, 595; Nuenlist 2011, 229.
82. J. Jackson 2018, 574.

In a gradual process that unfolded over the 1950s and 1960s, indirect rule in Western Europe evolved into domestic rule, but in ways that maintained alignment with the United States. As centrist coalitions consolidated within various West European countries, industries and workers both adapted to and became dependent on the open international economy, and institutions solidified around shared laws and practices, the need for the United States to support its political allies within Europe diminished and the people themselves elected and reelected these same allies. The United States morphed from ruler to leader. Exactly when and where this transition occurred is impossible to identify precisely. Ice on a pond does not freeze all at once. It begins at the edges and progresses at varying speeds depending on factors such as depth, temperature variations, and sunlight. The same with the invited empire. It "froze" into place a set of political coalitions at different paces across countries and even issue areas. Signposts included, perhaps, the Social Democrats in Germany adopting their Bad Godesberg program in 1959, which implicitly embraced *westbindung*, or even the Italian Communist Party in 1983 accepting membership in NATO. Slowly, gradually, below the level of consciousness, the invited empire was normalized, acquired a taken-for-granted quality, and was assumed to be the way things are and possibly should be. Interests within Europe congealed in ways very similar to those in the United States, allowing domestic rule to prevail.

But precisely because indirect rule was so beneficial to the United States, at least compared to the alternatives of direct rule and, in the initial postwar years, domestic rule, Washington feared opportunism by its new allies. To limit exploitation and entrapment, the United States imposed a set of rules on its ostensible partners that constrained their ability to conduct independent foreign policies, transforming shared interests into international hierarchy. It was these rules that most clearly rankled the allies and led to resistance, especially by France. Such resistance or, alternatively, opportunism, reduced US gains from indirect rule, likely accelerating the transition to domestic rule once pro-Western regimes were firmly ensconced in national capitals on the continent. Nonetheless, indirect rule and the rules of international hierarchy that followed suggest that the Pax Americana was more than just cooperation between equals and more akin to an invited empire ruled indirectly from Washington.

6

Indirect Rule in the Arab Middle East

The year 1979 was a turning point in the history of the Middle East. Iran's revolution unfolded with surprising speed, overthrowing Shah Mohammad Reza Pahlavi, a secular leader long allied with the United States; bringing a radical Shia cleric to power; and creating a second oil shock that upended the world economy.[1] That same year, Sunni religious zealots seized the Holy Mosque in Saudi Arabia, signaling the beginning of Islamist extremism in the Arab world. In the first major protest against the Saudi monarchy since its founding, the militants demanded the country cut ties with the West, including ending oil exports and expelling all foreigners, and reject the House of Saud and its clerics for failing to uphold the purity of Islam. Also in 1979, the Soviet Union invaded Afghanistan. Not only did this bring détente to a crashing halt, but the war drew in Muslim fighters from around the world—including some extremists unwanted by their home countries—and became the training ground for radical jihadists. Around this time, then, religious extremism emerged as a major force in the Middle East, and the Sunni-Shia divide—long papered over by claims of Arab unity and common opposition to Israel—opened up once again.[2] This same year saw the signing of a peace treaty between Egypt and Israel, which Islamic extremists used as a pretext to assassinate Egyptian president Anwar Sadat two years later. Regional regimes were now threatened in new ways at home and abroad. Though some were burgeoning with unprecedented oil wealth, nearly every regime began searching for new forms of external support.

---

1. On the regional consequences, see Gause 2010, chap. 3.
2. Ghattas 2020; Freedman 2009, xxviii. In addition to these events, in 1979, Saddam Hussein, long the power behind the "throne," formally seized power from his uncle, Ahmed Hassan al-Bakr.

The United States was unable to cope with the second oil shock, which sent its already troubled economy into a near fatal tailspin. Unmoored by the loss of its loyal ally, the shah, it was then humiliated by the seizure of its embassy and personnel in Tehran. Although it had already been practicing indirect rule for decades, by 1979 the United States clearly needed a new strategy and new allies. The convergence of Arab countries needing support and Washington's need for a revamped approach created new openings for US indirect rule.

The usual explanations for US policy toward the Middle East are many, varied, and ultimately incomplete. Some posit a residual antipathy from regional rivalries built up over decades fostered by bipolarity and the Cold War, which waned over the period examined here. Others focus on geopolitics, especially the region's strategic location as the hinge between Europe, Asia, and Africa, or on geoeconomics, including of course the crucial role of oil. Still others emphasize ties between various groups of Americans and their respective ethno-religious homelands in the region. These explanations help identify US interests in the Middle East, but they fail to explain how the United States pursues these interests, how it rules clients indirectly, and when this rule succeeds or fails.

This chapter argues that indirect rule is a primary means through which the United States exercises power in the Middle East.[3] Here, as elsewhere in this volume, specific assets drive hierarchy. Oil and the need to protect transit routes pull the United States into the region; these investments then lead to more intense interests, greater hierarchy, and yet more investments in specific assets. To secure these assets, the United States forms alliances with vulnerable elites in the region, who in return for US support adopt policies somewhat more favorable to US interests, thus creating systems of indirect rule. However, the interests of the United States and regional elites are less aligned here than elsewhere, or at least less aligned than in the Caribbean cases discussed in chapter 2 that otherwise bear many similarities. As a result, indirect rule in the Middle East is less than satisfactory to the United States. While it pulls policy in its favored direction, it is limited by how far elites themselves are willing to go. The net result is that policy remains quite distant from what the United States ideally wants. The governance costs of supporting these regimes are also moderately high and the domestic consequences of indirect rule are severe, with elite regimes governing undemocratically and repressing the human rights of their citizens. Overall, while the United States pursues indirect rule in the region, balancing the gains from more favorable policy at the margin against the costs, its empire remains incomplete, fragile, and ultimately disappointing. What this implies for US hierarchy in the region is examined in the next chapter.

---

3. This chapter draws heavily on ideas first formulated in Jamal 2012; Yom 2015; Zimmermann 2017.

Where to start any narrative is always a bit arbitrary. The United States has long been engaged in the Middle East, at least from the 1930s when it began developing Saudi Arabia's petroleum industry. Its involvement deepened from 1948 when it supported the creation of Israel, even more so from 1953 when it staged a coup in Iran, and certainly from 1967 when it sided with Israel against its Arab neighbors.[4] Yet, while current events always depend on the past, 1979 is as good a point as any to begin this analysis.[5] The Middle East is also an ambiguously defined region. For my purposes, I restrict the geographic focus to countries in and around the Arabian Peninsula. Although they are quite similar in many ways, I do not include countries in North Africa in which the United States has fewer specific assets and, thus, plays a relatively minor role. Iran and Syria are discussed only as counterexamples of domestic rule and indirect rule by Russia and Iran, respectively, during this period. Israel is a complex case that is left to a separate analysis for reasons of space and focus. For want of a better term and recognizing that it is at best an imperfect description, I refer to the relevant states here as the "Arab Middle East" (AME).[6] The chapter begins with an overview of the interests of the United States and AME countries, then outlines the mechanism of indirect rule in the region and concludes with the domestic consequences of the incomplete empire.

Interests

Although regional variations exist and are explored below, the interests of the United States and AME can be summarized in general terms as in figure 6.1. Compared to the other cases in this volume, the interests of the United States and the states of the region differ substantially, and even allied groups—oil monarchies and statist regimes—are not closely aligned with Washington's policy preferences. These elite allies are vulnerable, as demonstrated by the Iranian Revolution and Arab Spring revolts, and thus domestic politics alone would likely require considerable concessions to the opposition, suggesting that the outcome of domestic rule (x_q) would be unfavorable not only to the United States but also to its allies. At the same time, as discussed in the following chapter, direct rule is very costly. As suggested by the Afghan and Iraq

---

4. For a history of even longer US involvement in the region, see Oren 2011.

5. Iran under the shah is a most interesting case that gets excluded by starting the narrative in 1979. That case is certainly consistent with the theory here and has been examined at length by others, so I skip over it without significant loss. Good introductions to US-Iranian relations before 1979 are Bill 1988; Kinzer 2008.

6. Unless otherwise noted, I am referring to the following US clients by this designation: Bahrain, Egypt, Iraq, Jordan, Kuwait, Oman, Qatar, Saudi Arabia, the United Arab Emirates, and Yemen. There is variation among these subordinate states, and not all have been subordinate at all times since 1979.

Figure 6.1 Configuration of US and Arab Middle Eastern interests

wars, the United States would be likely to win any contest but the occupation costs of imposing its will upon the defeated society on an ongoing basis would be enormous. For this reason, the United States has been reluctant to consider military force against Iran, for instance, despite their deeply opposed interests and mutual hostility. The threat of war even relative to domestic rule would likely not be credible, such that in most cases $0 < x_w < x_q$. This configuration of interests opens the possibility of indirect rule. Almost any assistance from the United States would shift policy in a direction preferred by both elites and Washington itself, though the United States would still be dissatisfied with the policies enacted by its allies.

Interests in the United States

Unlike in the Caribbean Basin (chapter 2) where clear sectional interests existed, and postwar Europe (chapter 4) where bipartisanship prevailed, US interests in the Middle East lack clear lines of cleavage at home by party, region, or even ethno-religious group. Various ethnic or religious ties to countries in the AME have been important, but at present American Jews are increasingly split in their views, there are growing communities of Arabs in the United States, and Christian fundamentalists have emerged as major backers of Israel, all of which create competing pressures on US leaders. Overall, Americans were united by the terrorist attacks on September 11, 2001, but then split by the Iraq War in 2003, with some conservatives who initially backed the war increasingly questioning America's engagement in the region. These crosscutting cleavages might suggest that US policy lacks direction.[7] Yet the lack of clear divisions in society likely gives policymakers greater than normal freedom to pursue US interests as they see fit. In fact, US interests have been defined in ways that are surprisingly consistent over time. In July 1954, for example, the National Security Council identified US objectives in the region, which were essentially reiterated by the Reagan administration in 1981.[8] Suitably

7. Tyler 2009, 13.
8. Gelvin 2020, 304–315.

revised to reflect the post–Cold War era, these same interests lie at the core of US policy today.[9]

The primary interest of the United States is the steady supply of oil and natural gas at stable prices, including safe transit through strategic "choke-points" in the region, and economic integration and liberalization more generally. While oil is often believed to be an instrumental interest driving a US policy focus on protecting the assets of its oil companies, that is too narrow of a construction. Nor is the dependence of the United States on oil entirely a myth.[10] Rather, with energy the foundation for all industrialized economies, the interest is more general.[11] Today, approximately 35 percent of the world's energy is generated by petroleum and 23 percent by natural gas. That is, while nuclear power and renewable energy sources are increasing, and coal remains important, nearly 60 percent of the world's energy is generated by these two fossil fuels. In turn, 50 percent of the world's proven petroleum reserves and 38 percent of its proven natural gas reserves are in the Middle East, with the majority of both in the Persian Gulf.[12] The oil shocks of 1973 and 1979 demonstrated just how vulnerable countries are to disruptions in supply, as did Russia's 2022 invasion of Ukraine, which disrupted natural gas flows to Europe. It is the overall stability of the markets for oil and gas that matters, and despite (or because of) the global nature of the markets for these commodities this depends on a steady flow of both from the Middle East. To the extent that US or even foreign companies are critical cogs in the markets, the interests of firms will certainly be considered. But it is the stability of those markets that is the predominant concern of the United States. The US interest is much less about who "owns" the oil and gas or extracts it from the ground and much more about ensuring a continuous supply.[13]

The United States also has a general interest in opening the AME to greater trade and investment. Before 1973, the region was relatively poor with highly skewed income distributions, and thus was never a major consumer of American goods. After this date, new wealth drew in imports and investment at least for the oil-producing states. Given divergent interests, the United States has never pushed back hard against the state-owned enterprises, strategies of import-substituting industrialization, or the resulting crony capitalism that prevails in the region. The United States has been more concerned with opportunities for investment. Overall, US foreign direct investment in the

---

9. Freedman 2009, 31. One Obama administration official cites US interests as "preventing the proliferation of weapons of mass destruction, containing terrorism, ensuring the free flow of oil, preventing mass refugee flows, and saving human lives" (Gordon 2020, 23).

10. See Yetiv 2011; Vitalis 2020.

11. For a similar view, see Gause 2010. This parallels the distinction between instrumental and structural critiques of capitalism. In the former, policy favors capitalists because they lobby more effectively than workers. In the latter, policy favors capitalists because a capital "strike" would undermine the economy and hurt everyone. See Krasner 1978.

12. On the politics of oil, see Luciani 2019.

13. On the politics of oil, see Yergin 2009; Yergin 2012.

Middle East is relatively low, comprising only about 1 percent of the total stock of US investments abroad. Much of this FDI is in Israel and Egypt, followed by the oil-producing Persian Gulf states. The United States has also encouraged portfolio investment outflows from the region. Unlike in the Caribbean where the United States used debt to control states, in the AME the flow of finance is largely reversed, with the United States dependent on petrodollar recycling. All things considered, the United States has an interest in drawing the AME into the global economy, with itself as the linchpin in the process of economic integration, but as we shall see it has been relatively unsuccessful in this endeavor.

US Specific Assets

These broad interests are heightened by specific assets in the AME of concern to the United States. The US interest in the secure and steady supply of oil and gas depends, in part, on keeping open maritime chokepoints surrounding the Arabian Peninsula. The first and perhaps most important passage is the Strait of Hormuz at the mouth of the Persian Gulf. Just twenty-one miles at its narrowest point, the strait separates Arabia from Iran. It is the world's busiest shipping lane, and approximately 21 billion barrels of crude and refined oil now pass through the strait every day. Blocking the strait would be a massive undertaking no matter who attempted it, but threats and even occasional attacks on shipping can disrupt the flow of oil to the global economy.[14] The second major chokepoint is the Suez Canal, entirely within the territory of Egypt but connecting the Red Sea and the Mediterranean and cutting the route from Asia to Europe by half. About 10 percent of all international shipping goes through the canal, along with virtually all of Europe's oil imports. Finally, a third chokepoint is the Bab el-Mandeb Strait, which connects the Gulf of Aden and the Red Sea, separating Yemen from Djibouti and Eritrea. Keeping these strategic waterways open to shipping is a major interest of all countries, but one for which the United States has assumed special responsibility.

To protect these strategic passages and the region more generally, including its allied regimes, since the Carter administration the United States has increasingly invested in military bases around the Arabian Peninsula.[15] These bases have themselves become site-specific assets that intensify US interests in the region, creating a vicious cycle in which protecting the strategic chokepoints demands new bases, which then must be protected as well. Counting bases is difficult, as many sites in the region simply hold pre-positioned equipment or involve use rights in times of emergency. The system is not designed to house large numbers of US troops as in

---

14. Ma 2020.
15. On Carter, see McFarland 2020, 214.

postwar Europe, but to have the capacity to quickly flood the region with forces when necessary, as demonstrated in the Persian Gulf and Iraq wars. Critical to this capacity is the Al Udeid Air Base in Qatar, the largest US military installation outside North America and home to the US Combined Air Operations Center, US Air Forces Central Command, US Special Operations Command Central, and CENTCOM forward headquarters. Built in 1996, Al Udeid allowed for the relocation in 2003 of US troops and equipment previously stationed in Saudi Arabia.[16] While a simple count risks comparing different types of entities, the number of US bases bordering Arabia and covering the strategic chokepoints just noted rose from twenty-one in 1989 to sixty-six in 2015 and seventy-six in 2021, an increase of over 260 percent.[17]

As the United States has deepened its role in the AME it has also invested in specific economic assets that create further incentives for hierarchy. At one point in time, US investments in oil extraction in the region would have been specific assets. Starting in the 1960s and through the 1970s, however, countries nationalized their oil industries, transforming the Western oil companies from "owners" to contractors specializing in distribution and marketing.[18] Nonetheless, US firms continue to invest in the Middle East, especially in the mining sector, which includes oil exploration and drilling. Figure 6.2 depicts US foreign direct investment in the AME from 1999 (in constant 2019 dollars). Although less easily expropriated than the oil concessions that existed prior to the 1970s, current investments in the mining sector remain site-specific and continue to carry some risk. Unlike in other regions, US investments in manufacturing in the AME remain relatively low and flat. Overall, the strategic chokepoints—quintessential specific assets—have led to an expansion of the US military bases in the region, which are also specific, and which in turn have created conditions under which US economic investments can expand, creating further incentives for the United States to seek favorable policies. This is a clear example of the "chicken-and-egg" dynamic for specific assets and hierarchy discussed in chapter 1.

---

16. Wallin 2018. On Qatar's foreign policy, see Kamrava 2014. On the relocation of bases, see Gause 2010, 147.

17. List of bases from Vine 2022. Includes bases in Bahrain, Djibouti, Egypt, Eritrea, Ethiopia, Iraq, Jordan, Kuwait, Oman, Qatar, Saudi Arabia, Somalia, United Arab Emirates, and Yemen.

18. On the international market conditions that allowed producer countries to demand a switch from concessions to participation, see Yergin 2009, chap. 28, esp. 565. Under concessions, the oil firms de facto "owned" the oil under contract, which could be revoked by the country and constituted as a specific asset. Under participation, ownership was shared and the oil firms essentially "operated" facilities owned by the state. Though the country could now cancel the contract for operating the facilities, there was no real fixed investment that could be nationalized.

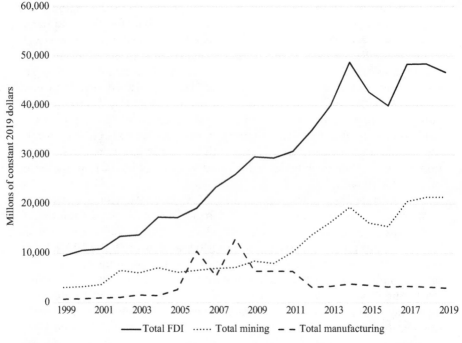

Figure 6.2 US foreign direct investment in the Middle East, 1999–2019

Source: Bureau of Economic Analysis, n.d. Converted to constant 2019 dollars using U.S Census Bureau 2022, CPI-U-RS.

Interests in the Arab Middle East

Interests in the AME are grounded in both history and place. Unified by the expansion of Islam in the seventh to ninth centuries, which provided a common legal structure and identity, most of the region was part of the Ottoman Empire for centuries. After World War I, Britain and France broke up the Ottoman Empire, creating the rump state of Turkey and dividing the remainder among themselves in the Sykes-Picot Agreement of 1916.[19] The states that emerged after 1945 retained their colonial-era borders but also a regional and Arab identity through their shared history.

As it had in the Caribbean Basin (chapter 2), the first period of globalization in the late nineteenth century transformed the economies of the region. As Europe expanded trade and later lending with the polities bordering on the Mediterranean, commercial agriculture displaced local farming. Politically powerful elites consolidated their control over land, creating larger farms worked by now landless peasants producing crops for export (cotton

---

19. Cleveland and Bunton 2018, 152–153, 310; Gelvin 2020, 90–91.

in Egypt, cereals in Syria).[20] The net effect was to concentrate wealth in the "notable" families in each country, often already prominent under Ottoman rule, whose interests were also relatively aligned with the new colonial powers.[21] In 1953, when the Egyptian Republic was proclaimed, for instance, 0.5 percent of the population owned over 33 percent of the cultivable land, while 72 percent of farmers owned only 13 percent.[22] States without a comparative advantage in agriculture, like Saudi Arabia, remained on the periphery of the global economy until after World War II, while others specialized in esoteric commodities, such as pearls in Kuwait, or became entrepots on the route to Asia, like Oman. None developed indigenous industries. Persian Gulf states were later drawn into the world economy with the development of the petroleum industry, which started in the 1930s but greatly expanded after the war. Having retained monarchical rule and many of their traditional social structures, these new petrostates concentrated growing oil revenues in their royal families, again increasing wealth and income inequality. These histories of political integration under Ottoman rule and economic integration under European imperialism combined to shape the politics of the region that the United States encountered in the twentieth century. Though countries of the AME have their own trajectories and particularities, four traits are common: rule by small, generally autocratic elites; highly skewed income distributions; artificial borders with conflicting territorial claims; and weak national identities.[23] As in the Caribbean Basin discussed in chapter 2, the United States did not create these characteristics but inherited them as it engaged more deeply in the region over time.

Given this history and the emergent political structures, all AME countries possess a deep cleavage that separates small elites that control the economy from mass publics that remain poor and dispossessed. Elites want to maximize their wealth from resource and market-distorting rents while redistributing as little as possible to the masses. The publics want land and wealth redistribution as well as economic opportunities to improve standards of living. Within this general cleavage, there are three types of regimes.[24]

In one archetype, found principally in labor-scarce, oil-rich states in the Persian Gulf, monarchs rule with the support of traditional families and, at least in Saudi Arabia, religious clerics.[25] The royal families seek to maximize their resource rents from the extraction and sale of oil and gas. In cases where they have excess production capacity, the monarchs are often willing

---

20. Cleveland and Bunton 2018, 54, 86.

21. E. Stein 2021, chap. 2; Gelvin 2020, 277; Mansfield and Pelham 2019, 96–101.

22. Mansfield and Pelham 2019, 275; Gelvin 2020, 277. Iraq had a similar land distribution. Cleveland and Bunton 2018, 310.

23. Hinnebusch 2014a, 21–27.

24. Cammett et al. 2018, see esp. table 1.1 on 17.

25. On deep ties between the House of Saud and Wahhabism, see Ghattas 2020, 67; E. Stein 2021, 48.

to defer short-term revenues to increase long-term returns, keeping prices below what could be charged in order to sustain the market for oil and gas into the distant future.[26] With large financial investments overseas, the royal families also have an interest in the growth and stability of the international economy as a whole. These monarchies use their resource rents to buy political support from their relatively small indigenous populations. Though real oil prices and revenues declined in the late 1980s and 1990s, rendering redistribution more difficult, they have since recovered, as have the politics of patronage.[27] These oil-monarchies import temporary labor that can be easily exploited, first from Egypt and Palestine and now from Asia.[28] Conservative in orientation, these monarchies either sided with the United States during the Cold War or remained neutral but leaned toward the West. Though subject to international market fluctuations, their economies are relatively more market-oriented, have lower levels of corruption, and—since they rely on buying off opposition—are less repressive than others in the region.

In the second archetype, of which Egypt is the exemplar, statist regimes came to power in the 1950s, typically led by soldiers from middle-class backgrounds who came up through the military academies created under European rule.[29] Statist regimes lack easily exploited natural resources but have abundant labor. These regimes, tied to the middle classes, embraced socialism and pledged to redistribute land and wealth to their broad populations but failed to do so to any significant extent.[30] Extensive nationalizations and confiscations of property along with import-substituting industrialization placed the levers of the economy in the hands of the regimes.[31] By the mid-1960s, for instance, the Egyptian government owned banks, insurance companies, textile mills, sugar-refining and food-processing facilities, air and sea transport, public utilities, urban mass transit, cinemas, theaters, department stores, agricultural credit institutions, fertilizer plants, and construction companies.[32] By the 1980s, the public sector broadly accounted for more than 40 percent of the total workforce and total public expenditures

---

26. On the political influence that arises from Saudi Arabia's position as a "swing" producer, see McFarland 2020, 184.

27. Cleveland and Bunton 2018, 469.

28. Cleveland and Bunton 2018, 410, 417, 467.

29. Cammett et al. 2018 refer to these states as resource-poor, labor-abundant economies. Solingen labels them statist-nationalist, which I partially follow here (1998, chap. 6). See also Gelvin 2020, 280–282; Cleveland and Bunton 2018, 288–289, 308. Statist regimes have also been described as "fierce" regimes. See Ayubi 1996.

30. Mansfield and Pelham 2019, 275–276; Gelvin 2020, 283; Cleveland and Bunton 2018, 301–302. On ties to the middle class, see Zimmermann 2017, 167–169. On the cooptation of clerics in Egypt, see Nielsen 2017.

31. Solingen 1998, 166; Cleveland and Bunton 2018, 300–301; Mansfield and Pelham 2019, 299.

32. Solingen 1998, 168; Gelvin 2020, 284; E. Stein 2021, 66. On Syria, see Cleveland and Bunton 2018, 425, 427–429.

were 61 percent of GDP.[33] By the 1990s, however, the statist regimes were facing fiscal crises. Egypt had borrowed heavily to sustain its model of state-led economic development, and its debt-to-GDP ratio rose to approximately 150 percent in 1990, among the highest in the world.[34] Under pressure from international financial institutions, statist regimes accepted structural adjustment programs designed to correct their macroeconomic imbalances, but that required them to privatize assets and reduce the role of the government in the economy. This did not, however, lead to major economic reforms.[35] Rather, many assets were sold to elite regime supporters, morphing their economies into crony-capitalist systems that were likely even more corrupt than the state-led systems they replaced.[36] Around five hundred firms now dominate the Egyptian economy and are controlled by only thirty-two businessmen, all of whom are closely connected to the regime and some of whom occupied political posts in the administration of President Hosni Mubarak. Indeed, the owner of the country's largest steel company chaired Mubarak's National Democratic Party and held other influential positions, and the second-largest real estate developer in the country served simultaneously as the minister of housing. The structural adjustment programs championed by the IMF and other institutions under the so-called Washington Consensus failed to produce the intended liberalization of these statist economies and simply led the regimes to shift from direct ownership of the commanding heights of the economy to indirect control through business elites.[37]

Between these archetypes are hybrid regimes comprised of resource-rich and labor-abundant societies (Iran, Iraq, and Yemen).[38] In this regime type, the resource curse, as it has come to be described, appears to bind tightly.[39] With a steady flow of oil revenues, these states do not need to build out administrative capacity and, in turn, collect few taxes and provide few public goods. At the same time, exports distort the exchange rate and inhibit investment in industries that would otherwise absorb labor.[40] Oil revenues are not large enough to permit large-scale redistribution to buy off political opponents, leading regimes to rely on repression. Although similar to the statist regimes in their politics, these hybrid regimes do not develop close ties to the business community and, overall, fare less well than either of the other archetypes in terms of growth, development, and human rights.[41]

---

33. Cammett et al. 2018, 242.
34. Cammett et al. 2018, 242, 293.
35. Cammett et al. 2018, 100.
36. Zimmermann 2017, 169–176.
37. Cammett et al. 2018, 285, esp. 296–297; Zimmermann 2017, 165.
38. Cammett et al. 2018, chap. 3.
39. Ross 1999.
40. Cammett et al. 2018, 24.
41. Cammett et al. 2018, chap. 3.

The cleavage between the mass public and rent-seeking regimes leaves regional states with weak domestic legitimacy. The monarchies are less than three generations old and cannot appeal to tradition to justify their rule. The statist regimes came to power through coups within the last two generations, and sometimes even more recently. Elites seek to build legitimacy by appealing to religion, unity against Israel, and anti-imperialism—currently, anti-Americanism. But in doing so, they walk a knife's edge.[42] While nearly all try to ground their right to rule in Islam, they all face Salafi fundamentalists at home who claim the regimes have strayed from the true religion of Muhammad. With limited means to justify their rule, regimes remain fragile. This implies that autocratic leaders and their support coalitions have strong, overriding interests in regime survival. As Marc Lynch writes, "with only a few exceptions, Arab leaders have proven that they would do virtually anything to hold on to power."[43] The Arab Spring protest movements struck fear into regimes across the AME and suggest just how tenuous is the hold of elites on power.[44]

In addition to this internal cleavage, the AME is also riven with external political rivalries. The breakup of the Ottoman Empire and the subsequent colonial regimes often left borders ambiguous. In 1990, for instance, Iraq could claim Kuwait as its nineteenth province with some degree of historical justification. Given the common identity of Middle Eastern societies, moreover, states can compete for leadership or make claims to reintegrate territories across the region. There have long been rivalries between Egypt and Saudi Arabia, especially in the 1960s when Nassar ruled in Cairo, and Saudi Arabia and Iran, particularly after the revolution in 1979. Until recently, all Arab states have tried to outdo one another in their opposition to Israel, which is perceived throughout the region as a neocolonial imposition. Unlike in the Caribbean discussed in chapter 3, where states were too small to pose much of an external threat to one another, in the AME the regional rivalries are strong enough to potentially spill over into war. Thus, states face significant internal and external threats to their regimes.

Overall, the United States and peoples and regimes in the AME share relatively few interests at either the mass or elite levels. As Lynch again observes, "It has become increasingly apparent that America has no real allies in the Middle East. America shares no values with the monarchies of the Gulf or nationalist military regimes like Egypt's. Nor does it share a diagnosis of the region's problems or even more national interests."[45] Critically, while the United States wants a steady supply of oil and gas at reasonable prices, oil-rich states want to exploit their market power. Although states with excess

---

42. Mandaville 2019; Hinnebusch 2014c, 36.
43. Lynch 2016, xv.
44. Ghattas 2020, 268.
45. Lynch 2016, 246.

capacity and wealth invested in the West can take a longer view more consistent with US interests, if a mass public were to assume rule it would likely seek to maximize returns in the short run by restricting supply and raising prices. In the statist regimes, though workers on average would benefit from greater economic liberalization, those already employed in the protected sectors would lose from greater openness, creating a cleavage within the working class. As interests between the United States and even its allies in the AME are distant, when the United States relies on indirect rule and elites succeed in moving policy to their ideal points, the results remain unsatisfactory for Washington.

Indirect Rule

Political systems in the Middle East are skewed in favor of elites, whether these be royal families and their supporters in the petrostates or military leaders and their business allies in the statist regimes. In all, elites remain firmly in control but weak. For good reasons, elites are sensitive to the so-called Arab Street, where demonstrations and protests remain one of the few ways in which mass publics can effectively threaten their regimes. The Arab Spring is only the most recent demonstration of the power of public opposition to autocratic elites. To enact the policies they want while strengthening their hand at home, elites seek support from the United States. As Lynch writes, "America's imperium rest[s] not on popular support, but on stolid alliances with the repressive regimes."[46] It is this internal weakness of all regimes in the region that the United States exploits for indirect rule.

To offset their domestic weakness, elites in the US sphere rely on external support and, in exchange, adopt foreign policies more favorable to themselves and the United States than otherwise. Historically, the external patron was Britain, today it is the United States, but for both the exchange of support for policy has been the basis for indirect rule. As Raymond Hinnebusch writes, regimes within the region "remain dependent on Western support, not domestic legitimacy."[47] In many cases, the Arab regimes themselves reach out to the United States and court Washington for support, in others the United States courts a reluctant regime. While the details of relationships vary according to which side needs the other more, in all cases the essence of the deal remains broadly similar. The United States guarantees the survival of its elite allies. In return, as Amaney Jamal states, "US ties to existing Arab regimes first and foremost guarantee [the]

---

46. Lynch 2016, 31.
47. Hinnebusch 2003, 231.

strategic priorities for the United States."[48] This mutual dependence en-sures that both sides live up to the deal.

Governance Costs

US support for its elite allies in the Middle East takes three primary forms. First, and perhaps most important, the United States guarantees each state's external security as well as the regime's internal security. Some guarantees are of long standing. On his way home from the Yalta conference, US presi-dent Franklin Delano Roosevelt met with King Abdul Aziz Ibn Saud, who had unified his country barely six years earlier. The two leaders agreed that Saudi Arabia would allow the United States to extract its oil in exchange for military protection and support.[49] In 1947, Truman expanded this pledge to Ibn Saud, stating that if his country were attacked or threatened, the United States would take "energetic measures under the auspices of the United Nations to confront such aggression."[50] In the midst of Yemen's civil war in the early 1960s, which saw Saudi Arabia and Egypt supporting oppos-ing sides, President John F. Kennedy assured the Saudi king that the United States would be there to "uphold Saudi Arabian integrity."[51] However, the most important guarantees were extended only after the Soviet invasion of Afghanistan and the Iranian Revolution. Following the fall of the shah, the Carter administration began talks about new bases in Egypt, Saudi Arabia, and Jordan in order to better protect them and its other subordinates in the region.[52] With the Soviet invasion of Afghanistan, however, President Jimmy Carter recognized that the Nixon Doctrine of relying on regional powers to enforce US interests was no longer sufficient and, in his 1980 State of the Union address, articulated what would come to be known as the Carter Doctrine. Echoing the famous Article 5 of the North Atlantic Treaty, the president declared that "an attempt by any outside force to gain control of the Persian Gulf region will be regarded as an assault on the vital inter-ests of the United States of America, and such an assault will be repelled by any means necessary, including military force." Soon thereafter, President Ronald Reagan extended this doctrine in what is sometimes referred to as the Reagan Corollary.[53] With a new recognition that the twin pillar strategy of reliance on Iran and Saudi Arabia was now a one pillar strategy, Reagan declared that the United States would not permit Saudi Arabia "to be an Iran." What exactly the president meant by this, of course, is unclear, but

---

48. Jamal 2012, 24.
49. Ghattas 2020, 52.
50. From a State Department cable summarizing the discussion, quoted in Yetiv 2011, 29. See also McFarland 2020, 51.
51. Quoted in Gelvin 2020, 316.
52. Tyler 2009, 233–234.
53. Ismael and Perry 2014, 11, 15; Yetiv 2011, 32.

the statement was widely interpreted then and now as a guarantee of the security of the regime not only against external threats but internal ones as well. As one analyst put it, US forces are now "the 'Republican Guards' of Saudi Arabia . . . . to protect the Saud family from its population."[54] Both the Carter Doctrine and Reagan Corollary were invoked—and gained credence—when Iraq overran Kuwait in August 1990. Making clear that it was not just guaranteeing the security of countries against "outside" threats but regional threats as well, the United States immediately rose to defend Kuwait and, by extension, Saudi Arabia, and in an important signal to others subsequently restored the Al Sabah monarchy. As Gary Sick concludes, "by the end of the twentieth century, the United States had become a Persian Gulf power in its own right. Its political, military, and economic footprint in the region was greater even than that of the governments of the region themselves. Its role as a security guarantor was not in doubt, and its prestige and influence were at their zenith."[55]

Traces of regime guarantees are evident in security and defense cooperation agreements (see table 6.1). While the terms of most security agreements are secret at the request of the clients, it is public knowledge that the United States does have agreements with its local allies, and the agreements and their broad terms are listed on the US Department of State website. To deter opponents both at home and abroad, the existence of at least some agreements must be public, though codicils may be kept entirely confidential. Although the exact number of agreements are unknown, the broad pattern in table 6.1 shows clearly that regimes in the US sphere have security and defense cooperation agreements with the United States, and countries outside the sphere—principally Syria and Iran—do not. Indeed, several client states have the rare designation of being "major non-NATO allies." These agreements not only facilitate joint military operations, increasing the odds of success if the need to defend the regime arises, but also make clear the commitment of the United States to the survival of the regime.

The US military presence in the region, along with actual joint military exercises, provides the means to honor these regime guarantees. The United States now has extensive bases throughout the region, as well as pre-positioned equipment at national bases, allowing for rapid deployment of military forces when necessary. As specific assets, these bases draw the United States further into the region, but they also commit it to the security of the host countries, and especially the regimes that permit these bases. Troop levels vary by year, but in the countries ruled indirectly by the United States deployments are often substantial.[56] Non-oil states like Egypt and

---

54. Nightline interview with Vali Nasr on October 25, 2001, quoted in Ismael and Perry 2014, 15.
55. Sick 2018, 249; Jamal 2012, 40–41.
56. Allen, Flynn, and Martinez Machain 2022.

TABLE 6.1
Instruments of indirect rule in the Arab Middle East

Country	Security-related treaties and agreements in effect, 1980–2012	Defense cooperation agreements, 1980–2010	Designated major non-NATO ally	Number of joint military exercises, 1980–2010	Arms sales, 1979–2019 (billions of current dollars)	Military aid, 1979–2020 (millions of current dollars)	Economic aid, 1979–2020 (millions of current dollars)	US military forces deployed, December 2020
				US subordinates				
Bahrain	5	1991–2032	2002	9	1.7	n/a	0	4,081
Egypt	17	1988–2010	1987	14	24.0	101,380.0	94,671.5	251
Iraq	11			0	4.9	70,058.9	92,042.4	Not disclosed
Jordan	11	1991–present	1996	10	3.1	17,644.6	34,880.3	206
Kuwait	3	1991–present	2004	33	5.4	n/a	0	1,862
Oman	8	1980–present		4	1.6	n/a	0	22
Qatar	0	1992–2023		6	3.3	n/a	21.1	460
Saudi Arabia	10	1982–1988 and 1999–2005		4	39.6	1.9	28.5	474
United Arab Emirates	4	1994–2034		9	12.3	n/a	0	197
Yemen	3	2009–2010		1	0.03	632.4	8,557.1	5
			Non-subordinates of the United States					
Iran	0			1	0.3	n/a	75.7	0
Lebanon	9			0	0.6	n/a	0	26
Syria	0			0	0	138.4	13,445.8	Not disclosed

Column 2: Kavanagh 2014; Kinne 2020; updated from U.S. Department of State 2021. Column 3: U.S. Department of State 2021. Column 5 D'Orazio and Galambos 2021. Column 6: SIPRI, n.d. Columns 7 and 8: USAID and U.S. Department of State 2023. Column 9: Department of Defense, n.d.

Jordan tend to rely on extensive training with and by US forces. Between 1980 and 2010, the last year for which systematic data are available, Egypt conducted fourteen and Jordan conducted ten joint military exercises with the United States.

The cost to the United States of these regime guarantees is difficult to estimate but appears to be substantial. The Department of Defense does not break down its budget by areas of operation and there are other agencies involved in supporting regional regimes. One systematic study of US military expenditures related to protecting the Persian Gulf as a whole suggests that US defense costs are approximately $27 to 73 billion per year (in 2004 dollars).[57] If the United States were called upon to honor its guarantee to various regimes, costs might resemble those of the wars in Afghanistan or Iraq, which totaled approximately $8 trillion, or about $400 billion per year from 2001 to 2021, when troops were finally withdrawn.[58] The actual cost of guaranteeing the security of regimes in the AME likely lies somewhere between these extremes but, regardless, the expenditure is not insignificant.

Second, the United States supports allied regimes through military and economic aid.[59] This is especially important for the non-oil regimes like Egypt and Jordan.[60] Since the Camp David Accords in 1979, the United States has provided Egypt with over $196 billion in total foreign aid.[61] Since signing its peace agreement with Israel in 1994, the United States has provided Jordan with over $52 billion in aid. Though the sums are not large relative to the US defense budget, the aid is large in comparison to each recipient's own resources and appears essential to keeping their economies afloat.

US military aid directly strengthens regimes by equipping and training military and police forces. It is through such aid that the day-to-day security needs of the regimes are enhanced. In the period from 1946 to 2019, the United States provided over $90 billion in military aid to countries in the AME and, in 2019 alone, over $2.9 billion.[62] Although the sourcing and definitions are sometimes different, the majority of funding appears to be in security force assistance.[63] In 2019, over 4,000 security personnel from AME states were trained by US forces; the United States currently has approximately 140 military advisers in Saudi Arabia alone coordinating weapons purchases and

---

57. Delucchi and Murphy 2008; Yetiv 2011, 167–168. This does not include non-oil producing states such as Egypt or Jordan.
58. Estimate from Watson Institute 2021.
59. The United States through the CIA also gives undisclosed amounts of aid to intelligence services of AME countries. Tyler 2009, 9.
60. Politically motivated aid is not always welcomed. On Nassar's imperviousness to aid, see Tyler 2009, 42.
61. Zimmermann 2017, 191.
62. USAID 2020.
63. See Center for International Policy, n.d.-a.

providing assistance across the defense spectrum.[64] This extends to the various internal security services that every regime possesses. The CIA has been deeply involved in developing and training Jordan's General Intelligence Directorate, for instance, one of the best but also most ruthless intelligence agencies in the region. As CIA director George Tenet later bragged, "We created the Jordanian intelligence service and now we own it."[65] Though these relationships are opaque, we can reasonably assume that similar ties exist with other security and intelligence services in other countries. All this aid increases the ability of a regime to protect itself against internal threats while adopting more favorable policies, but also contributes to frequent abuses of human rights.

Economic aid provides public goods essential to maintaining some public support and allows for continued patronage to critical constituencies. Even if aid is tied to particular projects, it allows the government to use the money that would have otherwise been required for that project for other purposes. Aid also permits regimes to forgo unpopular taxes that would normally be required. By failing to develop an indigenous tax capacity, in turn, aid creates a continuing dependence on additional aid, locking the regime into indirect rule.

Finally, and building on the first form of support, the United States provides access to advanced weapons. Although the most advanced systems are of little use in putting down urban riots and other forms of domestic unrest, they nonetheless deter both internal and external opponents. Since 1980, spurred by the Iranian Revolution, Saudi Arabia has made cumulative arms purchases from the United States totaling nearly $40 billion (in current dollars), Egypt has purchased $24 billion in arms, and the United Arab Emirates $12.3 billion (see table 6.1). Arms sales were critically important in repairing US-Saudi relations after the Camp David Accords.[66] By selling weapons, the United States enhances the capacity of regimes to defend themselves at home and abroad. It also signals its commitment to the security of the regime, and suggests the possibility of additional support should it be required.[67] Selling advanced systems not only facilitates interoperability with US forces, if necessary, but allows for relatively capital-intensive local militaries that reduce the need to recruit from domestic populations that the regimes mistrust.[68] Although some arms transfers to Egypt, Jordan, and other non-oil countries are covered under military aid, the Gulf states are, for the most part, "paying customers" for the arms they receive. Thus, arms sales are not a significant governance cost to the United States. Indeed, it is arguably the case that by

64. Center for International Policy, n.d.-b. On Saudi Arabia, see Springborg, Williams, and Zavage 2020, 26.
65. Quoted in Moore 2019, 247.
66. Freedman 2009, 123.
67. McFarland 2020, 94.
68. On variations in the capital intensity of militaries, see Caverley 2014.

extending production runs for various advanced weapons systems, foreign arms sales to US clients may lower the per unit costs to the United States for its own weapons, providing an indirect benefit. Although individual costs vary by country, the total governance costs of indirect rule for the United States in the AME are quite substantial, especially given the distance between regional elites and Washington in terms of policy preferences and the latter's inability to move policy beyond the ideal points of elites in the region. The United States pays a lot for policies that are still quite distant from what it prefers.

Indirect Rule in Jordan

The case of Jordan illustrates the pattern of support that allows allied groups to enact policies favorable to themselves. The Hashemite Dynasty that has ruled Jordan since 1921 is of relatively recent origin, with only four kings holding the throne and one of these for only a little over a year. In return for leading the Arab Revolt against the Ottoman Empire during World War I, Britain promised Hussein bin Ali, sharif of Mecca and the leading rival to the house of Saud, an Arab kingdom stretching north from the Hejaz. Controversy remains as to the scope of this promise, but Britain did reluctantly appoint his second son, Abdullah bin al-Hussein, as emir of Transjordan, after which he became king of independent Jordan in May 1946. Lacking any domestic basis of legitimacy, and in fact tainted by his association with British imperialism, Abdullah formed alliances with the small merchant community and the Bedouin tribes in his new country and, heavily subsidized by London, bought their support through extensive patronage.[69] The largely rural and agricultural Palestinian communities concentrated on the east and west banks of the Jordan River were left out of the political coalition. The Arab-Israeli War of 1948 and Jordan's annexation of Jerusalem and the West Bank added 800,000 Palestinians to the kingdom, overwhelming the preexisting population of 375,000 Transjordanians.[70] Rather than incorporating Palestinians into his coalition, Abdullah doubled down on his traditional supporters.[71] The patronage necessary to secure support, however, eventually overwhelmed the kingdom's resources, even with Britain's subsidies.

Hussein bin Talal, Abdullah's grandson, was elevated to the throne in 1952. Facing broad opposition from adherents of Nasserism, Ba'athism, and communism, Hussein suspended the constitution in 1957, proclaimed martial law, and requested US military support and economic aid.[72] The United States responded immediately with an emergency grant of $10 million, soon

---

69. Yom 2015, 156; Zimmermann 2017, 105–108.
70. Yom 2015, 159; Zimmermann 2017b 108–109; Cleveland and Bunton 2018, 314–315.
71. Zimmermann 2017, 109.
72. Zimmermann 2017, 110.

followed by another $10 million, starting a long stream of aid to the regime.[73] In return for adopting a staunchly Western-oriented foreign policy, Hussein was receiving more than $50 million annually by the early 1960s and close to $70 million per year by the 1980s—much of this in military aid for domestic security.[74] The CIA was also making cash payments directly to Hussein, ostensibly to fund the king's independent intelligence service.[75] With the loss of the West Bank during the 1967 Arab-Israeli War, 200,000 more Palestinians fled to Jordan. Once again, the regime relied on its traditional supporters in the Bedouin and merchant communities. Excluded from power and at odds with the regime, Palestinians revolted in 1970, leading to civil war, brutal repression, and the expulsion of the Palestine Liberation Organization—which relocated to Lebanon. When the growing Palestinian movement challenged the king's authority by hijacking four civilian airliners and landing three of them in Jordan in so-called liberated territory, the regime had to respond. In what is now known as Black September, over the course of ten days the Jordanian military bombarded Palestinian refugee camps and urban areas in pursuit of commando groups, killing some 3,000 civilians and guerrillas.[76] The United States threatened Syria and Iraq should they intervene on behalf of the Palestinians, resupplied Jordanian troops, and subsequently expanded aid programs. The United States also urged its other Arab subordinates to step up their aid to Jordan, which soon overtook actual US aid deliveries. By 1979, foreign aid was nearly twice what the government itself collected domestically in taxes.[77]

By the late 1980s, the kingdom was virtually bankrupt, having amassed foreign debts totaling 225 percent of GDP, half of which were likely incurred for military and security purposes.[78] After Jordan signed a peace treaty with Israel in 1994, however, the United States canceled its outstanding foreign debt.[79] At one point, about 20 percent of Jordan's gross national income came from US aid.[80] This aid, in turn, allowed the regime to rely on its traditional supporters and secure their loyalty through continued patronage without having to compromise with the opposition or build the administrative capacity necessary to survive as a state on its own.[81]

---

73. Yom 2015, 167; Zimmermann 2017, 130.
74. Cleveland and Bunton 2018, 315; Yom 2015, 173–174.
75. Moore 2019, 246; Zimmermann 2017, 129.
76. Cleveland and Bunton 2018, 344. The civil war led to a significant expansion of the Jordanian General Intelligence Directorate. See Moore 2019, 247–252.
77. Yom 2015, 187–192.
78. Moore 2019, 254.
79. Mansfield and Pelham 2019, 400.
80. Zimmermann 2017, 152.
81. Yom 2015, 8, 34–35; Zimmermann 2017, 112–116.

Despite some democratic reforms, the monarchy continues to rely on its traditional supporters.[82] Today, fear of Palestinian domination and religious extremism weds the monarchy to the United States, and vice versa. Popular support for Islamists is placed at anywhere from 20 to 50 percent of the electorate, in either case a significant constituency.[83] Knowing that if a Palestinian or religious opposition came to power Jordan's foreign policy orientation would shift significantly against it, the United States continues to support the Hashemite regime with aid, totaling some $3.7 billion in 2020. The cost to Jordan of defying the United States during the first Gulf War in 1991 was enormous. When the United States and Kuwait, one of its largest Arab supporters, cut all aid in retaliation for supporting Saddam Hussein, "the economic punishment of Jordan demonstrated the sheer magnitude of its reliance and dependence on external actors."[84] By the time Abdullah II assumed the throne in 1999, a consensus had emerged in Jordan that, without the alliance with the United States, "things could become considerably worse."[85] Indeed, after 2001, Jordan made clear that it would be a loyal ally in the war on terror, including supporting the invasion of Afghanistan. Though it did not join the Iraq War and refused to allow US troops to embark from its territory in 2003, it also did not oppose the war as it had in 1991.[86] In addition to aid and other forms of support for the monarchy, the United States signed a free trade agreement with Jordan in 2001, liberalizing trade between the two countries and building support among those sectors of the economy increasingly dependent on access to US markets.[87] Jordan now understood the rules of the incomplete empire, and was compensated accordingly, so that it could enact preferred policies even in the face of increased domestic opposition.[88]

Consequences of Indirect Rule

Given the conflicts of interest, the United States has been less successful in inducing its AME allies to adopt policies it favors than in the other cases in this book.[89] At the end of the Cold War, and in declaring his intent to liberate Kuwait, President George H. W. Bush envisioned a new world order, an era

---

82. Yom 2015, 195–205.
83. Jamal 2012, 69.
84. Jamal 2012, 47; Ryan 2014, 143.
85. Jamal 2012, 112.
86. Ryan 2014, 142–149. Cooperation between the United States and the General Intelligence Directorate greatly expanded during this period (Moore 2019, 259–260).
87. Jamal 2012, 31, 72, 105. The Jordanian currency is also strongly pegged to the dollar (Jamal 2012, 50). On vesting interests in the regime, see Yom 2015, 38.
88. Zimmermann 2017, 138.
89. Gelvin 2020, 314–315, offers a more positive assessment overall, as do Cleveland and Bunton 2018, 519.

of peace and fraternity in the Middle East under US leadership.[90] The vision was, in some ways, an expansion to the Middle East of the Pax Americana constructed in Western Europe after 1945. The United States would assume responsibility for security by maintaining a permanent military presence in the Persian Gulf, contain regional threats from both Iran and Iraq, provide development assistance as necessary, and adopt safeguards against the proliferation of conventional and unconventional weapons. Just as the United States had settled the age-old conflict between France and Britain, on the one hand, and Germany, on the other, Bush hoped to negotiate an Arab-Israeli agreement based on territory for peace and the recognition of Palestinian rights.[91] To top it off, Bush planned to induce the region to liberalize both its politics and economies. Much of this agenda was stillborn. As Michael Oren, a former Israeli ambassador to the United States, writes, "the Pax Americana [for the Middle East] the president had promised seemed almost as unattainable as it had before the [Gulf] war; the new world order appeared virtually indistinguishable from the old."[92] Nonetheless, the United States' plan to insert itself more deeply into the region with an eye toward promoting peace, stability, and economic exchange was still a bold initiative.[93]

Yet, Washington has, at best, enjoyed mixed success in realizing its ambition. Since 1979, the supply and price of oil have been generally favorable. As but one example, as oil prices spiked during the Iranian Revolution, Saudi Arabia increased its production by a million barrels a day at the request of President Carter.[94] The real price of crude oil peaked in 1980 and then fell through 1998, rising again until the Great Recession in 2008, peaking for a second time in 2011, then falling steadily until Russia's invasion of Ukraine in 2022.[95] Global prices declined significantly in July 2022, after Saudi Arabia chaired a meeting at which OPEC+ (OPEC plus other oil producing states) agreed to increase oil production to pre-pandemic levels. This meeting was timed to coincide with President Joseph Biden's first visit to the country after the murder of US citizen Jamal Khashoggi by Saudi security forces.[96] Nonetheless, less than three months later, Saudi Arabia, in conjunction with Russia, cut production levels, leading to bitter accusations in the United States that Riyadh had defected on the earlier agreement and sought to undermine the Biden administration immediately before the midterm elections. While over the long term cooperation on oil and natural gas has been reasonably positive, short-term relations remain volatile.

90. Freedman 2009, 229–231.
91. Oren 2011, 569.
92. Oren 2011, 571.
93. Hinnebusch 2014c, 54–63.
94. Tyler 2009, 260.
95. EIA 2022.
96. Tan and Stevens 2022.

An area of equal tension is that countries have adopted few market-based economic reforms as desired by the United States. While giving lip service to *infitah*, or the "open door," regional regimes have resisted actual economic changes.[97] Even today, the Egyptian government monopolizes power production, transport, heavy industry, and insurance, and owns and controls some 40 percent of the economy and 50 percent of manufacturing.[98] There, as elsewhere, the state remains by far the largest employer and, to the extent sectors have been privatized, most assets have been sold to "cronies" tied to the government.[99] State-owned industries have simply been replaced at the margin by crony-capitalist industries, using privatization as merely another way to reward elite supporters of the regime. To date, the United States has preferential trade agreements in the AME only with Bahrain, Jordan, and Oman.

Consistent with the theory, in these areas of overlapping interests the United States has not been able to pull policy further toward its preferences than what the regimes themselves want. By strengthening their regimes, the United States can assist elites in adopting something close to their ideal points, but it cannot move them beyond what they are willing to do. While it exercises indirect rule over states in the AME, it gets relatively little of what it wants in return. With its policy preferences and those of elites in the region still quite far apart, its leverage is severely limited. In the end, the United States is dissatisfied with the policies of its allies but can do little to change what they do.

Authoritarian and Repressive Regimes

While shifting policies in the direction desired by Washington, though not beyond what the regimes in the region are willing to countenance, indirect rule in the AME also has important consequences for publics in the region and the United States. Lacking broad public support, small elite-based regimes govern autocratically, repressively, and corruptly in ways that further alienate their publics. Despite a preference for democracy and considerable rhetorical support for it, in backing these regimes the United States ends up tainted by association and criticized for hypocrisy.[100] To the extent that elite regimes remain in power with the assistance of Washington, the United States and the American people are implicated in their repression—even if US influence is ultimately limited.

97. Mansfield and Pelham 2019, 420. In 1976, Egypt cut commodity supports and price subsidies in exchange for $450 million from the IMF (Gelvin 2020, 269).
98. Gelvin 2020, 290.
99. Gelvin 2020, 284, 288.
100. Lynch 2007, 202.

The United States does have an interest in promoting democracy and human rights in the region, all else being equal. While sincere in espousing support for democracy, however, the United States has done little in practice to advance it. Indeed, the United States has consistently avoided criticizing Saudi Arabia for its human rights abuses.[101] US clients in the AME are significantly less democratic and more likely to abuse human rights than the rest of the world. As figure 6.3 shows, on average US clients are more authoritarian and more likely to restrict access to justice than other countries in the world. Indirect rule is not the only cause of authoritarianism or human rights abuses, of course. Within the broader region, even countries such as Iran where domestic rule prevails can violate human rights. But in the AME, indirect rule helps support regimes that are typically less democratic and more repressive than elsewhere. Thus, while the United States supports in principle democracy and human rights, in practice its system of indirect rule sustains regimes that violate these principles.[102]

At the same time, when the opposition is moderate and benefits from the overall relationship with the dominant state, indirect rule can be consistent with greater political participation and freedom. In Kuwait, especially since the Persian Gulf War, the broad public has been more favorable to the United States than elsewhere even as the country's foreign policy has become increasingly aligned with US interests.[103] Given Kuwait's vibrant civil society, the monarchy has historically been pressed into participatory forms of rule, resulting in a long-standing parliament and increased political participation.[104] Partly under US pressure, but possible because of this broader engagement, the Kuwaiti regime has instituted a series of reforms that allow for even greater political participation than formerly. Because the populace is largely pro-American, democracy is not as threatening to the regime and its supporters or to the United States as it is elsewhere.[105] Though still a monarchy, Kuwait scores consistently above the regional average on indicators of political participation and human rights.

US hierarchy in the Middle East remains incomplete. In the AME, the interests of the United States and those of both elites and publics are further apart than in the other regions covered in this volume. The governance costs are moderately high, and the main instruments of indirect rule—regime guarantees and arms sales—move regimes close to their ideal points but provide little leverage in moving policy closer to US interests. This means that indirect rule will be too expensive in some cases, with relations defaulting to domestic rule as in Iran or Syria. It also means that even where indirect rule is pursued,

---

101. This is true from the Carter administration on. See McFarland 2020, 203.
102. Cammett et al. 2018, chap. 3.
103. Jamal 2012, 60.
104. Yom 2020.
105. Jamal 2012, esp. 33, 64.

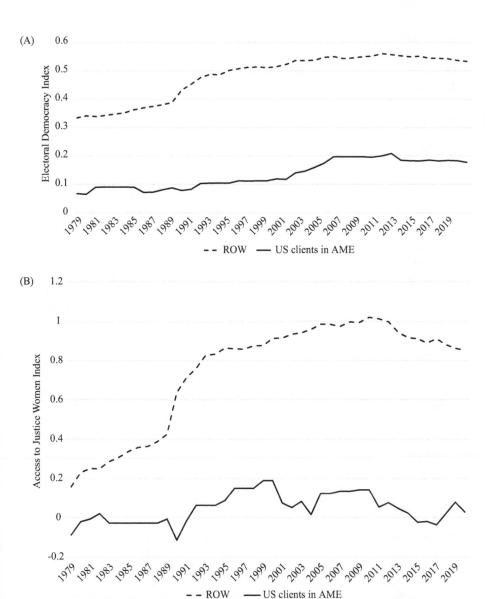

Figure 6.3 Democracy and human rights in the Arab Middle East compared to the rest of the world (ROW), 1979–2020. Panel A: VDem Electoral Democracy Index (v2x_polyarchy). Higher scores achieved when suffrage is extensive, political and civil society organizations can operate freely, elections are clean and not marred by fraud or systematic irregularities, and elections affect the composition of the chief executive of the country. In between elections, there is freedom of expression and an independent media capable of presenting alternative views on political matters. Very similar patterns are found in virtually all other measures of democracy. Panel B: VDem Access to Justice Women Index (v2clacjstw). Higher scores achieved to the extent women can bring cases before the courts without risk to their personal safety, trials are fair, and women have effective ability to seek redress if public authorities violate their rights, including the rights to counsel, defense, and appeal.

as in Saudi Arabia or any of the Gulf monarchies, the policy results will be limited and disappointing. Indirect rule survives in the AME only because, as we shall see in the next chapter, the alternatives of domestic and direct rule are even more unattractive to Washington.

In the Middle East, specific assets drive and then reproduce indirect rule. The dependence of industrialized nations on oil and gas focuses concern on the strategic passages through which they flow to world markets. To defend these chokepoints, the United States seeks to influence the policies of countries in the region and does so through relationships of indirect rule. The United States has built out a system of extensive bases in the AME to defend these chokepoints as well as its allied regimes, and these bases have become additional specific assets that require tighter indirect rule and yet more bases. Just as the defense of the Panama Canal required indirect rule in the Caribbean (see chapter 2), protecting the Strait of Hormuz and the Suez Canal require not only US naval bases but also friendly regimes in the region that permit those bases and help "police" the area. Although the geostrategic reasons for the US presence in the region are real, and not all US interests in the region stem from oil, the expansion of indirect rule is nonetheless a vicious cycle of Washington's own making.

The value of these specific assets is increasingly questioned. To see this, consider the following three questions. *If chokepoints and, in turn, allied regimes must be defended, why must this be done by the United States?* While the international oil market is deeply integrated, the United States is far less dependent on Middle East oil than other industrialized countries. The United States incurs the costs of indirect rule and the antipathy of local populations to provide the public good of steady access to oil at stable prices. Other countries have equal if not greater interests in this outcome. *Does the flow of oil actually need to be defended?* The industrialized economies are certainly dependent on imports of oil. But the states of the Persian Gulf are equally—perhaps more—dependent on exports of oil to generate income for their peoples and government revenues for defense and patronage. While oil exporters have incentives to act as a cartel and increase prices, and may, as they did in 1973, limit exports to gain political leverage, over the longer term they have incentives to sell as much oil as possible. States in the region have no incentive to close the strategic chokepoints. Neither Saudi Arabia nor Iran, for instance, would gain from closing the Strait of Hormuz, through which nearly all their oil exports flow. To do so might harm the other, but this would also choke off their own lifelines. Egypt is similarly dependent on revenues from ships transiting the canal. Letting international markets and mutual deterrence work is at least a plausible alternative to active defense of countries and strategic passages. *Finally, should the United States and the world more generally be encouraging continued dependence on oil?* Given anthropomorphic climate change, the trillions spent on war and defending US clients in the AME might be better used to advance renewable and alternative energy sources. If specific assets in the region drive international hierarchy, creating more intense interests and incentives for indirect (or direct) rule, it is worth debating the answers to these questions before continuing to acquire yet more assets in the region.

7

Hierarchy in the Arab Middle East

Having supported small elite regimes in the Arab Middle East, the United States faces a real threat of exploitation and entrapment from its subordinates. Although it has sought to establish rules limiting their behavior, both direct and domestic rule are relatively unattractive, which in turn allows subordinates considerable leeway in adhering to these rules. The United States not only gets limited policy concessions, as explained in the previous chapter, but extensive opportunism further undermines the gains from indirect rule, pushing Washington close to the point where it might be tempted to simply walk away from its relationships of indirect rule. Regional elites recognize this fact and hedge their bets, so to speak, by deepening their reliance on their narrow constituencies and seeking closer ties to other foreign powers, including Russia and China, further undermining the possible gains to the United States from indirect rule.

While the gains from indirect rule are small, the United States nonetheless becomes implicated in supporting elite regimes that repress their populations. Anti-Americanism is rife. In supporting weak and autocratic regimes that might otherwise fall or be forced to make greater concessions to domestic opponents, the United States has also become the "far enemy" that must be defeated or driven from the region if political change is to occur at home. As the United States has become a target in the global war *of* terror, it has doubled down in supporting its allies to gain their support in its global war *on* terror. As its allied regimes repress popular movements for change, the opposition turns even more anti-American and violent, reinforcing incentives for the United States to back existing elite regimes, which in turn creates more anti-Americanism and violence. The United States sits on the fence, wondering if indirect rule is worth the effort but equally unsure how to extricate itself from the region.

Opportunism and the Rules of the Incomplete Empire

In guaranteeing the security of regional elites, the United States faces two forms of opportunism in the AME. First, the allies can exploit the United States by doing less for their own security than they would otherwise, either by spending less on defense and police or redistributing less to their domestic support coalitions. Any of these actions would increase the likelihood that the United States would be called upon to honor the security guarantee. This is a concern but not a major worry, as it is in the interests both of the regimes and the United States to use any support received to suppress the domestic opposition up to the allied group's ideal point. Still, facing competing demands for scarce resources, elites may have an incentive to do less for themselves and to rely more on protection from the United States. Second, the allies could entrap the United States by acting more aggressively toward regional rivals. Knowing that the United States would likely come to their aid, allied regimes can take a tougher negotiating stance and make larger demands for concessions from others. As but one example, during the Iran-Iraq War, Iraq incurred huge debts to its neighbors. Kuwait then refused to forgive or renegotiate the terms of the loans, contributing to Saddam Hussein's decision to invade the country in August 1990. It is unlikely that Kuwait would have been so inflexible without some reasonable expectation of support from others, including the United States.[1] At present, Saudi Arabia may be escalating its regional rivalry with Iran, confident that the United States stands by its side. Indirect rule has the potential to draw the United States into regional conflicts it might otherwise have avoided.

To ward off opportunism, Washington offers only an implicit security guarantee to its allied groups. Regime guarantees are rarely stated openly or made ironclad. To limit problems of moral hazard, no guarantee can be absolute. Nonetheless, for decades it has been US policy to ensure the security of Arab states.[2] It should be noted, however, that the regime guarantee does not extend to individual rulers. It would be extremely difficult and costly for the United States to defend or replace any particular ruler, and it apparently has not been able to exert significant influence in secession struggles. Nonetheless, the United States builds bases, pre-places equipment, carries out joint troop exercises and engages in joint operations, and holds high-level military meetings. In some cases, it deploys a significant number of troops (see table 6.1). The absence of formal alliances, however, gives the United States greater discretion when it comes to honoring the guarantee and limits the domestic criticism of the regimes for being too close to Washington. The

---

1. On the causes and course of the war, see Freedman and Karsh 1993; Gause 2010, chap. 4.

2. The credibility of the guarantee, however, was called into question by President Barack Obama's decision not to back Egypt's president Hosni Mubarak in the Arab Spring, and this move was controversial for this reason.

lack of firm commitments, however, limits incentives for regional regimes to act opportunistically against US interests. None can know with certainty if and under what conditions the United States will come to their defense.

In similar ways, Washington controls its allies by retaining discretion over the provision of military hardware and, equally, ongoing maintenance, training, and resupply services—a spigot of resources that the United States can turn on or off at its discretion. Although it has sold large quantities of weapons to Gulf states, the United States has also stopped short of allowing them to obtain an autonomous military capability. Despite the billions spent, even Saudi Arabia was unable to defend itself adequately against the threat from Iraq in 1990 and ultimately had to invite in US forces. Without spare parts or US technicians on the ground, the weapons purchased by Saudi Arabia and others would soon become worthless. The provision of post-purchase services, which remain entirely at Washington's discretion, actually gives the United States greater control over military policy than arms purchases alone.

The United States also sets rules to limit opportunism by regional regimes, creating the hierarchy that governs relations. First, the United States aims to prevent states from forming security relationships with great powers other than itself. In seeking to bar other great powers from the region, Washington reduces the outside options of regional states and any additional leverage that might be brought to bear against the United States. During the Cold War, this rule was manifested in efforts to prevent the Soviet Union from playing a major role in the region. Moscow's refusal to withdraw from Iran in 1946 led to the first Cold War crisis. Its later overtures to Egypt and Syria, welcomed by the embattled leaders of both countries, prompted the United States to support either internal or external opponents of those regimes, drawing new Cold War lines in the sands. Concerned about the vacuum that might result as Britain and France unwound their colonial relationships in the region, the United States took over their mantle, especially after Britain retreated "East of Suez" after 1968. It then built up Saudi Arabia and Iran as twin pillars of anti-communism in the Persian Gulf. This "hegemonic" impulse was central to the Carter and Reagan doctrines (see chapter 6). Only since the end of the Cold War, however, has the United States been able to consolidate its position as the sole external power, creating a "profoundly American regional order."[3] President Anwar Sadat of Egypt explained his switch from the Soviet to the American sphere with the quip, "America holds 99 percent of the cards."[4] The biggest threat to US dominance in the region now is China, which is seeking greater influence over oil-rich states in the Persian Gulf as part of its Belt-and-Road Initiative.

As a corollary to this first rule, the United States also seeks to prevent the rise of regional hegemons, unless they are themselves closely allied with the

---

3. Lynch 2016, 11; Mansfield and Pelham 2019, 382–383.
4. Quoted in Gelvin 2020, 303.

United States. Not only does the United States want to exclude other great powers but it also wants to prevent the rise of any regional power unfriendly to its interests. President Gamal Nassar's regional ambitions, along with his ties to the Soviet Union—which were at least partly a response to Washington's hostility—led the United States to oppose his regime.[5] Conversely, the shah of Iran, closely tied to the United States, was cultivated as a proxy for US interests in the Gulf under the Nixon Doctrine not despite but because of his regional aspirations.[6] The same holds true for Saudi Arabia today.

The first rule implies a second, namely that states must avoid or settle interstate conflicts within the region. The United States is often described as a status quo power, which is true, but this depiction misses the underlying motivation. In a region of weak states, artificial borders created only during the interwar period, and uncertain national loyalties, any dispute either within or between countries has the potential to not only draw in outside parties but to entrap the United States into regional conflicts. This desire to limit conflict within the region and protect the status quo was most clearly revealed in the US-led effort to restore sovereignty to Kuwait in the Persian Gulf War of 1991.

This rule on stability and the status quo intersects with US policy on Israel and, in turn, the promotion of peace with Israel's neighbors. The commitment of the United States to Israel has many sources, of course. During the 1950s, support for Israel was quite tempered. Many State Department officials, including Secretary of State John Foster Dulles, reviled the Jewish state, and regarded it as a "millstone around our necks" when it came to relations with Arabs.[7] During the Suez Crisis (see chapter 4), the Eisenhower administration backed Egypt against Israel and its European coconspirators. In return, Israel initially adopted a position of neutrality in the superpower rivalry. As the Middle East was drawn into the Cold War, however, the United States found itself increasingly aligned with Israel against the forces for change within the region, deepening its relationship. After the Six Day War in 1967, mounting Cold War tensions developed into a more permanent alignment between Washington and Tel Aviv.[8] Regimes that were hostile toward Israel directed some of that hostility toward the United States, which reciprocated that hostility, and a spiral began that was and remains hard to reverse. As a central tension within the region, the Palestinian-Israeli dispute draws the United States into active conflict mediation and attempts at resolution. The creation of Israel was the most important and far-reaching disruption to the territorial status quo to occur in the region after World War II. Approved by

---

5. This was also true for other conservative and rival regimes in the region, especially Saudi Arabia (McFarland 2020, 48).
6. Bill 1988.
7. Dulles quoted in Oren 2011, 513.
8. Cleveland and Bunton 2018, 336–337; Oren 2011, 530–531.

the United Nations, the creation of the Jewish state on the historically integrated territory of Palestine is the one territorial change within the region
that was permitted by the international community and, indeed, encouraged
by the United States. Given that the 1973 war led to one of the most acute
crises of the Cold War, the United States is well aware that the conflict opens
the possibility for other great powers to intervene and has repeatedly sought
both to support Israel and to bring something resembling peace to the region. In essence, Washington seeks to create and legitimate a new territorial
modus vivendi that accommodates Israel while retaining as much as possible
of the older order. These goals are not necessarily consistent. Through its
support, however, the United States has allowed Israel to push against the
status quo by maintaining the occupation of the West Bank, which in turn
keeps the conflict alive. The unresolved tension between a US-backed Israel
and other states in the region sustains this central contradiction in US policy
and limits the ability of the United States to form tighter relationships with
its Arab clients. Recently, the United States has pushed its Gulf allies into
greater cooperation with Israel through the Abraham Accords.[9]

Third, allied regimes must not undertake independent military actions.
By prohibiting independent action, the United States seeks to limit the potential for entrapment. Although Saudi Arabia has chosen to ignore this rule,
the danger is illustrated by Riyadh's current war in Yemen. The Saudi regime
has long been concerned about its southern border and instability in the
neighboring state. It intervened in the civil war in Yemen in 1965, with Egypt
supporting the other side, and has intervened repeatedly from the 1970s,
supporting Ali Abdullah Saleh as president of North Yemen and then later
as leader of unified Yemen. At the urging of Saudi Arabia, the Carter administration began massive arms deliveries to Saleh's regime in 1979, beginning
a long but tenuous US involvement in the country.[10] After he lost favor with
Saudi Arabia in 2012, Saleh fell from power and sided with Houthi rebels
from the southern regions of Yemen who were backed by Iran. Saudi Arabia
then switched its support to Abdrabbuh Mansur Hadi. When the capital fell
to Houthi forces in September 2014, Hadi requested Saudi assistance, and
the situation escalated into a Saudi-Iranian proxy war that continues to this
day, creating one of the largest and most unpublicized humanitarian crises
on the planet. The Saudis have attempted to pull the United States further
into the conflict, but Washington has so far limited its involvement to supply-
ing additional military arms and intelligence, though it appears to be more
deeply involved in air operations including target selection.[11] In this case,
and despite the humanitarian outcry against the war, the United States has
been able to exert only limited influence over its subordinate.

---

9. Goldberg 2020.
10. McFarland 2020, 219–221; Brewer 2019.
11. Graham-Harrison 2016.

By the inverse logic, regional states must not support transnational terrorism directed at the United States or its facilities abroad. The concern with terrorism began in the 1970s when the Palestine Liberation Organization and other groups started to attack airplanes and tourists, but expanded dramatically as the United States became more deeply involved in the region. Since the attacks of September 11, 2001, the United States has waged a global war on terror, or more precisely a war on anti-American terrorism, much of which originates in the AME. As we shall see in the final section below, such terrorism should be understood at least partly as a response to US indirect rule in the region. Nonetheless, the willingness of allied elites to support the United States has become a major criterion in Washington for judging regimes within the region.

While the United States has only a limited ability to pull policies in its preferred direction, supporting the autocratic regimes of the region opens it to opportunism, especially entrapment. In attempting to safeguard its interests, the United States retains discretion and attempts to impose rules on its subordinates to limit their foreign policy independence. These rules, in turn, chafe against its allies and are often ignored or followed only partially. The United States is dissatisfied with this equilibrium but continues to sustain hierarchies through indirect rule because the alternatives are even less attractive.

Alternatives to Indirect Rule

Since domestic rule threatens even less favorable policies than indirect rule, and direct rule is prohibitively costly, allied elites can broadly exploit and entrap the United States into other conflicts almost with impunity. The region is far from an exclusive US sphere of influence, with Russia recently reentering Syria in support of the regime of Bashar al-Asaad and China making inroads into the Persian Gulf. The conflict with Israel persists, despite recent moves by the Gulf states to open diplomatic channels. Entrapment into regional conflicts is common. Saudi Arabia first drew the United States into the maelstrom of the Horn of Africa in early 1977, creating a continuing role for Washington in Somalia through the 1990s and into Yemen in 1979 and beyond.[12] The Iranian Revolution, which threatened Sunni regimes throughout the region, and the hostage crisis, which broke relations with the United States, prompted Washington and its regional subordinates to support Iraq during the Iran-Iraq War in the 1980s. As explained, debts from that war led Saddam Hussein to invade Kuwait and threaten Saudi Arabia, which in turn led to the Persian Gulf War, led by the United States. Saddam's

---

12. McFarland 2020, 216–217, 219–221.

continuing threat to the region spurred the Iraq War of 2003. Saudi Arabia helped draw the United States into Afghanistan in 1979.[13] Saudi Arabia's tensions with Egypt and especially the Muslim Brotherhood reinforced US hostility to President Mohamed Morsi and support for the coup against him. The United States has worked hard to avoid being drawn into Saudi Arabia's deteriorating relations with Qatar, the site of the largest US base in the region, and its war in Yemen, though it has not been entirely successful.[14] This is not to argue that the United States has been forced to fight wars in the AME against its will. In 2002, for instance, the United States had its own proponents in favor of the Iraq War. But in all cases, the commitment to regional stability, desired by regional states as well, has drawn the United States into conflicts it might otherwise have avoided. Finally, while they have invited in US forces onto their territories in various capacities, subordinates are only contingent allies in the war against terror, always acting in their own self-interest and sometimes even backing terrorists directly or turning a blind eye when their nationals fund various terrorist groups. Although it has "generally followed the US stance on diplomatic, political, and strategic issues," and "opened its military facilities for use by US naval and air forces," according to Gregory Gause, Saudi Arabia "has not completely followed Washington's stance on regional issues."[15] Likewise, Marc Lynch concludes that in recent years "leading Gulf states . . . [have] objected to and actively undermined virtually every dimension of American policy towards the region."[16]

The counterfactual is always hard to estimate. If Iran after the revolution is the baseline, then US indirect rule has induced a somewhat more favorable policy and tempered opportunism by states in the AME. But Iran's policies may themselves be influenced by US hostility and its support for its regional rivals, who are in turn supported by Washington. If Egypt under the democratically elected Muslim Brotherhood regime is taken as the baseline, the United States also found the policies it was adopting to be intolerable, though what might have evolved over time is unknowable. The United States has likely drawn policy closer to its interests under indirect rule than might otherwise have obtained, but its hierarchy in the region remains at best incomplete. As it nears the point of indifference between indirect rule with extensive opportunism and walking away from the region and letting domestic rule prevail, subordinates recognize the ambivalence and hedge their bets, seeking relations with other powers, now including China, and doubling down on their elite constituencies and strategies of repression, further lowering the benefits for the United States. Yet, indirect rule persists because the alternatives are worse.

---

13. McFarland 2020, 224.
14. Kamrava 2014.
15. Gause 2014, 188–189.
16. Lynch 2016, 246.

Direct Rule

Considering the history of imperialism in the Middle East and the rhetoric of anti-colonialism and independence that elites use to justify their rule, direct rule by the United States is nearly impossible to imagine. Although always understood as temporary hierarchies, the wars in Afghanistan and Iraq are suggestive of the difficulties that would be encountered under direct rule. In both cases, the costs in lives and money to overthrow the regimes were relatively low but mounted during the occupations. To sustain direct rule in the face of continuing resistance from an even more broadly opposed society would likely be untenable under all but the most extreme cases of interest divergence and specific assets.

The difficulties of direct rule in the face of resistance can be illustrated by the brief occupation of Iraq and its aftermath.[17] The Iraq War of 2003–2011 was complex, with many causes and unanticipated consequences.[18] Indeed, the administration of George W. Bush drifted into war, at no clear point making an explicit decision. While the US military planned and executed a successful campaign to topple Saddam's regime, there was virtually no formal planning for what would come next.[19] Although the thoughts and inner workings of the Bush administration remain unclear, and there were many competing agendas unfolding simultaneously, it was apparently assumed that a simple decapitation of the regime would suffice, with a new leader being "parachuted in" (almost literally) from the West.[20]

President George W. Bush and his advisers expected regime change in Iraq to be relatively easy for two reasons, both recognizably naïve in hindsight. First, the administration appears to have assumed that any policy adopted under domestic rule would be close to that desired by the United States, or to put this another way, the administration expected the median voter in Iraq would have policy preferences close to its own.[21] In reality, policy preferences within society were both ambiguous and fluid. Admittedly, the counterfactual here was difficult for the Bush administration to estimate at the time. After decades of severe repression under Saddam, and without significant access to Iraqi public opinion during the 1990s, what the various communities really wanted from politics and how strong one group was relative to others was hard to discern from afar. Generally speaking, Sunnis feared losing political power and access to oil revenues under a Shia regime, and the Shia sought retribution for decades of exploitation under Saddam's

---

17. The Iraq case is discussed at greater length in Lake 2016, chap. 4.

18. On the causes of the war, see, among others, Gause 2010, chap. 6; Harvey 2012; Yetiv 2018. For more analytic treatments, see Lake 2010; Debs and Monteiro 2014.

19. See esp. Lake 2016, 107–116; Freedman 2009, 429.

20. Gause 2010, 155–168.

21. In this case, in terms of figures 1.1 and 5.1, Saddam Hussein constituted the opposition. On anticipated interests, see Abootalebi 2018, 275–276.

rule and to consolidate their political dominance. Within each group, there were Westernized factions willing to work with the United States and more radical groups opposed to Washington's direction that included former members of Saddam's government who sought a Sunni restoration, and Shia with deep ties to Iran. Only the Kurds, long dependent on US support for their autonomous zone in northeastern Iraq, were reasonably aligned with Washington, though they too differed in their desire for national sovereignty. While the administration believed differences between groups were smaller than they were, with some officials famously predicting there would be no sectarian violence after the war, it does appear to have been understood that Sunnis and Shia had different policy preferences.[22] The problem arose in estimating the counterfactual policy that would emerge under domestic rule $\left(x_q\right)$—that is, where the median voter would be located. Ideologues in the administration believed their "freedom agenda" was universal. This line was reinforced by what the administration was hearing from exiles in the Iraqi National Congress. Nonetheless, there appears to have been a widely held assumption that domestic politics in Iraq would play out in such a way that policy would approximate and fulfill US interests $\left(x_q \approx d\right)$. Even though the counterfactual was unclear, the error was in not questioning this assumption more deeply.

Second, the Bush administration assumed that it could appoint a leader close to its own preferences who would, in turn, be accepted by Iraqis. This assumption was premised on the first. If the median voter in Iraq and the United States wanted the same set of policies, then a leader acceptable to Washington would also be acceptable to Iraqis. The candidate supported by the Pentagon, at least, was Ahmed Chalabi. An Iraqi exile who spent most of his life in the United States and United Kingdom, Chalabi had a long history of shady dealings, including bank fraud in Jordan, but rose to prominence as a founder of the Iraqi National Congress. Though Chalabi was distrusted by many in the intelligence community, he was a favorite of neoconservatives in the administration for his help in building the case for war—much of which subsequently proved to be wrong.[23]

This "decapitate and replace" strategy, however, quickly fell apart. While possibly important in the exile community, Chalabi lacked a following within the country. Those who had stayed in Iraq in opposition to Saddam refused to accept his leadership—or anyone else's for that matter.[24] The Iraqi Governing Council, composed of representatives from the major factions

---

22. On what the administration knew, should have known, and revealed to the public, see Isikoff and Corn 2007, 180, 194; Gordon and Trainor 2013, 6; Ricks 2006, 20; Allawi 2007, 12.

23. On early interactions between the CIA and Chalabi, see Tyler 2009, 429–441; Mansfield and Pelham 2019, 388–389; Freedman 2009, 399, 433. Appointed to lead the de-Ba'athification efforts, Chalabi was later suspected of spying for Iran (Gordon 2020, 120).

24. Mansfield and Pelham 2019, 444.

in Iraq during the transition, refused to anoint Chalabi as successor.[25] At a broader level, the state apparatus, including the Iraqi Army and crucial ministries, simply collapsed during the war and ceased to function. Soldiers took off their uniforms and disappeared. Widespread rioting and violence broke out within days of the fall of Baghdad, and government offices were looted and burned. There was no functioning government for Chalabi or anyone else to inherit. Even if a leader supported by the United States had been acceptable to domestic factions, the administrative capacity to recover from the war and lead the country forward had been eviscerated.

As a result, the United States had little choice but to impose direct rule, at least on a temporary basis. The occupation was expected to be relatively inexpensive, mostly because the administration assumed Iraq would pay for the costs of US forces from its oil revenues.[26] In April 2003, the Office of Management and Budget projected a total of $2.5 billion for postwar reconstruction—a figure that was closer to the weekly cost of the war for the next ten years.[27] The postwar transition, in turn, was supposed to be led by the Office for Reconstruction and Humanitarian Assistance (ORHA), headed by retired lieutenant general Jay Garner. As the title of this effort implies, the US role was envisioned as one of simple humanitarian relief. ORHA arrived in Iraq with limited staff and even fewer resources.[28] The early cost estimates were immediately proven wrong. Soon recognized as inadequate to the task, ORHA was disbanded after one month and replaced by the Coalition Provisional Authority, led by US ambassador L. Paul Bremer. On arriving in Baghdad in May 2003, Bremer immediately assumed the sovereignty of Iraq, declaring to the Iraqi Governing Council that he was the legitimate authority in Iraq under the law of occupation.[29] He then formally disbanded the military, though little remained, and abolished the Ba'ath Party, purging members from official posts and further gutting administrative agencies. Though he made clear that his most important task was to return sovereignty to a new government, he nonetheless wielded total authority over the country—a pure case of direct rule.

As violence and the insurgency spread, however, the Bush administration acknowledged that an indefinite occupation would be impossibly costly. When President Bush famously declared "mission accomplished" on May 1, 2003, the United States had incurred less than 1 percent of its eventual casualties and a small fraction of the final financial cost. Yet, even then, the occupation was understood to be unpopular in Iraq.[30] The prevailing assumption through 2007, especially within the US military, was that the growing

25. On the evolution and politics of the Iraqi Governing Council, see Lake 2016, 135–136.
26. Freedman 2009, 397.
27. Gordon 2020, 126.
28. Packer 2005, 143.
29. Gordon and Trainor 2013, 16.
30. On public opinion in Iraq, see Herring and Rangwala 2006, 201, 205.

insurgency was driven primarily by resentment toward the United States and that stability and withdrawal would follow one another in a virtuous cycle.[31] Accordingly, Bremer moved quickly, returning nominal sovereignty to an interim government in May and disbanding the Coalition Provisional Authority in June 2004. Nonetheless, the United States remained deeply involved in designing the new state, which would, it was hoped, reflect US values and accord with US interests in the region. Following the plan and schedule laid out by Bremer, elections for a national assembly to write a new constitution were held in January 2005. The new constitution was approved by national referendum in October 2005 and elections were held for the new legislative assembly in December 2005. After six months of tense negotiations, Nouri al-Maliki was selected as Iraq's new prime minister in May 2006. One common criticism of the occupation authority that arose later was that these elections were likely held "too soon," hardening sectarian divisions rather than mitigating them. Sovereignty and democratic elections did little to calm the growing violence that racked the country.

With direct rule waning, the US sought to move to indirect rule, but even this proved costly. Consistent with its broader interests in the region, and with the rules of hierarchy imposed elsewhere in the AME, Washington desired a regime that would be pro-Western, a stabilizing force in international oil markets, and open to economic liberalization and reforms; in turn, it would accept the territorial status quo in the Gulf and be an ally in the global war on terror. The United States hoped for the possibility of a regime that would be able to govern with the support of a majority of the population. Once the insurgency broke out and sectarian divisions within Iraq hardened, however, no leader or group met all the desired criteria. The "middle ground" that Washington sought proved elusive. When no leader both popular within Iraq and acceptable to the United States emerged in the December 2005 election, US ambassador Zalmay Khalilzad became "kingmaker" in the post-election negotiations over the choice of prime minister. After vetoing several possibilities as incompetent, too sectarian, or too close to Iran, Khalilzad eventually settled on Maliki as the least objectionable alternative. Although he had spent some time in Iran during his own period of exile, Maliki was a hardliner on de-Ba'athification and the Sunni insurgency, reportedly had deep concerns about Iranian influence, and had distanced himself from the more radical Shia, especially Muqtada al-Sadr and the Mahdi Army.[32] Yet, Maliki was undistinguished, a second-tier leader of Dawa—a Shia political party set up in the 1980s as a vehicle for Iranian influence—and critically lacking any base of support of his own.[33] Rather than lead from the center and close to

---

31. Lake 2016, 114–115.
32. Gordon and Trainor 2013, 183–198; Gordon 2020, 133–134. Subsequent reports suggest that the United States actually knew little about Maliki (Baker 2014).
33. Freedman 2009, 435–436.

US interests as desired, Maliki sought to build a personalist, Shia-only coalition and over time became increasingly aligned with Iran as an alternative source of aid and support.[34] As Philip Gordon summarizes the situation,

> Far from taking advantage of the relative calm [after his election] to reach out and bring Sunnis into the government or to reconcile with the Kurds in the north, the government of Prime Minister Nouri al-Maliki—now backed by tens of thousands of additional American troops—became increasing authoritarian, corrupt, and sectarian. . ... He never delivered on his pledges to incorporate [Sunni] fighters into Iraqi security forces, which he instead used as a tool to expand his own power. Nor was Maliki willing or able to take legislative steps to help heal Iraq's divisions, such as modifying the harsh de-Baathification laws, empowering Iraq's provinces, giving Sunnis a major voice in government, or implementing energy-sharing arrangements with the Kurds.[35]

In the eyes of the United States, at least, Maliki was also incompetent, unable to manage a larger coalition. Secretary of State Condoleezza Rice even traveled to Baghdad to tell Maliki that he was "a terrible Prime Minister. . .. Without progress and without an agreement [to maintain US forces in Iraq], you'll be on your own, hanging from a lamppost."[36]

The inability to influence Maliki and the failure of direct and indirect rule were structural. On the one hand, the administration sought to strengthen Maliki's regime enough that it could produce policy approaching the US ideal against the resistance of opposition groups, comprised of both more radical Sunnis and Shias. This implied a continuing regime guarantee provided by US forces and extensive military and economic aid to empower Maliki to sustain the regime against domestic opponents. In this way, Iraq looked to be a classic case of indirect rule. On the other hand, as it became clear to Washington that domestic rule would be unattractive, likely leading to policies it would find far from its interests, and as the costs of direct rule proved unsustainable, the United States feared that Maliki himself would turn against the United States and exploit and entrap it into unnecessary conflicts. With poor alternatives, Maliki had wide latitude to act opportunistically. The administration was, thus, caught between "Iraq and a hard place," as the canard went. If it withdrew support for Maliki, the regime would fall. But if it supported the regime, Maliki would turn that support toward his own ends. In the end, the Bush administration believed it had to support Maliki but limit that support to control his regime. As Bush asked in a National Security Council meeting, "If not Maliki, who?" As Secretary

---

34. Herring and Rangwala 2006, 33; Dodge 2012; Dodge 2013; Kaplan 2013, 209–210.
35. Gordon 2020, 133.
36. Quoted in Baker 2014.

of State Condoleezza Rice later admitted, there was "no Plan B."[37] Indeed, Bush hoped that constant reassurance would encourage Maliki to work with the Sunnis and build the kind of coalition that the administration—again, naively—still thought was possible. But in limiting its support, Washington drove Maliki into an alliance with more extreme Shia groups and with neighboring Iran, which was only too happy to act as a substitute for US aid and free up the prime minister to consolidate a Shia-only regime. Maliki's successors, all from the same Dawa Party, continued this Shia-only coalition strategy with Iranian support.

Given the high governance costs of supporting the regime and attempting to suppress multiple opposition groups, the United States eventually gave up and walked away. It got little in the way of favored policies in return for its support and suffered considerable opportunism, with Maliki taking US aid and using it for his own purposes and drawing the United States into internecine conflicts. Although it continues to meddle in the selection of prime ministers, Washington has essentially allowed the relationship to revert to domestic rule, no matter how unattractive that might be; alternatively, to the extent that Tehran has replaced the United States, Iraq might be better described as being indirectly ruled by Iran. When Maliki refused to sign an agreement regularizing the status of US forces within Iraq, President Bush agreed to withdraw all US troops by December 2011. Facing continued intransigence, President Barack Obama refused to renegotiate the deal and US forces left on schedule.[38] Although some US special forces returned in 2014 to help in the fight against the Islamic State, US troops and aid have been greatly reduced, and there has been little continuing effort to shape the regime. The case of Iraq clearly shows the limits of direct rule. Even the power the United States can exert through indirect rule is indeed quite limited in the AME. When direct rule is impossible, opportunism will be rife, and indirect rule may not be viable either.

Domestic Rule

The United States has not succeeded in establishing indirect rule everywhere in the Middle East. The Iranian Revolution of 1979 destroyed the system of indirect rule that the United States enjoyed under the shah, on whom it had pinned substantial hopes as a regional proxy for US interests.[39] With the Islamist regime securely in power, the influence of the United States is strictly limited and no hierarchy exists.[40] Although there are so-called moderate groups within Iran with preferences more aligned with the United States

---

37. Quoted in Gordon and Trainor 2013, 456–457.
38. Lake 2016, 129–130.
39. Bill 1988. On early relations with the shah, see Kinzer 2008.
40. Ehteshami 2014.

than those of the government, regime change is widely regarded as too difficult to contemplate. Even on the contentious issue of Iran's nuclear program, the United States resists forcible action and has attempted to negotiate a compromise solution, though this remains controversial. Any attempt to invade the country would likely unify the population against the United States and meet broad-based resistance potentially greater than that experienced in Iraq. Domestic rule prevails.

Likewise, Syria has long remained outside the US sphere.[41] Although it has received some aid from Russia and more recently from Iran, it has relied mostly on its own resources to sustain domestic rule under the Asaad family, who divide and rule the already factionalized society and coup-proof the regime by relying on relatives and trusted associates for key positions.[42] Even when the Arab Spring created a possible opening in Damascus, President Obama chose not to intervene. Stung by the difficulties of indirect rule in Iraq after the overthrow of Saddam Hussein and the chaos that unfolded in Libya, the president decided against any significant attempt to shape events, even accepting expanded roles for Moscow and Tehran. Having declared a red line regarding Asaad's use of chemical weapons, Obama chose to back down rather than intervene when it was crossed. President Donald Trump ordered US troops aiding the insurgents to withdraw in October 2019 but reversed himself under broad criticism and pressure from military leaders, leaving only a small residual force. As in Iran, the United States has been unwilling to expend the blood and treasure that would be necessary to change the regime in Damascus.

With Iran a clear example and Syria a mixed example because of Russian and Iranian influence, these members of what is sometimes called the "rejectionist bloc" suggest what domestic rule elsewhere might look like in the absence of indirect rule by the United States.[43] Both Iran and Syria are now defined by Washington as rogue states, unwilling to comply with US preferences and rules and serving as sources of disruption in the region. Indeed, as part of the so-called "axis of evil," Iran actively seeks to undermine the US presence and influence in the AME. These two cases suggest that Washington would face even greater problems and resistance in its subordinates if its allies were to fall.

As a result, the United States remains leery of and typically opposed to domestic rule, which necessarily incorporates popular preferences. In general, Islamist and nationalist groups oppose US goals in the AME. "Greater democratization could clearly bring groups unsympathetic to the United States into power," as Amaney Jamal writes, and "therefore it is in the interests of the United States and existing regime leaders to limit the ability of Islamists

---

41. See Hinnebusch 2014b.
42. Cleveland and Bunton 2018, 426–427.
43. Lynch 2016, 14.

to influence policy—a reality not lost on ordinary citizens."[44] As the United States becomes more deeply engaged in the region, supports unpopular regimes that lack domestic legitimacy, and attempts to pull policy closer to its own interests and further from the interests of the majority of citizens, the opposition becomes progressively more anti-American. Elites backed by the United States do not need to compromise with the opposition, and in fact become more repressive, which then deepens the opposition, making the United States even more fearful of any opposition regime.[45]

At least some of this fear may be rooted in exaggerated estimates of the strength of radical groups within AME societies. The terrorist attacks of 9/11 shocked Americans and have led, perhaps, to an unwarranted fear of mass publics in AME countries—the opposition, in my terms. The extent of this bias is hard to estimate, but like racism in the Caribbean Basin and anti-communism after World War II, a generalized fear of Muslim societies is likely distorting how the United States sees mass publics in the AME and, in turn, the consequences of democracy in the region. What really separates elites from the public in the AME is the fact that economic rents are concentrated in their hands, and they are willing to accept their subordination to US interests in return for regime guarantees and military and economic support (see chapter 6). On questions of economic and political reform, publics may be closer to the United States than the elites. Many Arabs argue that their interests are not that different from those of the United States. In this view, if only the United States would support democracy, more cooperative relations would be possible. This might be true. But when democracy has been tried in recent years, Islamists have come to power across the board. As Secretary of State Madeleine Albright once said, "Arab public opinion, after all, can be rather scary."[46] As she later elaborated, "We have been afraid to push too hard for democracy, especially in Arab countries. We worry, perhaps with reason, that if radical Islamists obtain power through an election, there would be no more elections . . . and instability might be created."[47]

Egypt after the Arab Spring is a particularly telling case in which the United States was open to the possibility of a long-time client turning to domestic rule. Egypt had been under US indirect rule for decades. After the 1973 war, Anwar Sadat broke with the Soviet Union, made peace with Israel, and allied with the United States, with his country becoming the second largest recipient of US aid (after Israel).[48] The close relationship and dependence on US support continued after Sadat's assassination and his replacement by President Hosni Mubarak.[49] Like his predecessors, Mubarak had risen

44. Jamal 2012, 4–5.
45. This is the main argument of Yom 2015, esp. 2.
46. Quoted in Norton 2019, 138.
47. Quoted in Yetiv 2011, 145.
48. Mansfield and Pelham 2019, 329, 324–325.
49. Freedman 2009, 125.

up through the ranks of the military to a position of national leadership.[50] Mubarak successfully led Egypt for three decades, following Sadat's turn to the West, nominally liberalizing the Egyptian economy, confirming the peace treaty with Israel, and supporting other US policy initiatives in the region all in exchange for US military and economic aid. Nonetheless, Mubarak became increasingly corrupt and repressive, even setting up his son to inherit an emerging political dynasty.[51] In Egypt as elsewhere, the root cause of the protests in 2011 "was the authoritarian regimes' glaring failure to meet the expectations of bulging youth populations."[52] Starting in Algeria, the Arab Spring quickly spread to Egypt with massive protests calling for the ailing dictator to resign.

As the Arab Spring swept through North Africa and into Cairo in early 2011, US president Obama decided that the increasingly corrupt and authoritarian Mubarak had to go.[53] The embattled president resigned days later. Some, impressed by the young, Westernized protestors in Tahrir Square, argued that the United States had an opportunity to finally be on the "right side of history" by backing popular demands for greater democracy.[54] Although many protesters still defined themselves as against the United States, the crowds in Tahrir Square shifted dramatically away from the traditional anti-imperialist and anti-Zionist chants and toward demands for democracy and freedom.[55] The popular uprising, led by a new generation of educated technocrats, appeared at least open to Westernizing reforms. Despite pressure from traditional allies in the region, and especially Saudi Arabia, Obama allowed this process of bottom-up regime change play out.[56] With Mubarak gone, the United States pushed for early elections and a rapid transition to democracy.[57]

The best-organized body in Egypt was the Muslim Brotherhood, an opposition movement formed in 1928 that combined a moderately conservative brand of Islam with a social justice orientation and a pan-regional ideology. Though hardly the most radical of Islamist organizations, the Muslim Brotherhood was long suppressed in Egypt, having been outlawed after one of its members attempted to assassinate President Gamal Nassar. It was

---

50. Cleveland and Bunton 2018, 398–400.
51. Hinnebusch and Shama 2014, 81–82, 91–93; Kheir 2014, 179–183; Gordon 2020, 150.
52. Cleveland and Bunton 2018, 539, 540–541.
53. Obama 2020, 986; Haas 2018, 408.
54. Obama 2020, 976–978. The administration was split on calling for Mubarak to step down largely by generation, with younger advisers (Ben Rhodes, Samantha Power, Denis McDonough, and Michael McFaul) calling for a more assertive stance and older advisers (Joe Biden, Hillary Clinton, Robert Gates, and Tom Donilon) more cautious out of fear of what might follow (Gordon 2020, 145).
55. Lynch 2016, 20; Hinnebusch 2014c, 69.
56. Lynch 2016, 22–25, 54.
57. It should be noted that the Egyptian constitution required an election within sixty days of Mubarak's resignation (Gordon 2020, 150).

anathema to other conservative regimes in the region.[58] At least some terrorists began their radicalization under the umbrella of the organization:
Hamas, demonized in the West, began as its Gazan affiliate. The United
States feared that the brotherhood might take Egypt in a policy direction
opposed to that desired by Washington. Nonetheless, domestic rule was to
be given a chance.

The Muslim Brotherhood won the crucial first elections after the fall of
Mubarak, winning 70 percent of the seats in the legislature after the first
ballots in 2011 and the presidency a year later.[59] Under President Morsi,
the brotherhood sought to retain good relations with the United States and
moderated its foreign policy program, even accepting the peace treaty with
Israel.[60] In July of 2012, Obama invited Morsi to visit the White House and
accelerated a $1 billion debt relief package to encourage the new presi-
dent's apparently constructive approach.[61] In a break with the past, according to one analyst, "Obama was prepared to pay the short-term costs of an
unsympathetic Egyptian president in order to achieve long-term consolidation of Egyptian democracy."[62] Yet, as security conditions deteriorated and
the Muslim Brotherhood turned more autocratic, the United States turned
against the new regime.[63] Although the military's extensive economic assets
and position in politics were protected under the new post-Mubarak constitution, defense minister and commander-in-chief General Abdul Fattah el-Sisi
overthrew the government in July 2013 in what has been described as "as
close to a textbook case of a military coup as it is possible to be."[64] A brutal
crackdown soon followed. Over 800 members of the Muslim Brotherhood
were killed while protesting the coup and the organization was banned. Tens
of thousands were imprisoned and Morsi was condemned to death, although
he died while in custody. Mubarak and his sons were acquitted and released.
International NGOs were especially targeted by the military, with some expelled from the country.[65] Sisi was elected president ten months later with an
unlikely 96 percent of the vote, and the military reasserted its control over
the economy.[66] Although no smoking gun has been revealed, given the very

---

58. Mandaville 2019, 186; Cleveland and Bunton 2018, 190–191; Mansfield and Pelham
2019, 426. On the attempted assassination, see Cammett et al. 2018, 99. While Salafists
reject democracy, the Muslim Brotherhood remains committed to popular rule (E. Stein
2021, 126).

59. Tadros 2012; Norton 2019, 148; Mansfield and Pelham 2019, 489; Cleveland and Bunton
2018, 543–546.

60. Kheir 2014, 194–195; Hinnebusch and Shama 2014, 99–101; Mansfield and Pelham
2019, 490–491; E. Stein 2021, 187–190; Gordon 2020, 159.

61. Gordon 2020, 159.

62. Lynch 2016, 147.

63. Kheir 2014, 176; Gordon 2020, 160–161. The United States was also under pressure
from Saudi Arabia and the UAE to break with the regime (see Ghattas 2020, 274–275).

64. Lynch 2016, 155; Mansfield and Pelham 2019, 491–492; Cleveland and Bunton 2018, 547.

65. Herrold 2020; Kheir 2014, 191.

66. Mansfield and Pelham 2019, 518–519, 536; Lynch 2016, 156.

close ties between the Egyptian and US militaries it is unlikely that a coup would have been carried out without at least the tacit consent of the United States.[67] US law prohibits the president from providing foreign aid to any government that takes power in a coup; consequently, the Obama administration simply refused to utter the word, approving new financial support to Sisi of $1.55 billion.[68] As this attempt at domestic rule threatened to take Egypt in a direction that might be against US interests, Washington at the very least accepted, and perhaps encouraged, a return to indirect rule with its traditional allies in the Egyptian military once again in charge. As Obama stated at the United Nations in September 2013 in reference to the new military regime, "the United States will at times work with governments that do not meet, at least in our view, the highest international expectations, but who work with us on our core interests."[69] The verdict of history notwithstanding, democracy was sacrificed for a regime that would more clearly toe the line. After experimenting with democracy, the United States reverted to indirect rule through an allied but authoritarian regime that would comply more fully with its policy preferences.

Egypt is not an isolated example, though it is unique in actually being allowed to experiment with domestic rule. Democracy in the AME threatens to bring to power groups opposed to US policy preferences. The election of the Muslim Brotherhood in Egypt is mirrored in the elections won by the Islamic Salvation Front in Algeria in 1992, Hamas in Gaza in 2007, and Ennahda in Tunisia in 2011.[70] The United States generally opposes domestic rule not out of some ideological allergy to democracy but rather because any democratic regime would likely be anti-American and adopt policies further away from the US ideal point. As long as the governance costs of indirect rule are not too large, the United States will continue to prioritize policy over democracy. However, since both direct and domestic rule are unattractive alternatives to indirect rule, countries in the AME have broad latitude to act opportunistically against the United States. In the end, Washington neither gets democracy nor compliant allies.

---

67. During the fall of Mubarak, the Obama administration was in constant touch with the Egyptian military, aiming to rein in the army and reassure its leaders that their relationship with the United States did not depend on Mubarak (Obama 2020, 988). There is some evidence that Saudi Arabia and the UAE provided financial support for the protests leading up to the coup (E. Stein 2021, 201; Mandaville 2019, 240–241; Lynch 2016, 141).

68. Baker 2013. See also Gordon 2020, 162. The United States did freeze the shipment of military equipment to Egypt after the coup, but released the hold in March 2015 (see Rampton and Mohammed 2015).

69. Quoted in Gordon 2020, 165.

70. Norton 2019, 143–144; Mansfield and Pelham 2019, 413; Cleveland and Bunton 2018, 496.

Resistance

By supporting regional elites, the United States does pull policy in its favored direction, but with distant preferences it has only so much influence over these elite regimes. It is unsuccessful in getting them to go beyond their own ideal policies, leaving Washington dissatisfied with the result. With direct rule nearly impossible and domestic rule problematic, the United States is also faced with considerable opportunism. The net benefits of indirect rule may be quite small. Nonetheless, in supporting elite regimes that govern autocratically and repress their populations, the United States faces considerable resistance from the broader society, including high levels of anti-Americanism and, at an extreme, terrorism.

Anti-Americanism

Not only are states in the AME less democratic and more repressive than average (see chapter 6), but they are also more likely to have public attitudes that are more hostile to the United States (see table 7.1). It follows from indirect rule under an elite regime that the broad public will oppose the United States as the dominant state that sustains a system that suppresses popular will. This opposition manifests as anti-Americanism, defined in chapter 1 as a deep hatred of the United States relative to other countries. Though protests and rebellion are normally repressed by the combination of elite regimes and external support from Washington, the broad public develops and displays attitudes that are hostile to the United States largely for the way it impinges on politics in the Middle East.[71] With indirect rule firmly in place, the road to regime change in Riyadh or Cairo is understood to lead through Washington.

According to Marc Lynch, there are a variety of anti-Americanisms in the AME. In the 1950s and 1960s, when the United States was less engaged in the region, anti-Americanism tended to be "transient and superficial." By the end of the Cold War and as the US presence expanded, Arabs felt increasingly "threatened by US power."[72] One style of anti-Americanism originates with secular-nationalist forces and appears to follow mostly from US policy toward the region. Another style is more religious and cultural, arising from Islamist circles.[73] Systematic polling results are available for only a handful of AME countries and only for the period after 2002. First, and consistent with expectations, the United States is regarded unfavorably by many in the region. In Jordan, Egypt, and the Palestinian territories, large majorities are highly critical of the United States, and even in Lebanon—itself threatened

---

71. Jamal et al. 2015; Makdisi 2002.
72. Lynch 2007, 198–200.
73. Blaydes and Linzer 2012. As competition from secular and religious elites becomes more intense, so does anti-Americanism, suggesting at least some domestic origins.

TABLE 7.1

Favorable attitudes toward the United States relative to China, by country and year

Full question wording: Please tell me if you have a very favorable, somewhat favorable, somewhat unfavorable, or very unfavorable opinion of the United States. Favorable combines "very favorable" and "somewhat favorable."

Country		2002	2003	2004	2005	2006	2007	2008	2009	2010	2011	2012	2013	2014	2015	2017	2019
Egypt	USA					30	21	22	27	17	20	19	16	10			
	PRC					63	65	59	52	52	57	52	45	46			
Jordan	USA	25	1	5	21	15	20	19	25	21	13	12	14	12	14	15	
	PRC				43	49	46	44	50	53	44	47	40	35	33	35	
Kuwait	USA		63				46										
	PRC						52										
Lebanon	USA	36	27		42		47	51	55	52	49	48	47	41	39	34	39
	PRC				66		46	50	53	56	59	59	56	53	52	63	68
Palestinian territories	USA		0				13		15		18		16	30	26		
	PRC						46		43		62		47	61	54		

Source: Pew Research Center 2022.

by Syria—approximately half the population consistently regards the United States unfavorably. In Saudi Arabia, one of the countries most closely tied to the United States, only 9 percent of respondents polled in 2007 approved of US leadership in the region.[74] Second, in all AME countries for which data are available, China is consistently regarded more favorably than the United States. This is true even for Kuwait, where the United States otherwise scores relatively well. The unfavorable view of the United States is not simply the product of anti-foreign sentiment. Rather, there is strong evidence—if limited in scope—of broad-based anti-Americanism. Year-to-year fluctuations suggest that some negative opinions of the United States may be influenced by actions undertaken by Washington, such as the Iraq War. In Saudi Arabia, for instance, confidence in the United States declined from more than 60 percent of respondents in 2000, before the war, to less than 4 percent in 2004.[75] Likewise, confidence in the US president was higher under Obama and Joseph Biden than either George W. Bush or Trump.[76] But the consistently high levels of unfavorable attitudes imply a deep, underlying hostility toward the United States. Importantly, this broad-based hostility appears to derive at least in part from opposition to the overweening power of the United States and its interventions in the Middle East.[77]

High levels of anti-Americanism in US clients like Egypt and Jordan might seem contradictory.[78] How could countries dependent on US aid be so negative about the United States? Why bite the hand that feeds you? But in the larger context of indirect rule, this makes perfect sense. Aid supports the regime, which in turn adopts policies more extreme than the public desires and suppresses dissent. Aid is not necessarily improving the lives of everyday people but, rather, is perpetuating the system of indirect rule. The public accordingly reacts negatively to the dominant state that keeps the regime in power.

Terrorism

Despite the hostility reflected in anti-Americanism, overt resistance to indirect rule is typically rare. In strengthening the allied group, indirect rule renders the regime more capable of suppressing dissent; knowing this, the opposition rarely challenges the regime openly. Anti-regime and anti-American sentiments run high, and there may be numerous "everyday" acts of resistance that occur below the threshold at which the regime responds, but open resistance simply calls forth the power of the regime and its patron

---

74. McFarland 2020, 247.
75. Yetiv 2011, 105.
76. See Wike 2020; Wike et al. 2021.
77. Jamal et al. 2015. Blaydes and Linzer argue that anti-Americanism is primarily a domestic, elite-led phenomenon (2012).
78. Lynch 2016, 208.

against those willing to risk public defiance. In equilibrium, the regime and the dominant state together usually deter active opposition.

Nonetheless, in the AME resistance surfaces in two ways. First, publics mobilize against the regime and the dominant state in demonstrations, protests, and other mass events. When successful, these mass mobilizations become revolutions, as in Iran in 1979, or lead to regime change, as in Algeria, Egypt, Libya, and Yemen during the Arab Spring.[79] In most cases, such public protest movements are eventually suppressed, as in Bahrain in 2011.[80] Mass movements like these are most likely in autocratic systems when there is significant "preference falsification."[81] Knowing that criticism of the regime is likely to be punished harshly, individuals keep their opinions to themselves. Once a "spark" brings people into the street against the regime, like the self-immolation of Mohamed Bouazizi in Tunisia in 2010, everyone quickly realizes that the regime is less popular than supposed and protests grow until the illegitimacy of the regime is revealed for all to see. Since preferences have been hidden or falsified, the regime is equally ignorant and will be surprised by the protests. At that point, it is hard to put the "genie" of public opinion back in the bottle, so to speak, and only severe repression can save the regime. Effective autocrats, as a result, attempt to suppress protests before they escalate.

In the case of Iran, Ayatollah Ruhollah Khomeini successfully linked his critique of the regime and popular opposition to the shah to the prior support of the United States. There were many grievances that led to the revolution, and we should be careful not to exaggerate the role of anti-Americanism. But Khomeini consistently charged "that the shah was selling Iran to foreign, and especially US, interests and that this was tantamount to the destruction of Iran's Islamic identity."[82] One of the goals of the revolution was to end Iran's dependence on the United States, according to Khomeini, and the most searing images during and after the fall of the shah were mobs in the street chanting "death to America."[83] Demonstrations during the Arab Spring did not take such an anti-American stance, perhaps because the United States did not attempt to suppress them and, indeed, encouraged them early on. These demonstrations did, however, reveal to publics and to the United States the depth of resentment toward the elite-based regimes found throughout the region. Although at first supportive, the United States soon reverted to indirect rule, staying its hand as Saudi Arabia brutally crushed demonstrations in Bahrain and as the Egyptian military carried out a coup against the democratically elected Muslim Brotherhood government.

---

79. Yemen is the under-examined case. See Haas 2018, 410.
80. Haas 2018, 410.
81. Kuran 1991; Kuran 1995.
82. Cleveland and Bunton 2018, 359.
83. Cleveland and Bunton 2018, 368.

Second, indirect rule exacerbates the broader problem of terrorism. With society repressed and unable to exert the political influence expected under the counterfactual of domestic rule, those most opposed to the regime who have a comparative advantage in organizing violence—those we call extremists—will take up arms against the regime and the dominant state that supports it. Precisely because they are weak relative to the repressive capacity of the regime and dominant state, however, extremists attack "soft" civilian targets, which defines them as terrorists.[84] In the AME today, terrorism is often associated with religious extremism. Religious sects, however, are no more or less likely to engage in terrorism than members of the opposition, but when they do turn violent they are more likely to be "successful" in actually carrying out attacks and to kill more people because of their prior organizational structures and devoted followers.[85] Given that religion has been the one form of social organization permitted under both Arab monarchies and statist regimes, religious terrorism has come to play a particularly salient role in the resistance to local regimes and indirect rule.

Modern terrorism emerged in the AME in the 1970s, largely in opposition to Israel and its Western supporters. Airline hijackings were initially a prominent form, at least until airport security measures raised new barriers. Islamist terrorism against local regimes began in the late 1970s, with the seizure of the Grand Mosque in Saudi Arabia the most startling example, but expanded as resistance movements developed against the Soviet Union's invasion of Afghanistan. With funding from Arab states and the United States, the mujahedeen deepened their religiosity and gained significant fighting experience. As that war ended, and emboldened by their success, these fighters sought new opportunities to bring about political change, returning home and challenging their local regimes. By the mid-1990s, decades of resistance to these apostate regimes had produced few results and the Islamist movement was beginning to crumble.[86] This was the opening that Osama bin Laden and al-Qaeda seized.

Al-Qaeda is the most prominent organization to have emerged from the Afghan resistance. The "money man" for the mujahedeen, bin Laden worked with Saudi intelligence services and funneled money from Saudi donors to the fighters.[87] When the war wound down, he and associates formed "the base" to broaden the resistance. When Iraq invaded Kuwait in August 1990, bin Ladin met with Saudi officials and offered to organize the resistance to a possible Iraqi attack. Promptly turned down in favor of a US defense of the kingdom and the liberation of Kuwait, and apparently deeply offended by the presence of US troops in the land of the Two Holy Mosques, bin Ladin

---

84. On strategies of terrorism, see Kydd and Walter 2006.
85. Berman 2009.
86. Gerges 2009, 25.
87. Freedman 2009, 346.

turned increasingly against the Saudi regime.[88] Indeed, his rejection by Saudi authorities appears to have been "the principal cause of the turn in bin Laden's worldview, leading him to concentrate on the malevolent international role of the United States and develop a seething contempt for the supine way that the Saudi elite had collaborated."[89] Expelled from Saudi Arabia in 1991, bin Ladin relocated to Sudan. Under increasing international pressure, he left Sudan in 1996 and returned to Afghanistan, where he agreed to help train Taliban forces in return for sanctuary. Al-Qaeda then attacked US embassies in Kenya and Tanzania in 1998, the *USS Cole* during a port visit in Yemen in 2000, and most spectacularly, the United States itself on September 11, 2001.

What distinguished al-Qaeda most clearly from other terrorist groups was its focus on the "far enemy."[90] Under the Salafist ideology that unites many religious extremists, local regimes are apostates who have deviated from the true Islam of Muhammad. Bin Ladin took the cause to a new level, however, connecting local regimes to support from the United States. To challenge the near enemy of the local regimes, he argued, resistance fighters also had to challenge the far enemy that supported them. Indeed, challenging the United States was a prerequisite to any attempt to overthrow the apostates themselves.[91] As Ayman al-Zawahiri, the theorist behind al-Qaeda, wrote in December 2001, "the United States will not allow any Islamic force to reach power in any of the Muslim countries. . ... Therefore . . . we must prepare ourselves for a battle that is not confined to a single region, one that includes the apostate domestic enemy and the Jewish-crusader external enemy," meaning the United States.[92] Bin Ladin declared war against the United States in August 1996 and issued a fatwa in 1998 titled "Declaration of War against the Americans Occupying the Land of the Two Holy Places." Three issues were presented to justify the war: US policy in the Arab-Israeli conflict, US sanctions on Iraq, under which the population was suffering, and US troops stationed in the Gulf. Of these, the last was central.[93] Thus began the global war *of* terror as an outgrowth of US indirect rule in the Persian Gulf.

While targeting the United States was part of this larger strategy of political change, the exact motives behind the attacks on the US homeland remain unclear. Bin Laden and his associates held the conflicting views that the United States was both weak and the main barrier to the advance of

---

88. Yetiv 2011, 69–74.

89. Freedman 2009, 351. See also Gerges 2009, 145–149; Tyler 2009, 379–380; Gause 2010, 139–142.

90. A small number of other terrorist groups also targeted the far enemy, including Egypt's Islamic Group and Islamic Jihad. Gerges 2009, 1; E. Stein 2021, 150.

91. Gerges 2009, 24–26, 131; Freedman 2009, 341.

92. Quoted in Gerges 2009, 32. Zawahiri assumed leadership of al-Qaeda after bin Ladin's death and was himself assassinated by the United States in Afghanistan in 2022.

93. Haddad 2018, 321; Gartenstein-Ross 2018, 366.

Islam.[94] Some analysts suggest that bin Ladin expected that attacks on the United States would lead Washington to withdraw from the region, much as the suicide attack that killed 241 US soldiers in 1983 caused the United States to withdraw from Lebanon or the death of eighteen servicemen in 1993 caused the United States to withdraw from Somalia.[95] Other analysts argue that bin Ladin sought to provoke the United States into retaliating against Muslim countries associated with the attacks, thereby revealing once and for all its truly imperialist nature and weakening public support within the AME.[96] Either way, attacking the United States was expected to undermine support for local regimes supported by Washington.[97] The United States did not withdraw—though it did relocate its troops in the region from Saudi Arabia to Qatar and the UAE in 2003. Rather, it responded by undertaking two costly and ultimately unsuccessful wars in Afghanistan and Iraq that were unpopular both at home and, more importantly, in the region. It also deepened its military presence in the Persian Gulf. The net effect has been to expand US indirect rule in the region while raising the governance costs of that rule and inflaming the passions of those opposed to Washington's interference in their domestic affairs.

The US empire in the Middle East remains incomplete and deeply unsatisfying to Washington. In the AME, the interests of the United States and those of both elites and publics are further apart than in the other regions covered in this volume. Although the governance costs are moderately high, the main instruments of indirect rule—regime guarantees and arms sales—move regimes to their ideal points but provide little leverage in moving policy closer to the US ideal. This means that indirect rule will be too expensive in some cases, with relations defaulting to domestic rule, as in Iran or Syria. It also means that even where indirect rule is pursued, as in Saudi Arabia or any of the Gulf monarchies, the policy results will be limited and disappointing to the United States. Extensive opportunism reduces the benefits of indirect rule even further. With both direct and domestic rule unattractive, regional elites are free to ignore US rules and, in turn, hedge their bets by sustaining systems of crony capitalism and pursuing relations with other great powers, notably Russia for oil and China for trade and investment. In the end, the United States gets little from indirect rule.

Nonetheless, as the United States becomes more deeply engaged in the region, supports unpopular regimes that lack domestic legitimacy, and attempts to pull policy closer to its own interests and further from the interests of the majority of citizens, the opposition in turn becomes progressively

---

94. Freedman 2009, 341.
95. Freedman 2009, 360–363.
96. Freedman 2009, 385; Cleveland and Bunton 2018, 524.
97. On strategies of terrorism, see Kydd and Walter 2006.

more anti-American. Fearing that the policies enacted by an opposition regime even under a democratic majority would be even more hostile to US interests, the United States doubles down on support for its elite allies. Backed by the United States, the elites do not need to compromise with the opposition, and in fact become more repressive, which then deepens the opposition, making the United States even more fearful of any opposition regime.[98]

Even if the opposition is hostile to the United States only because of Washington's support for autocratic and corrupt governments, were the United States to withdraw from the region the question would remain of how to get there from here. How can the United States be confident that the opposition would not be anti-American, that it would respect democracy and liberalize domestic markets, and that it would suppress any remaining terrorists?[99] This question took on greater importance after 9/11, which made all popular opposition to the United States seem more dangerous in the eyes of Americans. It also helped prevent the United States from engaging in the Syrian civil war, since there were a number of hardline Islamist groups fighting the regime.[100] In turn, how could opposition regimes be confident that the United States would not intervene in the future and restore elites to power who promised to protect US interests in exchange for renewed support? The brief Muslim Brotherhood interlude in Egypt suggests the difficulty both sides face in credibly committing to a new path. The question of how to build trust between social forces long suppressed by US-supported regimes and a United States fearful of extremists dominating the region remains open. Until some way forward is identified, indirect rule is likely to remain the default relationship.

98. This is the main argument of Yom 2015, esp. 2.
99. Lynch 2007, 204; Haas 2018, 412–420.
100. Haas 2018, 411.

Conclusion

From ancient empires to European colonies, Russia's near abroad, and the United States today, indirect rule has been a primary mechanism of international hierarchy. Indirect rule exchanges support for an allied group in a subordinate polity for policies favorable to the dominant state. By defending and aiding this allied group, the dominant state increases the ability of its client to enact policies that both prefer in the face of resistance from others—the opposition—in society. By strengthening the client regime at home, both the dominant state and the allied group are made better off while the opposition is rendered worse off than under autonomous or domestic rule.

Supporting allied groups is costly, however. Though the range of instruments available to support indirect rule is potentially large and contingent on local circumstances, the United States has typically relied on regime guarantees, including "boots on the ground" to support its allies, military aid and arms sales that increase the ability of the regime to defend itself, and economic aid and trade concessions that benefit businesses and industries within the allied group. All these forms of support require direct expenditures, the transfer of resources to the allied group, or policy concessions at home that would not otherwise have been made and that constitute the governance costs of indirect rule. The greater its specific assets in the subordinate—strategic military sites, site-specific economic investments, or portfolio investments at risk of default—the more the dominant state cares about the policies adopted by the allied regime and the greater the governance costs it will be willing to bear, all else being equal. The greater the governance costs paid by the dominant state, the stronger the allied group will become and the more favorable the policies it offers to its patron will be, up to a limit of the group's own preferred policies. Although this is difficult to show empirically, the dominant state presumably balances the incremental cost of supporting its ally against the marginal benefits of more favorable policies.

In supporting the allied group, the dominant state creates an opening for the group to act opportunistically, resulting in an additional cost to indirect rule. This is where mutual interests in policy are converted into international hierarchy. In strengthening the allied group, the dominant state enables its client to accept more risk, either by exerting less effort in its own defense or courting financial default and entrapping the patron into internal or external conflicts unrelated to its core interests. To offset these incentives for opportunism, the dominant state renders its support contingent and imposes additional rules that limit the foreign policy and economic autonomy of the subordinate. These additional rules are difficult to enforce directly, as doing so either undermines the policy of the allied group or raises the governance costs of indirect rule. As a result, opportunism is constrained mostly by the relative benefits of domestic or direct rule. The more attractive indirect rule is relative to these alternatives, the greater the scope for allied groups to exploit or entrap the dominant state. Conversely, when the differences between indirect rule and domestic or direct rule are relatively small there is less scope for opportunism.

The United States has employed indirect rule in all three regions covered in this study. In the Caribbean and Central America (CCA) in the late nineteenth and early twentieth centuries, Washington allied with landed elites to drive the commercialization of agriculture. In the CCA, the United States was relatively successful in extracting favorable policies from its subordinates. The interests of Washington and regional elites were well aligned. Precarious elites needed support and the United States could defend their regimes at relatively low cost. Geographic proximity, the overwhelming military capabilities of the United States compared to other countries in the region (except Mexico), and trade dependence concentrated in goods not produced in the United States all meant that Washington could influence politics within its informal empire without significant costs to itself. Yet, these same policy benefits meant that elites could potentially exploit its support and entrap it into internal, intra-elite struggles. As a result, the United States insisted its allies reorient trade and finance from Europe to the United States, yield control over foreign debt and customs receipts, and give up ties to other great powers, eventually producing the so-called "American Lake." These rules, in turn, were enforced by the very real possibility of direct rule by Washington, which was imposed whenever opportunism by the subordinate became too severe, as in the prolonged occupations of Nicaragua, Haiti, and the Dominican Republic. Opposition to indirect rule increased over time, producing a virulent anti-Americanism.

In the Arab Middle East (AME) today, the United States has likewise allied with elites in the Persian Gulf monarchies and statist regimes, helping preserve these fragile, rent-seeking coalitions in return for stable oil supplies.

In the AME, the United States has been less successful in realizing its preferences than elsewhere and is typically dissatisfied with the outcome of indirect rule. Its subordinates adopt the policies they want, which the United States accepts, but they are far from what Washington actually desires. Nonetheless, the United States has shifted policy in its favor, at least if we take the cases of Iran since 1979 or of Syria and Iraq in the 1990s as benchmarks of what would be likely in the absence of indirect rule. Washington has encouraged its regional partners to adopt pro-Western foreign policies, but it has not been able to induce its clients to reform their economies or make real peace with Israel. Nor has it succeeded in bringing all states in the region into its sphere, leaving its hierarchy at best incomplete. Nonetheless, direct rule is prohibitively costly and domestic rule is likely to produce even more unfavorable policies, so the United States perseveres and becomes entrapped in regional conflicts. Because of its role in propping up unpopular autocrats, the United States also becomes the "far enemy"—the target of strident anti-Americanism as well as terrorist attacks intended to drive it from the region.

In Western Europe after World War II, the United States backed conservative parties, creating the so-called Pax Americana of economic integration and collective security. With nearly every country on the continent facing vibrant left parties, some inclined toward the Soviet Union, and Social Democratic parties advocating neutrality in the emerging Cold War, the United States attracted voters to its conservative allies through aid, promises of security, and economic integration that permitted export-led growth. When necessary, it also sought to manipulate electoral outcomes. With policy preferences between Washington and its allied groups closely aligned, the United States was relatively successful in furthering its interests, and the continent consolidated behind economic and political integration and opposition to the Soviet Union. Though aid was generous and security expensive, once its clients were rebuilt politics coalesced into "centrist" regimes that embraced the Pax Americana. Even if observers and policymakers are prepared to recognize hierarchy and indirect rule in the CCA and AME because of the legacies of imperialist interpretations of US interactions with peripheral states, relations with Western Europe are more likely to be understood as those between equally sovereign states cooperating (or not) under international anarchy. Once seen through the lens of indirect rule, however, hierarchy becomes apparent even in Western Europe.

The consequences of indirect rule can be dramatic and raise important normative considerations. In Western Europe, with societies devastated by the war and divided on their future, the United States put its thumb on the political scale, so to speak, and built popular majorities around the foreign policy orientation and policies preferred by Washington. In this case, indirect rule was consistent with democracy, and the authority exercised by the United States was considered broadly legitimate, that is, accepted and possibly supported by a majority of citizens. By the late 1940s, centrist majorities held sway nearly everywhere in the US sphere. Although the Social Democrats were initially aggrieved and shut out of power, by the 1960s even left parties had embraced the Pax Americana, accepting membership in NATO that they had earlier shunned. There was and remains some residual anti-Americanism, sometimes directed at American culture and sometimes at the policies pursued by Washington. France under President Charles de Gaulle attempted to build support for a more independent European foreign policy, which has still largely come to naught. This case demonstrates above all that indirect rule can be regarded as legitimate by subordinate societies if it is consistent with the policy preferences of a majority of citizens.

In the CCA and AME, the consequences of indirect rule were and remain quite different. When allied groups are small elites, indirect rule must be autocratic and repressive. As support for the client pulls policy away from that desired by the majority, the elite must suppress its society. This is precisely the point of indirect rule under elite regimes: to enable a politically weak allied group to enact favorable policies in the face of resistance from the mass of society. In both the CCA and AME, authoritarian governments that abuse the human rights of their citizens have prevailed at least in part because of the support of the United States. Though the United States benefits from more favorable policies, its support for unpopular regimes breeds enduring anti-Americanism. In these cases, US indirect rule is broadly regarded as illegitimate. In the CCA, where repression effectively kept violence to a minimum, opponents of the United States attempted to limit its influence largely through international law, aiming to restrict the rights of intervention claimed by Washington. In the AME, popular protests have been a more common response to indirect rule and resistance has turned more violent, engulfing the United States in a transnational war of terror.

US indirect rule is not found everywhere. There are large swaths of the globe today where the United States does not seek indirect rule, either because it has few specific assets and thus does not care that much about the policies adopted by states, because its policy preferences do not differ that dramatically, or because the governance costs are too high. This is certainly true in its relations with great powers, notably Russia and China, but it also holds for relations with many countries in South America, South Asia, and Africa. Yet, indirect rule is more widespread than commonly recognized and likely to remain an instrument of international hierarchy.

The End of Empire?

It is often averred that the age of empires has passed, never to return. I will not speculate on the distant future, but today direct rule is well-nigh impossible. It is not that conquering a foreign land is too difficult or costly, at least for great powers. The United States defeated Iraq in 2003 in only a matter of weeks, though Russia's difficulties in Ukraine suggest that even middling powers can put up a significant defense if supplied with advanced weapons. Rather, direct rule is thwarted today by the almost unimaginable costs of occupying and ruling a subordinate people on a continuing basis. National sovereignty and self-determination are jealously guarded principles, even for weak elites. The United States expended trillions of dollars and incurred thousands of casualties in the Iraq War, and it withdrew in 2011 without having achieved much of note beyond overthrowing Saddam Hussein. Even in the case of West Germany in chapter 2, where the costs of war were absorbed for other reasons and the society's ability to resist was minimal given the destruction, direct rule was too costly, and the United States sought to transition to indirect rule as soon as possible. In a world where national identities have formed and self-determination is a goal to which many aspire, "alien rule" from some distant metropole is nearly impossible to sustain. Though we understand national identities and how they form only poorly, and therefore predictions about the future should be treated skeptically, nationalism and the desire for self-determination have today largely rendered formal empire and direct rule obsolete.

The same cannot be said for indirect rule. As described in preceding chapters, the United States continues to employ indirect rule because it works to produce policies more favorable to its interests than the strictly domestic alternative. Indirect rule continues in the CCA, although in weakened form, and Washington continues to pursue it in the AME, even reversing a move toward domestic rule in Egypt in 2013. Indirect rule is likely to remain a key instrument of US power into the indefinite future.

Other states also use and will continue to use indirect rule to build and sustain international hierarchies. Russia has long relied on indirect rule to control its subordinates. Under the Soviet Union, Russia implemented indirect rule across its informal empire in Eastern Europe.[1] The region had traditionally looked west rather than east. Before World War II, Eastern European states were integrated into the larger European economy and society, and during the war trade and relations were redirected to focus entirely on Germany.[2] With the costs of war absorbed in defeating the Nazis, Russia elevated small communist parties to power throughout its area of control. Lacking popular support, these allied groups governed autocratically and repressively, more heavy-handedly, it appears, than even US allies in the CCA.[3] The Russians, in turn, supported their communist allies against popular opposition, intervening in East Germany in 1953, Hungary in 1956, and Czechoslovakia in 1968. This system of indirect rule was formalized in

1. Triska 1986; Lake 1997.
2. Hirschman 1980. On Germany's empire in Eastern Europe, see Mazower 2008; Hollander 2017.
3. Triska 1986.

the so-called Brezhnev Doctrine, similar in spirit to the Roosevelt Corollary, which prohibited communist countries from escaping Russian control. Once President Mikhail Gorbachev abandoned the doctrine and refused to intervene against a wave of protests in Eastern Europe in 1989, indirect rule unraveled almost overnight. Without Russian support, the Eastern European communist parties could not survive on their own.

Similarly, President Vladimir Putin has pursued a mix of direct and, more generally, indirect rule in the former Soviet republics. All the Warsaw Pact countries escaped the Russian sphere and were quickly embraced by the West through enlargements to NATO and the European Union.[4] The Baltic republics, previously part of the Soviet Union itself, also bolted to the West and were similarly integrated into Western institutions. Other than the occasional rattling of sabers toward the latter, Russia has done little to challenge these moves. However, Russia has transformed the former Soviet republics of Central Asia and Belarus into an informal empire, ruled indirectly from Moscow.[5] Though these states do clash with Russia on some issues, and several allowed US bases on their territories during the Afghan War, their autocratic leaders—often officials under the previous Soviet regimes—know they are deeply dependent on Russian support and have oriented their economies and foreign policies toward Moscow. Russia intervened in Belarus in 2020 to prop up the regime of Alexander Lukashenko and in Kazakhstan in 2022, when the relatively new leader, Kassym-Jomart Tokayev, faced broad unrest. In the Caucasus, relations are more complicated, with ethnic and territorial conflicts dividing the former Soviet republics. Here, Russia has chosen sides in some cases and attempted to mediate disputes in others. In those post-Soviet states that have sought support from the West, like Georgia, Moscow has annexed Russian-speaking regions (Abkhazia and South Ossetia) in now rare cases of direct rule. In Ukraine, Russia ruled indirectly through Viktor Yanukovych, who fled to Moscow after massive protests supporting closer ties to the European Union. Russia subsequently attempted to reassert control, first by annexing Crimea in 2014 and supporting an insurgency in the Donbas shortly thereafter, and then invading the country in 2022. Whether President Vladimir Putin's aim is direct rule over the entirety of Ukraine or only to emplace a new Russian puppet in Kyiv under indirect rule remains unclear, and the fate of Ukraine is as of this writing undecided. But the attempt to subordinate Ukraine affirms the continuing relevance of international hierarchy. As but one indicator of continuing indirect rule, Belarus voted against UN General Assembly Resolution ES-11/1 (adopted March 2, 2022) condemning Russia's invasion of Ukraine—one of only five states (including Russia itself) to do so. The other Russian clients of Armenia, Kazakhstan, Kyrgyzstan, and Tajikistan abstained, and Azerbaijan, Turkmenistan, and Uzbekistan did

---

4. Albania is a member of NATO but not the EU.
5. Hancock 2001.

not vote. Of the former Soviet republics, only Georgia, Moldova, and—not surprisingly—Ukraine voted for the resolution. If anything, in its efforts to reestablish the Russian empire and promote its status as a great power, Russia under President Putin is likely to be ever more reliant on indirect rule. Tensions between the United States and Russia are likely to arise over where to draw the boundary between the Western sphere and the reclaimed Russian sphere of influence. Most Cold War crises revolved precisely around this question.[6] The United States and others have already ceded Central Asia and the Caucasus to Russia, but Ukraine is likely to remain a source of contention for the near future.

Looking forward, China is likely to adopt indirect rule as it expands abroad. To be clear, China today does not yet have extensive international hierarchies. We might consider it similar to the United States in the 1890s, before the Spanish-American War. But China is already on the road to international hierarchy and likely indirect rule. As but one emerging example, China recently renegotiated basing rights in the Solomon Islands in exchange for backing the increasingly unpopular regime of Manasseh Sogavare.[7] If it is difficult for Americans to think of themselves as an imperialist country, this will be even more disturbing for the Chinese, who both experienced domination by Western powers in the nineteenth and early twentieth centuries and positioned themselves as the vanguard of the anti-imperialist bloc of non-aligned states during the Cold War. But China will almost inevitably be drawn into creating international hierarchies in the future.

If the theory here is at all correct, it is almost certain that China will develop more intense interests in the policies of other countries as it expands abroad. China is greatly increasing its foreign investments through the Belt-and-Road Initiative (BRI), especially site-specific investments in infrastructure, energy, mining and metals, utilities, real estate, and finance (portfolio investment). Although many have focused on China's territorial and maritime disputes and President Xi Jinping's nationalist rhetoric, in my view the more consequential part of China's emerging grand strategy is the BRI.[8] Introduced by President Xi in 2013, the initiative is officially intended to strengthen policy coordination, expand infrastructure, open trade and finance, and connect peoples across diverse countries. As of February 2021, China had signed memorandums of understanding with 140 countries and invested roughly $4 trillion through the initiative.[9] Most of the funding comes from China's three government policy banks, large state-owned banks, and sovereign wealth funds, with 59 percent of the plan's projects owned

---

6. Lake 2018a.
7. Cave 2022.
8. Cavanna 2019; Custer et al. 2021.
9. The exact amount of BRI investment is difficult to calculate. Not all investments are announced or explicitly included as part of the BRI (see Baruzzi 2021).

by government entities, 26 percent by private firms, and the remainder by public-private ventures.[10] The largest recipients of BRI investments between 2005 and 2017 were Pakistan, Indonesia, Malaysia, Saudi Arabia, Ethiopia, Bangladesh, Iran, Kenya, Vietnam, and Egypt.[11]

Many BRI investments are in politically or financially unstable countries with poor credit ratings.[12] China's investments, in other words, are in sectors and often in countries that Western firms avoid because they are too risky and, in turn, too costly to govern indirectly. As China's investments expand, Beijing will be increasingly drawn into the politics of host countries to "stabilize" regimes that are willing to protect its investments or ensure the repayment of outstanding debts. At present, approximately $369.5 billion worth of these investments are described as troubled, meaning either that the collateral value of the investment is below its liabilities or loans are not performing.[13] To date, China has offset the risk inherent in site-specific investments in unstable countries by providing state-backed financing in one form or another; that is, the government is essentially insuring investments against foreign risk. If the investments fail, the government will—or is expected to—cover the loss. The Chinese government, however, cannot be indifferent to the actions of host governments that affect these investments. Even if Beijing covers the immediate loss, expropriation or default still transfers wealth from China to the host country, and this is money that might have been spent by the Chinese government or its citizens. While China's workers have so far been willing to forgo present consumption for greater growth in the future, how long they will accept deferring consumption to cover investments in foreign lands that have turned bad is unknown. Eventually, the government will have to act to protect these investments and ensure the loans are repaid.

Where investments in site-specific assets lead, international hierarchy and indirect rule are likely to follow. As China's overseas investments grow, so will its interests, and the likelihood of resorting to indirect rule. China decries imperialism but there is no reason to expect that it will respond differently to the challenges of rule than other great powers have in the past. Eschewing direct rule—"imperialism"—does not mean Beijing will not rely on indirect rule to protect its interests.

To the extent that China pursues indirect rule, the question becomes whether it will compete with the United States. The answer here is mixed. It is fortunate—at least for the purpose of minimizing conflict—that China is currently investing in countries that are primarily outside the traditional US spheres of influence and where US investments in site-specific assets have been relatively small. The fact that the Chinese are investing in places

---

10. Lee 2020.
11. OECD 2018, 21.
12. See Shi 2015.
13. OECD 2018, 29–30.

where Western firms fear to tread reduces the potential for conflict between Washington and Beijing. One possible source of contention, however, is that China is targeting energy and the Middle East, both a sector and region where the United States already has considerable investments and a sphere of influence. The "pivot" to Asia by the United States may also start to encroach on areas where China is already building out its sphere through the BRI. The greater the overlap in regions where both superpowers have site-specific investments, the greater the potential rivalry. The good news, if you will, is that competition between the United States and China will not necessarily be global in nature and could, if handled properly, be limited to particular areas, as it is at present to the Middle East. The bad news is that great power competitions have historically more often ended badly than well. Competition can be eased in overlapping regions, however, if the dominant states keep markets open rather than attempting to close them off to potential rivals.[14] Leaders in both Washington and Beijing would do well to anticipate the problem of rival hierarchies and begin addressing the question of how to manage relations between spheres now before the competition grows more intense. Conflict between the two twenty-first-century superpowers is not inevitable, but relations must be handled carefully by both sides with due regard for the difficulties of constructing spheres of influence through indirect rule.

Implications for International Relations Theory

Indirect rule both as a concept and practice challenges existing theories of international politics. Although the international system is anarchic, relations between states within that system take many forms, including hierarchies sustained by indirect or even direct rule. Moreover, hierarchy does not arise just between great powers and small powers, but can exist between large and powerful countries, as shown by the case of Western Europe after the war. International politics is a far more complex tapestry than is often acknowledged.

Scholars and especially policymakers have also misinterpreted the case of postwar Western Europe. Europe after 1945 may not have been a unique constellation of interests and capabilities, but it was a rare combination. As already noted, after a period of ferment, West European societies enjoyed interests that were, in general, closely aligned with those of the United States, a situation that allowed popular majorities to enact policies through democratic means that were supported by and favorable to the United States. This coincidence of interests allowed leaders and their populations to believe they

---

14. Lake 2017; Lake 2018a.

were acting autonomously and voluntarily even while the United States influenced their domestic political coalitions behind the façade of sovereignty and equality. In failing to see the role of hierarchy and indirect rule, scholars of international relations have interpreted the United States as a benevolent hegemon pushing on an open door to lead Western Europeans away from neutrality toward a Pax Americana that was facilitated by international institutions and enforced by reciprocity.[15] This view of "cooperation under anarchy" has become a mainstream position in international relations.[16] Yet, the United States played an influential role in tipping politics and policy within Western European societies in directions it desired. Behind the façade, the United States engaged in an active strategy of political manipulation that brought to the fore groups that favored its interests.

If scholars fail to understand indirect rule, they cannot properly assess the extent and effects of anarchy within the international system. When effective, international hierarchy through indirect rule is hidden from view and can easily be misinterpreted as cooperation between fully and effectively sovereign states. Once in power, governments with preferences more aligned with those of the dominant state look like they are adopting policies voluntarily and of their own accord. There is no direct coercion, no quid pro quos, no orders given or followed. Behind the scenes, the balance of power is shaped within the state before the policy-making stage. This is similar to second face of power arguments in which agendas are structured to bring about policies desired by the powerful.[17] In indirect rule, however, the preferences of groups within the subordinate are exploited by the dominant state to produce policies it favors. The actors—the dominant state, the allied group, and even the opposition—have agency and are understood to make choices, even if incentives are structured for the opposition in ways that are biased against their interests. Key, though, is that the dominant state has manipulated the domestic politics of its client to produce an outcome it prefers. This problem of observational equivalence suggests that analysts may be undercounting dyadic relationships that are hierarchical in nature and overcounting those supposedly based on anarchy. Relations between states may be more commonly based on hierarchy than is often recognized.

In turn, theorists have accepted a relatively benign view in which anarchy is not the inhibiting factor to better relations between states that it is sometimes assumed to be. Against the relatively pessimistic view of international relations held by neorealists and others, neoliberal institutionalists have developed a fairly optimistic view of anarchy as a constraint but not a barrier

---

15. Gilpin 1975; Gilpin 1977; Krasner 1976; Snidal 1985.

16. See the school of neoliberal institutionalism, esp. Keohane 1984; Oye 1985; A. Stein 1990; Ikenberry 2001.

17. Bachrach and Baratz 1962; Lukes 1977. See also James and Lake 1989.

to effective cooperation.[18] If Western Europe in the early years of the Pax Americana was a set of hierarchies rather than anarchies, however, what is taken as "voluntary" in a benign interpretation of anarchy must be reconsidered. Theorists who maintain that anarchy is a fundamental and invariant determinant of international relations are equally misled. In focusing on great power relations in which the potential for opportunism prevents investments in specific assets, these theorists fail to see how hierarchy emerges to solve problems that would otherwise thwart international cooperation.[19] When the gains from policy and the specific assets at risk are sufficiently large, dominant states will be willing to pay the costs of acquiring authority over other states, and groups within those states can be induced to yield a degree of their effective sovereignty in return. Anarchy is not just what states "make of it," but is a choice by states and groups within states.[20]

If the theory and evidence in this study are valid, four avenues for further research follow. While this book has, I hope, pushed research on international hierarchy forward and developed the mechanism of indirect rule within this approach, the research agenda is far from complete. Indeed, reflecting on what I have attempted here only highlights what remains to be done. I do not anticipate that any of the theoretical results nor empirics discussed above are likely to be significantly altered with additional work, but there are many ways in which the theory can be extended to produce additional insights.

First, in focusing on the governance costs of indirect rule, I have bracketed the costs and benefits of conducting "diplomacy" between countries under domestic rule. The fact that a potentially subordinate state is autonomous does not negate efforts by others to influence its policies. Rather than manipulating the constellation of groups within the society, another state may use coercion and inducements as one-offs—bargains made in the "spot market" of world politics. In such cases, there is no long-term relationship but merely a series of specific deals made under threats or rewards. Although we do not have a systematic accounting of the costs of diplomacy relative to indirect rule in the long run, the case of Britain is noteworthy in that it was both governed under domestic rule and a target of coercive pressure by the United States. Washington repeatedly used its financial advantage to press London to abandon imperial preferences and, especially, to withdraw from Egypt during the Suez Crisis. When Britain deviated from US interests, Washington forced it into compliance. Diplomacy is at the heart of traditional international relations theory and we have many useful approaches to understand its costs and benefits, even if comparing across instruments

---

18. For neorealist perspectives, see Waltz 1979; Mearsheimer 2001.

19. Waltz (1979) assumes states will never become dependent on others or "functionally differentiated."

20. Wendt 1992.

like economic sanctions and military threats remains challenging. Although I have concentrated on indirect rule here, theorizing compliance under domestic and indirect rule and the costs of each would benefit from more concentrated examination.

Second, the interests of dominant states can be disaggregated. Throughout, I have assumed that any dominant state has sufficiently well-established internal decision-making mechanisms that it would pursue consistent interests in world affairs, or that in pursuing its interests we can in practice treat the dominant state as if politics really did stop at the water's edge. I think this is a reasonable assumption given the cases examined here but it masks the possibility of transnational alliances between groups within the subordinate and dominant states. Even in the simple case of interests depicted in figure 1.1 and used throughout the book as a baseline, it is possible that some groups within the dominant state might be more or less closely aligned with the allied group in the subordinate or even—in extreme cases—with the opposition. Depending on the structure of power within the dominant state, this might have important implications for the mode of international hierarchy. Although this approach has been sidestepped here because such disaggregation did not appear necessary to understand the cases chosen, I suspect it will be a useful direction for further theorizing.

Third, other great powers and the effect of "imperial" competition should be integrated into the theory developed here. I have already touched on the importance of competition between the United States and Russia during the Cold War and possible competition between the United States and China in the future. Throughout and for simplicity, I have focused the theory and empirics in this book on dyadic relations between a single dominant and single subordinate state. This simplification was useful in highlighting the core logic of indirect rule. In working through the cases, I did not find that the presence of other great powers greatly challenged the theory or its predictions, though the potential for external competition showed up consistently in the rules imposed by the United States to safeguard indirect rule from opportunism by subordinates. When there are bipolar structures in which two potentially dominant states have diametrically opposed interests more extreme than groups within the subordinate society, we might expect a "bidding war" in which the resources transferred by one dominant state to group A are offset by resources transferred by the second to group B. It follows that the state with the larger specific assets or lower governance costs could be expected to "win" and pull policy in its preferred direction, albeit at higher cost and with less effect than with the involvement of a single state. This was likely the case in the Cold War between the United States and the Soviet Union in Europe, which resulted in two exclusive spheres of influence. Conversely, if both dominant states have closely aligned interests, we might expect a "peaceful transfer" in which one defers to the other. This likely occurred in the CCA, with Britain famously yielding to the United States around the turn of the century.[21] Nonetheless, in each case the United States placed a high priority on constructing an exclusive sphere of influence and, in essence, creating a monopoly over relations with its subordinates. This suggests indirect rule is possible and chosen in the "shadow" of other potential dominant states and that "external" powers should be incorporated more fully into the theory.

Finally, exploring the interests and strategies of resistance by subordinate states in more detail could be fruitful. As a study on US foreign policy written by a US scholar drawing largely on sources written by other US scholars, I have almost certainly created a limited and perhaps distorted depiction of the experiences and choices by groups within subordinate societies. I have been careful to check my understandings with regional experts and do not believe the narratives constructed here are incorrect, but they likely lack nuance—especially in terms of the political opposition within the subordinates. Here, as elsewhere, history is written by the victors, in this case the United States and its client regimes. Fleshing out subaltern perspectives in these international hierarchies will undoubtedly enrich our understanding. This will be especially important, I suspect, for strategies of resistance. Stepping beyond the dyadic theory here, cross-regional strategies of resistance are likely underdeveloped in my accounts. We see some inklings of such a strategy in the movement across Latin America to outlaw intervention into domestic politics (see chapter 3). A similar strategy was apparent in the non-aligned movement during the Cold War and in the reliance on multilateralism in Europe's efforts to constrain the United States after World War II. And of course, anti-American terrorism originating in the AME has gone global. Narratives of hierarchy should be written both from "above" and "below," and we have much to do on the latter. Although I hope to have made some progress in understanding indirect rule in this volume, there is much more to be done. If this book stimulates and perhaps provokes others to delve deeper, I will consider it a success.

Implications for Policy

If indirect rule is likely to remain a primary mode of international hierarchy, it is appropriate to consider its normative and policy implications. While indirect rule pulls policy toward that desired by the dominant state, it does so by suppressing the opposition within the subordinate society. As we saw in the theory and case studies, when the allied group is small, indirect rule reinforces authoritarian government and is associated with greater human rights abuses. Repression is not just an unintended by-product of but integral

---

21. Rock 1989; Lobell 2003; Schake 2017.

to indirect rule. In many of the countries today where the United States is most likely to seek international hierarchies, indirect rule is likely to take the form of elite-based regimes that must suppress the majority of their people. Resistance should be expected.

Support by the United States for such regimes also offends the values and principles of many Americans, although of course this offence pales in comparison to the harm done to the opposition in its subordinates. For normative and practical reasons, as explained in the introduction, Americans want to promote democracy abroad but frequently find themselves allied with autocratic regimes and sometimes odious dictators. As repression is integral to indirect rule, though variable in its extent, there will always be an unresolvable tension between US interests and the values of liberal democracy many Americans hold dear. Though the United States might strive to be the proverbial beacon on the hill for oppressed peoples everywhere, since indirect rule is an equilibrium exchange between allied groups who want support and a great power like the United States that wants more favorable policies, repression cannot simply be wished away. Nonetheless, the theory and cases of indirect rule examined here suggest three considerations that may slow the rush toward indirect rule and soften the tension even if they do not mitigate it entirely.

First, interests are rarely objective and clear; they should be actively contested, debated, and rigorously examined on an ongoing basis in any relationship of indirect rule. The divergence of interests between any dominant and subordinate state is a key determinant of indirect rule and policy. It is the distance between the political preferences of the states that matters, but this requires an assessment of the substance of those preferences and where they do or do not overlap. In each case, as explained in the final section of chapter 1, I have attempted to identify the interests of the various parties as understood by the United States and others at the time. This proves to be a difficult exercise as interests are seldom clearly formulated or stated. Even in retrospect, it is impossible to say with certainty what the interests of the United States were in each region. For actors at the time, this was likely even less clear—though contemporary proponents of different courses of action never admit this. Though I have treated interests as an independent variable, meaning they are exogenous and taken as given for purposes of exploring the theory, they are in practice subjective, susceptible to different frames and biases, and open to interpretation. In any current or future relationship of indirect rule, it is well worth examining and debating the interests of the United States in a particular region or country. As discussed in the conclusion to chapter 6, it is an open question in my mind whether US hierarchy in the AME is actually necessary. Although it is often taken as an article of faith that the United States has strong interests in the AME that must be protected, it is not obvious that those interests require US indirect rule given the governance costs and opportunism by regional partners. The fact that analysts differ in their views illustrates the difficulty of identifying interests. More important, it is precisely for this reason that it is worth debating the assumed interests of the United States before continuing to pursue indirect rule in the AME. The same holds for other regions and other cases of indirect rule. Though this is not necessarily a plea for isolationism nor for a limited offshore balancing role, a clear-eyed view of US interests may suggest there is less at stake in various countries around the world than we sometimes suppose.[22]

Second, the United States, at least, tends to exaggerate differences with or to "other" the opposition in subordinate countries, which reinforces the belief that the failure to support an allied group will bring a hostile alternative to power and result in a less favorable policy. The extent of bias against opposition groups is difficult to measure and I have thus not emphasized it in the cases, but it is hard to dispute that there is some bias at play in each. In the CCA, local elites were largely white and of Spanish descent while the opposition was mostly people of indigenous or African heritage. Given the prevailing racism of many Americans at this time, regime opponents were easily portrayed as less "civilized," alien, and incapable of self-rule. This created an affinity with Spanish elites who were more "familiar" and thus assumed to hold interests more closely aligned with the United States. In Western Europe, left parties were depicted as "communists" opposed to nearly everything the United States claimed to stand for. In the era of McCarthyism and the persecution of supposed communists in the State Department who were accused of purposely "losing" China, the United States would have been hard pressed to make the case for cooperation with any groups on the European left. In the AME, the Arab Street, as former Secretary of State Madeleine Albright has suggested, is "scary" and often assumed to be comprised of fanatic Islamists out to destroy the West.

"Othering" an opposition group may be a natural psychological trait.[23] To validate support for one group, we often portray any opponent as more extreme that it actually is. There are real conflicts of interest between the dominant state and the opposition in client regimes; indirect rule would be unnecessary and impossible to sustain without them. But like conflicts of interest between states, differences between the dominant state and an opposition within a subordinate are not objective and easily identified but subjective and open to debate. Before entering into or continuing a relationship of indirect rule, it is worth reflecting on whether the dominant state's differences with any opposition are as large as assumed or whether they are, at least in part, imagined. Again, a more clear-eyed understanding of US

---

22. On policies of restraint, see Posen 2014. For additional views, see the publications and scholars associated with the Quincy Institute for Responsible Statecraft at https://quincyinst. org.

23. Haidt 2012; Freeman, Kim, and Lake 2022.

interests and how they stand relative to any possible subordinate may render the United States more cautious in embracing indirect rule.

Finally, anti-Americanism is a long-term response to indirect rule, a festering of resentments large and small against the system of sometimes oppressive rule supported by the United States. Politicians—and especially US politicians responding to constant cycles of elections—typically focus on the short term, as does the public. Are our partners doing what we want, accepting US exports, helping deter Russia or other aggressors, and keeping oil flowing at reasonable prices? Seldom do leaders or the mass public focus on or want to admit the fact that anti-Americanism is the almost inevitable product of Washington's alliances with elite regimes that oppress their peoples. Developing over time and growing in the interstices of power, anti-Americanism is sufficiently divorced from any individual action of the United States or its allies that it appears inexplicable, a consequence without cause. After 9/11, Americans who pointed out our complicity in stoking terrorism against the "far enemy" were themselves charged with being anti-American! It seemed almost beyond comprehension that violence against the United States might be a response to our role and actions in the AME. Yet, if we understand indirect rule and take a longer-range view, we can see that a backlash to US support for small elites is almost inevitable.

The long-term consequences of indirect rule are especially acute when opposition groups come to power after decades of suppression by a US-supported regime. This can happen in out-of-equilibrium events, when either the allied regime or the United States itself miscalculates and does not respond effectively to unrest. This is especially likely in highly authoritarian systems where, with widespread preference falsification, both the allied group and the dominant state may be caught by surprise by the extent of popular opposition.[24] Castro's revolution in Cuba, the Sandinista revolution in Nicaragua, and the Bolivarian revolution in Venezuela, for instance, are all cases where the opposition overthrew a corrupt, decaying, but until the fall seemingly stable allied regime supported by the United States. The opposition may also come to power if US interests change and Washington rolls back its support for its ally, or some exogenous change in the world alters the governance costs of rule. The end of the Cold War and the rise of China have shuffled threat perceptions around the world, leading the United States to pivot toward Asia—or to at least try to redirect its focus and relocate its bases. Globally integrated supply chains have now fundamentally altered the pattern of specific assets in international economic relations. As conditions change, indirect rule is modified and sometimes abandoned entirely. Indeed, when indirect rule is eased and a new equilibrium sought, a formerly suppressed opposition may replace an elite regime. We would typically call

---

24. On preference falsification and surprises, see Kuran 1991; Kuran 1995.

this democratization and encourage it. Nonetheless, if and when the opposition comes to power, it will be more stridently anti-American and less willing to cooperate with Washington than if indirect rule had not been adopted in the first place. The opposition may also justifiably fear that the United States will intervene in an attempt to restore the allied group to its former position of dominance, as in Egypt. Opposition-dominated governments may also play upon lingering anti-Americanism to consolidate their own coalitions and authority, as has happened again and again in the CCA. This makes cooperation with the United States more difficult than otherwise even when interests are or become more closely aligned. At any moment in time, indirect rule may appear to be a reasonable choice compared to the alternatives of domestic or direct rule, but unanticipated events can impose hidden costs or "blowback" on the dominant state that render cooperation more difficult in the future.[25] This is a cost of indirect rule that is only realized at some future date, and thus too easily ignored by current decision-makers. Yet, the costs of future antagonism and missed opportunities for cooperation can be substantial. If properly anticipated, these long-run effects will allow us to more accurately assess the governance costs of indirect rule in any given case.

Indirect rule is not going away. A mode of international hierarchy that has been with us since the dawn of organized polities is likely to remain robust and to endure into the future. I see no circumstance under which the United States, Russia, China, and possibly other states would abandon the practice entirely. Nonetheless, a more reasoned and nuanced view of US interests and of the possible costs of unanticipated events may give the United States pause in rushing to support small elite regimes that provide favorable policies in the short run but create anti-American backlashes in the longer term.

---

25. On blowback more generally, see Johnson 2000.

Acknowledgments

A graduate student once remarked that this book is the final installment of my trilogy on international hierarchy. I hope he is correct. *Entangling Relations: US Foreign Policy in Its Century* (1999) proposed a theory of international hierarchy. That book had a disappointing start, dropping like a small pebble into a large pond. As I complained about this fact one evening, an astute colleague pointed out that I had written a theory about something that few believe exists. That remark (along with the Iraq War) spurred my second installment, *Hierarchy in International Relations* (2009), which laid a broader theoretical foundation and focused on the consequences of hierarchy for international politics. We might still not be able to "see" hierarchy, but we now had some evidence that it was real and important. As several critics pointed out, however, that volume relied too heavily on a naïve social contract theory. Challenged by that critique but consistent with the predictions of the first and second books, this third volume aims to explain the mechanism of international hierarchy and focuses more on the distributional implications of rule. I think I am done. But if the past is any predictor of the future, some reader will undoubtedly point out flaws in this work that will set me on a new course.

As this chronology suggests, I have been thinking about international hierarchy for a long time. My very first book, *Power, Protection, and Free Trade: The International Sources of US Commercial Strategy* (1988), pursued then current lines of inquiry about US hegemony, but I subsequently came to believe that this was not an especially profitable direction. One day at UCLA's Tuesday Political Economy Lunch group, we read some of Oliver Williamson's work on economic organizations, which proved to be a career-altering experience. The postdoctoral education I received at UCLA has guided virtually all of my subsequent work, and the intellectual debts I owe to the regular participants in that discussion group—Jack Hirshleifer, Ron Rogowski, Art Stein, the late Michael Wallerstein, and others—are virtually immeasurable. In particular, Jeff Frieden, a founder of the lunch group, has continued to be an unpersuaded critic as well as a wise counselor, collaborator, and dear friend. Although he bears none of the responsibility for my errors, Jeff's intellectual "fingerprints" are all over this volume from that initial push toward contract theory, my reliance on open economy politics, and so much more.

As this volume builds on the others, I have also incurred an enormous number of other debts. Many have contributed extended critiques, made passing but meaningful comments, or asked insightful questions at various talks or lunchtime conversations over the years. I cannot thank everyone. Three colleagues and—I am glad to say—friends deserve special recognition. As I once wrote to Peter Katzenstein, we have likely never agreed on anything. From my first graduate seminar to my dissertation and beyond, we have seen the world through different lenses. Though he has been a fierce critic, challenging my natural economism, Peter has been both extraordinarily generous with his time and an inspiration. Peter Gourevitch has lived inside my head for more than twenty-five years. Since our days editing *International Organization*, when we spent hours talking about and debating various submissions, Peter's view of the world has been absorbed into my own. I cannot read anything without immediately thinking, "Peter would say . . ." I know he wants me to unpack the domestic politics of not only the subordinate state, as here, but the dominant state as well, but he will have to settle for one half of the second image reversed. Finally, much of what I know about international hierarchy comes from Miles Kahler through our collaborations and, especially, co-taught classes. In particular, Miles has prodded me to think more deeply about authority and legitimacy, which I too often elided. This book is a small step, I hope, toward his more nuanced position.

For this volume, I am especially indebted to the late Robert Powell, a longtime friend and collaborator, who patiently corrected my various attempts at the model now confined to boxes in chapter 1; his humor and good nature were undoubtedly strained but his frustration with my inability to absorb his suggestions was never evident. He is greatly missed. I am also indebted to Jeff Frieden, Peter Gourevitch, Susan Hyde, Miles Kahler, Dorothy Kronick, Christina Schneider, and Sean Yom for participating in a book workshop in February 2022, as well as Bianca Freeman and Wendy Wagner who served as rapporteurs at that meeting. That one day of discussions on the book proved remarkably helpful. Christina Schneider went far beyond the obligations of collegiality to participate in a second mini-conference on the book in October 2022, along with Steph Haggard and Branislav Slantchev, and to provide additional readings when I lost confidence in my writing. I also received excellent comments and suggestions from Paul Drake, Sean Ingham, Michael Joseph, Melissa Lee, Brandon Merrell, Lauren Prather, and Wendy

Wong. Thanks also to Austin Beacham, Alex Lange, and Wendy Wagner for research assistance.

Three cohorts of graduate students at the University of California, San Diego endured early drafts of this manuscript. I am especially grateful to the students in POLI 248 in 2018, who did me the honor of ripping apart the first draft. Knowing that cutting and pasting is an irresistible temptation, I went home after the seminar and deleted every copy of the manuscript from every electronic device I could find and started over again from scratch. The second draft was vetted by the 2020 cohort; although it did not emerge unscathed, I did not feel compelled to start over again. The penultimate draft was read by Emilie Hafner-Burton's working group on international law and regulation. I also benefited from the opportunity to present parts of this book at several universities, including the University of California, Berkeley; University of California, Santa Barbara; University of Houston; Nankai University; Ohio State University; Texas A&M University; Tsinghua University; and Yale University. Though such opportunities were limited during the pandemic, I have always found these seminars to be extremely fruitful and I thank the participants in each. Finally, the comments and suggestions of two reviewers for Cornell University Press were critical in the final stages of revision. Jackie Teoh expertly handled the final stages of acquisition. Mary Kate Murphy adeptly managed the production process. Marlyn Miller copyedited the text with great skill. Kate Mertes prepared the index. My thanks to all, and my apologies to anyone I may have overlooked.

As always, my greatest debt is to my family. I am so proud of the men and fathers my sons, Brenden and Dylan, have become. They had the good fortune and, I must say, wisdom to marry amazingly strong, talented, and remarkable women, Tammy Kwan and Amily He, who have become much loved and integral parts of my life. This book is dedicated to them. With the births of Mirah, Logan, and Luna, my heart grew larger and my love deeper than I ever imagined possible; where it is common in acknowledgments to thank and simultaneously complain about the disruptions of children, I am fortunate to have been distracted during the pandemic and the writing of this book by wonderful grandbabies. At the base of all is my wife, Wendy, who has supported me from the beginning. Readers see only the words on a page. Behind each one is the world she has created for me with the freedom to think and write. None of this would be possible without her.

References

Abootalebi, Ali R. 2018. "What Went Wrong in Iraq?" In Lesch and Haas 2018, 274–288.

Acharya, Amitav. 2014. *The End of American World Order*. Cambridge, UK: Polity.

Adler, Emanuel, and Michael Barnett. 1998. *Security Communities*. New York: Cambridge University Press.

Adonis, Andrew. 2020. *Ernest Bevin: Labour's Churchill*. London: Biteback Publishing.

Allawi, Ali A. 2007. *The Occupation of Iraq: Winning the War, Losing the Peace*. New Haven, CT: Yale University Press.

Allen, Michael A., Michael E. Flynn, and Carla Martinez Machain. 2022. "US Global Military Deployments, 1950–2020." *Conflict Management and Peace Science* 39 (3): 351–370.

Allen, Michael A., Michael E. Flynn, and Julie VanDusky-Allen. 2017. "Regions of Hierarchy and Security: US Troop Deployments, Spatial Relations, and Defense Burdens." *International Interactions* 43 (3): 397–423.

Ambrose, Stephen E. 1990. *Eisenhower: Soldier and President*. New York: Simon and Schuster.

Arias, Luz Marina. 2011. "Analytic Narratives: The Method." In *International Encyclopedia of Political Science*, edited by Bertrand Badie, Dirk Berg-Schlosser, and Leonardo Morlino, 71–72. Thousand Oaks, CA: Sage.

Ashley, Percy. 1920. *Modern Tariff History: Germany—United States—France*. 3rd ed. New York: Dutton.

Ayala, César J., and Rafael Bernabé. 2007. *Puerto Rico in the American Century: A History since 1898*. Chapel Hill: University of North Carolina Press.

Ayubi, Nazih N. 1996. *Over-stating the Arab State: Politics and Society in the Middle East*. New York: I. B. Tauris.

Azpuru, Dinorah, and Dexter Boniface. 2015. "Individual-Level Determinants of Anti-Americanism in Contemporary Latin America." *Latin American Research Review* 50 (3): 111–134.

Bachrach, Peter, and Morton S. Baratz. 1962. "The Two Faces of Power." *American Political Science Review* 56 (December): 947–952.

Baily, Martin Neil, and Jacob Funk Kirkegaard. 2004. *Transforming the European Economy*. Washington, DC: Institute for International Economics.

Baker, Andy, and David Cupery. 2013. "Anti-Americanism in Latin America: Economic Exchange, Foreign Policy Legacies, and Mass Attitudes toward the Colossus of the North." *Latin American Research Review* 48 (2): 106–130.

Baker, Peter. 2013. "A Coup? Or Something Else? $1.5 Billion in U.S. Aid Is on the Line." *New York Times*, July 4, 2013. https://www.nytimes.com/2013/07/05/world/middleeast/egypts-arrests-of-islamists-pose-test-to-us-over-military-aid.html.

Baker, Peter. 2014. "For 2 U.S. Presidents, Iraqi Leader Proved a Source of Frustration." *New York Times* (national edition), August 11, 2014.

Barder, Alexander. 2021. *Global Race War: International Politics and Racial Hierarchy*. New York: Oxford University Press.

Barnes, Trevor. 1981. "The Secret Cold War: The C.I.A. and American Foreign Policy in Europe, 1946–1956." Part 1. *The Historical Journal* 24 (2): 399–415.

Barnes, Trevor. 1982. "The Secret Cold War: The C.I.A. and American Foreign Policy in Europe 1946–1568." Part 2. *The Historical Journal* 25 (3): 649–670.

Barnett, Michael, and Raymond Duvall. 2005. *Power in Global Governance*. New York: Cambridge University Press.

Barton, John H., Judith Goldstein, Timothy E. Josling, and Richard H. Steinberg. 2006. *The Evolution of the Trade Regime: Politics, Law, and Economics of the GATT and the WTO*. Princeton, NJ: Princeton University Press.

Baruzzi, Sofia. 2021. "The Belt & Road Initiative: Investments in 2021 and Future Outlook." Silk Road Briefing, February 10, 2021. https://www.silkroadbriefing.com/news/2021/02/09/the-belt-road-initiative-investments-in-2021-and-future-outlook/.

Bates, Robert H. 1997. *Open-Economy Politics: The Political Economy of the World Coffee Trade*. Princeton, NJ: Princeton University Press.

Bates, Robert H., Avner Greif, Margaret Levi, Jean-Laurent Rosenthal, and Barry R. Weingast. 1998. *Analytical Narratives*. Princeton, NJ: Princeton University Press.

Bates, Robert H., Avner Greif, Margaret Levi, Jean-Laurent Rosenthal, and Barry R. Weingast. 2000. "The Analytic Narrative Project." *American Political Science Review* 94 (3): 696–702.

Baynes, Kenneth. 2001. "Legitimacy." In *The Oxford Companion to Politics of the World*, edited by Joel Krieger, 495–496. 2nd ed. New York: Oxford University Press.

Beisner, Robert L. 1968. *Twelve against Empire: The Anti-imperialists, 1898–1900*. New York: McGraw-Hill.

Bemis, Samuel Flagg. 1943. *The Latin American Policy of the United States: An Historical Interpretation*. New York: Harcourt, Brace.

Bensel, Richard. 1984. *Sectionalism and American Political Development, 1880–1980*. Madison: University of Wisconsin Press.

Berg, Louis-Alexandre. 2022. *Governing Security after War: The Politics of Institutional Change in the Security Sector*. New York: Oxford University Press.

Berman, Eli. 2009. *Radical, Religious, and Violent: The New Economics of Terrorism*. Cambridge, MA: MIT Press.

Berman, Eli, and David A. Lake, eds. 2019. *Proxy Wars: Suppressing Violence through Local Agents.* Ithaca, NY: Cornell University Press.

Bessel, Richard. 2009. *Germany 1945: From War to Peace.* New York: HarperCollins.

Bew, John. 2017. *Clement Attlee: The Man Who Made Modern Britain.* New York: Oxford University Press.

Bill, James A. 1988. *The Eagle and the Lion: The Tragedy of American-Iranian Relations.* New Haven, CT: Yale University Press.

Blakeslee, George H. 1917. "True Pan-Americanism: A Policy of Cooperation with the Other American Republics." *Journal of Race Development* 7 (3): 342–360.

Blaydes, Lisa, and Drew A. Linzer. 2012. "Elite Competition, Religiosity, and Anti-Americanism in the Islamic World." *American Political Science Review* 106 (2): 225–243.

Block, Fred. 1977. *The Origins of International Economic Disorder: A Study of United States International Monetary Policy from World War II to the Present.* Berkeley: University of California Press.

Boone, Catherine. 2003. *Political Topographies of the African State: Territorial Authority and Institutional Choice.* New York: Cambridge University Press.

Boone, Catherine. 2014. *Property and Political Order in Africa: Land Rights and the Structure of Politics.* New York: Cambridge University Press.

Botting, Douglas. 2005. *In the Ruins of the Reich.* London: Methuen.

Bown, Chad P., and Douglas A. Irwin. 2015. "The GATT's Starting Point: Tariff Levels circa 1947." National Bureau of Economic Research Working Paper 21782.

Brewer, Ben. 2019. "Yemen, 2001–2011: Building on Unstable Ground." In Berman and Lake 2019, 210–237.

Britton, John A. 2013. "Intervention in the Mexican Revolution." In McPherson 2013, 390–394.

Buchenau, Jürgen. 2015. "The Mexican Revolution, 1910–1946." *Oxford Research Encyclopedia: Latin American History.* Published September 3, 2015. https://doi.org/10.1093/acrefore/9780199366439.013.21.

Bueno de Mesquita, Bruce, and Alastair Smith. 2009. "A Political Economy of Aid." *International Organization* 63 (2): 309–340.

Bueno de Mesquita, Bruce, Alastair Smith, Randolph M. Siverson, and James D. Morrow. 2003. *The Logic of Political Survival.* Cambridge, MA: MIT Press.

Bukovansky, Mlada, Ian Clark, Robyn Eckersley, Richard Price, Christian Reus-Smit, and Nicholas J. Wheeler. 2012. *Special Responsibilities: Global Problems and American Power.* New York: Cambridge University Press.

Bulmer-Thomas, Victor. 2012. *The Economic History of the Caribbean since the Napoleonic Wars.* New York: Cambridge University Press.

Burbank, Jane, and Frederick Cooper. 2010. *Empires in World History: Power and the Politics of Difference.* Princeton, NJ: Princeton University Press.

Bureau of Economic Analysis. n.d. "Balance of Payments and Direct Investment Position Data U.S. Direct Investment Abroad, U.S. Direct Investment Position Abroad on a Historical-Cost Basis." Bea.gov. Accessed September 19. 2020. https://apps.bea.gov/iTable/?reqid=2&step=1&isuri=1#reqid=2&step=1&isuri=1.

Bureau of the Census, U.S. Department of Commerce. 1975. *Historical Statistics of the United States: Colonial Times to 1970.* Washington: U.S. Department of Commerce.

Buruma, Ian. 2020. *The Churchill Complex: The Curse of Being Special, from Winston and FDR to Trump and Brexit.* New York: Penguin.

Bush, Sarah Sunn. 2015. *The Taming of Democracy Assistance: Why Democracy Promotion Does Not Confront Dictators.* New York: Cambridge University Press.

Butt, Ahsan I. 2013. "Anarchy and Hierarchy in International Relations: Examining South America's War-Prone Decade, 1932–41." *International Organization* 67 (3): 575–607.

Buzan, Barry, and Richard Little. 2000. *International Systems in World History: Remaking the Study of International Relations.* Oxford: Oxford University Press.

Cabranes, José A. 1967. "Human Rights and Non-Intervention in the Inter-American System." *Michigan Law Review* 65 (6): 1147–1182.

Cammett, Melani, Ishac Diwan, Alan Richards, and John Waterbury. 2018. *A Political Economy of the Middle East.* 4th ed. New York: Routledge.

Carnegie, Allison. 2015. *Power Plays: How International Institutions Reshape Coercive Diplomacy.* New York: Cambridge University Press.

Castle, William R. 1939. "The Monroe Doctrine and Pan-Americanism." *Annals of the American Academy of Political and Social Science* 204 (1): 111–118.

Castro, J. Justin. 2013. "Intervention and Occupation of Nicaragua (1912–1925)." In McPherson 2013, 431–435.

Cavanna, Thomas P. 2019. "Unlocking the Gates of Eurasia: China's Belt and Road Initiative and Its Implications for U.S. Grand Strategy." *Texas National Security Review* 2 (3): 9–37.

Cave, Damient. 2022. Why a Chinese Security Deal in the Pacific Could Ripple through the World. *New York Times,* April 20, 2022. https://www.nytimes.com/2022/04/20/world/australia/china-solomon-islands-security-pact.html.

Caverley, Jonathan D. 2014. *Democratic Militarism: Voting, Wealth, and War.* New York: Cambridge University Press.

Caves, Richard E. 2007. *Multinational Enterprise and Economic Analysis.* 3rd ed. New York: Cambridge University Press.

Center for International Policy. n.d.-a. "Security Assistance Database." Security Assistance Monitor. Accessed November 7, 2021. https://securityassistance.org/security-sector-assistance/.

Center for International Policy. n.d.-b. "Foreign Military Training Database." Security Assistance Monitor. Accessed November 7, 2021. https://securityassistance.org/security-sector-assistance/.

Cha, Victor. 2017. "Informal Hierarchy in Asia: The Origins of the U.S.-Japan Alliance." *International Relations of the Asia-Pacific* 17 (1): 1–34.

Chiozza, Giacomo. 2013. "Managing Difficult Allies: Domestic Institutions and Cooperation under Hierarchy." Paper presented at the Annual Meeting of the American Political Science Association, Chicago, IL, April 11–14.

Clark, Ian. 1989. *The Hierarchy of States: Reform and Resistance in the International Order.* New York: Cambridge University Press.

Clarke, Peter. 2008. *The Last Thousand Days of the British Empire: Churchill, Roosevelt, and the Birth of the Pax Americana.* New York: Bloomsbury.

Clausewitz, Carl von. 1976. *On War.* Translated by Michael Howard. Princeton, NJ: Princeton University Press.

Cleveland, William L., and Martin Bunton. 2018. *A History of the Modern Middle East.* 6th ed. New York: Routledge.

Cohen, Benjamin J. 2019. *Currency Statecraft: Monetary Rivalry and Geopolitical Ambition.* Chicago, IL: University of Chicago Press.

Connolly, William. 1984. *Legitimacy and the State.* New York: New York University Press.

Cook, Don. 1989. *Forging the Alliance: NATO, 1945–1950.* New York: William Morrow.

Cooley, Alexander. 2005. *Logics of Hierarchy: The Organization of Empires, States, and Military Occupation.* Ithaca, NY: Cornell University Press.

Cooley, Alexander. 2008. *Base Politics: Democratic Change and the U.S. Military Overseas.* Ithaca, NY: Cornell University Press.

Cooley, Alexander, and Hendrik Spruyt. 2009. *Contracting States: Sovereign Transfers in International Relations.* Princeton, NJ: Princeton University Press.

Costigliola, Frank. 1992. *France and the United States: The Cold War Alliance since World War II.* New York: Twayne.

Custer, Samantha, Justin Schon, Ana Horigoshi, Divya Mathew, Bryan Burgess, Vera Choo, Amber Hutchinson, Austin Baehr, and Kelsey Marshall. 2021. "Corridors of Power: How Beijing Uses Economic, Social, and Network Ties to Exert Influence along the Silk Road." Aiddata Policy Report, William and Mary, December 13, 2021. https://www.aiddata.org/publications/corridors-of-power.

Daggett, Stephen. 2010. "Costs of Major U.S. Wars." Congressional Research Service Report, June 29, 2010.

Darden, Jessica Trisko. 2019. *Aiding and Abetting: U.S. Foreign Assistance and State Violence.* Stanford, CA: Stanford University Press.

Debs, Alexandre, and Nuno P. Monteiro. 2014. "Known Unknowns: Power Shifts, Uncertainty, and War." *International Organization* 68 (1): 1–31.

de Ferranti, David, Guillermo E. Perry, Francisco H. G. Ferreira, and Michael Walton. 2004. *Inequality in Latin America: Breaking with History?* Washington, DC: The World Bank.

Delucchi, Mark A., and James J. Murphy. 2008. "US Military Expenditures to Protect the Use of Persian Gulf Oil for Motor Vehicles." *Energy Policy* 36 (6): 2253–2264.

Department of Commerce. 1918. Statistical Abstract of the United States, 1917. 40th ed. Washington, DC: Government Printing Office. https://www2.census.gov/library/publications/1918/compendia/statab/40ed/1917-05.pdf.

Department of Defense. 2020 "DoD Personnel, Workforce Reports and Publications." Manpower Data Center. December 2020. Accessed December 5, 2022. https://dwp.dmdc.osd.mil/dwp/app/dod-data-reports/workforce-reports.

Deutsch, Karl W. 1957. Political Community and the North Atlantic Area: International *Organization in the Light of Historical Experience.* Princeton, NJ: Princeton University Press.

Diaz, Jaquira. 2022. "Let Puerto Rico Be Free." *The Atlantic* 330 (4): 70–82.

Diggins, John Patrick. 1991. "From Pragmatism to Natural Law: Walter Lippmann's Quest for the Foundations of Legitimacy." *Political Theory* 19 (4): 519–538.

Dodge, Toby. 2012. "Iraq's Road Back to Dictatorship." *Survival* 54 (3): 147–168.

Dodge, Toby. 2013. "State and Society in Iraq Ten Years after Regime Change: The Rise of a New Authoritarianism." *International Affairs* 89 (2): 241–237.

Donnelly, Jack. 2006. "Sovereign Inequalities and Hierarchy in Anarchy: American Power and International Society." *European Journal of International Relations* 12 (2): 139–170.

Donnelly, Jack. 2009. "Rethinking Political Structures: From 'Ordering Principles' to 'Vertical Differentiation'—and Beyond." *International Theory* 1 (1): 49–86.

D'Orazio, Vito, and Kevin Galambos. 2021. "Multinational Military Exercises, 1980–2010." Harvard Dataverse. https://dataverse.harvard.edu/dataset.xhtml?persistentId=doi:10.7910/DVN/KHFODX.

Drake, Paul W. 1989. *The Money Doctor in the Andes: U.S. Advisors, Investors, and Economic Reform in Latin America from World War I to the Depression*. Durham, NC: Duke University Press.

Drake, Paul W. 1991. "From Good Men to Good Neighbors: 1912–1932." In Lowenthal 1991, 3–40.

Dunne, Tim. 2003. "Society and Hierarchy in International Relations." *International Relations* 17 (3): 303–320.

Earwicker, Benjamin J. 2013a. "Occupation of Cuba (1906–1909)." In McPherson 2013, 1:123–125.

Earwicker, Benjamin J. 2013b. "Occupation of Cuba (1917–1922)." In McPherson 2013, 1:126–127.

Eckstein, Harry. 1991. *Regarding Politics: Essays on Political Theory, Stability, and Change*. Berkeley: University of California Press.

Ehteshami, Anoushiravan. 2014. "The Foreign Policy of Iran." In Hinnebusch and Ehteshami 2014, 261–288.

EIA (U.S. Energy Information Administration). 2022. "Short-Term Energy Outlook: Real Prices Viewer." July 27, 2022. https://www.eia.gov/outlooks/steo/realprices/.

Eichengreen, Barry. 2001. "The Market and the Marshall Plan." In Schain and Judt 2001, 131–145.

Eichengreen, Barry. 2008. *The European Economy since 1945: Coordinated Capitalism and Beyond*. Princeton NJ: Princeton University Press.

Eichengreen, Barry. 2011. *Exorbitant Privilege: The Rise and Fall of the Dollar and the Future of the International Monetary System*. New York: Oxford University Press.

Elster, Jon. 2000. "Rational Choice History: A Case of Excessive Ambition." *American Political Science Review* 94 (3): 685–695.

Enloe, Cynthia. 1990. *Bananas, Beaches, and Bases: Making Feminist Sense of International Politics*. Berkeley: University of California Press.

Esposito, Chiarella. 1994. *America's Feeble Weapon: Funding the Marshall Plan in France and Italy, 1948–1950*. Westport, CT: Greenwood Press.

Fawcett, Louise, ed. 2019. *International Relations of the Middle East*. 5th ed. New York: Oxford University Press.

Fearon, James D. 1995. "Rationalist Explanations for War." *International Organization* 49 (3): 379–414.

Federico, Giovanni, and Antonio Tena Junguito. 2018. *Federico-Tena World Trade Historical Database: America*. Ministerio de Economia y Competitividad. https://doi.org/10.21950/UILNQU.

Finnemore, Martha. 2003. *The Purpose of Intervention: Changing Beliefs about the Use of Force*. Ithaca, NY: Cornell University Press.

Fisher, Michael H. 1991. *Indirect Rule in India: Residents and the Residency System, 1764–1858*. Delhi, India: Oxford University Press.

Freedman, Lawrence. 2009. *A Choice of Enemies: America Confronts the Middle East*. New York: Public Affairs.

Freedman, Lawrence, and Efraim Karsh. 1993. *The Gulf Conflict, 1990–1991: Diplomacy and War in the New World Order*. Princeton, NJ: Princeton University Press.

Freeman, Bianca, D. G. Kim, and David A. Lake. 2022. "Race in International Relations: Beyond the 'Norm against Noticing.'" *Annual Review of Political Science* 25 (1): 175–196.

Frieden, Jeffry A. 1994. "International Investment and Colonial Control: A New Interpretation." *International Organization* 48 (4): 559–593.

Frieden, Jeffry A. 1997. "Monetary Populism in Nineteenth-Century America: An Open Economy Interpretation." *Journal of Economic History* 57 (2): 367–395.

Frieden, Jeffry A. 1999. "Actors and Preferences in International Relations." In Lake and Powell 1999, 39–76.

Frieden, Jeffry A. 2006. *Global Capitalism: Its Fall and Rise in the Twentieth Century.* New York: W. W. Norton.

Frieden, Jeffry A., and Ronald Rogowski. 1996. "The Impact of the International Economy on National Policies: An Analytical Overview." In *Internationalization and Domestic Politics*, edited by Robert O. Keohane and Helen V. Milner, 25–47. New York: Cambridge University Press.

Friedman, Max Paul. 2012. *Rethinking Anti-Americanism: The History of an Exceptional Concept in American Foreign Relations.* New York: Cambridge University Press.

Gaddis, John Lewis. 1982. *Strategies of Containment: A Critical Appraisal of Postwar American National Security Policy.* New York: Oxford University Press.

Gaddis, John Lewis. 1987. *The Long Peace: Inquiries into the History of the Cold War.* New York: Oxford University Press.

Gaddis, John Lewis. 1997. *We Now Know: Rethinking Cold War History.* New York: Oxford University Press.

Gaddis, John Lewis. 2005. *The Cold War: A New History.* New York: Penguin.

Gardner, Roy. 2001. "The Marshall Plan Fifty Years Later: Three What-Ifs and a When." In Schain and Judt 2001, 119–129.

Gartenstein-Ross, Daveed. 2018. "The United States's Post-9/11 Fight against Al-Qa'ida and the Islamic State: A Losing Effort in Search of a Change." In Lesch and Haas 2018, 365–384.

Gause, F. Gregory, III. 2010. *The International Relations of the Persian Gulf.* New York: Cambridge University Press.

Gause, F. Gregory, III. 2014. "The Foreign Policy of Saudi Arabia." In Hinnebusch and Ehteshami 2014, 185–206.

Gelvin, James L. 2020. *The Modern Middle East: A History.* 5th ed. New York: Oxford University Press.

Gerges, Fawaz A. 2009. *The Far Enemy: Why Jihad Went Global.* 2nd ed. New York: Cambridge University Press.

Gerring, John, Daniel Ziblatt, Johan Van Gorp, and Julián Arévalo. 2011. "An Institutional Theory of Direct and Indirect Rule." *World Politics* 63 (3): 377–433.

Gerschewski, Johannes. 2018. "Legitimacy in Autocracies: Oxymoron or Essential Feature." *Perspectives on Politics* 16 (3): 652–665.

Ghattas, Kim. 2020. *Black Wave: Saudi Arabia, Iran, and the Forty-Year Rivalry That Unraveled Culture, Religion, and Collective Memory in the Middle East.* New York: Henry Holt.

Gibson, Carrie. 2014. *Empire's Crossroads: A History of the Caribbean from Columbus to the Present Day.* New York: Grove Press.

Gilley, Bruce. 2006. "The Meaning and Measure of State Legitimacy: Results for 72 Countries." *European Journal of Political Research* 45 (3): 499–525.

Gilley, Bruce. 2009. *The Right to Rule: How States Win and Lose Legitimacy*. New York: Columbia University Press.

Gilpin, Robert. 1975. *U.S. Power and the Multinational Corporation: The Political Economy of Foreign Direct Investment*. New York: Basic Books.

Gilpin, Robert. 1977. "Economic Interdependence and National Security in Historical Perspective." In *Economic Issues and National Security*, edited by Klaus Knorr and Frank N. Trager, 19–66. Lawrence: Regents Press of Kansas.

Goemans, H. E., Kristian S. Gleditsch, and Giacomo Chiozza. 2009. "Introducing Archigos: A Data Set of Political Leaders." *Journal of Peace Research* 46 (2): 269–283.

Goh, Evelyn. 2008. "Hierarchy and the Role of the United States in the East Asian Security Order." *International Relations of the Asia-Pacific* 8 (3): 353–377.

Goh, Evelyn. 2013. *The Struggle for Order: Hegemony, Hierarchy, and Transition in Post-Cold War East Asia*. New York: Oxford University Press.

Goldberg, Jeffrey. 2020. "Iran and the Palestinians Lose Out in the Abraham Accords." *The Atlantic*, September 16, 2020. https://www.theatlantic.com/ideas/archive/2020/09/winners-losers/616364/.

Gomez, Juan Pablo, and Bradley Hilgert. 2013. "Intervention in Nicaragua (1926–1933)." In McPherson 2013, 435–439.

Gonzalez-Cruz, Michael. 1998. "The U.S. Invasion of Puerto Rico: Occupation and Resistance to the Colonial State, 1898 to the Present." *Latin American Perspectives* 25 (5): 7–26.

Gordon, Michael R., and Bernard E. Trainor. 2013. *The Endgame: The Inside Story of the Struggle for Iraq, from George W. Bush to Barack Obama*. New York: Vintage.

Gordon, Philip H. 2020. *Losing the Long Game: The False Promise of Regime Change in the Middle East*. New York: St. Martin's.

Gowa, Joanne. 1994. *Allies, Adversaries, and International Trade*. Princeton, NJ: Princeton University Press.

Graham-Harrison, Emma. 2016. "British and US Military 'in Command Room' for Saudi Strikes on Yemen," *The Guardian*, January 15, 2016. https://www.theguardian.com/world/2016/jan/15/british-us-military-in-command-room-saudi-strikes-yemen?CMP=share_btn_link.

Granieri, Ronald J. 2003. *The Ambivalent Alliance: Konrad Adenauer, the CDU/CSU, and the West, 1949–1966*. New York: Berghahn.

Grovogui, Siba N'Zatioula. 1996. *Sovereigns, Quasi Sovereigns, and Africans: Race and Self-Determination in International Law*. Minneapolis: University of Minnesota Press.

Haas, Mark L. 2018. "The Arab Uprisings from the US Perspective." In Lesch and Haas 2018, 405–433.

Haddad, Yvonne Yazback. 2018. "Islamist Perceptions of US Policy in the Middle East." In Lesch and Haas 2018, 313–335.

Haftendorn, Helga, Robert O. Keohane, and Celeste A. Wallander. 1999. *Imperfect Unions: Security Institutions over Time and Space*. New York: Oxford University Press.

Hager, Robert P., Jr., and David A. Lake. 2000. "Balancing Empires: Competitive Decolonization in International Politics." *Security Studies* 9 (3): 108–148.

Haidt, Jonathan. 2012. *The Righteous Mind: Why Good People Are Divided by Politics and Religion*. New York: Pantheon.

Hancock, Kathleen J. 2001. "Surrendering Sovereignty: Hierarchy in the International System and the Former Soviet Union." PhD diss., University of California, San Diego.

Hancock, Kathleen J. 2009. *Regional Integration: Choosing Plutocracy.* New York: Palgrave Macmillan.

Harkavy, Robert E. 1993. "The Changing Strategic and Technological Basis, 1945–1962." In *U.S. Military Forces in Europe: The Early Years, 1945–1970,* edited by Simon W. Duke and Wolfgang Krieger. Boulder, CO: Westview Press.

Hartley, Keith, and Todd Sandler. 1999. "NATO Burden-Sharing: Past and Future." *Journal of Peace Research* 36 (6): 665–680.

Harvey, Frank P. 2012. *Explaining the Iraq War: Counterfactual Theory, Logic and Evidence.* New York: Cambridge University Press.

Hassan, Reem. 2016. "Hierarchy in International Relations: The Modern US Empire and Japan, Ecuador, and Bahrain." Bachelor's Thesis, Ludwig-Maximilians-Universitat, Munich.

Hechter, Michael. 2013. *Alien Rule.* New York: Cambridge University Press.

Heidenheimer, Arnold J. 1966. *The Governments of Germany.* 2nd ed. New York: Thomas Y. Crowell Co.

Herbst, Jeffrey. 2000. *States and Power in Africa: Comparative Lessons in Authority and Control.* Princeton, NJ: Princeton University Press.

Herring, Eric, and Glen Rangwala. 2006. *Iraq in Fragments: The Occupation and Its Legacy.* Ithaca, NY: Cornell University Press.

Herring, George C. 2008. *The American Century and Beyond: U.S. Foreign Relations, 1893–2015.* New York: Oxford University Press.

Herrold, Catherine E. 2020. *Delta Democracy: Pathways to Incremental Civic Revolution in Egypt and Beyond.* New York: Oxford University Press.

Hinnebusch, Raymond A. 2003. *The International Politics of the Middle East.* Manchester, UK: University of Manchester Press.

Hinnebusch, Raymond. 2014a. "Foreign Policy in the Middle East." In Hinnebusch and Ehteshami 2014, 1–34.

Hinnebusch, Raymond. 2014b. "The Foreign Policy of Syria." In Hinnebusch and Ehteshami 2014, 207–232.

Hinnebusch, Raymond. 2014c. "The Middle East Regional System." In Hinnebusch and Ehteshami 2014, 35–72.

Hinnebusch, Raymond, and Anoushiravan Ehteshami, eds. 2014. *The Foreign Policies of Middle East States.* 2nd ed. Boulder, CO: Lynne Rienner.

Hinnebusch, Raymond, and Nael Shama. 2014. "The Foreign Policy of Egypt." In Hinnebusch and Ehteshami 2014, 75–103.

Hirschman, Albert O. 1970. *Exit, Voice, and Loyalty: Responses to Decline in Firms, Organizations, and States.* Cambridge, MA: Harvard University Press.

Hirschman, Albert O. 1980. *National Power and the Structure of Foreign Trade.* Berkeley: University of California Press.

Hiscox, Michael J. 2002. *International Trade and Political Conflict: Commerce, Coalitions, and Mobility.* Princeton, NJ: Princeton University Press.

Hobbes, Thomas. 2017. *Leviathan.* New York: Penguin Classics.

Hobson, John M. 2014. "The Twin Self-Delusions of IR: Why 'Hierarchy' and Not 'Anarchy' Is the Core Concept of IR." *Millennium: Journal of International Studies* 42 (3): 557–575.

Hobson, John M., and J. C. Sharman. 2005. "The Enduring Place of Hierarchy in World Politics: Tracing the Social Logics of Hierarchy and Political Change." *European Journal of International Relations* 11 (1): 63–98.

Hoffman, Charles. 1970. *The Depression of the Nineties: An Economic History.* Westport, CT: Greenwood Press.

Hoffman, Kelly, and Miguel Angel Centeno. 2003. "The Lopsided Continent: Inequality in Latin America." *Annual Review of Sociology* 29 (1): 363–390.

Hogan, Michael J. 1987. *The Marshall Plan: America, Britain, and the Reconstruction of Western Europe, 1947–1952.* New York: Cambridge University Press.

Hollander, Ethan J. 2017. *Hegemony and the Holocaust: State Power and Jewish Survival in Occupied Europe.* New York: Palgrave Macmillan.

Hopkins, A. G. 2018. *American Empire: A Global History.* Princeton, NJ: Princeton University Press.

Hudson, Peter James. 2017. *Bankers and Empire: How Wall Street Colonized the Caribbean.* Chicago, IL: University of Chicago Press.

Huntington, Samuel P. 1996. *The Clash of Civilizations and the Remaking of World Order.* New York: Simon and Schuster.

Hurd, Ian. 1999. "Legitimacy and Authority in International Relations." *International Organization* 53 (2): 379–408.

Ikenberry, G. John. 2001. *After Victory: Institutions, Strategic Restraint, and the Rebuilding of Order after Major Wars.* Princeton, NJ: Princeton University Press.

Ikenberry, G. John. 2011. *Liberal Leviathan: The Origins, Crisis, and Transformation of the American World Order.* Princeton, NJ: Princeton University Press.

Irwin, Douglas A. 2014. *Tariff Incidence: Evidence from U.S. Sugar Duties, 1890–1930.* Cambridge, MA: National Bureau of Economic Research.

Isernia, Pierangelo. 2007. "Anti-Americanism in Europe during the Cold War." In *Anti-Americanism in World Politics,* edited by Peter J. Katzenstein and Robert O. Keohane, 57–92. Ithaca, NY: Cornell University Press.

Isikoff, Michael, and David Corn. 2007. *Hubris: The Inside Story of Spin, Scandal, and the Selling of the Iraq War.* Paperback with new afterword. New York: Three Rivers Press.

Ismael, Tareq Y., and Glenn E. Perry, eds. 2014. *The International Relations of the Contemporary Middle East.* New York: Routledge.

Ismay, Lord. 1954. *NATO: The First Five Years, 1949–1954.* Paris: North Atlantic Treaty Organization.

Jackson, Julian. 2018. *De Gaulle.* Cambridge, MA: Harvard University Press.

Jackson, Patrick Thaddeus. 2006. *Civilizing the Enemy: German Reconstruction and the Invention of the West.* Ann Arbor: University of Michigan Press.

Jamal, Amaney A. 2012. *Of Empires and Citizens: Pro-American Democracy or No Democracy at All?* Princeton, NJ: Princeton University Press.

Jamal, Amaney A., Robert O. Keohane, David Romney, and Dustin Tingley. 2015. "Anti-Americanism and Anti-Interventionism in Arabic Twitter Discourses." *Perspectives on Politics* 13 (1): 55–73.

James, Lawrence. 1997. *Raj: The Making and Unmaking of British India.* New York: St. Martin's Press.

James, Scott, and David A. Lake. 1989. "The Second Face of Hegemony: Britain's Repeal of the Corn Laws and the American Walker Tariff of 1846." *International Organization* 43 (1): 1–29.

Jay, Antony. 1996. *The Oxford Dictionary of Political Quotations.* New York: Oxford University Press.

Jervis, Robert. 1993. "International Primacy: Is the Game Worth the Candle?" *International Security* 17 (4): 52–67.

Johnson, Chalmers. 2000. *Blowback: The Costs and Consequences of American Empire.* Boston, MA: Little, Brown.

Jost, John T., and Brenda Major. 2001. *The Psychology of Legitimacy: Emerging Perspectives on Ideology, Justice, and Intergroup Relations.* New York: Cambridge University Press.

Judt, Tony. 2005. *Postwar: A History of Europe since 1945.* New York: Penguin Books.

Kamrava, Mehran. 2014. "The Foreign Policy of Qatar." In Hinnebusch and Ehteshami 2014, 157–183.

Kang, David C. 2003. "Hierarchy, Balancing, and Empirical Puzzles in Asian International Relations." *International Security* 28 (3): 165–180.

Kaplan, Edward S. 1998. *U.S. Imperialism in Latin America: Bryan's Challenges and Contributions, 1900–1920.* Westport, CT: Greenwood Press.

Kaplan, Fred. 2013. *The Insurgents: David Petraeus and the Plot to Change the American Way of War.* New York: Simon and Schuster.

Katzenstein, Peter J. 1987. *Policy and Politics in West Germany: The Growth of a Semisovereign State.* Philadelphia, PA: Temple University Press.

Katzenstein, Peter J., and Robert O. Keohane. 2007a. *Anti-Americanisms in World Politics.* Ithaca, NY: Cornell University Press.

Katzenstein, Peter J., and Robert O. Keohane. 2007b. "Varieties of Anti-Americanism: A Framework for Analysis." In Katzenstein and Keohane 2007a, 9–38.

Kavanagh, Jennifer. 2014. "U.S. Security-Related Agreements in Force since 1955: Introducing a New Database." Santa Monica, CA: RAND Corporation. https://www.rand.org/pubs/research_reports/RR736.html.

Keene, Edward. 2013. "International Hierarchy and the Origins of the Modern Practice of Intervention." *Review of International Studies* 39 (5): 1077–1090.

Kennan, George F. 1951. *American Diplomacy, 1900–1950.* Chicago, IL: University of Chicago.

Keohane, Robert O. 1984. *After Hegemony: Cooperation and Discord in the World·Political Economy.* Princeton, NJ: Princeton University Press.

Keohane, Robert O., and Joseph S. Nye Jr. 1977. *Power and Interdependence: World Politics in Transition.* Boston, MA: Little, Brown.

Keshk, Omar M. G., Brian M. Pollins, and Rafael Reuveny. 2004. "Trade Still Follows the Flag: The Primacy of Politics in a Simultaneous Model of Interdependence and Armed Conflict." *Journal of Politics* 66 (4): 1155–1179.

Kheir, Karen Aboul. 2014. "Egypt: The Continuing Storm?" In *The International Relations of the Contemporary Middle East: Subordination and Beyond,* edited by Tareq Y. Ismael and Glenn E. Perry, 174–201. New York: Routledge.

Kindleberger, Charles P. 1973. *The World in Depression, 1929–1939.* Berkeley: University of California Press.

Kinne, Brandon J. 2020. "The Defense Cooperation Agreement Dataset (DCAD)." *The Journal of Conflict Resolution* 64 (4): 729–755. https://www.brandonkinne.com/dcad.

Kinzer, Stephen. 2006. *Overthrow: America's Century of Regime Change from Hawaii to Iraq.* New York: Times Books.

Kinzer, Stephen. 2008. *All the Shah's Men: An American Coup and the Roots of Middle East Terror.* Hoboken, NJ: John Wiley & Sons.

Kisatsky, Deborah. 2005. *The United States and the European Right, 1945–1955.* Columbus: Ohio State University Press.

Kiser, Edgar, and Howard T. Welser. 2007. "The Microfoundations of Analytic Narratives." *Sociologica* 3 (3): 1–19.

Klein, Benjamin, Robert G. Crawford, and Armen A. Alchian. 1978. "Vertical Integration, Appropriable Rents, and the Competitive Contracting Process." *Journal of Law and Economics* 21 (2): 297–326.

Knock, Thomas J. 1992. *To End All Wars: Woodrow Wilson and the Quest for a New World Order.* New York: Oxford University Press.

Krasner, Stephen D. 1976. "State Power and the Structure of International Trade." *World Politics* 28 (3): 317–347.

Krasner, Stephen D. 1978. *Defending the National Interest: Raw Materials Investments and U.S. Foreign Policy.* Princeton, NJ: Princeton University Press.

Krasner, Stephen D. 1999. *Sovereignty: Organized Hypocrisy.* Princeton, NJ: Princeton University Press.

Kuran, Timur. 1991. "Now out of Never: The Element of Surprise in the East European Revolution of 1989." *World Politics* 44 (1): 7–48.

Kuran, Timur. 1995. *Private Truths, Public Lies: The Social Consequences of Preference Falsification.* Cambridge, MA: Harvard University Press.

Kurz, Aaron. 2013. "Shared Norms, Hierarchical Maintenance, and International Hierarchy." PhD diss., University of North Texas.

Kustermans, Jorg, and Rikkert Horemans. 2022. "Four Conceptions of Authority in International Relations." *International Organization* 76 (1): 204–208.

Kydd, Andrew H., and Barbara F. Walter. 2006. "The Strategies of Terrorism." *International Security* 31 (1): 49–80.

LaFeber, Walter. 1963. *The New Empire: An Interpretation of American Expansion, 1860–1898.* Ithaca, NY: Cornell University Press.

LaFeber, Walter. 1983. *Inevitable Revolutions: The United States in Central America.* New York: W. W. Norton.

LaFeber, Walter. 1985. *America, Russia, and the Cold War, 1945–1984.* 5th ed. New York: Knopf.

LaFeber, Walter. 1994. *The American Age: U.S. Foreign Policy at Home and Abroad, 1750 to the Present.* 2nd ed. New York: W. W. Norton.

Lakatos, Imre. 1978. *The Methodology of Scientific Research Programmes.* Philosophical Papers 1. New York: Cambridge University Press.

Lake, David A. 1988. *Power, Protection, and Free Trade: International Sources of American Commercial Strategy, 1887–1939.* Ithaca, NY: Cornell University Press.

Lake, David A. 1989. "Export, Die, or Subsidize: The International Political Economy of American Agriculture, 1875–1940." *Comparative Studies in Society and History* 31 (1): 81–105.

Lake, David A. 1996. "Anarchy, Hierarchy, and the Variety of International Relations." *International Organization* 50 (1): 1–33.

Lake, David A. 1997. "The Rise, Fall, and Future of the Russian Empire: A Theoretical Interpretation." In *The End of Empire? The Transformation of the USSR in Comparative Perspective,* edited by Karen Dawisha and Bruce Parrott, 30–62. New York: M. E. Sharpe.

Lake, David A. 1999. *Entangling Relations: American Foreign Policy in Its Century.* Princeton, NJ: Princeton University Press.

Lake, David A. 2009a. *Hierarchy in International Relations.* Ithaca, NY: Cornell University Press.

Lake, David A. 2009b. "Open Economy Politics: A Critical Review." *Review of International Organizations* 4 (3): 219–244.

Lake, David A. 2009c. "Regional Hierarchy: Authority and Local International Order." *Review of International Studies* 35 (S1): 35–58.

Lake, David A. 2010. "Two Cheers for Bargaining Theory: Assessing Rationalist Explanations of the Iraq War." *International Security* 35 (3): 7–52.

Lake, David A. 2016. *The Statebuilder's Dilemma: On the Limits of Foreign Intervention.* Ithaca, NY: Cornell University Press.

Lake, David A. 2017. "Domination, Authority, and the Forms of Chinese Power." *Chinese Journal of International Politics* 10 (4): 357–382.

Lake, David A. 2018a. "Economic Openness and Great Power Competition: Lessons for China and the United States." *Chinese Journal of International Politics* 11 (3): 237–270.

Lake, David A. 2018b. "International Legitimacy Lost? Rule and Resistance When America Is First." *Perspectives on Politics* 16 (1): 6–21.

Lake, David A., and Feng Liu. 2020. "Hierarchies in International Relations." In *Oxford Bibliographies in International Relations,* edited by Patrick James. Last modified April 22, 2020. https://doi.org/10.1093/OBO/9780199743292-0285.

Lake, David A., and Robert Powell. 1999. *Strategic Choice and International Relations.* Princeton, NJ: Princeton University Press.

Lee, Amanda. 2020. "Belt and Road Initiative Debt: How Big Is It and What's Next?" *South China Morning Post,* July 19, 2020. https://www.scmp.com/economy/china-economy/article/3093218/belt-and-road-initiative-debt-how-big-it-and-whats-next.

Leffler, Melvyn P. 1992. *A Preponderance of Power: National Security, the Truman Administration, and the Cold War.* Stanford, CA: Stanford University Press.

Lesch, David W., and Mark L. Haas, eds. 2018. *The Middle East and the United States: History, Politics, and Ideologies.* 6th ed. New York: Routledge.

Levi, Margaret, Audrey Sacks, and Tom R. Tyler. 2009. "Conceptualizing Legitimacy, Measuring Legitimate Beliefs." *American Behavioral Scientist* 53 (3): 354–375.

Levin, Dov H. 2020. *Meddling in the Ballot Box: The Causes and Effects of Partisan Electoral Interventions.* New York: Oxford University Press.

Lewis, Cleona. 1938. *America's Stake in International Investments.* Washington, DC: Brookings Institution.

Lobell, Steven E. 2003. *The Challenge of Hegemony: Grand Strategy, Trade, and Domestic Politics.* Ann Arbor: University of Michigan Press.

Lobosco, Katie. 2022. "Trump's Trade War Looms over Soybean Farmers 4 Years Later." *CNN Politics,* May 8, 2022. https://www.cnn.com/2022/05/08/politics/soybean-farmers-china-tariff-trump/index.html.

Loveman, Brian. 2010. *No Higher Law: American Foreign Policy and the Western Hemisphere since 1776.* Chapel Hill: University of North Carolina Press.

Lowenthal, Abraham F. 1991. *Exporting Democracy: The United States and Latin America.* Baltimore, MD: Johns Hopkins University Press.

Luciani, Giacomo. 2019. "Oil and Political Economy in the International Relations of the Middle East." In Fawcett 2019, 107–131.

Lugard, Lord Frederick J. D. 1965. *The Dual Mandate in British Tropical Africa.* Abingdon, UK: Frank Cass.

Lukes, Steven. 1977. *Power: A Radical View.* London: Macmillan.

Lundestad, Geir. 1986. "Empire by Invitation? The United States and Western Europe, 1945–1952." *Journal of Peace Research* 23 (3): 263–277.

Lundestad, Geir. 1990. *The American 'Empire' and Other Studies of US Foreign Policy in a Comparative Perspective.* New York: Oxford University Press.

Lynch, Marc. 2007. "Anti-Americanisms in the Arab World." In Katzenstein and Keohane 2007a, 196–224.

Lynch, Marc. 2016. *The New Arab Wars: Uprisings and Anarchy in the Middle East.* New York: PublicAffairs.

Ma, Alexandra. 2020. "How the Strait of Hormuz, a Narrow Stretch of Water Where Ships Carry $1.2 Billion of Oil Every Day, Is at the Heart of Spiraling Tensions with Iran." *Insider*, updated January 13, 2020. https://www.businessinsider.com/strait-of-hormuz-explainer-oil-us-iran-tensions-2019-7.

Mahoney, James. 2001. *The Legacies of Liberalism: Path Dependence and Political Regimes in Central America.* Baltimore, MD: Johns Hopkins University Press.

Makdisi, Ussama. 2002. " 'Anti-Americanism' in the Arab World: An Interpretation of a Brief History." *The Journal of American History* 89 (2): 538–557.

Mamdani, Mahmood. 1996. *Citizen and Subject: Contemporary Africa and the Legacy of Late Colonialism.* Princeton, NJ: Princeton University Press.

Mandaville, Peter. 2019. "Islam and International Relations in the Middle East: From Umma to Nation State." In Fawcett 2019, 180–200.

Mansfield, Peter, and Nicolas Pelham. 2019. *A History of the Middle East.* 5th ed. London: Penguin.

Martin, Garret. 2011. "The 1967 Withdrawal from NATO—A Cornerstone of de Gaulle's Grand Strategy?" *Journal of Transatlantic Studies* 9 (3): 232–243.

Martinez Machain, Carla. 2021. "Exporting Influence: U.S. Military Training as Soft Power." *Journal of Conflict Resolution* 65 (2–3): 313–341.

Maurer, Noel. 2011. "The Empire Struck Back: Sanctions and Compensation in the Mexican Oil Expropriation of 1938." *Journal of Economic History* 71 (3): 590–615.

Maurer, Noel. 2013. *The Empire Trap: The Rise and Fall of U.S. Intervention to Protect American Property Overseas, 1893–2013.* Princeton, NJ: Princeton University Press.

Mazower, Mark. 1998. *Dark Continent: Europe's Twentieth Century.* New York: Vintage.

Mazower, Mark. 2008. *Hitler's Empire: How the Nazis Ruled Europe.* New York: Penguin.

McCormick, Thomas J. 1989. *America's Half-Century: United States Foreign Policy in the Cold War.* Baltimore, MD: Johns Hopkins University Press.

McCune, Nils. 2019. "Nicaragua and Contemporary American Imperialism." In *The Palgrave Encyclopedia of Imperialism and Anti-Imperialism*, edited by Immanuel Ness and Zak Cope, 1–13. Cham, Switzerland: Springer Nature.

McDermott, Rose. 1998. *Risk-Taking in International Politics: Prospect Theory in American Foreign Policy.* Ann Arbor: University of Michigan Press.

McFarland, Victor. 2020. *Oil Powers: A History of the U.S.-Saudi Alliance.* New York: Columbia University Press.

McKinstry, Leo. 2019. *Attlee and Churchill: Allies in War, Adversaries in Peace.* London: Atlantic Books.

McPherson, Alan. 2003. *Yankee No! Anti-Americanism in U.S.-Latin American Relations.* Cambridge, MA: Harvard University Press.

McPherson, Alan, ed. 2006. *Anti-Americanism in Latin America and the Caribbean.* New York: Berghahn.

McPherson, Alan, ed. 2013. *Encyclopedia of U.S. Military Interventions in Latin America.* Santa Barbara, CA: ABC-CLIO.

McPherson, Alan. 2014. *The Invaded: How Latin Americans and Their Allies Fought and Ended U.S. Occupations.* New York: Oxford University Press.

Mead, Walter Russell. 2001. *Special Providence: American Foreign Policy and How It Changed the World.* New York: Alfred A. Knopf.

Mead, Walter Russell. 2007. *God and Gold: Britain, America, and the Making of the Modern World.* New York: Alfred A. Knopf.

Mearsheimer, John J. 2001. *The Tragedy of Great Power Politics.* New York: W. W. Norton.

Meyer, Lorenzo. 1991. "Mexico: The Exception and the Rule." In Lowenthal 1991, 215–232.

Milner, Helen V. 1991. "The Assumption of Anarchy in International Relations Theory: A Critique." *Review of International Studies* 17 (1): 67–85.

Moatsos, Michail, Joerg Baten, Peter Foldvari, Bas van Leeuwen, and Jan Luiten van Zander. 2014. "Income Inequality since 1820." In *How Was Life? Global Well-Being since 1820,* edited by Jan Luiten van Zanden, 200–216. Paris: OECD Publishing.

Monglin, Philippe. 2016. "What Are Analytic Narratives." HEC Paris Research Paper No. ECO/SCD-2016-1155. June 16, 2016. https://papers.ssrn.com/sol3/papers.cfm?abstract_id=2796567.

Monten, Jonathan, and Alexander B. Downes. 2013. "Forced to Be Free: Why Foreign-Imposed Regime Change Rarely Leads to Democratization." *International Security* 37 (4): 90–131. Online appendix: http://www.mitpressjournals.org/doi/suppl/10.1162/ISEC_a_00117.

Moore, Peter W. 2019. "A Political-Economic History of Jordan's General Intelligence Directorate: Authoritarian State-Building and Fiscal Crisis." *The Middle East Journal* 73 (2): 242–262.

Moran, Theodore H. 1974. *Multinational Corporations and the Politics of Dependence: Copper in Chile.* Princeton, NJ: Princeton University Press.

Morgenthau, Hans J. 1978. *Politics among Nations: The Struggle for Power and Peace.* 5th rev. ed. New York: Alfred A. Knopf.

Morrison, Toni. 1992. *Playing in the Dark: Whiteness and the Literary Imagination.* Cambridge, MA: Harvard University Press.

Musgrave, Paul, and Daniel H. Nexon. 2018. "Defending Hierarchy from the Moon to the Indian Ocean: Symbolic Capital and Political Dominance in Early Modern China and the Cold War." *International Organization* 72 (3): 591–626.

Narizny, Kevin. 2007. *The Political Economy of Grand Strategy.* Ithaca, NY: Cornell University Press.

Naseemullah, Adnan, and Paul Staniland. 2016. "Indirect Rule and Varieties of Governance." *Governance* 29 (1): 13–30.

New York Times. 1983. "Communists Back Italy's NATO Role." March 3, 1983.

Nichols, David A. 2011. *Eisenhower 1956: The President's Year of Crisis; Suez and the Brink of War.* New York: Simon and Schuster.

Nielsen, Richard. 2017. *Deadly Clerics: Blocked Ambition and the Paths to Jihad.* New York: Cambridge University Press.

Ninkovich, Frank A. 2001. *The United States and Imperialism.* Malden, MA: Blackwell.

Norton, Augustus Richard. 2019. "The Puzzle of Political Reform in the Middle East." In Fawcett 2019, 132–157.

Nuenlist, Christian. 2011. "Dealing with the Devil: NATO and Gaullist France, 1958–66." *Journal of Transatlantic Studies* 9 (3): 220–231.

Nye, Joseph S. 2004. *Soft Power: The Means to Success in World Politics.* New York: PublicAffairs.

Obama, Barack. 2020. *A Promised Land.* Large Print. New York: Random House.

OECD (Organization for Economic Cooperation and Development). 2018. China's Belt and Road Initiative in the Global Trade, Investment and Financial Landscape. OECD Business and Financial Outlook 2018. Paris: OECD. https://www.oecd.org/finance/Chinas-Belt-and-Road-Initiative-in-the-global-trade-investment-and-finance-landscape.pdf.

Office of the Historian. n.d. "Mexican Expropriation of Foreign Oil, 1938." Foreign Service Institute, US Department of State. Accessed April 22, 2023. https://history.state.gov/milestones/1937-1945/mexican-oil.

Olson, Mancur. 1982. *The Rise and Decline of Nations: Economic Growth, Stagflation, and Social Rigidities.* New Haven, NJ: Yale University Press.

Olson, Mancur, and Richard Zeckhauser. 1966. "An Economic Theory of Alliances." *Review of Economics and Statistics* 48 (3): 266–279.

Onuf, Nicholas, and Frank F. Klink. 1989. "Anarchy, Authority, Rule." *International Studies Quarterly* 33 (2): 149–173.

Oren, Michael B. 2011. *Power, Faith, and Fantasy: America in the Middle East, 1776 to the Present.* New York: W. W. Norton.

O'Rourke, Kevin H., and Jeffrey G. Williamson. 2000. *Globalization and History: The Evolution of a Nineteenth-Century Atlantic Economy.* Cambridge, MA: MIT Press.

O'Rourke, Lindsey A. 2018. *Covert Regime Change: America's Secret Cold War.* Ithaca, NY: Cornell University Press.

Owen, John M. 2010. *The Clash of Ideas in World Politics: Transnational Networks, States, and Regime Change, 1510–2010.* Princeton, NJ: Princeton University Press.

Oye, Kenneth A. 1985. *Cooperation under Anarchy.* Princeton, NJ: Princeton University Press.

Packer, George. 2005. *The Assassins' Gate: America in Iraq.* New York: Farrar, Straus and Giroux.

Padró i Miquel, Gerard, and Pierre Yared. 2012. "The Political Economy of Indirect Control." Quarterly Journal of Economics 127 (2): 947–1015.

ParlGov Project. n.d. "ParlGov Database." Accessed September 14, 2020. http://www.parlgov.org.

Patrick, Stewart. 2001. "Embedded Liberalism in France? American Hegemony, the Monnet Plan, and Postwar Multilateralism." In Schain and Judt 2001, 205–245.

Patty, John W., and Elizabeth Maggie Penn. 2014. Social Choice and Legitimacy: The Possibilities of Impossibility. New York: Cambridge University Press.

Paul, T. V., Deborah Welch Larson, and William C. Wohlforth, eds. 2014. Status in World Politics. New York: Cambridge University Press.

Peet, Richard Clayton. 1964. "De Gaulle's Force de Dissuasion." Air Force Magazine, June 1, 1964, 26–31.

Pew Research Center. 2022. "Opinion of the United States." Global Indicators Database. Updated March 2022. https://www.pewresearch.org/global/database/custom-analysis.

Philpott, Daniel. 2001. Revolutions in Sovereignty: How Ideas Shaped Modern International Relations. Princeton, NJ: Princeton University Press.

Pisani, Sallie. 1991. *The CIA and the Marshall Plan.* Lawrence: University Press of Kansas.

Pollard, Robert A. 1985. *Economic Security and the Origins of the Cold War, 1945–1950.* New York: Columbia University Press.

Pollins, Brian M. 1989. "Does Trade Still Follow the Flag?" *American Political Science Review* 83 (2): 465–470.

Posen, Barry R. 2014. *Restraint: A New Foundation for U.S. Grand Strategy.* Ithaca, NY: Cornell University Press.

Powell, Robert. 1999. *In the Shadow of Power: States and Strategies in International Politics.* Princeton, NJ: Princeton University Press.

Powell, Robert. 2006. "War as a Commitment Problem." *International Organization* 60 (1): 169–203.

Prados de la Escosura, Leandro. 2007. "Inequality and Poverty in Latin America: A Long-Run Exploration." In *The New Comparative Economic History,* edited by Timothy J. Hatton, Kevin H. O'Rouke, and Alan M. Taylor, 291–315. Cambridge, MA: MIT Press.

Raflik, Jenny. 2011. "The Fourth Republic and NATO, 1946–1958: Alliance Partnership or Idiosyncratic Nationalism?" *Journal of Transatlantic Studies* 9 (3): 207–219.

Rahlf, Thomas. 2016. "The German Time Series Dataset, 1834–2012." *Jahrbücher für Nationalökonomie und Statistik* 236 (1): 129–143.

Rahlf, Thomas, Paul Erker, Georg Fertig, Franz Rothenbacher, Jochen Oltmer, Volker Müller-Benedict, et al. 2015. "German Time Series Dataset, 1834–2012." Figshare. Dataset. https://doi.org/10.6084/m9.figshare.1450809.v1.

Rampton, Roberta, and Arshad Mohammed. 2015. "Obama Ends Freeze on U.S. Military Aid to Egypt." Reuters, March 31, 2015. https://www.reuters.com/article/us-usa-egypt-military/obama-ends-freeze-on-u-s-military-aid-to-egypt-id USKBN0MR2GR20150401.

Renshon, Jonathan. 2017. *Fighting for Status: Hierarchy and Conflict in World Politics.* Princeton, NJ: Princeton University Press.

Reus-Smit, Christian. 2005. "Liberal Hierarchy and the Licence to Use Force." *Review of International Studies* 31 (S1): 71–92.

Ricks, Thomas E. 2006. *Fiasco: The American Military Adventure in Iraq.* New York: Penguin Press.

Rock, Stephen R. 1989. *Why Peace Breaks Out: Great Power Rapprochement in Historical Perspective.* Chapel Hill: University of North Carolina Press.

Roeder, Philip G. 1993. *Red Sunset: The Failure of Soviet Politics.* Princeton, NJ: Princeton University Press.

Rogowski, Ronald. 1974. *Rational Legitimacy: A Theory of Political Support.* Princeton, NJ: Princeton University Press.

Rogowski, Ronald. 1989. *Commerce and Coalitions: How Trade Affects Domestic Political Alignments.* Princeton, NJ: Princeton University Press.

Rogowski, Ronald. 1999. "Institutions as Constraints on Strategic Choice." In Lake and Powell 1999, 115–136.

Rosenberg, Emily S. 1982. *Spreading the American Dream: American Economic and Cultural Expansion, 1890–1945.* New York: Hill and Wang.

Ross, Michael L. 1999. "The Political Economy of the Resource Curve." *World Politics* 51 (2): 297–322.

Rowand, Michael. 2022. "China Made a Failed Bet on Sri Lanka's Rajapaksa Family." *Foreign Policy*, July 13, 2022. https://foreignpolicy.com/2022/07/13/china-sri-lanka-rajapaksa-family-corruption/.

Ruggie, John G. 1993. *Multilateralism Matters: The Theory and Praxis of an Institutional Form.* New York: Columbia University Press.

Ryan, Curtis R. 2014. "The Foreign Policy of Jordan." In Hinnebusch and Ehteshami 2014, 133–155.

Sampson, Aaron. 2002. "Tropical Anarchy: Waltz, Wendt, and the Way We Imagine International Politics." *Alternatives: Global, Local, Political* 27 (4): 429–457.

Schain, Martin, and Tony Judt, eds. 2001. *The Marshall Plan: Fifty Years Later.* New York: Palgrave.

Schake, Kori. 2017. *Safe Passage: The Transition from British to American Hegemony.* Cambridge, MA: Harvard University Press.

Schelling, Thomas C. 1966. *Arms and Influence.* New Haven, CT: Yale University Press.

Schmidt, Brian C. 1998. *The Political Discourse of Anarchy: A Disciplinary History of International Relations.* Albany: State University of New York Press.

Schoultz, Lars. 1998. *Beneath the United States: A History of U.S. Policy toward Latin America.* Cambridge, MA: Harvard University Press.

Schoultz, Lars. 2018. *In Their Own Best Interest: A History of the U.S. Effort to Improve Latin Americans.* Cambridge, MA: Harvard University Press.

Scott, James C. 1985. *Weapons of the Weak: Everyday Forms of Peasant Resistance.* New Haven, CT: Yale University Press.

Shi, Weiyi. 2015. "The Political Economy of China's Outward Direct Investments." PhD diss., University of California, San Diego.

Shirk, Susan. 1993. *The Political Logic of Economic Reform in China.* Berkeley: University of California Press.

Sick, Gary. 2018. "The United States in the Persian Gulf: From Twin Pillars to Dual Containment." In Lesch and Haas 2018, 237–252.

Simpson, Gerry. 2004. *Great Powers and Outlaw States: Unequal Sovereigns in the International Legal Order.* New York: Cambridge University Press.

Singer, J. David, Stuart Bremer, and John Stuckey. 1972. "Capability Distribution, Uncertainty, and Major Power War, 1820–1965." In *Peace, War, and Numbers,* edited by Bruce Russet, 19–48. Beverly Hills, CA: Sage. Data available at: https://correlatesofwar.org/data-sets/national-material-capabilities/.

SIPRI (Stockholm International Peace Research Institute). n.d. "SIPRI Arms Transfer Database." Accessed August 27, 2021. https://www.sipri.org/databases/armstransfers.

Smith, Jean Edward. 1990. *Lucius D. Clay: An American Life.* New York: Henry Holt.

Smith, Peter H. 1996. *Talons of the Eagle: Dynamics of U.S.-Latin American Relations.* New York: Oxford University Press.

Smith, Tony. 1994. *America's Mission: The United States and the Worldwide Struggle for Democracy in the Twentieth Century.* Princeton, NJ: Princeton University Press.

Snidal, Duncan. 1985. "The Limits of Hegemonic Stability Theory." *International Organization* 39 (4): 579–614.

Snyder, Glenn H. 1984. "The Security Dilemma in Alliance Politics." *World Politics* 36 (4): 461–495.

Sokoloff, Kenneth L., and Stanley L. Engerman. 2000. "History Lessons: Institutions, Factor Endowments, and Paths of Development in the New World." *Journal of Economic Perspectives* 14 (3): 217–232.

Solingen, Etel. 1998. *Regional Orders at Century's Dawn: Global and Domestic Influences on Grand Strategy.* Princeton, NJ: Princeton University Press.

Springborg, Robert, F. C. "Pink" Williams, and John Zavage. 2020. "Security Assistance in the Middle East: A Three-Dimensional Chessboard." Working paper of the Carnegie Middle East Center, Carnegie Endowment for International Peace, Washington, DC, February 2020. https://carnegieendowment.org/files/Springborg_Williams_Zavage_-_Security_Assistance.pdf.

Srivastava, Swati. 2022. *Hybrid Sovereignty in World Politics.* New York: Cambridge University Press.

Stallings, Barbara. 1987. *Banker to the Third World: U.S. Portfolio Investment in Latin America, 1900–1986.* Berkeley: University of California Press.

Stein, Arthur A. 1990. *Why Nations Cooperate: Circumstance and Choice in International Relations.* Ithaca, NY: Cornell University Press.

Stein, Ewan. 2021. *International Relations in the Middle East: Hegemonic Strategies and Regional Order.* New York: Cambridge University Press.

Sylvan, David, and Stephen Majeski. 2009. *U.S. Foreign Policy in Perspective: Clients, Enemies, and Empire.* New York: Routledge.

Tadros, Samuel. 2012. "Egypt's Elections: Why the Islamists Won." *World Affairs* 174 (6): 29–36.

Tan, Weizhan, and Pippa Stevens. 2022. "OPEC+ Raises Output Faster Than Expected as Russia's War Roils Global Energy Markets." *CNBC,* June 2 edition. https://www.cnbc.com/2022/06/02/oil-prices-eu-sanctions-russia-saudi-arabia-output-opec.html.

Taussig, Frank W. 1931. *The Tariff History of the United States.* 8th ed. New York: Putnam.

Terrill, Tom E. 1973. *The Tariff, Politics, and American Foreign Policy, 1874–1901.* Westport, CT: Greenwood.

Thomas, Hugh. 2010. *Cuba: A History.* New York: Penguin Books.

Torreon, Barbara Salazar. 2017. *Instances of Use of United States Armed Force Abroad, 1798–2017.* Washington, DC: Congressional Research Service.

Trading Economics. n.d. "Soybeans." Accessed April 20, 2022. https://tradingeconomics.com/commodity/soybeans.

Trask, David F. 1996. *The War with Spain in 1898.* Lincoln: University of Nebraska Press.

Trías Monge, José. 1997. *Puerto Rico: The Trials of the Oldest Colony in the World.* New Haven, CT: Yale University Press.

Triska, Jan F. 1986. *Dominant Powers and Subordinate States: The United States in Latin America and the Soviet Union in Eastern Europe.* Durham, NC: Duke University Press.

Trubowitz, Peter. 1998. *Defining the National Interest: Conflict and Change in American Foreign Policy.* Chicago: University of Chicago Press.

Tulchin, Joseph S. 1971. *The Aftermath of War: World War I and U.S. Policy toward Latin America.* New York: New York University Press.

Tulchin, Joseph S., and Knut Walter. 1991. "Nicaragua: The Limits of Intervention." In Lowenthal 1991, 233–263.

Tyler, Patrick. 2009. *A World of Trouble: The White House and the Middle East—from the Cold War to the War on Terror.* New York: Farrar, Straus and Giroux.

USAID (United States Agency for International Development). 2020. "U.S. Overseas Loans and Grants: Obligations and Loan Authorizations, July 1, 1945–September 30, 2019." Report of the U.S. Agency for International Development, Washington, DC, document PB-AAJ-833. https://pdf.usaid.gov/pdf_docs/PBAAJ833.pdf.

USAID and U.S. Department of State. 2023. "Complete Dataset." ForeignAssistance.gov. Last updated April 7, 2023. https://www.foreignassistance.gov/data.

U.S. Census Bureau. 2022. "Current versus Constant (or Real) Dollars." Last revised September 12, 2022. https://www.census.gov/topics/income-poverty/income/guidance/current-vs-constant-dollars.html.

U.S. Department of State. 2021. "Major Non-NATO Ally Status." Bureau of Political-Military Affairs Fact Sheet. January 20, 2021. https://www.state.gov/major-non-nato-ally-status/.

Vernon, Raymond. 1971. *Sovereignty at Bay: The Multinational Spread of U.S. Enterprises.* New York: Basic Books.

Vine, David. 2022. "List of U.S. Military Bases Abroad, 1776–2021." American University Digital Research Archive. https://doi.org/10.17606/7em4-hb13.

Vitalis, Robert. 2000. "The Graceful and Generous Liberal Gesture: Making Racism Invisible in American International Relations." *Millennium: Journal of International Studies* 29 (2): 331–356.

Vitalis, Robert. 2015. *White World Order, Black Power Politics: The Birth of American International Relations.* Ithaca, NY: Cornell University Press.

Vitalis, Robert. 2020. *Oilcraft: The Myths of Scarcity and Security That Haunt U.S. Energy Policy.* Stanford, CA: Stanford University Press.

Vucetic, Srdjan. 2011. *The Anglosphere: A Genealogy of a Racialized Identity in International Relations.* Stanford, CA: Stanford University Press.

Wall, Irwin. 2001. "The Marshall Plan and French Politics." In *The Marshall Plan: Fifty Years After*, edited by Martin Schain, 167–183. New York: Palgrave Macmillan. https://doi.org/10.1007/978-1-349-62748-6_10.

Wall, Irwin M. 1977. "The French Communists and the Algerian War." *Journal of Contemporary History* 12 (3): 521–543.

Wallin, Matthew. 2018. "U.S. Military Bases and Facilities in the Middle East." American Security Project Fact Sheet, June 2018. https://www.americansecurityproject.org/wp-content/uploads/2018/07/Ref-0213-US-Military-Bases-and-Facilities-Middle-East.pdf.

Waltz, Kenneth N. 1959. *Man, the State, and War: A Theoretical Analysis.* New York: Columbia University Press.

Waltz, Kenneth N. 1979. *Theory of International Politics.* Reading, MA: Addison-Wesley.

Watson Institute. 2021. "Estimate of U.S. Post-9/11 War Spending, in $ Billions FY2001–FY2022." Costs of War Project, International and Public Affairs, Brown University. September 2021. https://watson.brown.edu/costsofwar/figures/2021/BudgetaryCosts.

Weber, Max. 1978. *Economy and Society.* 2 vols. Berkeley: University of California Press.

Wendt, Alexander. 1992. "Anarchy Is What States Make of It: The Social Construction of Power Politics." *International Organization* 46 (2): 391–425.

Wertheim, Stephen. 2020. *Tomorrow, the World: The Birth of U.S. Global Supremacy.* Cambridge, MA: Harvard University Press.

Weymar, Paul. 1957. *Konrad Adenauer: The Authorized Biography.* Translated by Peter de Mendelssohn. London: Andre Deutsch.

Wight, Martin. 1977. *Systems of States.* Leicester, UK: Leicester University Press.

Wike, Richard. 2020. "The Trump Era Has Seen a Decline in America's Global Reputation." Pew Research Center, November 19, 2020. https://www.pewresearch.org/fact-tank/2020/11/19/the-trump-era-has-seen-a-decline-in-americas-global-reputation/.

Wike, Richard, Jacob Poushter, Laura Silver, Janell Fetterolf, and Mara Mordecai. 2021. "America's Image Abroad Rebounds with Transition from Trump to Biden." Pew Research Center Report, June 10, 2021. https://www.pewresearch.org/global/2021/06/10/americas-image-abroad-rebounds-with-transition-from-trump-to-biden/.

Willard-Foster, Melissa. 2019. *Toppling Foreign Governments: The Logic of Regime Change.* Philadelphia: Pennsylvania State University Press.

Williams, Charles. 2000. *Adenauer: The Father of the New Germany.* New York: Wiley.

Williams, Philip M. 1966. *Crisis and Compromise: Politics in the Fourth Republic.* Garden City, NY: Anchor Books.

Williams, William Appleman. 1972. *The Tragedy of American Diplomacy.* 2nd rev. and enl. ed. New York: Dell.

Williamson, Oliver E. 1975. *Markets and Hierarchies: Analysis and Antitrust Implications.* New York: Free Press.

Williamson, Oliver E. 1985. *The Economic Institutions of Capitalism: Firms, Markets, and Relational Contracting.* New York: Free Press.

Yashar, Deborah J. 1997. *Demanding Democracy: Reform and Reaction in Costa Rica and Guatemala, 1870s–1950s.* Stanford, CA: Stanford University Press.

Yergin, Daniel. 2009. *The Prize: The Epic Quest for Oil, Money, and Power.* New York: Free Press.

Yergin, Daniel. 2012. *The Quest: Energy, Security, and the Remaking of the Modern World.* Revised and updated. New York: Penguin Books.

Yetiv, Steve A. 2011. *The Petroleum Triangle: Oil, Globalization, and Terror.* Ithaca, NY: Cornell University Press.

Yetiv, Steve A. 2018. "The Iraq War of 2003: Why Did the United States Decide to Invade?" In Lesch and Haas 2018, 253–273.

Yom, Sean. 2015. *From Resilience to Revolution: How Foreign Interventions Destabilize the Middle East.* New York: Columbia University Press.

Yom, Sean. 2020. "Roles, Identity, and Security: Foreign Policy Contestation in Monarchical Kuwait." *European Journal of International Relations* 26 (2): 569–593.

Zaller, John. 1992. *The Nature and Origins of Mass Opinion.* New York: Cambridge University Press.

Zarakol, Ayse. 2017. *Hierarchies in World Politics.* New York: Cambridge University Press.

Zimmermann, Anne Mariel. 2017. *US Assistance, Development, and Hierarchy in the Middle East: Aid for Allies.* New York: Palgrave Macmillan.

Index

Page numbers followed by an *f* indicate figures; *t*, tables; and *b*, text boxes.

Printed in the USA
CPSIA information can be obtained
at www.ICGtesting.com
LVHW091129220124
769605LV00008B/280